FORCING
CHOICE

OTHER BOOKS BY J. PATRICK BOYER

Foreign Voices in the House: A Century of Addresses to Canada's Parliament by World Leaders (2017)

The Big Blue Machine: How Tory Campaign Backrooms Changed Canadian Politics Forever (2015)

Our Scandalous Senate (2014)

Another Country, Another Life: Calumny, Love, and the Secrets of Isaac Jelfs (2013)

Raw Life: Cameos of 1890s Justice from a Magistrate's Bench Book (2012)

Solitary Courage: Mona Winberg and the Triumph over Disability (2010)

A Passion for Justice: How 'Vinegar Jim' McRuer Became Canada's Greatest Law Reformer (2008, revised paperback edition of 1994 hardcover edition)

A Man & His Words (2003)

Leading in an Upside-Down World: New Canadian Perspectives on Leadership (2003, editor and contributor)

"Just Trust Us": The Erosion of Accountability in Canada (2003)

The Leadership Challenge in the 21st Century (2002, editor)

Accountability and Canadian Government (2000)

Boyer's Ontario Election Law (1996)

Hands-On Democracy: How You Can Take Part in Canada's Renewal (1993)

La démocratie pour tous: le citoyen ... artisan du renouveau canadien (1993)

Direct Democracy in Canada: The History and Future of Referendums (1992)

The People's Mandate: Referendums and a More Democratic Canada (1992)

Local Elections in Canada: The Law Governing Elections of Municipal Councils, School Boards and Other Local Authorities (1988)

Election Law in Canada: The Law and Procedure of Federal, Provincial and Territorial Elections (1987, 2 volumes)

Money and Message: The Law Governing Election Financing, Advertising, Broadcasting and Campaigning in Canada (1983)

Lawmaking by the People: Referendums and Plebiscites in Canada (1982)

Political Rights: The Legal Framework of Elections in Canada (1981)

The Egalitarian Option: Perspectives on Canadian Education (1975, contributor)

FORCING CHOICE

The Risky Reward of Referendums

J. PATRICK BOYER

DUNDURN
TORONTO

Cover Image: shutterstock.com/hobbit
Printer: Webcom

Library and Archives Canada Cataloguing in Publication

Boyer, J. Patrick, author
    Forcing choice : the risky reward of referendums
/ J. Patrick Boyer.

Includes bibliographical references and index.
Issued in print and electronic formats.
ISBN 978-1-4597-3912-3 (softcover).--ISBN 978-1-4597-3913-0
(PDF).--ISBN 978-1-4597-3914-7 (EPUB)

1. Referendum--Canada--History. 2. Plebiscite--
Canada--History. I. Title.

JF493.C34B685 2017   328.271   C2017-904653-5
                                          C2017-904654-3

1 2 3 4 5   21 20 19 18 17

We acknowledge the support of the **Canada Council for the Arts**, which last year invested $153 million to bring the arts to Canadians throughout the country, and the **Ontario Arts Council** for our publishing program. We also acknowledge the financial support of the **Government of Ontario**, through the **Ontario Book Publishing Tax Credit** and the **Ontario Media Development Corporation**, and the **Government of Canada**.

Nous remercions le **Conseil des arts du Canada** de son soutien. L'an dernier, le Conseil a investi 153 millions de dollars pour mettre de l'art dans la vie des Canadiennes et des Canadiens de tout le pays.

VISIT US AT

dundurn.com | @dundurnpress | dundurnpress | dundurnpress

Dundurn
3 Church Street, Suite 500
Toronto, Ontario, Canada
M5E 1M2

For

Elise Marie Boyer

Sharing a Second Life

CONTENTS

UNDERSTANDING HOW TO ENHANCE OUR DEMOCRATIC LIFE

It is a pleasure to write a foreword for Patrick Boyer's new book on referendums. This book brings together much of the scholarship that informed the author's three earlier works on this subject and updates his account of the politics of referendums. This new volume includes discussion of the recent debate we have had in Canada about the need for a referendum to legitimize changing the electoral system. Boyer also has interesting things to say about the surprising (and, for many, disturbing) results of the Brexit referendum in the U.K. and the referendum on the peace process in Colombia.

Indeed, Patrick Boyer is without doubt the doyen of referendum scholars in Canada. No other Canadian has written so much and so thoughtfully on this subject. My own discipline, political science, has largely neglected researching the use of referendums in Canada. This has not prevented political scientists from having strong views, for and against, the use of referendums. But these views are usually based on a few referendums that are thought to have turned out well or badly, or on a simplistic admiration or revulsion of referring issues to the public.

That is how I thought about referendums myself, until I went to school with Patrick Boyer. His resourceful scholarship and careful analysis puts these simplistic views about referendums or plebiscites (he teaches us that there is really no difference between the two any longer, at least in Canada) to shame. His work shows that referendums are woven into the fabric of our democratic life. While there have been only three Canada-wide referendums (prohibition, conscription, and the Charlottetown Accord), we have had hundreds and hundreds of them — maybe thousands — at other levels of government (including aboriginal governments), and we have used them to resolve issues as disparate as marketing agricultural products and drawing new boundaries in northern Canada.

It is not that Boyer is simply gung-ho about referendums and thinks they are always the best way of resolving contested public issues. On the contrary, as he puts it, "This valuable instrument is not needed to resolve most issues. Its significant and symbolic purpose is reserved for those prepared to take the risk and reap the rewards of forcing choice, in the mature working of Canadian self-government, on a transcending issue for which there is no electoral mandate from the people yet that will affect us all in a major way."

Unlike so many critics of referendums, Boyer sees them not as an alternative to parliamentary democracy but as complementing parliamentary government. It is Parliament and the country's other legislative assemblies, after all, that decide if and when a referendum is to be held, and that will be responsible for implementing a positive referendum result. Boyer wants us to think of the referendum as a tool that enables parliamentary bodies "to give reality to the basic principle of the sovereignty of the people."

Referendums do not take place in a legal vacuum. They must be regulated by laws that among other things determine the wording of the question to be voted on, the timing, the organization and financing of contending sides, and what constitutes a win for the yes side. Most jurisdictions in Canada, including the federal Parliament, have shirked this law-making responsibility. Referendum legislation is introduced by private members (and Boyer is a veteran of these efforts) but is defeated by solemn homilies that taking issues directly to the people will undermine parliamentary democracy.

No one has thought more carefully about what should go into a good referendum law than Patrick Boyer. Two points he highly recommends. One is that the referendum debate should be between official "yes" and "no" sides, and not just a free-for-all. Equally important, each side should be required to prepare a clear message setting out the benefits of voting for or against the referendum proposition, and these concise educational pamphlets should be sent by electoral officials to all eligible voters. Boyer argues that a referendum conducted in this manner goes a long way to enabling the electorate to cast their votes intelligently.

The publication of this book is timely. The Brexit and Colombia Peace Accord referendums have cast a dark shadow over the use of ballot questions. The populist style of the Trump regime in the United States has added to doubts about the wisdom of the populace. This new book by Boyer on referendums is a healthy antidote to fears of doom and gloom about ever seeking the people's view on a matter of public policy. Referendums, as Boyer shows, can be used in an abusive way — especially when they deal with the rights of a vulnerable minority, like aboriginal people or Muslims. And they can produce bad policy. But then so can parliamentary votes.

Dundurn is to be congratulated for publishing a book that enables Canadians to transcend the shocks of recent events and understand how and when direct appeals to the people (who are supposed to be sovereign) can enhance our democratic life.

Peter Russell
University of Toronto

ON DEMOCRACY

Democracy may be likened to beautiful architecture, for every part of the tracery and sculpture, supreme in its individuality, claims a permanent place on its own merit and then surrenders it to the entire composition, thereby enriching the whole and retrieving it from the tameness of mere qualitative perfection.
— *Madame Chiang Kai-shek, First Lady of China, House of Commons, Ottawa, June 16, 1943*

The Canadian Parliament combines the quest for the democratic perfection of the nation and the desire for its people's active participation in the tasks of the state.
— *Miguel de la Madrid, President of Mexico, House of Commons, Ottawa, May 8, 1984*

We must use democratic means in our search for a democratic result.
— *Nelson Mandela, House of Commons, Ottawa, June 18, 1990*

Democratic societies require more than democratic governments.
— *The Aga Khan, House of Commons, Ottawa, February 27, 2014*

Democracy allows our most precious rights to find their fullest expression, enabling us, through the hard, painstaking work of citizenship, to continually make our countries better, to solve new challenges, to right past wrongs.
— *Barack Obama, President of the United States, House of Commons, Ottawa, June 29, 2016*

PREFACE

A WORD ABOUT WORDS

The words *referendum* and *plebiscite* have been interchanged so much that the legal distinction between them is gone. Originally, plebiscite results would *guide* those running government, as advice from the electorate, while a referendum would *direct* a government to do something, or specifically refrain from doing it, as a binding order from the sovereign people. For both the *process* is identical: a ballot question answered by voters to determine which option a majority favours. Only the *outcome* is (or was) different in how the results got applied.

Nobody was more ambitious to reimpose this fading distinction than French scholar Jean-Marie Denquin. His 350-page law book *Référendum et Plébiscite* in 1976 explained numerous distinctions between referendums and plebiscites based on a hierarchy of classifications and subcategories — classic Continental European scholarship. A jurist, Denquin believed these legal distinctions had to be respected. Two years later, however, political scientists David Butler and Austin Ranney looked at the same subject through a different lens. Their 1978 book *Referendums: A Comparative Study of Practice and Theory* focused on the political phenomenon of referendums rather than their legal implications. "Since there does not seem any clear or generally acknowledged line that can be drawn to distinguish the subject matter, the intent, or the conduct of a referendum from that of a plebiscite," they said — a Briton and an American eschewing continental scholarship's formalism — they'd just use "referendum."

Four years after that, in my 1982 work of legal history *Lawmaking by the People*, I suggested at least lawyers and drafters of statutes ought to uphold the distinction, and classified ballot questions based on Canadian political experience and case law. That was three and a half decades ago. Today the old legal distinction is too fogged over to be relied upon. Our governments, legislators, commentators, and even those drafting laws use *referendum* and *plebiscite* interchangeably. Statutes that invert the meanings include those in Quebec, Yukon, and Newfoundland and Labrador, employing *referendum* to mean what, in other Canadian jurisdictions, is a non-binding plebiscite.

The muddle is not, however, only legal. In advance of a non-binding plebiscite, government leaders might announce their intent to be bound by the voting results, thus converting the ballot question, politically if not legally, into a referendum whose outcome will oblige, rather than merely advise, the government to take a specific course. Other times, leaders wriggle out of a result they do not cherish. "It's only a plebiscite, so we're not bound by the outcome."

Another effort to classify Canadian issue-voting was proposed in 2001 by Julien Côté of Quebec's election office, categorizing them as *ratification* (citizens voting to approve a bill adopted or measure taken by the government, with binding results upon the government), *consultative* (citizens expressing opinion on policies as non-binding advice to government), and *arbitration* (citizens voting to resolve a conflict between public authorities).[1] The first is another name for *referendum*, the second a nickname for *plebiscite*, and the third a German type of referendum never used in Canada. These distinctions and terminology did not clarify our muddy waters in this country but reminded us how much people still struggle to understand what this whole subject is really all about.

Because common speech now employs *referendum* for all purposes, including non-binding voting, this book follows that usage except where historical context requires *plebiscite*. I also use the terms *ballot question*, *issue-voting*, and *ballot-box democracy* because they aptly describe the concept, handily cover both meanings, and add welcome variety of expression to an already turgid topic.

•   •   •

Sticklers for linguistic purity might admonish that the plural of *referendum* ought to be *referenda*. Although both plural forms are used, contemporary authority favours the Anglo-Saxon *referendums*. The meaning of the Latin plural gerundive *referenda* is "things to be referred," necessarily connoting a plurality of issues, that is, *a number of questions* on a ballot, which is seldom the case. Even Prince Edward Island's five-option ballot in 2016 pertained to the sole issue of changing the province's electoral system. British Columbia's eight questions on a single ballot in 2002 dealt exclusively with negotiating principles for aboriginal land claims.

Finally, about the use of words, what is often called *direct democracy* is nothing of the kind. But to explain that — and to deconstruct other misconceptions about the reward that comes, in tandem with risks, when Canadians vote on big issues that affect us — entire chapters are required.

1

HIGH-RISK DEMOCRACY

Television cameras are waiting in the heart of Centre Block inside the historic Reading Room. Evening blurs to night. Voting results bring surprises from Nova Scotia and Ontario, bitter chagrin in Quebec's numbers. Ballots will soon be counted in British Columbia.

The news cameras are in here, primed to capture Canadian history in the making, because Brian Mulroney knows the importance of venue gravitas for moments of state. This elegant heritage room was made over as a vast committee room two years ago. Gone are the Reading Room's dramas of public events and news reportage captured in 1920s murals celebrating the spirit of the printed word in diffusing knowledge and portraying the skills and pride of Canada's printers. In their place hangs a painting of the Fathers of Confederation.

It is the 1990s, and the newspapers themselves, fewer in number, are entombed in a smaller room a floor below along the north corridor. Now the people's elected representatives mostly receive only a small daily fix of printed news, a second-hand pastiche of articles in French and English from Canadian papers clipped by Commons research staff and reproduced on a dozen or so letter-sized sheets of white paper entitled *Quorum*. Everybody nowadays gets news from television.

Parliamentary Press Gallery reporters drift in, joining the cameramen, the soundmen with boom microphones, lighting technicians, and uniformed security guards. They check with one another, stand in sombre expectancy for a black limousine to reach Parliament Hill, resigned to wait as one must at a state funeral. They report to viewers that the PM is expected momentarily. Producers cut to another camera panning the elevated Main Entrance to the Parliament Buildings at the Peace Tower's base. People are there. The pavement is empty. It is now almost midnight.

Producers cut away from the vacant parliamentary stage, ready to return for the leading actor's appearance. They restore viewers to ongoing coverage of referendum results as they become breaking news, the people's verdict in a country-wide vote on far-reaching constitutional changes. Studio anchors bridge to the latest numbers in today's astonishing results. We get an update first from British Columbia, where the No vote is climbing higher as more polls report.

• • •

It has taken more than a quarter century to get to this night, a mostly wearisome, intermittently tension-filled roller-coaster ride for Canadians. We've been captive spectators watching the country's political class waltz through interminable conferences discussing makeovers of our Constitution.

It began after the Second World War when Quebecers resumed their perpetual mission to preserve French-language culture in North America's swollen sea of English speakers. The 1867 Constitution enshrined this imperative by ensuring education and social programs remained a provincial jurisdiction so that Quebec, though not home to all French-speaking Canadians, could at least be "master of its own house" where a majority of Francophones lived.

During the economic depression of the 1930s and the world war of the 1940s, Ottawa used emergency powers and instituted programs in provincial jurisdiction, using a new key called "the federal spending power" to unlock this entrance and extend federal control over social programs and other fields of provincial responsibility. Federal consolidation of power even included a constitutional amendment that transferred provincial responsibility for unemployment insurance to Ottawa.

Predominantly English-speaking provinces, especially the poorer ones, welcomed any new spending by the national government because it saved money they didn't have. Quebec, however, to fulfill its almost primordial mission, had to return to the Constitution's original plan. It was not a radical move but a profoundly conservative one: respect the Constitution, end "temporary" wartime measures, and get Ottawa out of provincial jurisdictions.

This was interpreted elsewhere across Canada as "unrest" in Quebec. It puzzled most Anglo-Canadians, some of whom also melded anti-French bigotry into their complaint about Quebec wanting "special status." So Ontario Premier John Robarts, fancying himself a latter-day Father of Confederation, convened his nine fellow premiers in Toronto for a November 1967 "Confederation of Tomorrow" conference, acting as if it were still the 1860s and organizing a new federal state was a concept waiting to be teased into proper shape from scratch.

John Robarts was probably the only twentieth-century Canadian premier who had read *The Federalist Papers*, a record of American constitution-makers debating how best to structure powers of state, and one of the few to be candid about what made him tick politically: "I'd rather govern than be governed." To reinforce the Ontarian's fantasy universe of ten principalities having carte blanche to fashion a Confederation of tomorrow, Premier Robarts pointedly did not invite Prime Minister Lester Pearson. His presence would have reminded the premiers that an actual living person was in charge of a nation already a century old.

Quebec Premier Daniel Johnson, a conservative man, outlined in a luncheon address to Toronto's Empire Club how cultural and constitutional imperatives of French-speaking peoples in Canada led to this impasse. Then he told the other premiers, facing them around a conference table on the top floor of the city's newest sky-scraping bank tower, they had to revisit Canada's Constitution because for Quebec it was *égalité ou indépendance*, "equality or independence." Equality had been the original bargain, with linguistic rights, political representation, and double-majority rules, and since 1875, a supreme court with three Quebec judges to accommodate the province's long-embedded civil law system with a three-member panel of justices, the same way common law provinces get an odd-numbered bench to decide their cases.

For the next quarter century, constitutional negotiations then ran through the Victoria Charter constitutional agreement, the constitutional package negotiated by Prime Minister Pierre Elliott Trudeau with ten divergent premiers to add a Charter of Rights and Freedoms and an amending procedure to the Constitution, and next the Meech Lake constitutional accord negotiated by Prime Minister Brian Mulroney to address the fact that the Trudeau accomplishment had excluded Quebec. After that came the anguishing three-year death throes of this agreement because the Mulroney government refused to promptly ask in a national referendum if *Canadians* agreed with the Meech Lake Accord's five clear points. The traumatic death of Meech was followed by resurrection of constitutional negotiations that produced wholesale changes by 1992 in the Charlottetown Accord, itself touched up with even more tweaking in Ottawa by the Langevin Agreement.

Over those twenty-five unrelenting years, Canada's governing class had increasingly sought to "constitutionalize" the country's political issues through this self-reinforcing alternate vehicle of so-called "executive federalism" with "first-minister" conferences, rather than address and resolve problems through normal politics in our legislatures or, for really big questions, force a specific choice at the ballot box. By the time this unstoppable locomotive hurtled into the early 1990s, every Canadian issue of significance had been sucked into its vortex.

The same government that brilliantly negotiated an executive agreement at Meech Lake in 1987 dismally misunderstood the statecraft of gaining constitutional ratification. By not taking the risk of a referendum, it failed to claim its reward. By 1992, Brian Mulroney's government had no choice except to hold a referendum on the infinitely more complex Charlottetown Accord.

This nationwide referendum on the Constitution had not arisen because Ottawa finally grasped the necessary role of participatory democracy and citizen ratification of major constitutional change, but only because three major and democratic-minded provinces were submitting this fundamental change to direct vote of their people. British Columbia, Alberta, and Quebec had each enacted statutes requiring a province-wide ballot question on any proposed constitutional change *before* the people's elected representatives in their legislatures themselves voted to formally approve or reject the measures. Unless Ottawa itself embraced this normal democratic procedure, the country would have two-tier citizens: those with a right to vote on changing our Constitution, and those denied that right.

Prime Minister Mulroney had accepted inevitability. Just three days earlier he'd told the *Globe and Mail*'s editorial board, "I always thought, quite frankly, that under the British parliamentary system a referendum was a kind of abdication of responsibility." He'd changed his mind over the years, he said on October 23. "I've come to recognize that in a modern, plural-istic society like ours, people do indeed require a much greater degree of participation than a kick at the can every four years. And they have propri-etary rights in respect to the constitutional document. And that indeed there should be public consultation and the ultimate in that is a referendum."

Tonight the historic price exacted by his failure to be "converted" five years earlier, at the time of Meech, is being doubly paid by the PM's still incomplete grasp of the referendum process. It is a condition extending far beyond Mulroney himself, involving, too, most of his cabinet and Ottawa's political establishment. The democratic instrument Canada's prime minister has belatedly embraced is designed to *separate* policies from personalities. Brian Mulroney, who'd invested so much political capital in herculean constitutional bartering to create this dense thicket of amendments, saw the Charlottetown Accord as one of his crowning achievements. It just had to get implemented. And our PM knew himself to be one of the best election campaigners in Canadian political history.

Growing desperate over the Yes campaign's lacklustre effort, he'd hero-ically flung himself into a crusade for ratification. It was a push for victory that ironically paved the way to defeat. His intense identification with the Yes side coloured voters' evaluation of the accord because Brian Mulroney's low personal standing with Canadians by 1992 diminished objective con-sideration of the changes on their own merits.

Reporters continue to stand by for the PM to address the nation. They know it will be grim. The verdict is being excruciatingly revealed, from east to west, through the country's four-and-a-half-hour spread of time zones. Even by the time ballots were counted in Atlantic and Central Canada, it seemed the accord's future all lay behind it.

• • •

Culminating his exhausting campaign's public appearances and backroom strategizing, Brian Mulroney with his wife, Mila, cast their Yes votes early this morning then spent the day quietly at Harrington Lake, Canada's col-onial revival retreat for prime ministers in the Gatineau Hills.

He'd taken a call from pollster Allan Gregg around 4:00 p.m., then telephoned Quebec Premier Robert Bourassa to pass along his info that Yes "should win 51.5 percent of the popular support," but it would take "almost a miracle to pull through in Quebec, Manitoba, and B.C." As the sun set, the Mulroneys started watching two televisions set up in the dining room for French-language and English-language coverage, while sharing an informal supper and analysis with a half-dozen insiders.

As the results from Quebec and Ontario made the accord's fate clear, the PM went upstairs to the den with two others, L. Ian MacDonald and Paul Terrien, to work on remarks he'd deliver in the Reading Room. Before long, the PM's motorcade passed the RCMP guards at the gate of the Harrington Lake compound and proceeded southwest along Quebec Autoroute 5 to Parliament Hill. When he and Mila arrived, they walked with slow dignity up the stone entrance steps, through brass doors held open by guards, into the high vaulted rotunda with its oil portraits of past prime ministers, along the Hall of Honour's highly polished marble floor, through the corridor honouring Canadian journalists, and into the Reading Room. The television cameras' red lights signalled they were recording. The prime minister of Canada made only brief solemn comments as one day turned into the next. In conclusion, he declared to Canadians, "The Charlottetown Accord is now history."

This was not the legacy he'd intended. Canadians had derailed the juggernaut that for three and a half decades drove a country's political issues into an arena of relentless constitutional discussion, a wrong track taken. Only a direct vote by the people managed to close that down. As further reward, the democratic verdict would redirect Canada's public agenda back into parliamentary forums where elected representatives could resume their rightful roles.

Brian Mulroney described in his personal diary his intention to resign: "… the bullet had indeed been removed from the chamber by a democratic vote … time for me to move on …"

LONDON: JUNE 24, 2016

Reporters crowd against a metallic street barricade and gaze across Downing Street to a lacquered black door with the over-polished yet discreet brass numeral *10* on it. David Cameron steps into the fresh air with his wife, Samantha, at his side. The couple stride practised brisk steps to a curbside podium on which every photographer's lens holds a well-tested focus. The prime minister's stylish wife moves off to his left, out of immediate camera frame for her husband's singular moment of history.

"I have always believed that we have to confront big decisions," he asserts, "not duck them."

"That is why we delivered a fair, legal, and decisive referendum in Scotland," the PM continues, "and it's why I made the pledge to renegotiate Britain's position in the European Union and to hold the referendum on our membership."

More than thirty-three million people in England, Scotland, Wales, Northern Ireland, and Gibraltar had just voted on whether Britain should remain in the union. Each elector had offered his or her specific, unequivocal choice. The ballots had been counted. Their collective verdict — not what pollsters predicted — sent a shock wave through Britain, across Europe, and around the world.

Cameron describes the referendum as a "giant democratic exercise, perhaps the biggest in our history." Britons, he adds, should be "proud of the fact that in these islands we trust the people for these big decisions."

"We not only have a parliamentary democracy," stresses a leader who wields immense power within that governing system, "but on questions about the arrangements for how we're governed, there are times when it is right to ask the people themselves, and that is what we have done. The British people have voted to leave the European Union and their will must be respected."

This idea is so significant that Prime Minister Cameron reformulates and restates it: "The will of the British people is an instruction that must be delivered."

•　•　•

Astonished Canadians are among those absorbing the drama. Word that a majority of voters support "Brexit" — the No side's popularized portmanteau for "Britain exit" from the European Union — is genuine news: something unexpected. Despite the "dead heat" reported by pollsters on the eve of voting, media savants and political elites considered this outcome so improbable as to be virtually impossible.

Brexit resonates in Canada. Some twilight colonials, even yet, think about British affairs as our own. Apart from that, it is a commanding news story, big enough even to displace talk about playoffs, weather, and Donald

Trump. And beyond cultural ties and sheer news impact, another reason Brexit makes Canadians take heed is that our government is concluding negotiations for a Canada–European Community trade treaty — the opposite direction from Brits who'd now negotiate *out* of their E.U. membership.

The story also plays for entirely domestic reasons. Brexit fascinates Quebec's diehard separatists, keen for portents to push fresh wind into their own luffing sails. A number of our commentators toss off glib generalizations about Brexit in their rush to say something significant-sounding, their banal understanding of referendum politics deserving to be quickly forgotten. But ironically, their bromides gain extended life because Brexit's supposed "lessons" feed a rising Canadian debate over Prime Minister Justin Trudeau's government holding a referendum on changing the system for electing MPs. In a deeper way, perhaps, Brexit even touches a subconscious undercurrent in Canadians about Confederation itself.

• • •

Britain set a new course in the early 1970s under Prime Minister Edward Heath after former colonies achieved independence and could no longer be economically exploited as before. "Britain has lost an empire," it was observed, "and failed to find a role." Ambivalence appeared on many fronts. Powers of government would be "devolved" to the United Kingdom's national parts, but without giving Scotland, Wales, Northern Ireland, or England complete independence. The United Kingdom would join the European Common Market, but without the spirit of devotion needed for complete adhesion, keeping the British pound as currency and refusing to join the Eurozone. Centuries of being a "distinct society" within Europe, fostered by the island mentality of a people set apart, ensured that the United Kingdom would never embrace and become part of a united Europe in the manner of Germany, France, Italy, and the others. Even more, the United Kingdom had joined without popular ratification of its government's historic decision.

"Muddling through" is a core principle of British planning and management, but even so, the United Kingdom's failure, at the very outset, to ask if electors consented to their country joining Europe's Common Market fostered unrelenting disquiet and forced an oddly timed referendum in 1975, *after* the United Kingdom's Common Market relationship was in place but still in a tentative early stage. People's experience was fresh, feelings were mixed but hopeful, and voters approved staying in the Common Market, but in Britain's aloof and limited way. As decades passed, European integration accelerated with Britain remaining, both officially and culturally, a reluctant partner. Keeping the pound rather than embracing the euro was more than monetary and economic. It excluded Britons from the thinking and politics driving creation of the Eurozone, leaving shopkeepers and citizens to feel the local impact of decisions from Brussels without comprehending why change was necessary or justified. Of the risks with a referendum, one of the greatest is just not using it soon enough, to test buy-in from the sovereign people. The 2016 referendum on the treaty's renegotiated terms didn't create this ancient dichotomy; it merely revealed its current manifestation.

Meanwhile, for the United Kingdom to ditch the Commonwealth common market in the 1970s and seek a new future with Continental Europe left Canada and other Commonwealth countries, our economies meshed through decades-long trade patterns with the United Kingdom, to fend for ourselves. Canada entered into a Free Trade Agreement with the United States, later expanded as the North American Free Trade Agreement (NAFTA) to include Mexico, and most recently a trade treaty with the European Community — all to deal with the aftermath of being abandoned by the so-called Mother Country. The deeper subconscious link, however, is perhaps found in the United Kingdom's referendums on being part of Europe and Canada's recurring cycle of voting on choices about Confederation from 1866 to the present — whether to join, leave, or somehow change the arrangements. For both the United Kingdom and Canada, the question about being part of a larger sovereign entity, or not, has to be asked sooner or later. Forcing choice by referendum brings clarity, the way nothing else can, its reward a true measure of where people really stand and what should be done next.

Britain would cease to be part of the European Union. David Cameron confirmed he'd no longer be prime minister.

ROME: DECEMBER 4, 2016

In wintry darkness, reporters stream through Sunday night's raw chill air to Palazzo Chigi, palatial sixteenth-century residence of Italian prime ministers, for a midnight press conference. In strides Matteo Renzi, Italy's youngest ever prime minister, alone, dressed in funereal black suit and black tie. He moves quickly across the front of the chamber, dizzying in its overheated atmosphere, temperature rising from the crowd's body heat, reporters' breath, and hot lights of television cameras. He passes between the claustrophobic crowd and a large wall's baroque mural of a medieval battle scene. He stops at a clear Plexiglas podium, draws a single folded sheet from his inside breast pocket, pats it flat by repeated strokes, and looks up. Behind the PM in one direction slants Italy's green, white, and red flag; in the other, the European Union's flag, its blue field emblazoned with a circle of more than two dozen gold stars for each member state, a fourfold increase from the original half-dozen who'd signed the Treaty of Rome here sixty years ago.

The prime minister still has energy, even bounce. But his emotions are imploding. "I lost. I wasn't able to win. I beg you to believe that I did everything I could. I say that with a lump in my throat, because we are not robots." The referendum defeat humiliates the ambitious leader of Italy's Democratic Party, prime minister for only two years.

· · ·

Renzi progressed from mayor of stately Florence to prime minister in 2014 with a promise of constitutional change and parliamentary reform. As months passed, that focus increasingly made their PM seem, to many Italians, detached from their more urgent imperatives. Additionally, the referendum proposals to reduce parliamentary checks and concentrate more power in the prime minister's own hands gave many Italians the impression of personal power hunger on the part of Renzi, reviving memories of Benito Mussolini's Italy and what my cousin, Giovanni Brenciaglia, a youth in wartime Italy, called "historical fears."

Throughout the day, Italians turned out in large numbers to vote on the constitutional changes to Parliament's upper house. As long ago as 1973, Costantino Mortati, respected veteran constitutionalist and Christian Democrat member of Italy's earlier constituent assembly, had called Italy's senate a "useless replica" of the Chamber of Deputies, creating constant governance problems by exercising powers equal to those of the lower house. Senators regularly defeated measures for economic and financial overhauls needed for Italy to prosper in Europe's Common Market. The referendum campaign, like the U.K. Brexit vote earlier this year, has been rife with emotional appeals and competing political interests, the Yes and No sides appearing in a virtual dead heat in the opening weeks but, as December's voting day neared, a No win seeming probable.

"If you fight for an idea, you cannot lose," Matteo Renzi had asserted with a whiff of arrogant superiority, casting himself heroically at the vanguard of historical inevitability. But you can. And you can even make loss inevitable if, as an unpopular PM, you personalize the ballot question by identifying yourself too closely with its central idea.

If one didn't know much about referendum dynamics, didn't appreciate that the essence of a ballot question is to isolate a single issue and force a specific choice *apart* from personalities and party affiliations, Renzi's decision to insert himself into the voting equation might have seemed correct. Italy ached for reforms. The black-market economy was bigger and more efficient than Italy's official open economy. Italy's networks of entrenched interests perpetuated long-standing problems by resisting change to preserve their power and privileges. So by appealing over their heads, Renzi believed his all-out role in the Yes campaign would connect directly with the people. He expected to tap their frustration about a gridlocked Parliament unable to implement reforms for modernizing the country's relic banking system, and other overhauls needed for Italy to succeed. The prime minister even believed he could win support for the institutional changes by staking his political future on the referendum's outcome.

Forcing choice by referendum again brought its reward of clarity, and once more revealed the risks of its operating dynamics. In this case, the risk hadn't come from seeking consent of the governed but from a leader who didn't understand the art of getting it. By announcing at the outset he'd resign if his proposed reform of Italy's twin-chamber parliament failed to win voter approval, Prime Minister Renzi converted a referendum on senate reform into a proxy vote on his own performance in office. The stratagem imperiled whatever relief constitutional reforms might have given the stagnating country and its sclerotic Parliament, because Renzi's approval rating was steadily declining.

With their PM now in play, Italian voters paid closer attention to his nature, which seemed to fluctuate between joviality and arrogance. It would be easy to change that.

• • •

Today's heavy voter turnout has yielded a convincing No win — almost 60 percent of the ballots, to 40 percent for Yes. Some commentators said the outcome echoed the United Kingdom's Brexit June vote; others, that it replicated Donald Trump's November win in the United States. All political events share common surface appearances, but the intimate complexity of Italian affairs defies such simplistic comparisons.

Besides Prime Minister Renzi's soaring unpopularity, Italy's major opposition parties, rivals to Renzi's Democratic Party, all supported No. Among the most ardent were the populist Five Star Movement, which seeks policies aligned with people's needs and challenges Italy's political elites, and the Northern League, which channels Italians' reactions against an unrelenting influx of refugee immigrants. They joined forces against Yes to drive Renzi from office.

Beyond this partisan battle, many Italians concluded that the constitutional and parliamentary "reforms" spelled an end to Italy's constitutionally limited government, much desired in the wake of Mussolini's dictatorship and modelled on the U.S. Constitution's division of powers and its many checks and balances. Believing the proposed changes would give Italy a neutered senate and concentrate excessive power with the prime minister, they said No.

Italy's referendum also tapped into Euro-sceptic attitudes and channelled them to the No side — simply because Renzi, strongly pro–European Community, was fully identified with Yes. Finally, many voters believed that lifting Italy out of its economic swamp demanded stronger political leadership and changes in the economy, not second-order changes to the Constitution.

Canadian interest in this referendum is slighter than for Brexit. We'd already voted down reforms to our Senate that would have made it elected, accountable, more effective, and equally representative across Canada. We'd already seen, with Prime Minister Mulroney's active role in the Charlottetown Accord referendum campaign, how an unpopular PM can sideline attention from the policy issue itself. Most germane for Canadians, in this moment, is Italy's future as a pillar member of the European Union and what the country's rising anti-E.U. sentiment portends for European unity, just as we're establishing a trade treaty with the European Union.

In Rome, Prime Minister Renzi's brief press conference remarks late Sunday night acknowledge the "convincing win by the No side," describe the referendum as "a feast of democracy," and express his hope the winners would "work for the good of Italy and Italians." He adds that he'll meet his cabinet in the morning, "thank them for an extraordinary adventure," and then tender his resignation to the president. His parting words: "Long live Italy, and good luck to us all."

A fraught Renzi walks off hurriedly, stuffing his single sheet of paper into a suit pocket while exiting stage left, taking no questions. At the culmination of a major referendum, the country's prime minister addressing the world had no message about the process, the principle, or the future. From the campaign's outset to his cameo finale, Italy's 2016 referendum has been all about him.

Italy's senate reform is rejected. Within the week, Matteo Renzi is no longer prime minister.

2
ANVIL OF A
SELF-GOVERNING PEOPLE

A referendum is the place a democracy sends hard issues to get hammered out.

Sometimes the result is as surprising as a jury not returning a guilty verdict when the accused already stands convicted in the court of public opinion, as an election result nobody saw coming, as a coroner's inquest disclosing a shockingly unexpected cause of death.

That a verdict in ballot-box democracy is unknowable until those examining the matter have deliberately chosen between possible outcomes makes the referendum — as it does juries, elections, and coroner's inquests — indispensable in a functioning democracy. The bonus is how these established procedures remind us not to make assumptions about what people think. Ballot questions force spark-flying debates about hard issues. They culminate in a deliberate choice by the full electorate through our democratic rituals and secret ballots.

HOT POTATOES FOR THE PEOPLE

"People are grumbling the government is not doing things right," Prime Minister Pierre Trudeau said, shrugging, in 1978. "Well, it might be time for the government to throw a few hot potatoes back at them. There are some elementary questions that could be answered Yes or No."[1]

It was no quip. The exasperated PM, mired in never-ending negotiations with provincial premiers about the Constitution, had his intergovernmental affairs minister, Marc Lalonde, draft referendum legislation and introduce it in the Commons. The Referendum Act could provide democracy's zipline —

ballot questions by which citizens could embrace Canada and glide above the politicians' self-generated quagmire. As events unfolded, however, no air-clearing referendum was instituted — something the PM later regretted as the constitutional imbroglio continued festering and got transported to Britain, where aboriginal chiefs in full headdress and provincial premiers in high dudgeon provided embarrassing proofs of a country unable to get its politics together.

Pierre Trudeau was not our first prime minister to envisage the referendum as a useful means, perhaps the best method, if indeed not the *only* way, to force choice on a contentious matter.

Wilfrid Laurier launched Canada's first national ballot question by throwing voters the "hot potato" of choosing whether to prohibit alcohol. The referendum wasn't borne out of frustration nor taken on a whim. It was as deliberate as anything a self-governing democracy could muster. A national vote on the contentious liquor issue had been proposed, debated, and approved by a majority of cross-country representatives attending the Liberal Party's 1893 national convention. In the party's platform for the 1895 election, two years later, this policy was something Liberals campaigned for. Voters gave them an electoral mandate to form a government and implement its program. Prime Minister Laurier carried through on the commitment. Voting took place September 29, 1898.

WAR ISSUES AND BALLOTS

In 1914 Prime Minister Robert Borden was preparing a ballot question on Senate reform. Public interest had focused not so much on the Senate as on the nature of a Canadian navy, because our extensive ocean frontiers required naval security and the need for warships was real. Disagreement erupted over whether Canada should pay money to help Britain build more ships for the Royal Navy (Borden's imperial-minded plan) or spend funds on a navy of our own (Laurier's Canadian-minded alternative). After Borden's Naval Bill was approved by the elected Conservative majority in the Commons, appointed Liberals in the Senate thwarted it. This reminded the PM that doing something about Parliament's relic second chamber could be delayed no longer. However, that summer the Great War sidelined the PM's plans for a referendum on the Senate.

Referendums were in the air for other issues, though. Laurier believed Canadians ought to vote approval for sending our soldiers to foreign wars before the government dispatched them, even though in this era Canada couldn't make foreign policy and Britain automatically made colonies part of its wars. Already in 1899, when the British Empire's war of conquest of Dutch territory began in South Africa to seize newly discovered diamond and gold resources, Prime Minister Laurier believed a new principle was involved: ordering Canadian soldiers not to defend our country but to fight beyond our borders required public debate and a mandate from the people. It couldn't be. The imperial drumbeat stirred British-minded Canadians into frenzy to kill Boer (Dutch for "farmer") colonists in South Africa, thinking it was for the glory of the Union Jack, not seeing the strings being pulled behind the flag by British companies greedy for diamonds and gold. Prime Minister Laurier couldn't withstand this pro-British sentiment in colonial Canada. The best he managed was having his government never officially endorse the Boer War. Even so, popular war lust discounted Ottawa's stance: Canadian volunteers *over-enlisted* in British forces to fight and die half a world away.

The South African war ended in 1902, but the bellicose rhythm remained unbroken when a new war in 1914 again excited British-minded Canadians with the adventure of distant battle. Parliament enacted measures, patterned on statutes from Westminster, to censor the press, force "enemy aliens" into concentration camps, commandeer national resources under a War Measures Act, and impose a "temporary" income tax to help with war costs.

Only by 1917, when the war had become an aching womb of death, could Laurier, now leading the Opposition, manage a motion in the Commons calling for a national referendum on conscription. The former PM had failed to get a ballot question on sending Canadian *volunteers* to foreign wars but knew it was essential for *mandatory* war service overseas. From neutral Acadians refusing to swear allegiance to kings of either France or England as their Maritime lands alternated under control of these rival powers, to French Canadians not taking up arms to defend against north-ward U.S. expansion in the 1860s, through Britain's war against South African farmers, to the Great War when Canada's initial plan in 1914 to send twenty-five thousand volunteer soldiers had since exhausted ten times that number, a strong impulse to not take sides between warring foreign powers ran through French Canadians, Canada's farming communities, and settlers from Central and Eastern Europe. Any drive to conscript the unwilling for probable death in uniform would be resisted.

Laurier saw a principle to be hammered out on the anvil of public debate, with a democratic choice forced at the ballot box after all perspectives had been heard. His motion in the Commons didn't succeed. Instead, Liberal MPs wanting conscription deserted him to make a "Union" government with Borden's largely pro-conscription Conservative caucus. This majority enacted a revised Election Act that preordained a pro-conscription majority in 1917's election. The Union government enacted conscription laws, and the recruiting hunt for unwilling soldiers began, with men hiding in the countryside and riots erupting in Quebec cities, jails filling, and Canadians shot within our borders over conscription. Justice Minister Arthur Meighen dispatched a unilingual English-speaking regiment from Toronto to Quebec City with its machine guns to uphold the law against rioters.

Two decades later Meighen, a top minister in Borden's wartime government who'd become prime minister in the 1920s, reflected on the tragic insanity that took hold from 1914 to 1918 when more than sixty thousand Canadians died. He admitted it would have been better if the overseas military service issue had been thrashed out at the beginning, with the people voting on it. Meighen envisaged such a verdict coming through a general election in which the issue was central, rather than a referendum, which was in line with some British thinking about how "issue mandates" were obtained. Belatedly, Meighen acknowledged that, as David Cameron would put it with Brexit, "Big decisions have to be confronted, rather than ducked."

UNADDRESSED CONTROVERSY DOES NOT DISAPPEAR

Controversy doesn't vanish if its causes go unaddressed. It festers below the surface, waiting for an opportunity to erupt, then surprises those who see only society's thin veneer of civilization and delude themselves that all is well — which is why the smouldering issue of conscription resurfaced in the depths of another world war.

Prime Minister William Lyon Mackenzie King instituted a referendum in 1942 forcing Canadian voters to confront the life-and-death choice of military conscription. The Liberal PM won re-election in 1940, early in the war, promising no conscription. Like Meighen, he'd learned the First World War's lesson and let people express their verdict, through a general election, on his policy that only volunteers would wear a soldier's uniform. Liberals swept ridings with French-Canadian majorities, farming constituencies in Southwestern Ontario, Prairie ridings with large Central and Eastern European populations, and other voters ardently opposed to forcing men to fight.

Conditions changed by 1942, in the normal pattern of wars extending themselves and demanding more lives than anyone first dared to contemplate. The spectre was real that the Allies would lose the war. Canada's military commanders stressed their increasingly urgent manpower needs. King accepted the prospect of conscription, which he'd sought and obtained a specific mandate to never impose. To his credit, the prime minister respected electors and the mandate given him. Rather than blithely reversing his unequivocal election pledge, he went back to the people. Canada's second national referendum, conducted in the midst of an intense war, asked if voters would release him from his election pledge.

In 1992 Prime Minister Brian Mulroney arranged for Canadians to decide, with our country's third national ballot question, another of the country's long-smouldering issues. Before, during, and after he placed the package of Charlottetown Accord constitutional changes on democracy's anvil, complainers bitterly urged that such major matters ought never to be decided by folks unable to comprehend a constitution's complexities. Joining that chorus were the voices of risk-averse politicians who saw "their" Charlottetown Accord a satisfying culmination of careers consumed by Canada's long-running constitutional makeover project. All ardent and nervous, they opposed citizens scrutinizing their work, this constitutional amalgam.

However, had Canada's national government not asked *all* Canadians *Do you agree that the Constitution of Canada should be renewed on the basis of the Agreement reached on August 28, 1992?* then we'd have had two-tier citizenship. British Columbians, Albertans, and Quebecers all had a legal right to vote on constitutional change. Canadians in other provinces and territories did not. Partial use of "the anvil" in those three provinces alone would have created another, longer-term problem. Had the Charlottetown Accord's far-reaching changes of fundamental arrangements governing us been adopted, or rejected, without *full* participation of all citizens, the Constitution's political legitimacy itself would have been weakened.

Not all prime ministers have thought much about referendums, in either sense of that expression: reasoning through a referendum's risks and rewards, or holding them in high regard. A number have changed their minds, recognizing the benefits for a democratic society to hammer out a wide consensus on a major issue. None explained their conversion more precisely than Brian Mulroney. Three days before the October 26, 1992, referendum the PM acknowledged that the sovereign people of a "modern, pluralistic society like ours" need more than a vote for a representative every four years.

3

OUR OWN DEMOCRATIC LANDSCAPE

Canadian referendums, a long-standing, under-utilized, and ill-understood component of our public life, aren't the same as those in other countries — something missed by those who look sideways at others but not back into our own history of participatory democracy. Every time referendum news from abroad gets refracted through their lenses, we suffer extraneous and misleading commentary paraded as insight about ballot-box democracy in our own country, the usual predicament of bad translation.

THEY ARE NOT US

The news in 2016 about U.K. voters endorsing withdrawal from the European Community, Colombian voters rejecting a peace accord to end a half-century civil war, Hungarian voters registering a desire to keep refugees out of their country, Italian voters rejecting constitutional reform of their senate, and Australians voting down legal recognition of same-sex marriage all cued Canada's stage-worn chorus to sing its downbeat lament about why we don't want referendums *here.*

Canada's political culture and domestic conditions are not those of Colombia, Hungary, and Italy, and differ dramatically from those of the United Kingdom and Australia. Yet those widely dissimilar experiences in diverse foreign lands got blended, for Canadian consumption, into universal condemnation of referendums in general. Certainly nobody seized on them to argue that Canadians should have more referendums, only as evidence for never having any ballot questions in Canada. These opinion leaders were preachy, superior, yet anxious — as if even the shadow of overseas issue-voting was somehow subversive to our decision-making practices here in North America. Those writing bleak editorials for the *Globe and Mail* could only see, on October 10, 2016, "the dark side of modern referendums."

Much is lost in translation. When it comes to interpreting other countries' referendums, the loser is any Canadian taking at face value glib comparisons and shallow punditry. At a very minimum, one must adjust the methods and factor the experiences of others to our own political landscape. That's why, fifteen years ago, British Columbia's referendum office cautioned, when preparing the public for a provincial referendum on whether to establish a "recall" mechanism for elected representatives, that this proposed democratic tool "may require adjustments to a parliamentary system of government."

This book — rather than interpreting referendum experiences of others, appraising their relevance to our political life, and hypothesizing Canadian lessons from votes in other places — primarily addresses our own reality.

BRIEF SYNOPSIS OF CANADIAN REFERENDUM EXPERIENCE

One hundred and forty years of national, provincial, territorial, and local referendums show us where the unwelcome swamps of issue-voting lie, just as they reveal the mountain peaks of participatory democracy where Canadians have been lifted to broadening perspectives, a more cohesive sense of community, and sounder verdicts on major issues.

In 1980 I began looking into the use of ballot questions and realized one reason for relatively little use of this democratic tool was the absence of enabling legislation. By 1982, in *Lawmaking by the People*, I documented the nature of referendum statutes for federal, provincial, municipal, and band council jurisdictions. There was no referendum statute federally, also the case in some provinces. Several provinces with referendum-enabling laws either embedded them within their election statutes or had enacted very short acts adapting election act provisions *mutatis mutandis*, a phrase meaning "as they are relevant and apply, with adjustments as required." Glamorized by Latin, it's a lawmaker's lazy way of sloughing off work to harried election officials in the pressure cooker of a referendum campaign when they must figure out how to apply the transposed rules. In this pattern of absent or inadequate enabling laws, I saw how a minimalist legal framework for ballot questions was an administrative way of discouraging referendums from ever being held.

Most statutes providing referendums were for municipal affairs. The plethora of such measures revealed local democracy to be alive and well across much of Canada, an interesting disconnect because the preponderant national political culture evinced strong disinterest in them.

One entire crop of statutes had been repealed — the Direct Legislation Acts of Manitoba, Saskatchewan, Alberta, and British Columbia. Several were spent, such as the Canada Temperance Act. All these laws had provided, at earlier stages of Canada's democratic life, the use of ballot questions and the right of citizens to bring on a referendum by petition.

The list of Canadian direct votes on national, provincial, and territorial issues printed at the back of this book yields several observations. First, we've made use of ballot questions for fourteen decades. Referendums are a venerable and integrated part of our political system. Second, these referendums took place under governments of more than a half-dozen different political parties, establishing that ballot questions aren't "off-the-wall" efforts from the political fringes. Third, we've only used the referendum mechanism sparingly. This infrequency explains, in turn, why most politicians, political scientists, reporters, public commentators, and members of the public are generally unfamiliar with this democratic practice — the way we'd be if just three general elections had been held since Confederation instead of forty-two.

This unfamiliarity fosters mute apprehension about the unknown, a threshold problem nowadays for Canadian democratic practice. I discovered this first-hand when I introduced a private member's bill in Parliament to establish a permanent legal framework for referendums, the way the Canada Elections Act sets all the rules for elections of representatives. I encountered politicians as awkward discussing referendums as a child and parent having their first conversation about sexual intercourse. There were some supporters. My former professor and friend Eugene Forsey, a constitutional expert and independent senator, came to my press conference to endorse the Canada Referendum and Plebiscite Act I'd introduced in the Commons. Some parliamentarians were curious, many opposed, while others sought outright to derail the project.

The absence of enabling legislation for referendums was mute testimony to the political establishment's determination to control democratic expression, confine those having voice about the public agenda, restrain political participation — and turn its back on our own history.

TEACHERS FAIL TO TRANSLATE OUR OWN EXPERIENCE

The problem with public commentators who, striving for instant analysis of non-Canadian referendums, fail to adjust their observations to a Canadian context even though they intend to educate citizens of this country, also occurs in the academic world, even without the rush to a news-day deadline.

Ignorance of our own political history spawns simplistic generalities about Canadian democratic impulses. It denies the grounding that can help individuals in public life today be more constructive leaders, since knowing where we've come from is a big help for setting a course into the future. Tentativeness about the role for citizens voting on important public issues, though long an effective working part of Canadian democracy, has repeatedly created a negative vibe, buttressing unwarranted resistance to ballot questions.

This has serious implications. Lack of practical experience with referendums, or even clear understanding of their role in shaping today's Canada, contributes to errors in political judgment about such votes. It causes bungled strategy. It leads to counterproductive campaign tactics. The "risks" of referendums are often less about holding them, more about doing so badly, repeating prior mistakes because lessons were never learned.

Professor Robert Jackson, who has influenced thousands of Canadian students of politics and governance through successive editions of his textbook *Politics in Canada: Culture, Institutions, Behaviour, and Public Policy*, devotes two pages of his 750-page work to referendums in other countries, a single page to referendums in Canada. Referendums in non-democratic countries such as Egypt, where nine referendums between 1965 and 1976 never yielded a Yes vote below 99.8 percent, are rightly seen as "primarily symbolic devices which give the illusion of popular participation without any meaningful choice." Jackson suggests they "may be useful in lending an air of legitimacy to decisions on which the ruling elite is already agreed." But where there is "meaningful choice," he adds, referendums "may be considered to enhance the democratic process." Voters have "a much more immediate influence on public decisions than is possible through the election of representatives." The legitimizing function of referendums "is particularly important when it comes to fundamental changes in the political system" such as constitutional amendments.

Then Jackson lists a half-dozen arguments from critics of referendums: referendums downgrade Parliament as "the sovereign law-making body"; uninformed citizens have neither time nor expertise to evaluate complex issues; consulting voters on every issue that might be considered fundamental is impossible; a Yes/No decision might oversimplify complex problems; unscrupulous politicians might appeal to populist sentiments; and such appeals to the masses pose a threat to minorities. He suggests these "drawbacks" account for "the infrequent use" of ballot questions in most countries.

From that analysis he segues to "Referendums in Canada," which begins, "Federal politicians in Canada share the mistrust of referendums and concerns for parliamentary sovereignty displayed by their counterparts elsewhere." A very brief synopsis of several referendums in Canada follows, concluding, "In general, the referendum has not been widely used in Canada."

Members of Canada's political class opposed to referendums, alleging that ballot questions are not part of our system and are incompatible with parliamentary government, are comforted by Jackson's superficial message, since all of them share a predilection for quiet resolution of matters in an accommodating interface restricted to our country's power brokers. An enthusiastic and committed teacher, Robert Jackson has, over the decades, imparted to Canadian students, many of whom came to occupy governance roles, the lesson that Canadian politicians "mistrust" referendums and view them with "concerns for parliamentary sovereignty."

Yet *our* referendums come from the realities of Canada, hold a mirror to our most contentious issues, and have helped us come to terms with raw, practical issues. They are as intrinsic to parliamentary government as elections themselves. They are more compatible than ever now that "parliamentary sovereignty" is an increasingly empty wheelbarrow — constrained by the Constitution, by the higher authority of the Supreme Court, which is empowered to interpret laws in light of the Charter of Rights and Freedoms (providing for the first time in our history an effective "sober second thought" on statutes that Parliament's appointed and unaccountable second chamber still fraudulently claims as its reason for existing), and by a Parliament weakened through iron party discipline.

REFERENDUMS AND THE ART OF STATECRAFT

Not every issue should be litigated in court or made the subject of a royal commission. Not every person suited to a task needs appointment to a public body or a consultant's contract. Not every major decision needs a parliamentary committee … or a referendum. A ballot question is just one of many instruments in our democratic toolbox. The art of statecraft resides in choosing the best tool for a particular job.

One reason this precision tool for democratic governance might not be selected when it could serve a good purpose, or even if chosen might not be deployed skillfully, is that its infrequent use has resulted in a poor understanding of the place and utility of referendums, of government leaders and members of the public not knowing how best to devise and conduct a ballot question. Whereas Californians have dozens and sometimes hundreds of "ballot propositions" accompanying their general elections — seemingly pushing this voting mechanism to the limit the way they do diets, religion, exercise regimes, and special-effects movies — Canadians haven't overdosed on direct democracy. Rather, we've rusted out. From surgery to sports, lack of continuous experience imposes a penalty of lost expertise. It's the same rule for democracy, from the art of public speaking to the statecraft of ballot questions: use it or lose it.

In provincial and municipal referendums, ballot issues placed before voters have ranged from the transcendent to the trivial, minor matters getting onto ballots because of unfamiliarity with applicable criteria or because campaign opportunists imagined an electoral advantage. That, in turn, has left a residue of confusion about which types of issues are suitable or necessary for ballot questions, and distaste for a shoddy exercise. On the other hand, a bonus of renewed Canadian use of referendums is how increased experience imparts lessons and provides a comforting level of familiarity. In short, the cure for democracy is more democracy.

Ballot questions in Canada are a component of hands-on and accountable local government in many municipalities and aboriginal reserves. The desire for democratic accountability at the local level, combined with the relative ease of holding votes in smaller geographic centres, cumulatively accounts for thousands of ballot questions across Canada over the decades — most of them off the radar screens of the national or even provincial news media and political class. The municipal arena also boasts a strong history of local citizens requiring, by petition, that a ballot question be submitted to them on a particular issue — a tangible example of what is often just a metaphor about "grassroots" democracy.

Participatory democracy helps us address contentious issues, and in the process, shapes the steady evolution of Canadian values. Complex issues have been resolved by ballot-box democracy in several instances thanks to repeated votes over time.

The bottom line: ballot questions have long-standing use in our country, have been turned to by governments of many partisan stripes, have addressed a wide variety of issues, and have helped self-governing citizens make decisions whose consequences we pay for and live with.

This specialized instrument in our democratic toolbox has even proven to be a uniquely beneficial procedure when, sometimes, nothing else would work. Even more, voting on public issues highlights the institutional ambiguities that are fused in our political culture about who is really in charge.

4

THE SOVEREIGN PEOPLE
OF CANADA

One reason Canadian public affairs seem so muddled is that constitutionally we have not one but *two* sovereigns. This leaves a lot of people confused about who's in charge.

Thirteen of England's North American colonies united in the 1700s to overthrow the monarchy and became an independent republic, the United States of America, where sovereignty resides *exclusively* in the people. Quite simply, *We the people* … are in charge.

In contrast, our loyalty premium for not making that clean break was inheriting the United Kingdom's historical residue known as a "constitutional monarchy." This power structure emerged as that country's institutional compromise was battled out over centuries, shifting from an absolute monarch to a more restrained setup with "sovereignty" vesting simultaneously in both the Crown *and* the people. That arrangement was exported to North America in colonial times and endures to this day as the divided arrangement in Canada. Another country's historic necessity became our operational legacy: a twin source of legitimizing state power perpetuated by the institutionalized ambiguity in our enduring 1860s Constitution.

THE JANUS-LIKE FACE OF A CONSTITUTIONAL MONARCHY

Being a constitutional monarchy creates the ambivalent two-directional context for all Canadian governance. We, as sovereign people, must coexist with visible symbols of this other sovereign power. The Queen's image is on our currency and stamps. In our courts, the Queen's framed portrait gazes out as charges brought under her austere Latin designation, *Regina*, are prosecuted by a Crown attorney. Governments that screw up hide from liability behind the thick skirts of "Crown immunity," a governmental version of papal infallibility. In daily life we acquire resource rights on Crown lands and pay "royalties" to exploit them. Our private property is subject to expropriation under historic powers of the Crown. The British lapsed into "muddling through" as a modus operandi and inevitably, given that we have the same institutional muddle, this became our preponderant method of operation, too. Except in Canada, locating the locus of power is further compounded by division of power between various levels of government, often with duplication or overlap, seldom with clarity, direct acceptance of responsibility, or true democratic accountability.

We look to our Constitution and statutes to clarify which of our various governments has jurisdiction for a particular field of activity, but when it comes to the *source of governing authority*, we have to look in two places. In one, we find ourselves: a self-governing democratic people. In the other, we see a represented Crown. Although both are sources of sovereign power, there is, of necessity, a hierarchy: the people rank above the Crown.

Those wielding the powers of state do so in the name of the Crown, most prominent among them elected representatives who have been named ministers of the Crown. However, nobody gets to exercise any of these Crown powers or prerogatives until *after* the people first elect representatives of a political party with enough votes in the legislature authorizing them to form a government. Then, and only then, can a group of elected Canadians exercise power in the name of the Crown — appointing judges; launching royal commissions; and naming officials to run banking, communications, armed forces, police, transport, and foreign relations. Deputy ministers of government departments, and heads of all Crown corporations, boards, commissions, and agencies, are appointed by those we elect. Our *elected* prime minister designates an individual for the monarch to *appoint* vice-regal representative as governor general or as lieutenant governor of a province.

Moreover, the elected representatives exercising these Crown powers only get to do so for five or fewer years. Then, in another election, the sovereign people assess performance and scrutinize new job applicants. Even between, while in office, the ministers of the Crown and officials answering to them are directly held to account by the people's elected representatives in the House of Commons and the provincial and territorial legislatures.

THE PEOPLE, NOT THE GOVERNMENT, ARE MASTER

Today's overriding focus on prime ministers and premiers, and the politicians and players who guide them, tends to eclipse citizens as the ultimate sovereign in all matters of state. Despite such obscurity, only electors hold the ultimate key to power.

"The people, not the government, are master," emphasized Winston Churchill. "The will of the British people is an instruction that must be delivered," reiterated David Cameron about the political and constitutional status of electors. Despite our considerable and growing differences, Britain and Canada share this democratic foundation: the people are the country's ultimate boss despite the remnant presence of a monarchy.

Textbook charts resembling pyramids show the structure of Canadian government as a mass of people at the bottom with ever fewer numbers of individual office holders triangulating through institutional groupings to the pointed top where the prime minister and, at the side, the governor general, occupy individual boxes. However, as already described, citizens first elect representatives so parliaments can convene, with selected MPs sworn in as ministers of the Crown to then exercise governing powers. Canada's democratic power structure better resembles an *inverted pyramid*.

Seen in this *correct* constitutional context, having citizens vote on important issues is appropriate and unexceptional. This is why Canada and Britain, as well as Australia and New Zealand, all incorporate referendums within parliamentary systems. Even so, when citizens vote in the United Kingdom about the European Community or in Canada on the Charlottetown Accord, the process sparks almost primordial anxiety in some who, thinking the sovereign people to be interlopers, challenge our citizen-centred democracy by angrily demanding, "Who is running the country?"

THE OUTDATED DOCTRINE OF "PARLIAMENTARY SOVEREIGNTY"

Referendums earned their place in 1800s Canada as a deliberate process to channel, arbitrate, and resolve contentious public questions. Some referendum opponents, preaching an outdated gospel of "parliamentary sovereignty" and invoking "the Westminster model" despite its significant dissimilarities to Canadian parliamentary forms, allege that a ballot question posed by elected representatives to the people is a dodge, "an abdication of responsibility." Their contention fails to recognize that both the MP and the ballot question are not juxtaposed opposites, but rather common features of sovereign people exercising power.

Senior legal counsel to the House of Commons Gregory Tardi discerned how a referendum is "the symbiosis of political and legal aspects which endows this vehicle of governance with its democratic pedigree."[1] Voting on a ballot question is a political exercise, to be sure, but one deliberately shaped by legally binding rules, conducted in harmony with Canadian legal norms, having legal outcomes, and compliant with statutory provisions enacted by the people's elected representatives.

Even so, referendums aren't immune from attack on constitutional grounds. Canada's 1898 vote on prohibiting alcohol faced a court challenge from the country's prospering liquor interests. Although distillers, vintners, and brewers knew they'd forfeit everything if booze was banned, they also understood the folly of challenging Canada's first national ballot question as, somehow, an invalid democratic exercise. After all, asking the people for a specific mandate on prohibition had been adopted as policy by an open Liberal Party convention, advocated by the Liberals in Canada's 1896 general election, and become part of the government's electoral mandate when Laurier formed a majority government. Moreover, ballot questions had been taking place under the Canada Temperance Act in Canada's municipalities and provinces for decades. So their constitutional challenge didn't attack the referendum device itself but was framed on grounds that had become a hallmark of that era's constitutional law: that one level of government was "trenching" on the jurisdiction of another. Their argument was that the division of federal and provincial responsibilities in sections 91 and 92 of the Constitution meant Ottawa lacked jurisdiction to impose prohibition. The courtroom contest wasn't to prevent 1898's vote taking place. The plaintiffs only hoped to prevent the Laurier government from implementing prohibition if the people voted to ban alcohol. Eventually, the challenge reached our colonial era's ultimate appellate court, the Judicial Committee of the Privy Council in Britain, where the Law Lords sustained prohibition as a valid federal power should Parliament choose to invoke it.[2]

Our modern era also sparks constitutional challenges about referendums, but both the context and substance of constitutional law has changed. In 1948 appeals to the Law Lords in England was ended by the decolonizing

Liberal government of Louis St. Laurent so that our own Supreme Court, in existence since 1875, finally became Canada's highest court of appeal. Then, in 1981, as the result of initiatives by Pierre Trudeau, the Charter of Rights and Freedoms became integral to determining constitutionality. These twin developments changed the very character of "constitutional law" in Canada: first, from being the product of interpretations by a court of foreigners in Europe to a body of decisions by resident Canadians; second, from mostly battles over jurisdiction to primarily rights-based litigation. To the benefit of Canadian democratic life, the political-legal dimensions of public issues grew more sharply defined — because, finally, they were more closely entwined. In the process, the ancient concept of "parliamentary supremacy" was overtaken by the supremacy of courts interpreting, in light of the Charter, laws enacted by Parliament. One constant over all these decades has been *Canadian* judges displaying, subject to upholding the rule of law, reluctance to intervene in the workings of elected legislatures and democratic processes.

CONTROLLING ACCESS TO REFERENDUMS

Referendums complement the overall operation of parliamentary government in several ways. First, as constitutional authority A.V. Dicey noted in the 1800s when arguing for direct balloting in Britain, it provides a rounding out of parliamentary democracy wholly consistent with the theory and practice of representative government. It does so by providing a democratic check, rather than a monarchical veto, on government. Referendums are democracy's way of holding a mirror to the community, reflecting people's considered outlook on a specific question at a particular time.

A second benefit, given the natural limitations of Canadian parliamentary operations, is the indispensable role ballot questions intermittently play in enabling institutions of self-government to continue operating. This has included transferring issues, too explosive to be contained within traditional parliamentary confines, from the assembly to the people for a direct and comprehensive vote. As well, this safety valve of Canadian democracy has also been welcomed for turning over to ballot questions issues that had stalemated the assembly.

The full electorate of sovereign Canadians is a greater forum than a legislative assembly because it is the real thing, not a "representative" body. As the people who elect governments to exercise power in the name of the Crown are the highest sovereign authority in our *constitutional* (meaning "limited" or "restricted") monarchy, the referendum is our ultimate recourse.

However, this raises the crucial issue about who controls access to the referendum device. Mostly, in Canada today, the ability to get a significant issue before the public on a ballot is controlled by the political parties, especially by the party in office. This risk that use of referendums will only be self-serving for the party controlling government is a temptation that hasn't always been resisted.

The right of citizens to initiate ballot questions themselves for a broader vote than can occur within the assembly of elected representatives exists today in British Columbia, our country's leading jurisdiction for enhancing participatory democracy. When this right for citizens to initiate ballot questions becomes more widespread, that will be wholly in keeping with fundamental constitutional principles of our country and consistent with Canadians being a self-governing sovereign people.

CANADA'S SOVEREIGN PEOPLE CONTRASTED WITH "WE THE PEOPLE ..."

Is it not significant that American voting on ballot propositions never generates the angst familiar to Canadians? Americans spend time debating policies, not whether it is proper for citizens to share law-making with their elected representatives. In many states, governments submit ballot propositions to voters and the people themselves also launch ballot questions. All it takes is enough people signing a petition to initiate the process and a judge certifying the question constitutionally valid. Then state electors debate, educate themselves on the issues, and divide between minority and majority support for policy propositions such as those on the ballot in November 2016 about legalizing marijuana, extending health benefits, raising the minimum wage, controlling firearms, recognizing rights of LGBT people, and dozens more. Voting on propositions is a recognized, normal, healthy component of American citizenship.

Beyond the United States, in Southeast Asia, I also witnessed a contrasting example of constitutional *inclusion* of the referendum device within the political system. Like other Canadians, I'd been acculturated by our country's open-ended cycles of constitutional negotiations from 1967 to 1992 and supposed that "muddling through" was normal. But in Thailand, helping draft the country's new referendum law, I discovered an alternate pattern for rewriting a constitution: a clearly defined process with specific deadlines.

To launch the project, full-page ads appeared in Thai newspapers. Flyers were widely distributed, and posters filled public notice boards from Bangkok to Chiang Mai. All showed a year-long calendar for public meetings, completing an initial draft, further input from people interested in the constitution, the process of second-round review, revision, and final approval. If the people's representatives in Thailand's parliament didn't ratify the constitution by a stipulated date, it would go to a national referendum so that the people could render their verdict on it instead. There was ample time for each stage. There were deadlines to focus completion and force choices. There were alternate pathways to bypass any stalemate.

A Canadian conceit is that we have lessons to teach others about democracy.

5

REFERENDUM LAW NORMALIZES DEMOCRATIC LIFE

If you wanted to thwart democratic accountability through regular elections, you'd make sure no Election Act was on the statute books. That way, whenever somebody suggests a trip to the polls, there would be debate about why an election was even necessary since the Commons already has MPs. Disagreement would erupt over what a proposed election bill should cover. The legislation would flounder amid self-interested cross-currents of incumbents. Delay would sideline the effort.

If you were part of Canada's networked political and policy establishment, keeping at bay the unpredictable and ignorant masses you're smoothly governing, resolved to ensuring that they'd never get a direct say on *anything*, you'd likewise make sure no Referendum Act was on the statute books.

A ONE-OFF STATUTE FOR 1898'S PROHIBITION VOTE

Canada's first national ballot question in 1898 about prohibiting alcohol certainly riled those convinced that asking voters to make a choice violated parliamentary democracy as practised by "the Mother Country."

Yet by then Canadians had already used referendums for decades in harmony with parliamentary and municipal government systems, because involving "the people" in significant decisions was vital for democratic life, and because in our constitutional system the sovereign people have the ultimate say, anyway. The people had representatives in the Commons, provincial legislatures, and municipal and band councils routinely handling regular business, but when they could help resolve important issues of widespread consequence by saying Yes or No to something specific, that was a way democracy worked, too.

Prime Minister Laurier knew the task at hand was to build a country of our own, chucking a colonial mindset that stubbornly adhered to the increasingly irrelevant "Westminster" model with its misunderstood cluster of antiquated doctrines. Not until 1911, a third of a century after Prince Edward Island conducted a province-wide ballot question and miraculously survived, would the value of referendums be debated for the first time in Britain's parliament at Westminster. Only in 2000, under Prime Minister Tony Blair, would Westminster enact a *permanent* statute to provide the mechanisms for country-wide referendums.

In Canada it had been no stretch in the late 1800s for the Liberal Party's modernizing vanguard to see referendums as entirely compatible with the work of the people's elected representatives. Even so, Canada was still populated by "British subjects" so colonial-minded they could never imagine leading Mother, only following her. This mentality was on full display when Parliament debated the Prohibition Plebiscite Act, a threshold step for holding a national ballot question because Canada needed a law to govern referendums and didn't have one.

George Elliott Casey, a Liberal MP and a declared opponent of citizens voting on ballot questions, represented Ontario's Elgin West — a riding in which municipal voting on issues occurred, as had already been common in Ontario since 1850. He'd even lived through province-wide issue-voting in 1894. Yet this Ontarian ardently rejected the practice at the national level because, contended Casey, ballot questions were "foreign" to Westminster parliamentary government.

On May 3, 1898, Casey joined debate. About the Liberal's 1898 prohibition ballot, he said people shouldn't be asked to vote for a broad proposition but instead indicate whether or not a specific scheme of prohibition suited them. "Anybody who knows anything of the popular vote knows it is easy to get people to vote for an abstract proposition like Free Trade, or Protection, or Prohibition, or anything else," he hypothesized, "while you could not get them to agree by the smallest majority upon some particular plan of carrying out the principle that might be adopted." On those grounds, Casey urged the government to adopt the legally binding referendum rather than the merely advisory plebiscite, then pass a bill that wouldn't become law until approved by a majority of Canadian voters.

Having been Liberal whip, George Casey knew all Grit MPs had to fall in line with Liberal measures, so he told the House he felt "compelled to support the bill" because the government itself was "compelled to keep their promises" and, "as a supporter of theirs and one who shared in their pledges," he could do nothing else. Then clouding matters more, he said the bill had "my hearty support in its general features … though in opposition to my judgment in its principle." How much simpler for the anguished parliamentarian if he'd just accepted that, in a democracy, the quest for a specific mandate on a policy so profound as completely removing beverage alcohol from society is how things should work, regardless of what people did or thought in Britain.

The difficulty that modernizing Liberals faced in 1898 — just getting legislation through Parliament for a vote on prohibition — showed it would help normalize democratic life tremendously to have a general enabling statute on the books, rules that would be available when needed for a national referendum the way the Dominion Elections Act was at the ready for elections. However, because so many parliamentarians cleaved to outdated British thinking in 1898, only a compromise one-off statute got enacted for the prohibition vote, expiring when the event ended.

ANOTHER ONE-OFF STATUTE FOR 1942'S CONSCRIPTION VOTE

The identical problem faced Mackenzie King's Liberal government in 1942. His imperative for a vote on conscription required first getting Parliament to enact the requisite enabling law. A new generation of Canadians zealously asserted loyalty to British parliamentary doctrines, imagining incorrectly that they precluded referendums. Debate continued for days. Anxious, King was displeased by the lacklustre performance of some Liberals, who limply defended his government's plan. But on February 4, the PM was heartened by "a splendid speech" in which finance minister J.L. Ilsley vigorously refuted all arguments against a ballot question.

To the charge a referendum represented "a cowardly negation of responsible government," the Nova Scotia lawyer retorted that "the essence of responsible government involves not only a government responsible to Parliament, but a Parliament responsible to the people; not a government which makes its solemn pledges to the people who elected it, but a government which, if elected on a particular pledge, seeks the consent of the people to free it from that pledge if changing conditions seem so to require."

To objections that a referendum would dangerously delay war preparations, Ilsley answered that the voluntary system of recruitment would continue operating, all other war plans would proceed, and the three months for the campaign and verdict from the people wouldn't stop any of these operations. Ilsley then delivered his finishing punch: "Surely the cowardly government or Parliament is one, rather, which fears to ascertain the views of the people."

On February 25, King himself joined the debate. He'd become annoyed how colonial deference to Britain's hallowed "Westminster model" led many MPs to challenge the appropriateness of issue-voting by the people in a parliamentary system, claiming it would alter the role of elected representatives. "There is a distinction to be made between the legal powers which the government has and the moral authority which it possesses," he stated. It was "inescapable" that a people's mandate was required to provide legitimizing authority for the exercise of power in a democracy. "With respect to the legal power, there can be no question whatever that this Parliament has full power to do whatever it may decide to do in the management of matters pertaining to the war," he told the elected representatives.

"The one limitation which exists on that power, so far as this parliament is concerned, is not a legal limitation but a moral obligation," stated Canada's prime minister. "To say that the Parliament of Canada, which derives its powers from the people, after a solemn pledge has been given to the people on a matter which is of deep concern to them, is released from this pledge the moment the people have elected it, is for Parliament itself to create a precedent which would be subversive of parliamentary institutions."

The Dominion Plebiscite Act, 1942, made it through Parliament, a statute only ten sections long, most provisions adopted by *mutatis mutandis* reference to the Dominion Elections Act. Rules for electing MPs would need painstaking reconfiguration by officials conducting the ballot question vote. Much worse, this 1942 act was again a one-off statute for a particular issue, not general enabling legislation that, in addition to governing the conscription vote, could apply to future ballot questions.

A REFERENDUM STATUTE TO NORMALIZE DEMOCRATIC LIFE

To create enabling legislation *after* a government is already contemplating citizens voting on a particular question guarantees that referendum procedures will become conflated with the controversial issue itself.

The Laurier and King governments struggled hard just to get referendum legislation through Parliament, two powerful PMs only managing compromises, one-time statutes for those votes. As these two "case studies" made clear, a looming crisis distorts the perspective of lawmakers, produces a compromised law because subjective considerations dominate thinking and shortage of time precludes careful reflection. For a mature democratic country, why not enact referendum legislation in a calm atmosphere and deliberate manner?

After getting elected to Parliament in 1984, I drafted a referendum bill, a full set of integrated rules for conducting referendums in a single self-contained statute. On July 21, 1988, I introduced the Canada Referendum and Plebiscites Act, Bill C-311, in the House of Commons. It provided four ways to initiate ballot questions and governed everything such as voting, fundraising, advertising, broadcasting, voters' lists, voting procedures, duties of referendum officials, spending limits, registration of Yes and No umbrella committees, providing information to voters, and other elements and safeguards needed for modern Canadian campaigns. Senator Eugene Forsey, a recognized scholar on constitutional affairs and educator about democratic government in Canada, came to my press conference that morning and told reporters, "I am here to express my support for this bill. Ballot questions would allow voters to have *their* say when all three parties take the same stand on a major issue."[1]

My bill drew on the British Referendum Act 1975 and U.K. lessons of the good that flows from having two opposing umbrella organizations, one for the No and another for the Yes side of a ballot question, as well as Quebec's Referendum Act, which incorporated the same British umbrella organizations but added contemporary Canadian provisions to finance and register referendum groups. Another helpful source for detailed provisions was the 1978 Canada Referendum Act that Marc Lalonde, minister for federal-provincial relations, had introduced in the Commons for the Trudeau government. I next adapted "publicity pamphlet" provisions from Manitoba's 1916 Initiative and Referendum Act, by which Yes and

No sides would get equal space to state their case in a brochure distributed by the chief referendum officer to all voters, updated for 1988 technology to include videotapes for voter education. Bill C-311 included provisions empowering citizens to initiate a referendum, based on principles I'd distilled from Canadian legal history when writing *Lawmaking by the People.*

Finally, I "modernized" my legislation by incorporating provisions from Bill C-79, introduced by the Mulroney government in 1986 to amend the Canada Elections Act. It was an amalgam of Charter reforms, accumulated recommendations from Chief Electoral Officer Jean-Marc Hamel's annual reports, and suggestions by Progressive Conservative MPs contained in the report of a caucus committee on election law reform that I chaired. Our caucus report became the government's White Paper on Election Law Reform, tabled by Justice Minister Ray Hnatyshyn in 1986, which in turn became the basis for Bill C-79. That government bill never got enacted, but its relevant bits made it into my private member's Canada Referendum and Plebiscite Act. As a result, my bill incorporated equality provisions required by the Charter, such as level access to polling stations for people with disabilities, and proposals by the chief electoral officer, such as distinctions between urban and rural voters.

Under Bill C-311, no more than one referendum could be held during the life of a Parliament (up to five years) on the same, or a substantially similar, subject. A national referendum couldn't take place concurrently with a general election.

FATES OF A PRIVATE MEMBER'S REFERENDUM ACT

Getting Bill C-311 enacted was hard. A number of MPs told me referendums were a bad idea because members of the public are too ignorant to vote intelligently on complex issues, so it would be a danger for public affairs to start down this ill-conceived path. They couldn't support my bill. Why didn't I just withdraw it? "You should, you know, if you want to be taken seriously in national politics."

Perseverance helps. After 1988 I kept the Canada Referendum and Plebiscite Act continuously before Parliament, reintroducing it each time a new session began. Bill C-311 of July 21, 1988, became Bill C-2 on December 14, 1988; C-257 on September 26, 1989; C-201 on May 15,

1991; and C-287 on September 23, 1991. It was debated on June 18, 1991, but "talked out" rather than brought to a vote. By unanimous consent of the House, however, I could get it referred to committee for second-reading review. Working behind the scenes to line this up, I first got the PCs to agree, not too hard because, despite opposition from individual ministers and MPs, the government itself was under mounting pressure to get referendum legislation in place for a ratification vote on the package of constitutional amendments that was then in the process of becoming the Charlottetown Accord.

Next I met with Opposition Leader Jean Chrétien in his parliamentary office to get Liberal agreement. We talked so long about Quebec's 1980 referendum on sovereignty, and how an annual Chrétien family reunion had erupted into fist fights between federalist and sovereignist cousins, that a growing cluster of backed-up Liberal MPs outside the closed door for their appointments with the leader fantasized us having a protracted discussion, I later learned, about me crossing the floor to sit as a Liberal. I was willing to do just about anything to get my bill passed, but there are limits.

After that I got willing consent from MP Deborah Grey, the Reform Party's lone member in the House, a referendum on the Constitution being Reform policy. Then I sought out Independent MPs J. Patrick Nowlan and Alex Kindy, long-time acquaintances and former PC colleagues, either of whom by a single "Nay" could deny the unanimous consent needed for my bill to advance to committee. Both gave their support. With the NDP, I anticipated a hurdle because my socialist friends such as John Rodrigues, MP from Sudbury, adamantly opposed referendums, a streak more widespread in the socialist party's ranks than one might suspect from champions of a "new democracy." But other New Democrats, including MP Svend Robinson who'd served on the equality rights parliamentary committee I chaired, spoke with his new party leader, Audrey McLaughlin, who promised that there would be no opposition from that quarter.

This left only the Bloc Québécois. Most of its MPs, including leader Lucien Bouchard, had been in our PC caucus and were personal friends. I spoke with them individually and won conditional consent, each one stipulating that I'd need Lucien on side. Now it was down to a single individual.

The small table in the parliamentary restaurant where Lucien and I sat over lunch gave him the opportunity to demonstrate his case by holding the tip of his tie out over the white linen tablecloth toward me. "If I agree, it will be like the tip of my tie getting into the wringer. Soon the entire tie and everything else gets pulled in. I can't agree." As the separatist leader in Parliament, Lucien knew he wanted only Quebecers to vote on leaving Confederation. He didn't want Ottawa having recourse to a referendum with its own ballot question for Quebecers, or for voters across the rest of the country since all Canadians would be impacted by the breakup of Confederation. My bill remained stalled.

STRANGER FATES AWAIT A GOVERNMENT'S REFERENDUM ACT

The May 13, 1991, throne speech contained the Mulroney government's commitment to referendum legislation. So it seemed we'd get a Canada-wide ballot question on constitutional amendments one way or another.

The minister responsible for constitutional affairs, Joe Clark, said referendum legislation confined to constitutional questions would be brought before Parliament, but delayed. In the spring, Joe said the legislation would come in the fall. In early autumn, he said October. By November, after meeting with the Quebec Progressive Conservative caucus, he appeared to unilaterally reverse the Mulroney government's policy by declaring to journalists the referendum was "no longer an option." Joe formulated his stunning circled-wagon stance this way: "If we have national consensus, there's no need for a referendum. If there's no consensus, we don't want a referendum." Just how we'd discern "consensus" remained a mystery he didn't explain.

In the interim, I had again reintroduced my private member's bill, to keep something before Parliament. I believed it, or some government version of the bill, had to be enacted so Canadians could vote on the pending constitutional package directly. Meanwhile, the Liberals had withdrawn from a joint Commons-Senate committee studying the government's constitutional proposals, in protest against its proceedings and the government's inexplicable stalling on referendum legislation. Time passed. Opposition Leader Chrétien and Constitutional Affairs Minister Clark struck a deal: as a condition for Liberals rejoining the committee, the government would introduce its long-promised referendum legislation. Despite this, however, no government referendum bill materialized.

The Liberals had been advocating a referendum to ratify any constitutional package that ultimately got negotiated. Faced with the government's continuing postponement, Opposition Leader Chrétien urged in the

Commons on April 7, 1992, that my Canada Referendum and Plebiscite Act, since it constituted a comprehensive code for a national referendum on the Constitution, be called for debate and enacted. To advance this plan, I tabled my bill with the special parliamentary committee on electoral law reform. This cohesive group of MPs, already up to speed dealing with voting legislation, was focused and particularly well-suited to review the referendum bill.

Finally, on May 15, a full year after it had been promised, the government introduced its own Referendum Act, Bill C-81, rushing it through the Commons using closure. In the brief interval that C-81 was being debated in the Commons, my PC colleague from Quebec, MP Jean-Pierre Blackburn, and I introduced many amendments, as did Opposition MPs. The government intended the Referendum Act to expire after three years, to placate ministers like Joe Clark, who opposed any public scrutiny and vote by citizens on changes to the country's Constitution. The expiry date was Mulroney's concession, the way Laurier and King had to compromise to get a single law for holding a referendum. One of my amendments changed that to require a parliamentary committee review the statute in three years, instead. That kept the Referendum Act on the books and subsequently, following that review, led to several amendments.

Blackburn and I, as well as the Liberals, had two other strong concerns: (a) effective spending limits weren't provided; and (b), no umbrella committee structure was mandated to organize the Yes and No sides. In the controversy over correcting this, our amendments to the bill were defeated by the government majority. Jean-Pierre and I refused to vote the party line.

WHY UMBRELLA COMMITTEES AND SPENDING LIMITS MATTER

Use of umbrella organizations for Quebec's 1980 referendum on sovereignty-association and Northern Quebec's 1987 referendum on the region's constitutional future made sense for political, legal, administrative, and structural reasons. Drawing together as teams those who support and oppose a ballot question enables them to effectively coordinate their campaigns within an overall structure. In addition to maximizing campaign strategy, tactics, messaging, and finances, the common organization provides order and context for each campaign to raise funds, spend money, sponsor advertising, divide up free airtime broadcasts, and organize supporters for voting.

Political parties provide similar structures to give shape to elections. Political parties also constitute an identifiable entity to fix with legal consequences for statutory violations. A referendum campaign, arguably needing even more organizational coordination, requires this umbrella structure for those same purposes.

However, in 1992, critics of the umbrella concept contended "freedom of association" was the overriding democratic value. They asserted no law could oblige one group or organization to associate with another. They invoked "freedom of expression" also, contending an umbrella committee would limit people's ability to freely express their political views, a libertarian school of thought articulated by the National Citizens Coalition (NCC) and holding sway with nervous Mulroney cabinet ministers and those drafting Bill C-81.

Behind the scenes, it was embarrassing to witness how timid a Canadian majority government became, actually paralyzed by fear that the National Citizens Coalition would constitutionally challenge the Referendum Act as infringing freedoms of assembly and speech if it contained the umbrella provisions. Because the Mulroney government had delayed so long to bring referendum legislation before Parliament, its back was now against the wall. Quebec had long been on track to its own referendum on the Charlottetown Accord in October 1992, a timetable by which Quebec Premier Robert Bourassa had provided ample warning and time for the Mulroney government to get its act together and its referendum law enacted. Now Ottawa's excruciatingly tight timetable for organizing a Canada-wide referendum led the government's closeted ministers and their advisers to remove any risk of the Referendum Act getting tied up in court over a constitutional challenge. The government cut the umbrella committee provision. It would avoid chaos in the courts, only to get chaos in the campaign.

FREEDOM AND FINANCES IN A CAMPAIGN FOR VOTES

In 1974, when election finance provisions were first added to the Canada Elections Act to impose spending controls, the law still allowed independent-minded individuals to express themselves during an election campaign. In 1982 Parliament changed this safety valve in the law to close what the Trudeau government considered a loophole — it restricted all non-party paid political expression during election campaigns. This new restriction was challenged by the National Citizens Coalition and struck down in court, rightly, as an unconstitutional legal straitjacket. As a result, election finances were restored to a balanced position in the Canada Elections Act, which would govern all political parties in which like-minded supporters function as one, while allowing individuals not affiliated with a particular party to independently exercise their constitutional freedoms of association and speech.

This effort to achieve "reasonable accommodation" of individual independence and freedom of expression ought to have prevailed within the Mulroney government's Referendum Act to maintain balance with the equally valid requirement for order, structure, financial accountability, and legal responsibility in national campaigns.

However, the Mulroney government asked six eminent lawyers from prestigious firms across Canada for legal opinions to bolster the Justice Department's in-house conclusion that umbrella committees might not withstand a Charter challenge. The Department of Justice asked outside counsel whether "exclusive" umbrella committees would violate the Charter. Of course they would. All six legal opinions predictably stated this obvious conclusion. The point about exclusivity and thwarting individual rights had already been made by the court deciding the NCC's challenge to the 1982 changes to the Canada Elections Act. That case alone ought to have pointed competent government lawyers to a Charter-proof way to draft umbrella committee provisions.

No one who has seriously examined the trade-off between freedom of expression and workable campaign spending rules simplistically suggests the choice is black and white (as "exclusive" umbrella committees would be). The Lortie Royal Commission spent two years and $18 million dealing with these issues, emerging with a balanced approach favouring the structure needed for campaigns while allowing the necessary "escape valve" for individuals of independent views who require alternate, non-party means of expression. In my 1983 law book *Money and Message*, I canvassed the same issues at length, then concluded: "As long as Canada is a democracy and we have laws which regulate campaign spending to ensure that politics is not just a rich man's game, there will be debate about the exact location of the line which must be drawn between freedom of expression and the efficacy of the legal regime for campaign financing." Anyone taking account of competing interests recognizes that a balanced trade-off is required. Bill C-81, the Mulroney government's referendum legislation, intentionally refused to seek that balance. A reasonable campaign structure, made possible by two umbrella committees, was sacrificed to dubious political expediency.

At this very time, it is worth remembering, Quebec's Referendum Act was being constitutionally challenged over this identical issue by the province's Equality Party. The Superior Court of Quebec upheld umbrella committee provisions as being constitutional. Had they been struck down under the Charter, the Quebec government was standing by to have the National Assembly invoke the Charter's "notwithstanding" clause and re-enact the provisions a second time, so committed was it to this balanced and sensible system for a properly functioning democracy.

In the Commons debate on Bill C-81, we connected our umbrella committee amendments directly to the issue of spending limits. Bill C-81 *appeared* to set spending limits because it set a $5,000 expenditure ceiling on each registered referendum committee. However, making a complete farce of spending controls, there was no limit on the number of committees that could be formed!

Despite these shortcomings in the legislation, the government fulfilled its pledge that "the men and women of Canada could participate directly in the process of constitutional change." The Mulroney government succeeded where the Trudeau government had twice failed in getting legislation for a national direct vote on the Constitution. As a result, Canada today has enabling law for direct votes on the statute books. Confined to constitutional matters, it governed the Charlottetown Accord referendum of October 26, 1992.

STILL FACING THE SAME STATUTORY CONUNDRUM TODAY

After 2015's general election, a number of Canadians urged a referendum on electoral change. On December 2, 2016, the parliamentary committee studying electoral reform recommended the government hold a referendum in which the first-past-the-post system would be on the ballot. The twelve-member committee had not, however, achieved unanimity in its recommendations. A "Supplementary Opinion of the Liberal Party of Canada" by MPs John Aldag, Matt DeCourcey, Sherry Romanado, Ruby Sahota, and Francis Scarpaleggia, himself the committee's chair, dissented from and qualified their own report, saying the timeline was rushed. They did not recommend a referendum. They urged more study, paving a way for no electoral change by 2019, despite the Liberals' electoral mandate to do exactly that.

The Canada Referendum Act is exclusively for voting on constitutional questions, which, strictly speaking, changes in the electoral system are not. Chief Electoral Officer Marc Mayrand rightly pointed out that the Referendum Act would have to be changed for it to govern a referendum on electoral change, although this threshold difficulty seemed to float past most everyone who heard his cautionary report. Advocates ardent for a referendum on the electoral system, who numbered many, skipped right over the necessity of enabling legislation.

Perhaps, if they thought about it at all, they figured getting the legislation drafted and through Parliament to be a mere technicality.

6

REFERENDUMS IN HARMONY WITH THE CONSTITUTION

Referendums *about* the Constitution are one thing, but how referendums fit *within* the constitutional regime of our country is something else. Does a referendum undermine "parliamentary supremacy," threaten minority rights, or challenge constitutionally established roles of legislatures? Is voting in a referendum a citizen's constitutional right?

Slicing through these topics reveals how referendums operate most of the time in harmony with the *Constitution of Canada*, a term that broadly defined includes the customs, conventions, and enactments of the written constitutional text as well as Canadian political and judicial institutions and processes.

THE RIGHT TO VOTE ON BALLOT QUESTIONS

A citizen's democratic right to vote on public questions is provided in statutes enacted by the people's elected representatives. Although not included among other constitutionally enumerated political rights in the Charter of Rights and Freedoms, such as the Section 3 right to vote for one's representatives, the Charter isn't a closed list and doesn't confine our rights and freedoms so much as express most of them. For instance, the Supreme Court of Canada ruled in the 1989 *Andrews* case that Section 15 equality rights are available to groups even though not explicitly enumerated in the Charter. Again in 1995 in the *Egan* case, the Supreme Court established that sexual orientation is a prohibited basis for discrimination, despite not being specifically mentioned in the Charter. This was the same unanimous conclusion reached in 1985 by an all-party Commons committee I chaired on Section 15, in our report *Equality for All*, that the Charter does not constitute a closed list. Case law in Ontario more than a century ago confirmed municipal electors have a right to vote on a local matter, even in the absence of statutory authority, akin to a citizen's "natural right" if living under a democratic system of government.

The extent of one's right to vote on issues varies quite a bit from one province to the next. Each jurisdiction imprints its own political culture on province-wide issue-voting through a referendum act and balloting about municipal matters by means of a variety of other statutes, which deal with such issues as libraries, adding fluoride to the local water supply, or other identifiable concerns. Some enactments also specify subset categories of provincial voters for such sectoral issues as milk production and distribution, or fruit and vegetable growing and marketing.

Case law has established some protective ground rules. The right to vote on a ballot issue, as a fundamental democratic right created by a legislature, can't be altered by a municipality or local board. In the 1929 Ontario case of *Eldridge v. Southhampton*,[1] the court held that unless expressly empowered to do so, a municipality couldn't itself define the class of voters entitled to cast ballots. That was a matter for the legislature. In 1958 another Ontario court ruled in *Freeman v. Farm Products Marketing Board*[2] that when the legislature has enacted law entitling persons who engage in farm production to vote on a ballot question, the Ontario Farm Products Marketing Board couldn't circumscribe those rights, nor could it disfranchise persons the legislature said were entitled to vote.

Through the twentieth century this trend to statutorily codify and judicially confirm the legal right of citizens to vote on ballot questions accelerated. A particular reason was that province-wide referendums, which were increasing, required more structure than municipal plebiscites. In this drive to expand voting rights, the Direct Legislation League, which was especially active from Ontario to British Columbia, became a catalyst to get referendum and initiative statutes enacted in all four western provinces. This movement began in 1898 when South Dakota added referendum and initiative rights to its state constitution, a manifestation of the Progressive Movement then on the ascendant in response to the political and economic needs of rural areas in Canada and the United States.

This early twentieth-century quest for "direct legislation" in Canada wasn't developing because people thought it might be nice to exercise the legislative function themselves. It was happening because they distrusted their legislatures where large corporations and powerful individuals corrupted general legislation by their self-serving interests in an era of raw political power without any rules addressing conflict of interest, let alone controlling who paid for elections. As a needed counterbalance, this new referendum power made legislation subject to ratification by the people, with necessary exceptions for tax bills, some spending measures, policing, health, and public emergencies.

In the United States, this right of citizens to initiate ballot questions by petition was becoming embedded, either in state constitutions or in statute law. In Manitoba, Saskatchewan, Alberta, and British Columbia, these measures took the form of statutes, although they could have been made part of provincial constitutions. However created, this referendum right provided people a vehicle to express their opinion on legislation before it took effect, while the power of initiative gave people an avenue to propose their own laws. In effect, these two democratic instruments made citizens a component of the legislature, because they could both initiate laws and overturn laws already enacted but not yet in force. Voting non-ratification of new law was akin to a state governor's veto power, a Swiss suspensory referendum, or a lieutenant governor's refusal to sign an enacted statute into law.

During the 1970s, election finance laws and conflict-of-interest guidelines removed some of the most blatant corruption from our legislatures and the backrooms of government and politics, ending the original impetus half a century earlier for these four western Canadian Direct Legislation statutes. Cleaning up elections and the legislature did not, however, remove the importance of electors having a direct say by ballot on issues of importance.

THE RIGHT TO INITIATE BALLOT QUESTIONS

The right of citizens to initiate a ballot question has existed several times in Canada — a century ago under those Direct Legislation Acts of the western provinces, and country-wide from 1878 to 2000 under the Canada Temperance Act.

Today the only province providing a right of initiative is British Columbia. The Recall and Initiative Act of British Columbia was promised by the Social Credit government. A referendum to determine if British

Columbians favoured the measure was called by Socred Premier Rita Johnston, and in 1991, it received overwhelming electoral support. Her successor, New Democrat Premier Mike Harcourt, brought forward the legislation, which became law in 1995. The initiative provisions have since been used, most notably by another former premier, William Vander Zalm, in his capacity as a private citizen, to challenge the B.C. government's move to harmonize federal and provincial sales taxes.

At the municipal level across Canada, the statutory right of electors to petition for ballot questions on issues has remained more fully intact, although how often this right actually gets exercised ebbs and flows. In recent years, ballot issue-voting has been removed from specific statutes, and it has also been discouraged politically in municipalities where entrenched councillors with four-year terms increasingly look to consultants, more than to constituents, for guidance.

THE RIGHT TO VOTE ON LEGISLATION IN MANITOBA

Assessing the fit between referendums and the Constitution requires a closer look at what happened in western Canada. The Liberal government of Tobias Norris in Manitoba, having gotten elected on a pledge to enact a direct legislation statute, did so in 1916 but then referred the act for judicial review of its constitutionality. In the first round, Manitoba's chief justice, Thomas Graham Mathers of the Court of King's Bench, upheld the act's validity.[3] Then Manitoba's Court of Appeal reversed Mathers's decision.[4] On higher appeal, the Judicial Committee of the Privy Council in a 1919 decision rendered by Lord Haldane upheld the Court of Appeal's decision, agreeing the act was beyond the legislature's constitutional powers.[5]

Manitoba's act wasn't judged unconstitutional because it augmented the structure of the province's parliamentary system by enabling electors to democratically work in harmony with their elected representatives in specific qualifying cases. It was deemed unconstitutional only because provinces are unable, said Manitoba's Court of Appeal and the Judicial Committee of the Privy Council in Britain, to alter powers of the Crown's representative, the lieutenant governor.

The Judicial Committee's archaic and formalistic reasoning about a narrow symbolic point allowed their British judicial minds to pivot into a realm alien to North American democratic life and Canadians' constitutional evo-lution. The Law Lords in England attributed more, in the way of changed duties for the lieutenant governor, than the Manitoba statute provided. They burnished a brighter role for the monarch's provincial representative than he occupied in the evolving democratic landscape of western Canada. They alluded obscurely to "legal theory" about the lieutenant governor yet ignored that by 1919 the political reality in Canada had evolved to the point that its government, though still technically described as being a constitutional mon-archy was, in fact, more constitutional than monarchical. The right of the monarch's representative to give Royal Assent to legislation wasn't a real power for the Crown's representative to exercise; it was just an honorific formality.

No lieutenant governor would refuse to sign an elected government's law duly enacted by elected representatives in the legislature once it landed on his desk. So it was a bogus argument to contend, as the British Law Lords did, that the referendum result "renders him powerless to prevent it becoming an actual law if approved by a majority *of these voters*" when he was already "powerless to prevent legislation becoming an actual law if approved by a majority of" *members in the legislature* who are but elected representa-tives of those very same voters. The decision about when to send a bill for Royal Assent always rests with the government and legislature.

Even after a new statute is "signed into law" by the Crown's represen-tative, the elected government alone decides when, or even whether, to pro-claim the statute in force. The ceremonial vice-regal signature, preserving notional vestiges of a reigning monarch still in control, has the same substan-tive significance as someone throwing confetti on a bridal couple after they've already exchanged vows and become legally married. This narrow point over a symbolic role, juxtaposed with sovereign citizens potentially approving a law, was enough to slay the Initiative and Referendum Act of Manitoba.

ALBERTANS MORE DECISIVE ON THE SAME FRONT

Albertans prevailed in a similar contest over the constitutionality of their Direct Legislation Act. When electors voted their province "dry" in 1915, voting for prohibition under Alberta's Direct Legislation Act, Nat Bell Liquor Company contended that the Direct Legislation Act, which required that a proposed law approved by electors be enacted by the legislature, and the Liquor Act, which had been enacted in consequence of this arrangement, were both unconstitutional.

The case of *R. v. Nat Belt Liquors Ltd.* gained fame and Prohibition Era notoriety all the way to the final court of appeal.[6] The Judicial Committee of the Privy Council upheld the legality of the Liquor Act, with the crucial implication that the Direct Legislation Act itself was also valid. Lord Sumner, delivering judgment in 1922, reaffirmed that, constitutionally, a law is made by a provincial legislature when it has been passed in accordance with its regular procedure and received Royal Assent by the lieutenant governor on behalf of the monarch. "It is impossible to say that it was not an Act of the Legislature and it is nonetheless a statute because it was the statutory duty of the Legislature to pass it," elaborated Lord Sumner about the logical conundrum facing Nat Bell's case. "Unless the Direct Legislation Act can be shown, as it has not been shown on this occasion, to interfere in some way formally with the discharge of the functions of the Legislature and of its component parts [meaning the lieutenant-governor], the Liquor Act, 1916, being in truth an Act duly passed by the Legislature of Alberta and no other, is one which must be enforced."

This judgment became a landmark ruling in Canadian constitutional law as reaffirmation of "parliamentary sovereignty" — in the sense that law-making by the people's elected representatives, when done in compliance with institutional practice and the Constitution, is not to be interfered with by judges. It recognized the primacy of a legislative body made up jointly of the sovereign people's elected representatives and the monarch's appointed representative. Professor Berriedale Keith, a Scottish constitutional lawyer and author of *Responsible Government in the Dominions*, surmised that Sumner's view "suggests the Court would look with favour on the Direct Legislation Act if its validity were directly challenged." This, he continued, indicated "a change of view in comparison with the treatment meted out to the Initiative and Referendum Act, 1916, of Manitoba." The Judicial Committee's reasoning, contended Keith, overlooked the vital point that the procedure under the act deprives the legislature of any deliberative function whatsoever and turns it into a mere machine for registering the decrees of the people. He found it "wholly contrary to British political views to treat a member of the Legislature as sent there simply to carry out the instructions of his constituents."[7]

Professor Keith's hostility to accommodating a rising form of *Canadian* democracy echoed the oft-quoted view, earlier articulated by Edmund Burke, that a parliamentarian is more than a mere delegate sent to do the bidding of the constituency's electors, that he is, rather, someone who owes them, and owes Parliament and the country, the exercise of his own intelligence and independent thought. It's a sublime theory. But even by 1916 the notion of an MP or MLA exercising independent thought had been vaporized by the iron party discipline wielded in Canada's legislative assemblies. Keith also ignored that the legislature itself had enacted the statute by which it agreed to share and limit the scope of its law-making powers.

A different "British political view" that Berriedale Keith might more aptly have considered was the doctrine of parliamentary supremacy: if a legislature wishes to exercise its powers in a way that curtails them, so be it. Forty years after the Scotsman's stultifying critique of provincial direct legislation statutes, the Parliament of Canada and provincial legislatures amended our Constitution by entrenching in it a Charter of Rights and Freedoms to significantly limit the way they themselves could shape a law. Not only did Prairie legislatures enact self-limiting laws in favour of direct democracy, not only did Canada's lawmakers with the Charter rank constitutional rights of citizens ahead of the powers of legislators, but all our legislatures have created dozens of Crown corporations, commissions, boards, and agencies to which they devolved extensive powers they'd previously exercised themselves. Constitutionalists like Berriedale Keith simply provided irrelevant fodder for Canadians clinging to non-relevant British concepts, those who in adhering to the outdated Westminster model sought to suppress our democratic vitality.

REFERENDUMS HELP MAINTAIN CONSTITUTIONAL OPERATIONS

For the working of our institutional arrangements, the referendum also plays a helpful role in Canadian parliamentary democracy's "due process" when issues become too hot for elected representatives.

Manitoba illustrated with the complex and inflammatory issue of prohibiting alcohol how referendums can help legislatures cope with problems too volatile to be contained within them. The provincial assembly sank deep into years of turmoil trying to find a balanced public policy on liquor. The contentious question divided the legislature, fractured the political parties, and split cabinet.

Too explosive to be contained within a "traditional" parliamentary framework, not amenable to any compromise, the liquor question went to the people for province-wide balloting. As it turned out, a single referendum wasn't enough. But a half-dozen were, over a number of years, until everyone was sufficiently worn down by the intractable hardline positions. Except for zealous "dry" and "wet" diehards, the majority of Manitobans recognized the need for compromise, which the government and legislature were then able to achieve.

Manitobans had voted directly on liquor issues, beginning with a prohibition plebiscite on July 12, 1892, continuing in the national plebiscite of 1898, and next facing a ballot choice between alcohol's control or prohibition on March 13, 1916. After that came a ballot question on government control of liquor sales on June 22, 1923, a round of voting next topped up on July 11 that same year by whether to ratify or reject amendments to the Temperance Act. Then followed a three-question finale about the sale of beer on June 28, 1927. Over these thirty-five years, eleven general elections took place in the province, generally clear of the divisive liquor question and more focused on a wide range of other important issues. Also over those three and a half decades, as the souring cultural experience with prohibition was being worked out with full public participation and observation, came eventual resolution that would have been impossible if the issue was confined to workings in the provincial assembly, or to parties' election campaign stances.

The reason the referendum is compatible with our legislative system is because it complements, rather than competes with, our democratic processes.

HOARY FEAR OF "MOB RULE" AND TYRANNICAL MAJORITIES

The essence of Canadian democratic life is that majorities rule while the rights of minorities are protected.

Fear of mob rule seems a stretch in Canada nowadays, although opponents of citizens voting on important issues continue to invoke this scare tactic. When Parliament was debating a 1973 motion to hold a referendum on capital punishment, New Democrat MP Ed Nelson said the death penalty "must be decided from a logical and philosophical point of view, rather than from emotional motivation." Then he asserted, with more emotion than logic, "This type of referendum is little more than an invitation to mob rule."

Even in 2016, the alarmist term *mob rule* was raised in a televised Canadian panel discussion, as if a referendum somehow brings into the streets thousands of rioting people who successfully take over the powers of government. What quality in Canadians would foster a mob surge that is absent from Californians, the Swiss, Australians, and so many others whose political culture successfully accommodates ballot questions?

A second spectre raised by referendum opponents is "the tyranny of the majority." The rights of minorities in Canada warrant more serious attention.

7

CHARTER PROTECTION OF MINORITY RIGHTS

Safeguarding minority rights in referendums is of a piece with our larger democratic framework of majority rule with protection for minorities. Canada's history shows the risk to minorities has been greater from laws enacted by legislatures than from any questions asked in referendums. But 1981's constitutional entrenchment of a Charter guaranteeing rights and freedoms of individual Canadians ushered in a new universe in which neither legislative action nor referendum question can trump the standing of minorities.

Today, any catechism against referendums that includes "the danger to minorities" not only ignores our Canadian experience with ballot questions but more importantly fails to recognize the dramatically new era of "Charter" Canada that has existed for more than a third of a century. Our constitutional reality, not lingering fears from other countries and earlier eras, should allay the fear of ballot questions as an instrument for minority suppression.

Even so, constitutional protection of minority rights mustn't give rise to complacency. Any question pertaining to Canadians who might be subject to discrimination on any of the prohibited grounds specified by Section 15 of the Charter — race, national or ethnic origin, colour, religion, sex, age, or mental or physical disability — or such additional grounds specified in human rights codes as sexual orientation, must be monitored and addressed. The ongoing work of the Canadian Civil Liberties Association and others supports this "eternal vigilance" as the price of our liberty.

Five case studies in this chapter from our history and current events — involving linguistic minorities, religious minorities, and racial minorities — underscore this raw reality about referendums.

FRENCH-LANGUAGE MINORITY RIGHTS IN MANITOBA MUNICIPAL REFERENDUMS

Acrimony spread across Manitoba in 1983 over use of the French language. No province-wide referendum took place, but nearly thirty municipalities, which together contained a majority of Manitobans, asked voters, in conjunction with their October 16 council elections, about French-language services. The ballot question was ambiguously worded, challenged minority linguistic rights, and was beyond municipal jurisdiction to deal with.

As such, this 1983 event is a case study not only about ballot questions on minority rights but, more broadly, it is also a lesson about the risk when referendums are wielded unwisely. It's a microcosm of Canada's enduring challenges for English-language and French-language services and minority rights. And, like all contentious matters focused by a referendum, background is key to the story.

When it was created a province in 1870, Manitoba's two official languages were French and English. However, in 1889, Manitoba Liberal Premier Thomas Greenway had the provincial legislature pass measures removing the right to use French in courts, the legislature itself, and other forums and circumstances. Next, in 1890, the Liberal majority audaciously legislated English as the province's only official language. These enactments went unchallenged by Liberal Prime Minister Wilfrid Laurier, despite Ottawa's power of disallowance in an era when that constitutional provision was still being invoked to set aside or "disallow" provincial statutes the federal government deemed unconstitutional.

The issue smouldered; most of a century passed. Then one day a speeding ticket was issued to Robert Bilodeau of St. Boniface. Bilodeau's blood boiled to see an English-only ticket in his francophone city. Being a lawyer, he decided, rather than pay up, to challenge the ticket's validity. Contesting the underlying validity of Manitoba's English-only laws themselves, his case got all the attention it deserved.

While advancing through the courts toward the Supreme Court of Canada, Bilodeau's challenge spread into the political arena. In May 1983, Premier Howard Pawley unveiled plans to amend the province's constitution by declaring French and English the official languages of Manitoba, confirming as valid all Manitoba laws enacted before the end of 1985, requiring new statutes to henceforth be in both languages, and completing a bilingual general revision of statutes before 1994. As well, he announced that from 1987 onward every Manitoban would have the right to service in English or French from the main offices of government departments, courts, quasi-judicial bodies, Crown corporations, and government agencies. Also, such service would be provided in local government offices whose nature made bilingual service reasonable and where significant demand warranted. Finally, the amendment would define and restrict the province's obligation to translate its statutes into French. These dramatic changes had been agreed upon by the federal government, the Société Franco-Manitobaine, and Robert Bilodeau who, if still not happy about being charged with committing an infraction, was grateful that he'd challenged the unilingual ticket. Those three parties, and the NDP provincial government, all recognized that ameliorating steps taken in advance of a Supreme Court decision might more satisfactorily address the long-smouldering issue of French-language rights in Manitoba.

However, when word of this plan became public, anti-French backlash spread. The provincial government responded to the criticisms, saying it would modify the amendment by curtailing the official status of the two languages, deleting reference to main offices, modifying the test of "significant demand," and ensuring existing rights to use other languages. During the intense summer heat of 1983, Manitoba's legislature ground to a halt with a series of Opposition walkouts until the premier reversed his earlier decision to not hold public hearings. As soon as they got under way, the meetings became a political disaster for the government. Most testimony was "hostile to the planned amendment, often expressed in the strongest possible terms."[1]

For October 16's council elections, more than thirty municipal jurisdictions, including Winnipeg, where more than half of all Manitobans reside, a ballot question on the issue was handed to voters. In most of these municipalities, the government's French-language proposal was rejected by margins of three to one or four to one, though in some, as high as sixteen to one. In Winnipeg three-quarters of voters opposed Manitoba entrenching French-language services in the province's constitution. Turnout at the polls was 52 percent of eligible voters. Usual municipal participation in council elections was about 29 percent.

"The result," said Manitoba's attorney general, Roland Penner, "was not unexpected." He discounted the outcome, noting it was not binding on the government. Penner reiterated that "minority language rights should not be settled by a popular vote of the majority."[2]

The municipal voting on Manitoba's provincial linguistic policy illustrated what *not* to do when it comes to referendums. First, municipalities inexcusably strayed outside their jurisdictional powers, just as municipalities in Canada have held ballot questions on declaring themselves "nuclear-free zones" — a much-coveted state to achieve, but beyond any municipal council's powers to bring about. Second, by initiating a democratic process knowing it wouldn't produce a concrete result, these municipalities made a mockery of referendums as a proper means for citizens to participate in governance.

Third, and most serious, this setup was an attack on minority linguistic rights, which Anglican, Jewish, United Church, and Roman Catholic leaders jointly condemned as "deeply undemocratic." Respect of minorities, they declared, "is the very essence of democracy," admonishing that "a referendum or plebiscite is not an appropriate means of determining minority rights." Dr. Victor Goldbloom of Montreal, president of the Canadian Council of Christians and Jews (and subsequently a member of Quebec's National Assembly, provincial cabinet minister, then official languages commissioner for Canada), was the group's spokesperson. He advocated "durable protection" for minority rights that would not be "subject to the opinions which may prevail at a particular time in a particular part of the country."[3]

A fourth bad thing about the referendum was the shoddy ballot question. Wording in most municipalities violated even basic rules of fairness and simplicity. Winnipeg's, which was typical, asked: "*Should the provincial government withdraw its proposed constitutional amendment and allow the Bilodeau case to proceed to be heard and decided by the Supreme Court of Canada on the validity of the English-only laws passed by the legislature of Manitoba since 1890?*"

Don Sellar of Southam News called it "legalistic in tone, double-barrelled in construction, and dynamite in content."[4] Voters were asked to agree with two statements at the same time: that the resolution to amend the Constitution be withdrawn, and that the Bilodeau case proceed to the Supreme Court. U.S. courts rule, in advance of voting, on a ballot question's constitutionality by applying the "single-issue" test: a ballot should ask but one question, and deal with just one issue, because a voter can only give a single answer, Yes or No.

Confusion resulting from not even asking a clear question made the exercise more farcical. Pollster Angus Reid surveyed six hundred Winnipeg voters for the CBC, finding confusion so widespread "all sides of the issue can claim a

victory on election night with this question." Some 32 percent of Yes supporters believed they were endorsing entrenchment of French-language rights in
Manitoba; 34 percent of No voters believed they were doing the same thing.[5]

The language issue attracted national attention. The House of Commons
passed a resolution, with support of all three national parties, endorsing the
Manitoba government's proposed constitutional amendment. Across the
country, editorialists evaluated the process and its outcome. Canadians have
"seldom distinguished themselves in matters of language," said the *Vancouver
Sun*. "It brings out prejudices greatly out of proportion to the amounts of
money and inconvenience involved." Such a referendum, the newspaper suggested, would probably have produced similar results in British Columbia,
Saskatchewan, or Yukon, where extension of French-language rights was also
being sought, adding, tit-for-tat, that many Quebec leaders seemed "less than
cognizant of English-language rights" in seeking to preserve the French language. "Referendums are a bad way to make public policy," concluded the *Sun*,
"especially when it comes to protecting minorities." The *Windsor Star*, noting
that the municipal balloting was orchestrated by opponents of the government's
plan with intent "to embarrass the government," said it had backfired because "it
is the electorate which is being embarrassed in front of the rest of the country."[6]

Those municipally run ballot questions on provincial policy for French-
language services in Manitoba demonstrated a "potential danger" of referendums even though the exercise had no legal consequences. Every democratic
instrument, referendums included, must be used with intelligent care and be
opposed when that isn't the case.

ABORIGINAL RIGHTS AND COMMUNITY RIGHTS IN THE NORTHERN QUEBEC REFERENDUM

A 1987 referendum in "Northern Quebec" took place in territory the province acquired in 1912 when its boundaries were extended into the Arctic to
encompass land populated by Inuit peoples and by one Cree community on
the eastern shore of James Bay. The largest of Quebec's seventeen administrative districts, Northern Quebec constitutes 55 percent of the province's land
surface, its people dwelling in fourteen widely scattered villages. Beginning
in the middle of the twentieth century, non-aboriginal people also moved
into the region. The 1987 referendum not only dealt with aboriginal

self-government but also became a landmark event leading to the creation of Canada's third self-governing territory, Nunavut, a decade later.

The saga of this ballot question began with the James Bay and Northern Quebec Agreement of 1975, enabling Hydro-Québec to resume its electricity-generating megaproject, halted by aboriginal action to prevent their lands being flooded behind power dams on major rivers running into James Bay. The saw-off produced $90 million for the aboriginal peoples affected. But with the purse strings controlled by non-Aboriginals in southern Quebec, the Northerners pushed for regional government of their own so they could administer the funds and run their affairs. Besides money, the James Bay and Northern Quebec Agreement granted local government powers to the Inuit, giving rise to a municipal system by 1978. Its success, as evaluated in 1983 by the provincial legislature with Inuit participation, fuelled the drive for greater Inuit autonomy. Premier René Lévesque found it hard to dispute their quest for a mild version of "sovereignty-association."

In 1984 a task force began working on this goal, and by 1987, agreed that the best form of autonomy would be a regional government. A constituent assembly was to determine its constitution, but disagreement over how to establish this body created an impasse. Those concerned agreed unanimously to force the choice, about forming a representative body to draft the regional government's constitution and structure, by referendum.

With no directly applicable governing referendum law, Quebec's chief electoral officer, Pierre-F. Côté, deployed his skills to fill the void and make the North's first-ever referendum a success. Côté became coordinator and arbitrator between the two contending groups, Citizens for a Responsible Government led by Harry Tulugak from the community of Povungnituk, and Timiujuit headed by Simeonie Nalukturuk representing mayors and regional organizers. "Harry's Group" wanted constituent assembly members elected by universal suffrage and financed by the local population and businesses through their taxes. Timiujuit favoured an appointed constituent assembly funded by private-sector donations. Both leaders signed, with Chief Electoral Officer Côté, a tripartite agreement establishing all rules for voting, and agreed to abide by the majority decision.[7]

The chief electoral officer and his staff ran the referendum according to the agreement, adjusting for northern conditions such as the vast distances between widely separated villages. A leaflet on basic principles of the referendum, and posters summarizing key stages, were posted in all fourteen communities. A "publicity pamphlet," stating the position of each group in their own words, was printed in Inuktitut, French, and English and distributed by each village's returning officer. A video about the referendum was taken to every village for cable broadcast, as was audio material for local FM stations, the North's communications system consisting mainly of radio and community television stations.

With umbrella committees for the Yes and No sides, the campaign unfolded and on October 1, 1987, voters chose, by 53 percent, to have a constituent assembly whose members would be elected by universal suffrage and financed by the local population and business through taxes.[8]

The outcome of this "clash of ideas," noted Rudy Paltiel, "has broad implications because it could go beyond what happens in Northern Quebec and set a new model for native self-government in Canada's North."[9] Jean-Jacques Simard, sociology professor at Laval, celebrated the referendum as "one more step away from the concept of a purely native ethnic government."[10] Despite having differences over the form of government, the Inuit insisted that non-Aboriginals have the same voting rights as Inuit, rejecting the concept of a racially based government.

An exclusively ethnic government would shield Inuit culture and language, but as the *Edmonton Journal* observed, it would do so "at the expense of non-native rights." Conversely, a "mixed government" could raise alarm in the aboriginal community. "Would the entitlements accorded the Inuit in the 1975 Agreement," asked the paper's editors, "be diluted if non-natives are included in future self-government plans?"[11]

The willingness of Quebec's legislators to authorize this referendum enabled those directly concerned to have a say themselves. Also significant was the genuine interest of officials in the northern communities to become more adept in the use of voting procedures. The constructive, respectful approach adopted by the two northern leaders, Harry Tulugak and Simeonie Nalukturuk, who'd negotiated an agreement to fill procedural gaps in the referendum procedure and who honoured their voters' verdict, was another hallmark. Those doubting the capacity of individual Canadians to be entrusted with ballot-box democracy can rightly take inspiration from this Northern Quebec example.

"The parties showed a clear desire to proceed in a democratic manner," Pierre-F. Côté told Quebec's National Assembly, "a reality in keeping with the democratic evolution of this community." The Inuit of Northern Quebec proceeded, with a mandate from the people that included non-aboriginal voters, and with provincial approval, to set up an autonomous regional government, according to the constituent assembly's realistic plan for "aboriginal self-government" within a public government framework. The aboriginal majority respected the rights of the non-aboriginal minority, from voting rights in the referendum through to the operation of their common government.

MINORITY RIGHTS AND FAITH-BASED SCHOOLS IN NEWFOUNDLAND REFERENDUMS

Two referendums on the same question in mid-1990s Newfoundland raised uncommon issues about religious freedom, secular freedom, and the rights of minorities. In seeking voter approval to repeal constitutional guarantees for denominational schools, arguments about *protecting* religious freedom made by the No side were counterbalanced by arguments for *expanding* religious freedom from the Yes side. Supporting religious freedom for some meant ending centuries-old systems that enshrined religious freedom for others. Again, historical background is needed to ground the issue.

In 1995, Premier Clyde Wells sought to get at the root of divisiveness in Newfoundland (officially renamed Newfoundland and Labrador in 2001), fostered by faith denominations antagonistic to one another — a system entrenched from children's early years by religious education in the province's denominational schools — which erupted in fights at elections, bloodletting brawls at hockey matches, vindictive discrimination in housing and rental accommodation, and revenge-taking in the workplace.

Newfoundland's long saga of emphasizing religious differences through schools had begun when Anglicans first opened classrooms in the 1720s. Organized religion's unrelenting *political* control of this arrangement ever since — Christian churches having the right to own and operate schools using public money supplied by the government — was enshrined in Article 17 of Newfoundland's 1949 "Terms of Union" for joining Confederation. That made the religion-based school system a constitutional right for particular denominations. To improve education and remove denominational warfare from society, the entrenched guarantee of the churches' rights to administer education in Newfoundland would have to be repealed.

The premier called a referendum on ending the denominational school system for September 5, 1995. The campaign highlighted controversies, but the referendum didn't *create* divisions. They'd existed for decades. By 1980, as the number of adherents to Anglican, Catholic, Methodist, and other Christian religions continued to shrink, a significant number of Newfoundlanders belonged to non-Christian faiths or weren't believers in any organized religion. For this increasingly secular and multicultural society, Newfoundland's publicly funded denominational school system had "religious discrimination" stamped all over it in the eyes of many. Others saw it for what it also was: an inefficient antiquated structure. True believers of the established religious denominations, however, saw the arrangement as their best last bastion of religious freedom.

"The greatest single threat to equality of religion and freedom of worship is the restrictive nature of the denominational educational system," the Newfoundland-Labrador Human Rights Association said in a 1984 brief to the minister of justice. Human-rights advocates saw denominational schools "discriminating on the basis of religion." In 1990 a royal commission began its two-year study of the matter. Following interviews with more than a thousand Newfoundlanders in all corners of the province, it reported that 79 percent favoured a single school system for all children. The recommendation was to modernize the education structure.

The issue for the No side was "religious freedom." Christian advocates opposed any change to their costly privileges. Zealous Catholics and Pentecostals rallied in their churches to hear god's messengers exhort them from their pulpits like gang leaders priming before a rumble. On the streets, the devout canvassed door to door. Churches directed weekly collections of money toward high-profile ad campaigns. Bonaventure Fagan, a Catholic administrator fiercely opposing change, didn't turn his Christian cheek or seek the brotherhood of Christ-inspired love. Catholics couldn't "be indifferent to their system and think that they're going to have it," he admonished. "You have to be committed to it and have an active faith. You're only going to fight when you're committed."[12]

It was fighting commitment, after all, that for centuries had kept faiths alive far more effectively than rituals of religious practice and hallowed worship of some nebulous divinity. The fighting ardor championed by Bonaventure Fagan elevated religion's role through visceral social antagonism. The No side's intense campaign for religious freedom was not about justice; it was about justification — religion as a cloak rather than a calling.

Supporters of the Yes side documented the need to change a bank-rupt and fragmented school system unable to provide quality education. Non-believers emphasized their inability to get a religion-free education in Newfoundland. The province itself needed to save millions of dollars by ending overlap and could no longer justify funding four or five separate church school systems when the government had no evidence that they pro-vided quality education. As numbers of denominational adherents dwin-dled, children were being bused greater distances to half-filled classrooms that were exclusively one denomination.

Overshadowing the campaign were feelings of disgust and shame about the entrenched criminal patterns of sexual abuse that had been protected and covered up by the Roman Catholic Church at Mount Cashel, a church-run orphanage where the devout brothers preyed on boys who had no way out and nobody to guard them. Evidence was now also public about the abuse and deaths in residential schools of aboriginal children that churches ran for the federal government. Growing numbers of many Newfoundlanders real-ized the challenge posed to society's vulnerable members by exclusive religious institutions, and resolved to get churches out of their province's school system.

Prime Minister Jean Chrétien began the push for Parliament to do its part, in tandem with Newfoundland's legislature, to amend Article 17 in the Terms of Union. However, the Newfoundland government's plan was unravelling on the ground. Its policy still allowed religious schools to operate where numbers warranted. Not only did that put an effective public school system at risk, but court challenges were also causing new problems.

After the September 5, 1995, referendum, Roman Catholic and Pentecostal school boards, upset they'd lost, sought an injunction to stop implementation of the result. In response to this, Premier Brian Tobin, who'd replaced Clyde Wells, called a second referendum for September 1, 1997. The question asked if voters agreed to amend Article 17 to enable disbanding the Catholic and Pentecostal school systems and bringing them into the public system. This time, the choice being forced was all or nothing.

Voters approved the measure by a convincing 73 percent of ballots cast. Then, after Newfoundland's House of Assembly and Parliament passed resolutions amending Term 17, but before the constitutional amendment proclamation could be issued, another injunction was sought, this time to enjoin the governor general from making the proclamation. This application was dismissed. The amendment to Term 17 was made, underpinned by the approval of the people of Newfoundland in two referendums. By 1998 all Newfoundland schooling operated within a single, secular system.

Every young person in the province had the freedom to get a better education. Freedom to practice one's religion by worshiping in church, synagogue, mosque, or temple — previously eclipsed by the full-bore Christian schooling system — was also enhanced. "Freedom of conscience" likewise meant, more than it previously had, enhancement of minority rights for those desiring secular education in Newfoundland but who'd been restricted to attending denominational schools.

The Charter's guarantee of "freedom of conscience and religion," subject "only to such reasonable limits prescribed by law as can be demonstrably justified in a free and democratic society," had not been infringed by removing schools from the grip of churches.

However, a third court challenge, made after Newfoundland's schools had been integrated into a single public educational system, attacked aspects of the September 5, 1997, referendum, as well as the legal instruments that flowed in consequence of the voting outcome. Applicant Robert Hogan, in line with Fagan's two prior cases, sought a three-part court order (a) quashing the proclamation authorizing the September 1, 1997, ballot question; (b) declaring that failure to provide government funding for the No side in the referendum campaign was an infringement of Hogan's Charter rights under Section 2(b), Section 15, and other sections pertaining to freedom of religion and equality; and (c) declaring the 1997 vote invalid under Section 171 of Newfoundland's Election Act pertaining to technical requirements for counting ballots.[13]

The Newfoundland Supreme Court refused to quash the proclamation that initiated the ballot question. It held that plaintiffs were entitled to funding for the No side. It denied a declaration that the referendum was invalid. In doing so, the Newfoundland court followed the Supreme Court of Canada's *Quebec Secession Reference* decision, which held that a referendum is a democratic way of ascertaining the views of an electorate on important political questions, but it doesn't play a *legal* role in constitutional amendment.[14] The court emphasized *legal* role because it recognized that when the sovereign people vote on constitutional questions, that alone doesn't result in the amendment taking place, but it does give a clear signal to their elected representatives in the provincial House of Assembly and

Parliament about how to vote on the motions that are legally required by the Constitution's amending procedure.

Hogan appealed this decision to Newfoundland's Court of Appeal, but the higher court dismissed it, confirming the validity of the constitutional amendment.[15] The Court of Appeal also had to deal with the lower court's ruling, under Section 15 of the Charter, that Hogan had been entitled to government funding in the referendum campaign, a conclusion the Newfoundland attorney general had cross-appealed. It responded to this contention by ruling, "While government cannot act to restrain access to a medium, it is not required to make the medium available."[16] The Court of Appeal held that the actions of the Newfoundland government hadn't restricted appellant Hogan's freedom of expression, and that the government didn't need to undertake further measures to provide funding. Thus ended the ironic saga of how religious freedom and open education could only be achieved by removal of constitutionally entrenched religious rights — following the due process of one royal commission, two referendums, three court cases, and measures enacted by legislatures in St. John's and Ottawa. The problem had not been tyranny of the majority, but of the minority.

FIRST NATIONS MINORITY RIGHTS IN BRITISH COLUMBIA'S LAND CLAIMS REFERENDUM

In the era of colonization following the arrival of non-aboriginal peoples on their lands, most First Nations in British Columbia either didn't sign treaties, or if they did, saw them dishonoured. As a result, negotiating treaties, or renegotiating old ones, remains a current event. In the province's diverse demographic makeup, the First Nations number some 155,000 people, or 3.6 percent, amid a total population of 4.4 million. When combined with Métis, Inuit, and individuals of mixed aboriginal identities, the total aboriginal population of British Columbia numbers 232,290 people, or 5.4 percent of all those living in the province. By any standard, the aboriginal people of British Columbia are a minority.

Several hundred bands of First Nations, from urban Vancouver to British Columbia's remotest corners, occupy extensive territories and claim the natural resources of their "traditional lands." The ill-defined geographic boundaries, uncertain nature of "aboriginal title" in the legal context of a land ownership system imposed under colonization, and expanding activity and presence by non-aboriginal Canadians in these territories meant these spaces became used by a wide mixture of people and companies for camps, roads, lumbering, pipelines, mining, and other private and public purposes. Although fraught with ambiguity, the matter is riddled by strongly held beliefs.

To address what since the 1800s has been called "the Land Question," a regime is today operating in British Columbia to negotiate land claims by protecting constitutional rights while balancing unavoidable compromises. This three-part structure working to disambiguate the complex relationships embraces First Nations, the Government of Canada, and British Columbia's provincial government. Operating this forum for negotiating agreements, and the channel for ratifying land claim treaties, is the B.C. Land Claims Commission. The stakes are high. Cultural values jostle. Negotiations resemble trying to figure out how to turn an omelette back into eggs. The process drags on over years, decades.

In 2002 Premier Gordon Campbell called a referendum on eight ballot questions to guide B.C. negotiators in developing land claim treaties with First Nations peoples. Debate began over what aboriginal rights mean in today's context but quickly spread to controversy over whether it was appropriate, or even constitutional in terms of minority rights, for all British Columbians to vote in a province-wide referendum on principles, or issues, touching land claim negotiations. Aboriginal communities again felt threatened by an entire provincial electorate voting on the government's stance about their claims, just as they had in 2001 when some British Columbians advocated a province-wide referendum to approve the Nisga'a land claim treaty. The Nisga'a stayed discreetly quiet in 2002 because their well-developed treaty had been concluded on a different track from the tripartite negotiating structure Premier Campbell was now addressing. However, other First Nations leaders fought back through litigation and a boycott of the referendum.

In March 2002, Chief Ke-Kis-Is-Uks of the Hupacasath First Nation at Port Alberni, known outside First Nations communities as Judith Sayers, sought an injunction to keep British Columbia's chief electoral officer from conducting the referendum until her case was decided. Among the issues raised, Chief Ke-Kis-Is-Uks contended the Treaty Negotiation Referendum Regulation was inconsistent with the government's obligation to negotiate treaties in good faith and in conformity with the honour of the Crown.

Another argument was that the referendum about treaty principles would destroy British Columbia's treaty process. For instance, one of the ballot questions sought to limit the inherent right of aboriginal self-government, guaranteed under Section 35 of the Constitution, by characterizing it as "delegated" and thus no different from municipal governments created by the province under provincial statute.

"As a First Nation," said Chief Ke-Kis-Is-Uks, "we believe our inherent right to self-government is not delegated but recognized by the Constitution, and that even the powers we now possess are greater than local governance." Because the referendum was legally binding, another of her arguments was that "a majority vote will not allow the provincial government to negotiate beyond a delegated local government style of government."

On March 27, Justice Robert Hutchison of British Columbia's Supreme Court denied Chief Ke-Kis-Is-Uks's application for an injunction. Sticking to the general rules for granting this extraordinary remedy, rather than dealing with the issues of a political process, the judge said he wasn't convinced there was a serious question in issue and opined that the irreparability of the harm was speculative and hypothetical.

The chief had also argued that racism could result from holding the referendum. Whether use of ballot questions would create racist views or rather reflect existing ones wasn't addressed. Instead, Hutchison noted that British Columbia, at that time, comprised 3.9 million citizens of whom 139,655 were Aboriginals whose minority rights under the British North America Act and the Charter of Rights were constitutionally protected. He confirmed that nothing in the Referendum Act or the Treaty Negotiation Referendum Regulation could abrogate those entrenched rights.

Justice Hutchison found merit in the argument that "the questions are in some respects ambiguous and misleading" but added "it is difficult to see how the mere asking of eight somewhat benign questions will cause the plaintiffs irreparable harm, particularly since they have entrenched rights that cannot be interfered with." In the end, he added, the provincial government in its negotiations "will still have to deal with the problem of those entrenched rights no matter how the questions are answered."

While this matter was proceeding, Justice Hutchison had requested British Columbia's chief electoral officer to hold off mailing the ballots. The very day after his decision, Chief Ke-Kis-Is-Uks submitted her application for leave to appeal to British Columbia's Court of Appeal as a matter of extraordinary emergency, which a single judge of the Court of Appeal heard on March 28 and immediately denied. But in the intervening twenty-four hours, the chief electoral officer had delivered all the ballots to Canada Post. This enabled the Court of Appeal to say her appeal had become moot. But even if that hadn't occurred, the court said, it wouldn't have granted her the injunction anyway. Any question about constitutionality of the referendum, based on the vagueness of the ballot questions, it said, could be advanced "in the fullness of time in an action to prevent either the counting of the ballots or to bring about a setting aside of the whole process."

Chief Ke-Kis-Is-Uks's campaign to legally challenge the referendum was reinforced on April 14, 2002, by Wilson Bob and four other First Nations individuals. They applied for declarations that the Treaty Negotiation Referendum Regulation violated the equality rights guaranteed by the Charter of Rights and Freedoms and that the regulation was of no force or effect, being a law in relation to "Indians and Lands reserved for Indians," which is an exclusive constitutional power of the federal government and thus unconstitutional as an act of the government of British Columbia. The applicants also sought an interlocutory injunction to prevent the chief electoral officer from holding the referendum, pending final disposition of their action.

Getting an injunction, which is an "extraordinary" legal remedy, requires proving that it is justified by urgency, irreparable damage about to be done, severe costs that will be incurred, and the issue's gravity. The applicants advanced the political argument that the issue was discrimination.

At the same time that this new request for an injunction was being heard, the other legal challenge to the referendum resumed in a different courtroom. On April 16, Chief Ke-Kis-Is-Uks, having failed to get an injunction to stop the vote, renewed her campaign by filing a statement of claim seeking a judicial declaration that the Treaty Negotiation Referendum Regulation, and the Referendum Act itself, were unconstitutional.

"The purpose of the Referendum Act is to promote democratic decision-making and to elicit public opinion on specific questions," she argued. On the other hand, she said, the referendum being held under that statute, pursuant to the Treaty Negotiations Referendum Regulation, "seeks to *procure public endorsement* of a mandate for conducting treaty negotiations based on principles pre-established by the provincial government, a purpose not contemplated by the Referendum Act."

The B.C. Supreme Court heard argument in her case on May 11, and Justice James Shabbits issued judgment on June 27, 2002, denying the application and upholding the constitutionality of both the Treaty Negotiations Referendum Regulation and the Referendum Act. He said the provincial government could elicit public opinion as to what principles should guide its participation in treaty settlement negotiations. In his opinion, "the question of whether it ought to hold a referendum, and whether it has appropriately participated in the process of treaty settlements, are political matters for which it is accountable to the electorate, not to the courts."

Justice Daphne Smith of the B.C. Supreme Court rendered her decision in the legal challenge by Wilson Bob and others, requesting an injunction and a judicial declaration about the provincial referendum's constitutionality, on May 15. In addition to legal perspectives, she did consider political dimensions, as well.

The plaintiffs, Judge Smith noted, claimed the ballot questions were loaded, biased, and leading, reflecting a design of assimilation and ethnocentrism. They also claimed the preamble to the questions was crafted to evoke a Yes response, substantively promoting discrimination. They contended the questions were confusing, with one framed in the negative, another incorporating two questions, and a third unclear about the answer it sought to elicit. Judge Smith noted that, indeed, witnesses for both the plaintiffs and the Crown agreed the questions could have been worded better, and that wording can slant voting.

Turning to their arguments for an injunction, she found their challenge "neither frivolous nor vexatious." Indeed, the judge deemed the constitutionality of the Referendum Regulations a serious issue, meriting further examination at a trial. However, she held the plaintiffs had been unable to show "irreparable harm," a key test for getting an injunction. Their submissions about how reporting the referendum results could have detrimental impact — as demonstrating irreparable harm — were, in her view, theories unsupported by evidence. She concluded that the attitudes, feelings, and opinions of B.C. residents, as indicative of their propensity for racism, couldn't be proven except by expert testimony. As for the "burden of inconvenience" needed to support an injunction, Judge Smith held that, in the balance of inconveniences, the public interest should be given great weight. Plaintiffs had to demonstrate that public interest would benefit from suspending the referendum. In the end, she saw greater benefit to the public interest in holding the referendum rather than suspending it, which she felt was justified by the province's stated commitment to "negotiating workable, affordable treaty settlements that would provide certainty, finality, and equality." She dismissed the case.

Meanwhile, the Union of British Columbia Indian Chiefs (UBCIC) organized an "active boycott" of the referendum. Rather than just not voting, the "active" boycott entailed electors sending their unmarked ballots in a plain envelope to collection points specified by the UBCIC, including union halls and churches, rather than mailing them back to Elections BC.

The chiefs urged this course of action, they said, because the ballot questions "are problematic not only for what they include, but also for what they exclude." Included, said the UBCIC, were "recycled status-quo positions, which the Province has advanced to deny constitutionally enshrined aboriginal rights," and arguments that "when advanced through the courts were resoundingly rejected." Excluded from this provincial negotiating "mandate" being voted on, the chiefs said, was "any reference to acknowledge Crown obligations owed to aboriginal peoples, or attempt to address a century of denial of rights and title." The mandate did not include "steps to ensure the survival of distinct First Nations within their territories by focusing on language survival, education for non-aboriginal people about aboriginal peoples, or access to higher education for aboriginal peoples." The "right of self-determination" was entirely absent, and the ballot questions did not address, either, "how reconciliation will occur between the pre-existence of Aboriginal societies and the assertion of Crown sovereignty; how Aboriginal peoples can make decisions as to how the land will be used while, at the same time, co-existing with federal and provincial laws."

Their ultimate justification for boycotting the referendum, said Chief Stewart Phillip of the Union of Chiefs, Vancouver, and Chief Ke-Kis-Is-Uks (Judith Sayers) of Hupacasath First Nation, was that the ballot questions asked nothing about "providing a path for Aboriginal Peoples and the Federal and Provincial governments to achieve a just resolution of the Land Question and thereby accomplish an enduring and lasting reconciliation between all parties."[17]

As for votes not part of that result, the chiefs gathered for a protest finale on April 4, 2002, and in a public ceremony, burned the unmarked ballots of the thousands who'd boycotted the province-wide referendum.

For more about this critical dimension of minority rights in a referendum, see Chapter 24, "Voting on Aboriginal Questions."

MINORITY RIGHTS OF MUSLIMS IN QUEBEC

On January 29, 2017, at Quebec City's Islamic Cultural Centre, following evening prayers, six worshippers were killed and nineteen others wounded, shot by university student Alexandre Bissonnette, who turned himself over to police and was charged with six counts of murder. Public support of Muslims in the province immediately coalesced in vigils and rallies. Quebec Mayor Regis Labeaume asserted that the city would stand with the victims' families. Premier Philippe Couillard ordered flags to half-mast, called for "unity," and next day told Quebec's Muslims "We're with you. You are home. You are welcome in your home. We're all Québécois." The victims had established themselves in Quebec as Canadian citizens. They spoke French and sought to integrate into provincial life. They were a local grocery store owner, a professor at nearby Université Laval, three civil servants, and a pharmacy worker.

Their bodies were taken either to Montreal or the country from which they'd emigrated for burial in accordance with Islamic rites and cultural beliefs. Quebec has some two-hundred-and-fifty thousand Muslims, but only one dedicated Muslim cemetery, in Montreal. Religion-based burial places exist for Catholics, Protestants (various denominations), and Jews, plus mixed-denomination cemeteries, several with Muslim designated plots.

On July 16, 2017, a referendum to authorize opening a Muslim cemetery in the Quebec City area municipality of Saint-Apollinaire, on land owned by the Islamic Cultural Centre, produced a majority No vote.

Quebec municipal law permits referendums on rezoning if enough people oppose the project. Anti-Muslim elements seized on the issue to force Saint-Apollinaire's referendum, then fear-mongered misinformation during the campaign. The only voters were forty-nine people living or working nearby, of whom thirty-six cast ballots: nineteen No, sixteen Yes, with one spoiled.

This unresolved case of religious discrimination mixing with ballot box democracy, greeted by silence or impotence of leaders whose grandiose pledges remain in fresh memory, is stark evidence of a risk with referendums and why those in high public office must match their words to actions.

8

JUST WHAT CONSTITUTES A "MAJORITY"?

It's easier to say "in a democracy, the majority rules," than to know what a majority actually is. The significance of this to referendums is that, because ballot questions address transformative change, some believe the level of support required for "majority" approval should be higher than the "simple majority" norm. Our general "majority" standard is a number higher than half, even as close as 50 percent plus one of all votes cast. In Canadian history, a number of significant decisions have turned on a single vote.

This threshold concern about "majorities" was discussed in 1991 by the Beaudoin-Edwards parliamentary committee on constitutional amendments. In 1992 parliamentarians again debated the issue when considering the Mulroney government's enabling legislation for a referendum on the Charlottetown Accord. The debate about numbers that count has posed a challenge ever since 1898 when the concept that a referendum focusing on fundamental change required not just an overall majority of votes but also a majority of provinces. It has continued since, as well, in B.C. and P.E.I. referendums where governments imposed higher vote requirements, and in the ongoing battle between Ottawa and Quebec's separatists over what is meant by "a clear vote" being needed for a province to leave Confederation.

TOSS A COIN OR CALL A NEW VOTE IF RESULT TIED?

Sometimes in voting to elect a representative, or on a measure in a legislature or council chamber, a tie vote occurs. The rules for breaking ties vary. One simply stipulates that the measure getting equal Yes and No votes is defeated on the grounds that it didn't gain majority support.

Another rule, however, calls for a "deciding vote" to be cast by an identified official, such as chairman of the council meeting or the legislature's presiding officer. In some cases, this rule might stipulate that this presiding official not vote *except* to break a tie. In other cases, though, where that isn't the case, this person might end up casting a second vote to tip the balance one way or the other.

Tied elections for a representative in our legislatures have sometimes come under a third rule: the toss of a coin. This efficient expedient saves the time and cost of a second election with all voters having to cast ballots again. Rather than imposing a personal burden on a single individual to cast the "tie-breaking vote," the heads-or-tails verdict lets fate decide.

However, sometimes an electoral tie is broken simply by a recount, when errors in counting, or in deciding whether or not a ballot was properly rejected as "spoiled" according to a list of criteria, will reverse the original count by a few votes. This is why election and referendum statutes in Canada refer to "valid votes cast" as being the only ones that can be counted. Validity pertains to both the qualifications of the voter *and* to proper marking of the ballot paper. A voter is determined to be eligible on the basis of being (i) a Canadian citizen, (ii) of the age of "majority," and (iii) "resident" in the voting area, which means "ordinarily resident" and has a dozen indicia for determining "residency" in the case of temporary workers and seasonal students, new arrivals, and homeless people. That "age of majority" to qualify for voting, sometimes called "legal age," itself has changed over time, with intermittent amendments to the Election Act reducing voting age from twenty-four, to twenty-one, then nineteen and eighteen, even in some instances sixteen. As for creating a "valid" ballot paper, these rules, too, have changed over time. They've included marking the ballot with pencil only; marking with an *X* only; marking inside the square or circle beside a candidate's name, not outside; marking the ballot for no more than a specified number of candidates; and not writing anything on the ballot. Any ballot paper breaking these and other rules was deemed "spoiled." So for many years was an unmarked ballot, although now these are deemed "declined" ballots in some Canadian jurisdictions and counted and reported separately as such. Ever since the right to a secret ballot was introduced, replacing the earlier Canadian practice of an elector openly declaring his support for a particular candidate at the "hustings" or voting place, a host of other administrative and security standards have also been developed to prevent voter fraud and preserve sanctity of the ballot.

Sometimes a tie between two candidates, following recounts, is resolved through a second election.

All these rules about voter qualification and validity of cast ballots apply to referendums just as to elections, although the conundrum of a dead tie hasn't yet arisen, except with some municipal ballot questions. There are more wrinkles, but that's enough to make the point that even a "simple majority" doesn't quite live up to its name.

RAISING THE BAR: "SUPER-MAJORITY" MAKES CHANGE ABNORMALLY HARD

Sometimes a constitution or statute dealing with balloting to approve a change stipulates that a measure will only carry if approved by a higher than "simple majority" count, such as 60 percent, or sometimes even two-thirds, of the votes. This super-majority exception is imposed because powers-that-be have determined certain changes are so significant they must clear a higher hurdle of voter approval than normal.

The criteria in our Constitution governing amendments, for instance, depend first on what the subject is, and second, how many approval votes are needed by Parliament's two houses and the ten provincial assemblies. For some measures, motions of approval must be voted by both houses of Parliament and also reach or exceed approval with motions passed by legislatures in "seven provinces having more than half the population of Canada." For other measures, such as abolishing the Senate, "unanimity" is required, meaning approval in all twelve of these legislative bodies. However, these "unanimity" votes don't require that every last member in Parliament and each provincial legislature approve — just a simple majority of them in each assembly.

Basically, the "super-majority" requirement adds a surcharge, the price that those defending the status quo exact for making change. For example, referendums in British Columbia on changing the electoral system had to be approved by 60 percent of voters in 75 percent of the electoral districts. This abnormal standard was replicated for Prince Edward Island's referendum on the same subject. It can be called "abnormal" in light of other significant referendum decisions in British Columbia, such as granting women voting rights or harmonizing federal and provincial sales taxes, which needed only 50 percent plus one, aggregated across the entire province, to win.

Referendums on electoral reform where an exceptional super-majority is required are a ruse. The legislatures enacting such higher hurdles themselves pass the measure by simple majority, as they do all other matters, including many of transcending nature. While it might thus appear that a government is turning an important issue over to the people so electors themselves can make the choice, this double standard "majority" approval requirement is a taunting abuse of the ballot-question process. When major voting system changes were previously made in Canada, at the federal and provincial levels — for everything from proportional representation to multi-member ridings — it was by a simple majority vote in the legislature. For the electoral system referendum in British Columbia, the people's assembly that prepared the new voting system urged that it be endorsed by a referendum and didn't want anything other than a simple majority to decide the matter. It was the same in Prince Edward Island where a similar process occurred. In both provinces, imposing the super-majority hurdle was the incumbent government's idea — governments now self-protective of the existing electoral system under which they'd been elected.

ANOTHER HURDLE AS SAFEGUARD: THE "DOUBLE MAJORITY"

Similar to the concept of a "super majority" in providing a restraint on change is the requirement for approval by a "double majority." While this latter term can generally describe needing a majority vote in a majority of ridings, it is also used in Canada for measures requiring consent of *both* French-speaking and English-speaking communities, and so is related to questions of protecting minorities. This concept was much in play in Canada during the 1850s and 1860s when Canada East (Quebec) and Canada West (Ontario) legislated together. More recently it has had a number of specific formulations. One was the concurrent or double-majority requirement embedded in the Charlottetown Accord to approve measures materially affecting the French language or culture of Quebec. Any such measure, to carry, needed a double majority in the Senate, meaning approval by both the majority of francophone senators voting, and a majority of all senators voting, on the matter.

Another example relates to separation referendums, and the provisions of the Chrétien government's Clarity Act, a statute based on concepts argued before the Supreme Court of Canada and adopted in the justices' ruling on requisite levels of approval for a province to separate from Confederation.

SHOULD CONCURRENT OR DOUBLE MAJORITIES BE REQUIRED?

A fear in Canada's regions is that, though a population might be strong within its locale — farmers on the Prairies, fishers in the Maritimes, French-speaking Canadians in Quebec — it risks being swamped by a single electoral tsunami. To counter that possibility, the concept of "concurrent majorities" emerged.

The concurrent majority doctrine requires approval from each of two conflicting interests in society on any major proposal, which in some respects makes it similar to the "double-majority" idea. The concurrent majority system was most comprehensively outlined in the mid-1800s by American John C. Calhoun, a political theorist and Democratic vice-president of the United States, who was devoted to ensuring that the more populous North wouldn't override the interests of the American South, including the matter of owning human slaves. Calhoun's formulation incorporated both qualitative and quantitative elements so that no government action could be taken except with widespread consent across all sectors and strata of the community. Despite elaborate elements in Calhoun's formula for "concurrent majorities," it boiled down to the southern and northern communities having veto power against the other, meaning the South's numeric minority couldn't be trumped by majority rule. Calhoun asserted that this system could more fully "collect the sense of the community" and therefore "aid and perfect" the right of suffrage — a Democrat's grandiose cloak for preserving slavery.

THE CONSTITUENCY OF VOTERS ALSO DETERMINES "MAJORITY" OUTCOME

Of overriding importance, if a referendum is to produce a legitimate and accepted outcome, is determining the "constituency" of voters qualifying for a say on the ballot issue.

Voting for MPs and provincial legislature representatives is organized by electoral district, with geographic boundaries that are redrawn every decade or so (after new census reports are available at ten-year intervals) to ensure community of interest for areas within the borders, ease of travel and communication for electors in each district, and relative population balance between all districts. When it comes to voting on ballot issues, using electoral district boundaries is often done, yet it isn't always the pattern.

For prohibition votes under the Canada Temperance Act, the constituency was a municipality, a subunit of a normal provincial or federal electoral district. For some provincial-sponsored referendums, the constituency has been a region within the province consisting of several electoral districts, but not all the province's ridings. For votes on farm issues, the "constituency" is based on the agricultural product rather than geography, for example, a vote on wheat and barley marketing by farmers of the three Prairie provinces and Peace River district of British Columbia who grow these crops and fall under the jurisdiction of the Canada Wheat Board. Likewise, for marketing issues to be decided in sectoral referendums by votes of producers of peaches, pears, plums, asparagus, or other such produce in Ontario, the "constituency" qualifying to ballot on those questions are producers of those fruits and vegetables no matter where they farm within the province, but those farmers only.

In British Columbia, where First Nation leaders felt only aboriginal peoples should constitute the constituency voting on land claim settlements, not the entire provincial electorate, defining the "constituency" of voters merged with related considerations about voters needing to have a direct interest in the issue at hand and about minority rights being safeguarded. That is why holding a province-wide referendum on land claim negotiations, or indeed on any settlement agreement resulting from negotiations by a First Nation with the provincial and federal governments, was opposed in British Columbia when first proposed in 2001. The provincial legislature's Committee on Aboriginal Affairs conducted public hearings at Chilliwack and Vancouver on treaty referendum questions that October to listen "to all British Columbians" and engage "in a constructive and useful discussion to reinvigorate the treaty negotiation process."[1]

At that time, among First Nations leaders opposing a province-wide referendum on the agreement that the Nisga'a had finally reached after a quarter century of negotiation was Wally Braul. President of the Victoria-based

Aboriginal Rights Coalition, Braul called such a voting constituency not only "ill conceived" but one that amounted to "an act of bad faith." With twenty-five years of negotiations, and many compromises being made "by all sides" to reach the Nisga'a treaty, including significant concessions by the Nisga'a, a province-wide referendum could not, he said, "adequately portray the real choice that must be made to obtain closure on these land rights negotiations."[2]

The following year, when the Liberal government of Premier Gordon Campbell presented such a ballot question to the entire provincial electorate, the Union of British Columbia Indian Chiefs led a boycott of it, as already discussed, while other First Nations representatives initiated court challenges based on grounds that essentially boiled down to their belief that the voting constituency wasn't appropriate.

A different kind of "battle of the constituencies" arose on the Prairies when voting took place on the monopoly marketing system for wheat and barley. Only directly affected farmers qualified as the constituency for casting ballots about the Canada Wheat Board. This vote was intended to counter the Conservative government of Prime Minister Harper, whose policy was to end the Wheat Board's monopoly and provide grain growers freedom of choice in marketing, either by continuing with the Wheat Board or selling on the open market themselves. In this contest of ballots, the federal government pointed to its electoral mandate — from a constituency that included more than grain farmers — as its trump card to proceed.

"COUNTING AREAS": ANOTHER FACTOR IN DETERMINING MAJORITY APPROVAL

Electing our representatives is necessarily tied to geographic entities, and so the reporting of elections is done by riding, but there is no reason why the results of voting on a ballot question by the relevant constituency need be *reported* on a riding basis, even though the electoral districts are the most efficient units for actually conducting the balloting using established voters' lists, polling stations, and trained officials.

With referendums, indeed, one can make a strong case for reporting the aggregate vote on the largest unit possible: provincially for province-wide referendums, all of Canada for national votes. Because the electorate has been deemed to form a unity, the collective verdict will, by majority count, determine approval or rejection. In provincial and federal elections, the overall result is reported for party popular support and seat counts on a province-wide or Canada-wide basis, because this larger picture is essential. The largest counting area is even more germane to referendums, a point that has long been understood in the politics of ballot totals.

"Unless there is a majority in every province in the Dominion in the affirmative," asked George Foster, a New Brunswick MP who'd been Canada's finance minister in John A. Macdonald's Conservative government and in 1898 was debating Laurier's prohibition plebiscite from the Opposition benches, "would the government consider it did not have a mandate from the electorate of this country to introduce a prohibition bill and carry it into law?"

Or, as an alternative, might the *total popular vote alone* count as the majority view? "Is it to be considered that the decision of the majority of the total electorate," Foster pressed, "if given in the affirmative, will constitute a mandate to this Government sufficiently clear to demand for the people of Canada a prohibitory law?"

Clearly, the "counting area" from which referendum results are reported adds a significant dimension when interpreting voter support. It is different from an election count that chooses one representative per electoral district to a legislative body. In a referendum, the people in all electoral districts collectively make a decision about a single issue. For a representative, the edge of victory depends on the count in the riding; for the referendum, it's generally the overall popular vote, unrelated to constituency boundaries, that determines if Yes or No wins. The recent Canadian exception is provincial referendums on electoral systems with a double-majority requirement. Thus a strong case can be made that the votes counted in each electoral district should be tabulated centrally, for the entire province or the whole county, and reported that way. We voted on the Charlottetown Accord as Canadians, not as residents of particular electoral districts, even though that subdivision served the practical administration of casting and initial counting of local ballots. Even in electoral districts, the numerous polling districts make their count and then report it to the central office of the returning officer. For referendums, the better approach is to apply this very same idea on a larger scale.

In our diverse regional land, whether for national or provincial referendums, there are reasons to use counting areas larger than individual constituencies, even if smaller than the single aggregated whole. A reward of holding a referendum is for citizens as well as governments to see and appreciate regional differences, because that reality must be accommodated in governing a federal state. Our three national referendums used provincial boundaries as midpoint tabulating areas, even though votes were first counted in the electoral districts. In 1898 and 1942, this method revealed the gulf between Quebec voters and those in other provinces on alcohol prohibition and wartime conscription. This information in turn enabled all Canadians to understand, even if they didn't agree at the time, why Prime Ministers Laurier and King proceeded with extreme prudence in light of the recorded differences in "majority" support.

NO SUCH THING AS "DIRECT DEMOCRACY"

Ballot questions are intrinsically part of our constitutional practices, established democratic procedures, and the rule of law. The referendum is a valid instrument of governance in a democracy, enabling sovereign people to exercise fundamental choice about decisions affecting the future everyone will share. However, this democratic tool is not a free-standing phenomenon. So-called direct democracy, or what Canadian academic Janice Stein disdains as "pure democracy," is nothing of the kind.

In Switzerland, constitutional lawyers use the more accurate term *semi-direct democracy* precisely because traditional law-making procedures remain an intrinsic part of the county's referendum and initiative processes. Peter Stüder, editor of Zurich's newspaper *Tages-Anzeiger*, describes his country's ballot-issue procedure as "a unique combination of representative and direct components."[1]

That's also true in Canada. Although *semi-direct democracy* is too cumbersome for everyday speech, it correctly defines the reality of all our referendum procedures. Voting in which citizens play a role deciding issues or enacting laws *only* occurs in concert with our elected representatives. Rather than posing any challenge to representative democracy, this partnership expands and enriches it.

PARTNERSHIP BETWEEN CITIZENS AND ELECTED REPRESENTATIVES

Canadians who denigrate referendums, saying "our legislators should not abdicate responsibility," betray their embarrassingly shallow knowledge of what is really going on. Legislators remain intrinsic to the referendum process *every step of the way*.

The referendum process is conducted entirely within a statutory framework enacted by legislators. The right to vote on a ballot question, or even to initiate one, is conferred only by statute, no other source. Whether it's the Canada Referendum Act as debated, studied, and made law by Parliament, or a similar provincial statute enacted by a legislature, these deliberately constructed laws guide, regulate, and contain the exercise of ballot-box democracy.

This power to confine the debate, and thereby direct people's thinking, is in the hands of the elected representatives, not the people themselves: wording of the ballot question is approved by votes of elected representatives.

Balloting on a referendum measure doesn't end the matter. If the outcome requires a change in some law, it will have to be implemented by elected representatives — be they members of Parliament, a provincial or territorial legislature, municipal council, or band council. This pattern of elected representatives and electors interacting in democratic partnership, each connected to and depending on the other to make Canada's referendum system work, is an institutionalized and long-standing control ensuring that power can't pass to "the mob."

British Columbia, Alberta, and Quebec each signalled their democratic maturity by stipulating in statutes passed by elected members of their provincial assemblies that citizens would get to vote on constitutional change *before* the elected representatives themselves dealt with the Charlottetown Accord. When this democratic right was then extended to all Canadians, it was Parliament that did so, according to legislation enacted by the people's elected representatives (and in the second chamber by appointed senators, even though they aren't representatives of the people).

POWER OF CITIZENS TO LAUNCH BALLOT QUESTIONS

The "initiative" is another semi-direct form of democratic engagement by which citizens launch ballot questions themselves. The value of this balloting mechanism resides in citizens being able to trigger it, not having to depend on those in office to start the process.

Even so, where citizens can initiate a ballot question municipally, or provincially in British Columbia, the process is still not "direct" because statutes enacted by legislators, and detailed regulations made pursuant to them, prescribe everything from the number of signatures required on the petition to launch a vote, to the requirement that a judicial officer certify the ballot issue as constitutional and compliant with all statutory criteria, and so on through other rules governing voting procedures and spending limits.

VOTING TO RECALL AN ELECTED REPRESENTATIVE

Another semi-direct balloting mechanism, provided only by duly enacted statute, gives voters the possibility of triggering a mid-term vote on whether to "recall" their elected representative. Rather than just waiting for the next election when there would be an opportunity to simply not "re-elect" an incumbent, recall accelerates the timetable. It enables voters to "de-elect" a member of the legislature and then replace that person through a fresh election. In jurisdictions where this procedure exists, it might be invoked by constituents to get someone supposedly more akin to their electoral district's perceived needs and interests to represent them — a dubious criteria. More serious, however, are cases in which removal might be instigated for a representative because of corruption or some other type of malfeasance.

The recall mechanism has limited Canadian history. In Alberta the procedure was invoked against member of the legislature William Aberhart, whose Social Credit government had itself enacted the measure. The chagrined premier recalled "recall" by having the statute repealed in 1937. Apart from other lessons this example imparts, it is clear how these procedures can't kick in unless elected representatives in the legislature first enact a law through which, according to rules they provide, it must operate.

In British Columbia, recall has been on the provincial statute books since 1995 after being strongly approved in an October 1991 referendum. Under the Initiative and Recall Act, a registered voter in the electoral district can petition to remove that constituency's member of the legislative assembly from office. The petition needs signatures from more than 40 percent of eligible voters in the district. To safeguard against recall being used to perpetuate a hard-fought election campaign, petitions can't be submitted to Elections BC during the first eighteen months after the member was elected.

British Columbia's chief electoral officer administers the recall petition process, according to rules established by statute. No criteria are specified to recall an MLA. An applicant must state, in no more than two hundred words, grounds for recalling the member. By 2017, twenty-six recall petitions had been initially approved, but on verification five lacked enough valid signatures. Another was halted because the member, under threat of recall, resigned before the process was completed.

A LEGISLATIVE VETO AT THE BALLOT BOX

The legislative veto, a component of Swiss-style democracy, has made it onto the statute books of several provinces. Manitoba Liberals campaigned in 1914 on the idea of empowering citizens to ratify a law after the legislature enacted it but before it came into force.

Working to perfect their democracy, the Swiss adopted a facultative-style referendum in the 1830s enabling voters to petition for a popular vote on a law passed by a legislative assembly and, potentially, to then override the legislature. By the 1860s, they'd progressed to an obligatory referendum for this sort of thing, stipulating certain classes of enactments that positively had to be referred to voters for approval or rejection. This was the measure Manitoba Liberals won election in 1914 pledging to implement.

In 1916, having an electoral mandate for it, Premier Tobias Norris's government introduced "An Act to Enable Electors to Initiate Laws, and Relating to the Submission to the Electors of Acts of the Legislative Assembly." The Liberal measure passed unanimously. Conservatives, who'd previously opposed referendums, had become converts.

This new democratic partnership being pioneered between the sovereign people and their elected representatives was challenged on constitutional grounds pertaining to the secondary sovereign, the Crown. Three years after its unanimous enactment by the legislature the act was declared unconstitutional on the ground that the Crown's powers — as represented by the lieutenant governor, whose vestigial role included formally signing provincial statutes into law — couldn't be altered by Manitobans. If electors voted approval of legislation and thereby authorized it becoming law, the appellate court felt, this could be interpreted as bypassing the monarch's pen-holding representative. The justices seized upon this antiquated royal power to thwart a province's elected representatives in democratizing their constitution. The discouraged Manitobans didn't redraw their law to overcome this technical formality, as adept draftsmanship could have accomplished. The episode was unhelpful for an evolving nation seeking to clarify and enrich representative democracy and connect our country's law-making process with the people governed by those laws.

THE MINIMAL RISKS OF SEMI-DIRECT DEMOCRACY

No referendum in Canada takes place until a legislature has enacted the enabling legislation to establish all parameters for it — from approval of the ballot question to formation of Yes and No umbrella committees, from voting procedures to rules about campaign advertising, broadcasting, and financing.

No referendum result in Canada is self-executing. Whatever might be decided by electors, it is the elected representatives of the people who must act through normal legislative procedures to implement the results. In our country, the term *direct democracy* actually describes something quite different — a multi-stage operation between elected representatives and the people, with a series of interlocking democratic components.

The various instruments of "semi-direct democracy" are important adjuncts to existing legislative procedures, supplementing and reinforcing them in win-win ways for all concerned. Canadians never chose exclusive representative government, nor did we pick a citizens-at-large democracy, but rather, a blend of both. For truly significant decisions that make it onto ballots, we've complemented and supplemented the process normally engaged in by the elected few who represent the many. The common denominator for both referendums and elections is a sovereign citizenry expressing itself through the deliberate act of ballot-box democracy.

10

REFERENDUMS AND ELECTIONS: ALIKE, YET SO DIFFERENT

Almost nothing about referendums makes sense unless seen in the context of general elections.

Canada's sovereign people engage in broad-based voting on public issues in two ways:

1. General elections, when parties present themselves atop a "campaign platform" built of "planks" — policies, programs, and pledges — and citizens respond by electing to govern us the candidates whose platform, party, and leadership achieve the most support.
2. Referendums, when a substantive issue is publicly debated and we guide its resolution by collectively answering a specific ballot question about it.

Elections and referendums, like conjoined twins of Canadian democracy, are two dimensions of the same thing: the people of a self-governing political community accepting responsibility for the working of our system and taking *an indirect yet participatory role* in shaping our common future.

The "indirect" nature of this entails, first of all, having chosen representatives who will debate issues and make laws on our behalf for the duration of the electoral mandate we've given them; and second, in the case of referendums, voting on measures according to procedures established by legislators, on questions proposed by others, the outcome of which must be addressed by government — the "semi-direct" democracy already described.

The "participatory" element is the driving force that makes all this work, because neither elections nor referendums happen unless we the people yield to our democratic instinct and take part as our democratic institutions and political rights and freedoms empower us to do.

Both these democratic events are similar in many respects. Elections and referendums are initiated by a formal procedure, lead toward a specific voting day, with lists of voters, polling stations, ballot boxes, and officials in charge. Each has a campaign period with a specific sequence of deadlines for filings, registrations, and paid advertising. Election campaigning is mostly run by political parties, referendums primarily by "umbrella committees" that consolidate the factions into party-like Yes and No entities. Elections and referendums have various spending limits for advertising and campaign expenses. News media focus on both events with similar patterns of coverage, combining in-depth background stories with breaking news, pollsters' predictions, voting day drama, commentary, and analysis.

A general election embraces every contending party's past performance, present character, and future promises. It is a verdict on the suitability of all party leaders and everyone's local candidates. It is open season on all conceivable issues and every variant of solution. A properly conducted referendum is none of these. It is, instead, the epitome of a microscopic procedure: a single clear question that can only be answered Yes or No, the paradox of a referendum's blunt precision.

ONLY CONTENTIOUS ISSUES MAKE THE CUT

Whether national, provincial, or local, ballot issue-voting is a serious matter. Every society has touchy subjects. But when an issue is "ripe," or the political will is present, or necessity calls for it, the referendum's unique qualities might make it the most suitable way to confront reality and, rather than avoid discussion and delay decision, help force the necessary choice.

Some might think "forcing" people to decide a public policy is unpleasant, even coercive. Yet choices have to be made by individuals every day, some personal, others in the wider arena of community. Seen in the positive way that befits a people gifted with freedom, a referendum actually offers exhilarating opportunity to do more than vote once every four or five years to elect somebody else to make decisions for us. A ballot-question campaign, and its news coverage, can restore a citizen's hands-on power to make a difference, the opportunity to shape a vital decision and influence others about it, too. It reminds us that, even in mass society, we matter.

Citizens aren't asked in a referendum to vote about whether to go on a picnic in the sunshine at the beach. What makes it onto ballots are challenging issues, the more contentious the better because citizens' answers are part of a democratic process assisting governments to resolve hard questions of a transcending, and often traumatizing, nature.

Perhaps a reason referendums strike a negative reaction from some is the association of this anvil-like public process with subjects they'd prefer to avoid. "Parliament should deal with that," they protest at being forced to face something discomforting. "That's what we elect our MPs for." But self-reliance and citizenship entail more than delegating difficulties to others. If we use our democratic right to choose between candidates for office, it is fully consistent to also make a ballot choice about some fundamental characteristic of our country or province, municipality or reserve.

• • •

The more contentious a subject, the more likely it is to be framed as a referendum question, the more certain to spark discussion with neighbours and debate within families. Forcing choice through a ballot question is a full-fledged component of what Patrick Watson called "the tangled, messy, and unpredictable story of democracy."

The purpose of a referendum is not to reassure those atop the power hierarchy or comfort those in high administrative positions; it is to confront a matter of widespread impact with which we all must live. Hammering out a *collective* decision, amid the flying sparks of open debate, not only measures the maturity of a political society but reflects true understanding of Canada's constitutional reality that, ultimately, it is the people who are sovereign.

ELECTIONS ALL-IN, REFERENDUMS EXCLUSIVE

When painting, we use a roller brush for a huge living room wall, but for the narrow trim around windowpanes, a small bristle brush — different instruments to get the job done well and efficiently. Picking the right tool makes sense in the exercise of statecraft, too.

Just as a general election is an all-in event, a referendum is exclusive. With a ballot issue, the way elected representatives and parties have behaved is beside the point — or should be, if political leaders know how to comport themselves in this non-election, election-like event. We don't, as in an election, try to imagine possibilities in a shimmering future when election promises *might* translate into government performance. Rather, we study and debate a specific issue in real time, preparing for the hard choice the ballot question is forcing us to make. We are, generally, liberated from partisan consideration — making our choices more on merit than undercurrents of human loyalty or antipathy.

Electors can't reach their ballot verdict until a series of steps, stipulated by law, have been taken, many of them similar to our general elections. Procedures might be parallel in many respects, but they aren't identical: political parties are central to the conduct of elections, but in a referendum many other groups seek to get involved while party members might not.

Sometimes putting off a decision, if the issue isn't yet ripe for resolution, has merit. But too often those in office hope other events will overtake the agenda and spare them choosing one solution over another. Because the institutionalized ambiguity of Canadian politics causes matters to drag on a long time before resolution, something bringing clarity to an issue and forcing a public decision is welcome.

Governance and statecraft require making decisions, though no significant measure is free of trade-offs, and few issues yield to an "easy" answer. *Any* decision taken will have consequences, not all of them favourable or popular. But once a choice is committed to, one has to proceed to implementation and ensure the new course is as good as it can be. After the Brexit decision in June 2016, Prime Minister David Cameron stated, "The British people have made a choice. That not only needs to be respected, but those on the losing side of the argument, myself included, should help to make it work."

Our political parties carry the heavy freight through general elections. The referendum device only intermittently helps carry issues forward. But both fit together. The interaction of elections and referendums, though under-examined and little appreciated in our country, represents a "division of labour" in Canadian politics. The deep value of a decision-clarifying referendum about some proposed course is that it incorporates consultation while simultaneously producing a verdict.

WEIGHING THE FINANCIAL COSTS OF REFERENDUMS

One reason voters should *not* be asked to answer a ballot question when voting for elected representatives is that a referendum is meant to focus choice on a particular issue, while a general election includes every issue as well as political personalities and party records. It makes sense to keep the two segregated to best fulfill their distinctive roles. One reason for combining them, however, is financial cost.

Both these democratic events require extensive organization, deployment of personnel, renting of facilities, setting up communications systems, expenditures for publicity, and dozens of other costs that push today's price tag for a referendum into the multi-million-dollar bracket. The 2015 Canadian general election cost $443 million. Estimates for a national referendum today are $300 million. Combining the two would save millions because the voters would be the same, the polling stations could double for both purposes, and the only extra expense would basically be for communications and printing twenty-four million ballot papers to ensure enough for all registered voters.

British Columbia, undisputed leader in Canada on ballot-question practice, offers instructive comparisons in this department. In 2005 British Columbians, voting in a general election, simultaneously cast referendum ballots on a proportional electoral system. The cost of administering the general election was $22.9 million, the extra cost for the referendum just over $1 million. The cost savings of such two-in-one events are more than impressive.

A second way to cut costs dramatically yet preserve the significant advantage of keeping the referendum separate from an election, also recently used in British Columbia but pioneered in Prince Edward Island at least as early as 1954, is voting by mail. In the 1950s, the P.E.I. ballot concerned the potato marketing board's monopoly. The mail-order referendum held to decide the issue cost a tiny fraction of a regular election procedure. In 2015 British Columbia used a postal ballot for its referendum on harmonized sales tax. British Columbia's 2013 provincial election, the closest in time for cost comparison, required some $35 million. The cost of the HST referendum with mail-in balloting was just over $8 million. When conditions seem to call for postal ballots, there is, reports B.C. Chief Electoral Officer Keith Archer, a further benefit. People, he ascertained, "have confidence in the integrity of a referendum process that uses mail-in ballots."

A third money saver, at least for provincial referendums, is voting in conjunction with municipal elections. They are typically all held on the same day throughout the province. In March 2017, this is what New Brunswick Premier Brian Gallant proposed for a 2020 provincial vote on revamping the electoral system. In doing so, he was following precedent, not breaking new ground. British Columbia long ago showed that this could be a cost-effective way to have the best of both worlds. The core idea is that, generally, voting for local councillors involves sufficiently different considerations than arise in a provincial election, so independent focus on the ballot question isn't lost. Some even see a further benefit in boosting normal voter turnout for municipal elections thanks to the greater interest and importance of a contentious ballot issue. One hesitates to cite the malodorous Manitoba case when a series of *municipally* conducted ballot questions about French-language services all took place on the same day as council elections, but the focused attention on the linguistic issue more than doubled normal voter participation that day.

Financial cost can never be the sole criteria, however. So, in crafting referendum-enabling laws, the most prudent approach to permit a panoply of options in statecraft is to provide all possible ways for conducting them, including the matter of timing.

HUMANS ARE EMOTIONAL

Another common feature of referendums and elections is that people get emotional. Humans respond to what frightens or stimulates us, and while some reactions are more cerebral than others, medical science suggests all human behaviour springs from feelings and conditioned reflexes.

Citing "emotionalism" has become one of the new arguments against referendums. Pollster Mario Canseco of Insights West, when reporting 2016 opinion sampling about Canada's electoral system, referenced the United Kingdom's Brexit vote to observe that a referendum "can turn into a very emotional exercise." Robin Sears, former NDP official turned lobbyist, said referendums on conscription and Quebec's separation caused "deep wounds and lasting damage for Canadian public life." Like Canseco, Sears didn't fail to use Brexit as a hook for his view that a referendum "can turn into a very emotional exercise" — as if that observation seals the fate of ballot questions. It is apparently un-Canadian to display emotion about public issues.

Being logical thinkers, the pollsters and backroom political strategists who conclude we should avoid referendums because of the high levels of emotion they induce, will next recommend that general elections themselves be banned. They are, after all, both alike in this regard.

SECOND THOUGHTS, REPEATING VOTES

As the vote on the Charlottetown Accord showed, a referendum can yield a conclusive verdict on a question, its collective decision bringing a complex issue to resolution. Even the most ardent supporters of a side that loses are usually satisfied they'd had full opportunity to persuade a majority to support their view, but could not. They reconcile themselves to accepting, and living with, the will of people who openly debated and reached a collective verdict different from their own. This cathartic finality that a referendum brings to an issue is, generally, one of its rewards.

And yet ballot questions on the same subject might recur, either in a general election or a repeated ballot question on the issue. Such "rounds" of balloting show another way elections and referendums are tightly interwoven, similar yet different methods by which democratic societies grapple with issues and power and seek to work out a consensus about how to live together and make progress. Such an entwined relationship between these two democratic exercises counters those who argue referendums in Canada are "not part of democracy" and are "an abnegation of responsibility by elected representatives."

Elections to the House of Commons, our legislatures, and municipal and band councils must occur at regular intervals, giving voters a chance to reconsider who we want running our affairs. We reappraise our collective decision about who can best represent us, wield power, and make decisions on our behalf. Because politics and public issues are not hermetically sealed but comingled, we reconfirm or reject elected representatives, renew or replace governments, and in the mix, revisit or let rest our electoral mandate on a specific issue. In Canada this has happened on prohibition of alcohol, use of Daylight Saving Time, whether Newfoundland should join Confederation, the retention of parochial schools in Newfoundland, electoral system changes in Prince Edward Island and British Columbia, and Quebec's constitutional connection with Canada.

In both elections and referendums, a verdict from voters at one date is the right choice, but time and changing circumstances can recast how we judge a political leader's personality, a party's policies, or a referendum's conclusion. Canadians, sometimes, take second bites of the apple. Conscription was voted on twice, once in the general election of 1940, a second time in the national ballot question of 1942. Political and military conditions required reconsideration.

In Quebec votes on separation were dubbed "neverendums" because, though only two trips were made to the polls to cast ballots on the issue, ever since the 1970s talk was recurring about votes to leave Confederation. After the 1980 vote failed to authorize the separatist Parti Québécois government to negotiate "sovereignty-association" with the Government of Canada, Premier René Lévesque simply said, the night the votes were counted, *"À la prochaine!"* — "Onward to the next time!" Before, between, and since the 1980 and 1995 separation referendums, sovereignist governments have been elected, and defeated, in general elections.

Nor are Quebecers the only ones to vote twice on membership in our political union. In 1948 Newfoundlanders made two trips to the polls in run-off balloting that ultimately produced a majority for joining Confederation. Doubts about the benefit of being in Confederation, when not able to be channelled through a specific ballot question, also found expression in Maritime general elections, as Nova Scotians demonstrated in several trips to the polls electing representatives to the House of Commons and provincial assembly in the 1870s. Absence of a referendum on this question turned a number of Atlantic provinces' general elections into a facsimile of one.

For a long stretch of our history, the votes on liquor questions encompassed all the problematic aspects of trying to conclude a public policy on beverage alcohol in Canadian society, with voting taking place in general elections and referendums as well as in the legislative assemblies. When prohibition was imposed but resisted, people responded by creating an alternate, illegal system for the manufacture, distribution, and sale of alcohol. From Prince Edward Island to Manitoba, voters faced a half-dozen ballot questions about booze over many decades, the outcomes cumulatively helping us evolve workable policies. Referendums played their part in the much larger struggle by a democratic society to resolve a deep-seated dilemma.

Newfoundlanders not only took two rounds at the ballot box, weeks apart in 1948, to work through their three options for future constitutional government, but also two rounds, a couple of years apart, to vote on shifting from religious-based schools to a public school system, in 1995 and 1997. The need for further referendums in that case arose not from confusion on the part of voters but problems in the government's policies that were being put to a vote. We've also had cases in which electors got to vote on measures already in place. In Saskatchewan this arose with whether to continue public funding for abortions performed in hospitals, while in New Brunswick a referendum was held on whether province-wide gambling, using already operating video lottery terminals the government had previously decided to allow, should continue.

A decision adjudicated by one court might be appealed to another. One doctor's diagnosis might give rise to a second opinion. An umpire's call about a tag at second base, like a referee's judgment on whether a puck really crossed the goal line, might be overturned on video review. It's in our nature to reconsider and reappraise in light of new or better evidence, and it is the democratic nature of our society, as well — regularly recurring elections, routine amendment of statutes by our legislatures, even repeated ballot questions to hammer out a truly obdurate matter. Canada is seldom a country of finality, more a place of perpetual second chances.

11

"MANDATES" FROM THE PEOPLE

"To say that the Parliament of Canada, which derives its powers from the people, after a solemn pledge has been given to the people on a matter which is of deep concern to them, is released from this pledge the moment the people have elected it, is for Parliament itself to create a precedent which would be subversive of parliamentary institutions."

Perhaps no statement more sharply etches the political ethics framing an electoral mandate than the above words, addressed by Prime Minister King to the House of Commons seventy-five years ago.

The concept of an electoral mandate is so enshrined in the belief system of Canadians that it is part of our unwritten Constitution. A huge part of our public debate concerns the sanctity of pledges given to gain electoral office, and whether or not they are honoured.

Because governing is the most serious work anyone can undertake, the conditions of employment, for a democratic society such as ours, are grounded in trust. On one side, this involves voters who entrust power to duly elected representatives, and on the other side, the trustworthiness of those elected. What you say you'll do during the bargaining session of an election campaign, when those wanting votes appeal to those with votes to give, has to be honest. If it is dishonest, the exercise is a sham and democracy becomes a fraud, or as our longest-serving prime minister put it, "subversive of parliamentary institutions."

The bargain struck at the ballot box is a democratic contract based on performance promised and undertakings given. This pledged agreement is so central to the legitimacy of those governing that we dignify it as an "electoral *mandate*" — not a "wish list," but an *order* to perform according to the election-time negotiation and authorization of a particular course of action.

However, nothing is more encrusted by self-interested interpretation, enshrined in elusive parliamentary doctrines, enriched by constitutional fiction, or politically fatal to get wrong than our Canadian concept of a "mandate" from voters.

BRITISH COLUMBIA'S COSTLY LESSON ABOUT ELECTORAL MANDATES

In the summer of 2011, British Columbia voters told their government not to "harmonize" the province's sales tax with the federal government's goods and services tax. Fifty-four percent of 1.6 million voters cast mail-in referendum ballots during June and July rejecting harmonization. By this date, Ottawa had somehow managed to spend $1.6 billion helping British Columbia's administrative changeover to the combined taxes.

Opponents of referendums held up this result as proof that "people are resistant to change" and why ballot questions are thus a bad thing. *Globe and Mail* editorial writers in Central Canada derided the outcome as "government by plebiscite." On our West Coast, however, British Columbians were more attuned to the working of their democracy. The issue had a history.

Two years earlier, during the 2009 provincial election campaign, Liberal leader Gordon Campbell told voters he had no plan to introduce a harmonized sales tax: "It's not on my radar." Two months after winning a majority government Premier Campbell announced that harmonizing the provincial and federal taxes was exactly what his government was going to do.

The reversal provoked outcry from political opponents, news media, and British Columbians at large. Their ire arose from Campbell's dishonesty with voters about harmonization and his betrayal of his government's electoral mandate. The electorate had been duped into voting for his party's candidates, giving Campbell's Liberals authority to govern on the pledge of no tax harmonization. B.C. Finance Minister Kevin Falcon openly acknowledged the moral conundrum created by reversing an explicit electoral mandate conferred by voters.

It got worse. That autumn documents surfaced revealing that British Columbia's Liberals had HST-related plans prior to the 2009 election, contradicting their campaign statements in the spring. Campbell's approval rating plummeted to 9 percent, a record low. Minister of Energy, Mines, and Petroleum Resources Blair Lekstrom resigned over "fundamental disagreement with the B.C. Liberals on the harmonized sales tax." Rumours indicated the premier was losing the support of more ministers. At the start of November, Gordon Campbell addressed British Columbians from the safety of a television studio to announce he was resigning as premier.

Meanwhile, a referendum was in the works. Amid the outrage over the violated electoral mandate, former B.C. premier Bill Vander Zalm launched a referendum petition for a ballot question on HST under British Columbia's Initiative Act. On August 11, 2010, Elections BC confirmed his campaign had succeeded in clearing all procedural hurdles. Now the provincial government *had* to hold a referendum on the tax issue. Business organizations supporting HST went to court to challenge Vander Zalm's petition. Elections BC kept the referendum process in dramatic abeyance until the case was decided. On August 20, B.C. Chief Justice Robert Bauman ruled Vander Zalm's petition opposing HST was valid and that Elections BC had been correct to approve it. That is what produced the 2011 referendum for British Columbians to decide the fate of their sales tax system.

Meanwhile, in her campaign to replace Gordon Campbell as Liberal leader and premier, the province's former education minister, Christy Clark, said she wouldn't proceed with blending the provincial and federal sales taxes if she won. By December 2010, believing the upcoming referendum would reject sales tax harmonization, Clark advocated cancelling the vote so that, instead of a verdict at the ballot box, a free vote in the legislature could settle the question. "Let our MLAs do their jobs and let our MLAs vote down the HST," she said. "Do it by March 31 and get it over with and get on with life in B.C."

However, after she became premier, the Liberals proceeded with HST, despite Christy Clark's statements when seeking the leadership that she didn't intend to blend the two taxes. She now campaigned for harmonizing the two sales taxes. As the province readied for the referendum, which would be conducted by mail, the Liberals warned of the high cost of returning to separate GST and PST systems. In April 2011, Premier Clark launched a province-wide "engagement initiative" to hear British Columbians' ideas for how to "fix" the HST. Mostly she learned the Liberals faced plummeting support for being two-faced about HST.

To counter this, Finance Minister Falcon tried bribery. If British Columbians would vote to keep HST, he promised, he'd drop the sales tax rate by 1 percent on July 1, 2012, and by another point in 2014. Why stop there? The provincial government next promised to mail vote-enticing "transition payments" of $175 per child to families with children and $175 for low- and middle-income seniors. It was money they'd only get if harmonization took place. Translation: we'll pay you to vote Yes.

After Elections BC announced on August 26 that 55 percent of voters favoured abolishing the HST, the Liberal government proceeded to reinstate the two-tax GST/PST system.

"We are better off for having had this process," said Premier Clark, "whatever the outcome." The premier was putting a positive face on things, to be sure, but she was right: the province was better off clearing the air on the principle of combining two sales taxes into one, and more profoundly, restoring integrity to B.C. public life in terms of political promises, electoral mandates, trust of the people, and consent of the governed. Finance Minister Falcon acknowledged, "We should have stopped and had that discussion with the public first before we made that decision to go forward. We never fully recovered from not having done that."

The B.C. government repaid Ottawa its $1.6 billion — only part of the price tag for misleading electors and violating its electoral mandate.

CANADA'S REPUDIATED MANDATE FOR ELECTORAL REFORM

On October 19, 2015, when a majority federal Liberal government was elected, the party's "campaign platform" — the metaphorical stage hammered together from campaign promises upon which the party's leader and candidates "stand for office" while pledging to implement such measures if elected — was translated by constitutional custom into an "electoral mandate." The sovereign people of Canada had given powers of state to identifiable individuals for specified purposes — one of them clearly being to change the system for electing MPs.

In addition to speeches and brochures, the 2015 election campaign included websites through which the country's parties outlined, for millions researching the best recipient of their vote, the programs and policies they promised to deliver if elected to govern. The Liberal Party's site, highlighting its "Real Change!" theme, was explicit: "We are committed to ensuring that 2015 will be the last federal election conducted under the first-past-the-post voting system. Within eighteen months of forming government, we will introduce legislation to enact electoral reform." The Liberal leader, now become prime minister, repeatedly affirmed this promise in public appearances, which was reassuring to many who'd voted Liberal for this specific reason, a party not otherwise their first choice.

The Liberals' mandate was reinforced by throne speech alchemy at the opening of Parliament on December 4, 2015. Governor General David Johnston's text, provided to him by the PM, outlined ways the government would implement its contract with voters, making the sovereign people's mandate now Her Majesty's, as well, through this ritual for formal sanctification of electoral promises offered and accepted. "To make sure that every vote counts," confirmed the Crown's spokesperson, "the government will undertake consultations on electoral reform and take action to ensure that 2015 will be the last federal election conducted under the first-past-the-post voting system."

Prime Minister Justin Trudeau's "mandate letter" to Maryam Monsef, minister responsible for democratic institutions, outlined what she had to do to fulfill the electoral mandate the Liberals had been granted by Canadian voters: "Bring forward a proposal to establish a special parliamentary committee to consult on electoral reform, including preferential ballots, proportional representation, mandatory voting, and online voting."

The campaign promise to replace the electoral system because it was "unfair" had not been made by an ill-informed fringe group but by a major political party with institutional memory. Liberals knew (1) the timetable was tight for a new voting system to be in place for 2019's election; and (2) during the prior decade in-depth work, including exhaustive public consultation, had already devised explicit alternatives to our first-past-the-post system.

For the first, Chief Electoral Officer Marc Raynard confirmed early on that the new voting system would have to be law by 2017 to complete the switchover in time for the 2019 election. Time was of the essence. That well-understood reality was why the Liberals, from the outset, had promised legislation "within eighteen months" of forming a government — April 2017 at the latest.

As to the second, the Liberals also knew Canadian-developed "proportional" systems were available and that they had to implement one — because that's what they'd sought a mandate to do. Nationally, the Law Commission of Canada had completed a top-calibre four-year study, drawing from its extensive public consultation sessions across Canada and hundreds of briefs from electoral system experts, to recommend "mixed-member proportional" or MMP as superior to first-past-the-post. In British Columbia, Quebec, Ontario, New Brunswick, and Prince Edward Island, extensive efforts had likewise gone into devising better electoral systems, drawing from thorough public consultations and even constituent assemblies. Each had recommended a specific alternative, generally mixed-member proportional, to first-past-the-post. Research and study of suitable proportional electoral systems, at the cost of millions of dollars, was already a national asset. Well-developed Canadian alternatives to first-past-the-post were available to implement.

However, the PM directed his minister to start over from square one. She was only to see a parliamentary committee established that would "consult on electoral reform." What could this mean? In May 2016, Minister Monsef underscored the government's fundamental understanding of its electoral mandate, saying, "Our commitment to end the first-past-the-post system was clear" in the election and thus "the will of the people" is for a new electoral system to be implemented. But what followed wasn't action based on that mandate; instead, the government proceeded to kill time at public expense and people's inconvenience through open-ended consultations. The process appeared to be an effort to enshroud a clear mandate in meaningless clouds of unfocused possibilities.

Had commitment to "real change" been as real as Liberals held out during the 2015 election, the democratic renewal minister would have been asked to bring forward legislation to implement the mixed-member proportional system recommended by the Law Commission of Canada. Then this specific bill could be referred to a parliamentary committee for focused hearings, a precise report, and parliamentary debate on the committee's recommendations in the course of enacting the measure and fulfilling the Liberals' mandate. If the prime minister and his cabinet didn't want mixed-member proportional, other options developed in Canada through extensive public consultation were also available. But *one had to be chosen*. That was implicit in the promise made during the election. Leadership requires making a choice and then making the best of it.

Once the Liberal government replaced its mandate to act with open-ended consultations, however, electoral reform drifted into a political twilight zone. The history of electoral system changes in Canada, from decades-long periods of operating experimentation with systems based on proportional representation, to significant protracted attempts to alter voting systems by deliberate consensus-seeking, made clear that Prime Minister Trudeau's approach, whether innocent or intentional, would doom his oft-repeated pledge to Canadians.

Given our well-honed proclivities, consulting one another about electoral reform was an ideal formula for sucking Canadians into a swamp of paralyzing indecision, resulting in no electoral system change. Gradually, through mid-2016, the government shifted its concrete plan to replace the "unfair" voting system to a vague seeking of "consensus" about what to do.

The Liberals now claimed to want an informed consensus on diverse and complex electoral systems. But this consensus-seeking gambit stirred discussion without any contextual framework beyond the "unfairness" of the existing system. The parliamentary committee on electoral reform heard from hundreds of experts during 2016. Other MPs dutifully engaged citizens about electoral reform or sent questionnaires to constituents. All the while, Canada's minister of democratic renewal was taking her own soundings with Canadians — even as she simultaneously had a parliamentary committee doing this work. In late August 2016, Monsef lamented that "no consensus was emerging." Was this unfolding scenario a calculated effort to nurse the electoral system project beyond time available for action? Had the Liberals, like others before, decided a system that could elect them to majority government with only 39.74 percent of the popular vote wasn't so flawed, after all?

Several Liberal MPs began to push a revisionist line that electoral pledges weren't really meant to be implemented, just to start public dialogue on a subject.

By December, in the Commons, the minister for democratic renewal berated the all-party parliamentary committee for not recommending an alternate electoral system, something it had expressly *not* been asked to do. The committee recommended the government study electoral systems further, which was akin to asking Campbell's to review other recipes for tomato soup. The report wasn't even unanimous, with a couple of appendices expressing dissents and qualifications. Some of the MPs recommended a referendum to approve any new voting system once the government figured out what it should be.

In January 2017, Maryam Monsef was moved to a different portfolio. Rather than close down the now-functionless "Ministry of Democratic Renewal," Prime Minister Trudeau handed the empty title to Karina Gould, who told Canadians that a series of town halls and online consultations had shown "a range of views" about replacing the first-past-the-post system. That, she stated, made it "evident that the broad support needed among Canadians for change of this magnitude does not exist." She added, as if it had been ordained, that "electoral reform is not in my mandate." That was the "mandate" as revised in a letter to the new minister from the PM, not the mandate as given by voters, the mandate she and her predecessor minister, as well as the prime minister and all other elected Liberals, had campaigned for and received to change the unfair electoral system.

In the Commons, Prime Minister Trudeau stated that a "lack of consensus" indicated there was no sense in proceeding, adding "a divisive referendum at this time is not what Canada requires." Nor, he threw in, did Canada require "an augmentation of fringe voices" that could hold the balance of power in Parliament, one of the alarmist fears typically cited by those *opposed* to proportional representation. No apology was offered, no suggestion that a longer time frame was needed for the promised reform. Electoral system change under the Trudeau Liberals was dead. Its mandate violated, the Liberals would run for re-election in 2019 under a system they'd repeatedly condemned as "unfair" — statements seemingly attesting to their own illegitimacy as an "unfairly elected" Canadian government.

New Democratic MP Nathan Cullen, vice-chair of the all-party committee on electoral reform, called the renunciation of the electoral mandate a "cynical display of self-serving politics" and that "Mr. Trudeau proved himself today to be a liar." Green Party leader and MP Elizabeth May, who'd also run the fool's errand on which the Liberal government dispatched the hard-working committee of MPs, was "more shocked by the brazen reversal than anything else in my adult life." Public protests erupted across Canada, petitions were signed, and letters sent in the thousands to Liberal MPs. A constitutional challenge to the first-past-the-post system, placed in abeyance when the Liberals promised and got a mandate to change the electoral system, was revived, with donations pouring in to support the legal costs.

Meanwhile, the very same first-past-the-post electoral system that Prime Minister Trudeau now decided to save, so that "fringe voices" could not hold the balance of power, had produced in British Columbia's May 2017 election just three Green Party representatives in the legislature. They not only held the balance of power; they used it to oust the governing Liberals and install the NDP in office under a governing pact that includes a pledged 2018 referendum on a new electoral system based on proportional representation. At times irony is almost poetic.

HOW ELASTIC CAN A MANDATE BECOME?

Gordon Campbell broke his mandate on sales tax doing what he'd promised not to. Justin Trudeau broke his mandate on electoral reform by not doing what he'd promised he would. Both violated the voters' trust that a leader would make good on promises given. Both provoked outrage from citizens saddled with top office holders who'd deliberately violated electoral contracts. Both had strong majorities in their legislatures, so there was no barrier in that department to prevent honouring their commitments.

Interpreting a mandate might in some ways be the winning party's prerogative, but Canada is a democracy, not a dictatorship, a place where rule of law (including constitutional conventions that treat electoral mandates as being real) takes precedence over the self-interested whims of those wielding power. Opposition parties, political pundits and pollsters, special interest groups, and journalist commentators do their best to watch governments and juxtapose their actual performance with earlier election promises.

If voters fill the legislature with an avalanche of a party's members, we accept this as overwhelming endorsement of its program and expect the government to take bold action. But what if a party just squeaks into office with a minority? Does that mean the people have given only tepid approval and that the government ought to go slow? We saw, when Prime Minister Pierre Trudeau governed from a minority position with support from the New Democrats, enactment of measures the Liberals had never campaigned for. It was the same with Ontario's minority Liberal government under Premier David Peterson, who signed a specific agreement on measures to enact with NDP leader Bob Rae, their pact completely scrambling the "electoral mandate" doctrine.

As to just how "elastic" an electoral mandate can be, there seems to be a shifting pastiche of variables. First, the electoral system might result in large distortions between a party's level of support with voters and the number of seats it gets in the legislature, a prevailing Canadian pattern. Second, the purity of an electoral mandate might get diluted by a minority government embracing policies of its political opponents to hold on to power, not what voters endorsed but what political manoeuvring engineers. Third, a government in Ottawa might face the impediment of having to implement its mandate through an unaccountable second legislative chamber whose appointed members, though lacking legitimacy as representatives of the people, thwart the legislated will of elected MPs in the Commons, something that doesn't embarrass or confound governments operating within the framework of our single-chamber provincial legislatures.

A fourth source of confusion about the nature of an electoral mandate derives from whether the party in government outlined a detailed program to electors, or merely presented a slogan tying together several general propositions. If the former, such as the 223 specific Liberal Party promises in 2015, the government has a more precise mandate and its task is primarily one of implementation. If the latter, "It's Time for a Diefenbaker Government!" in 1957, or "The Land Is Strong!" in 1972, the government has more latitude interpreting its "mandate" and might exaggerate a meaning, obscure passages, or invent new importance for a trite phrase.

Fifth is the wild card of changed circumstances. This can be played at any time to rationalize changing an electoral mandate, whether the new context is manifest to all, such as an outbreak of war, or a spurious excuse the public can't test, such as allegations the public finances were discovered to be much worse than expected and therefore promised actions must be shelved.

IS THE MANDATE DOCTRINE JUST A FICTION OF CONVENIENCE?

To keep the machinery of government working and to sustain plausible parliamentary operation, we cling to the idea that a government, after gaining power by virtue of winning the most seats in a general election, and even if its popular vote was less than majority support in the country, has some kind of mandate to deal with *any* issue that comes up during the life of that parliament, provided it retains the confidence of the legislature.

Our country's political scientists and journalists operate within this open-ended construct. Compliant politicians sustain it. Everybody shrugs and goes along because … well, the government does have the power — and because this mandate doctrine offers pragmatic cover for dealing with issues never debated or anticipated during the election.

Political scientists studying Canada's general elections of 1974, 1979, and 1980 concluded in their book *Absent Mandate* that campaigns had become no more than horse races between contending leaders, and because electors lacked alternate policies to choose from, they couldn't give a clear policy mandate to any government, nor judge its record appropriately when the next election came around.[1] "The workings of the Canadian party system," they found, "cannot produce any clear mandate for development of policies to deal with the country's significant problems."

The same conclusion was reached by political scientist Vernon Bogdanor, who wrote in *The People and the Party System* that a voter can at best give a judgment only "on the general political colour of the government" and can only rarely "make views felt on particular issues."[2] Adding further to this line of analysis, another political scientist, Jon Pammett, observed that although issues are important in campaigns and central to voting decisions for many Canadians, "these issues are infrequently defined with a degree of precision that might approximate public policy." He concluded that "voting patterns based on issues are frequently not in any concerted direction" and that this causes "difficulties in trying to connect an issue mandate with any particular group of representatives."[3]

Even if all parties outlined with impeccable precision policies on ten or fifty or one hundred issues, it would still be impossible to infer from voting results which policies had been approved and which rejected. That is why most parties seek to offend the fewest voters by pledging nothing more than is needed to win, and keeping pledges at the highest level of general abstraction. Occasionally, parties are even elected to office *despite*, rather than because of, some of their policies. Did Canadians really want a changed electoral system in 2015, or just the end of a Stephen Harper government?

A development not anticipated during an election might confound a stated policy of the party once in office, sometimes spawning an opportunistic change, even necessitating a complete reversal. So we go along with a watered-down version of the mandate idea. We hold simply that a government in office has received authority from the electorate in the most recent election to govern as it must and as it chooses before the next election — conditional upon maintaining the voting support of a majority of the people's elected representatives in the legislature. We contrive to make the mandate doctrine a loose-fitting garment over a generously proportioned body, concealing bumps here, revealing some shape there, and generally giving, at a casual glance, the impression of having the whole thing covered.

"RESPONSIBLE GOVERNMENT" DEMANDS SOME KIND OF ELECTORAL MANDATE

However, the assertion that a government can go to war, amend the country's Constitution, reverse an entire regime of trade policies or immigration programs, impose price-and-wage controls it said it wouldn't, or cancel promised procurement of military equipment stretches the electoral mandate doctrine beyond reason. To reverse clearly promised policies made during the campaign that are, hence, part of the government's general mandate challenges the very doctrine on which that government depends for its political legitimacy.

The idea of a government having a specified electoral mandate goes to the heart of responsible government. Without some kind of program, how can anyone follow the concert? The Official Opposition might be an institutionalized component of our parliamentary system, but unless there is a reasonably clear sense of what a government in power is expected to do, how can "holding power to account" be anything more than a freelancer's field day? The campaign pledges, and the speech from the throne, offer at least a plot outline for the drama of democratic accountability.

Sometimes an election contains so many ambiguities and cross-currents that no party could truly claim an explicit mandate from it. But to hold that Canadian general elections resemble nothing more than politicians pushing empty wheelbarrows is to deny the essence of a democratic society and disregard that, quite often, enough is said clearly in bargaining for votes that must be taken as the pledged word of an individual reliable enough to become prime minister or premier, as was nailed by Nathan Cullen.

The overwhelming volume of legislation, former prime minister Arthur Meighen observed in 1937, comes not from a popular mandate but merely the routine working of government over the term of its life.[4] Meighen stated that there was "no question of a mandate at all in the case of at least 98 percent of the measures" coming before Parliament, that virtually all matters could be routinely dealt with by the elected representatives under the general electoral mandate of the previous election.

Yet every now and then, as Meighen also observed, an issue of transcending national importance comes along, a measure that if implemented would "affect positive principle going to the root of our institutions," for which no government in office can be said to have a mandate, and on which it would act at its peril without seeking some direction from the people.

The referendum, unnecessary for routine matters, is a tool for that special "2 percent" category of exceptional measures. Meighen believed the people had to be consulted on such exceptional measures through the ballot box. He saw a general election as the method for "consulting" the people, because like many others, he was slow to recognize the merit of direct voting on an issue. He conflated general elections with specific issue determination.

Difficulty in discerning a specific mandate from a general election really highlights the referendum as an appropriate mechanism for a democracy such as ours, in these cases, on three grounds: (1) the legitimacy of the government depends upon the consent of the governed, (2) the major issue of transcending importance hasn't previously been addressed by the public, and (3) the government in office can't be said to have an express electoral mandate to deal with it.

This conundrum of general elections and specific mandates is continuous. Our 1988 general election was fought extensively, but by no means exclusively, on the multi-dimensional issue of a Canada–U.S. trade treaty. The Mulroney government, championing the plan, was re-elected with a majority of seats. The Liberal Opposition introduced a motion contending the government lacked a mandate to proceed with free trade. Council of Canadians Chair Maude Barlow cautioned the PM not to go ahead because a "majority of Canadians voted for parties opposed to the free-trade agreement."[5] Paul Grant, a private citizen, responded that Barlow was "exhibiting disdain for democracy when it doesn't suit her purposes." Barlow would like to draw inferences from the "popular vote," he said, but they would be "based on fallacious assumptions, namely that every vote for a Progressive Conservative candidate was a vote for the free trade agreement and every vote for another candidate was against it."[6]

Debate over the people's mandate in 1988's election was aggravated by the electoral system's distorting results of voting in our multi-party system and its inability to translate votes into seats in a manner honouring "representative democracy." With the same electoral system still in place today, the outcry about "majority governments with minority support," or "fake majorities," cannot be confined to 1988 and Canada's trade treaty with the United States. It endures and is increasingly raised by those wanting to challenge a course of action in the ambiguous aftermath of Canadian elections and our foggy doctrine of an electoral mandate.

People understand if extreme changes intervene that neither voters nor office seekers could have anticipated during the election. People will acknowledge the impossibility of proceeding as mandated if a leader candidly reviews why a pledge has to be varied, or its implementation delayed, because of a radically altered context. But to violate a promise without any cause beyond political self-interest and without any clear and sincere explanation breaks faith with the people by those in positions of authority. Trust is soluble in opportunism; power to govern that lacks legitimacy becomes tyranny.

Voters complain, based on experience and observation, that politicians promise anything to get elected, then break their promises once in office. That's not always the case but is often true. Some political leaders act as if winning a majority of seats is a carte blanche "mandate to govern" and proceed to exercise power with little or no connection to pledges given during the election campaign.

A government asserting it has a clear mandate might, in fact, lack credibility, even legitimacy, should its leader defiantly justify a change of course by saying, or implying, "We can do this because we won the power to govern!" Especially if that's said about an issue of overriding importance not even mentioned during the election, or that was pledged to be handled differently; such a brazen stance rips away the increasingly fictional veneer of the "electoral mandate" doctrine.

The Canadian catalogue of broken election promises began long ago. Conservatives, Liberals, Social Credit, New Democrat, Parti Québécois, United Farmers, Progressives, and Union Nationale have each formed governments and then failed to uphold commitments to voters. Election campaigns are such a grab bag of issues that it might not really be possible to separate from voting returns a clear mandate for, or against, a specific project. But whether the electoral mandate is stretched beyond recognition or shrinks to nothing, whether it's allowed to slip into administrative oblivion or is dramatically broken, the political morality isn't mystifying. Breaking promises erodes a government's legitimacy.

All problems considered, more intelligent use of referendums would be good medicine for this "mandate" ailment of Canadian politics, and more compatible with our existing system of governance than other suggestions being advanced as cures.

CONSTITUTIONAL UNDERPINNING OF REFERENDUMS TO CLARIFY A MANDATE

All of which brings us to the constitutional underpinnings of interpreting how people vote. One of the denigrating raps against referendums — that this democratic exercise is mere "populism" — is advanced by those who seem to suggest that early use of ballot-box democracy in Prairie Canada was an unsophisticated expression of agrarian protest by hayseed characters and rural rubes. Such critics often contrast radical populism to "parliamentary sovereignty" doctrines from Britain to make their case that populist forms of participatory democracy are profoundly wrong for our country.

The truth, however, is that when the United Kingdom's deep thinkers began to realize that more was needed to establish democratic government than constitutional stances against "monarchical sovereignty," it was esteemed constitutional lawyers such as A.V. Dicey and major political leaders such as Prime Minister Benjamin Disraeli who argued for referendums.

Unlike plain-spoken Canadian farmers, high-born Albert Venn Dicey was educated at King's College, Balliol College, and Trinity College. After his call to the bar, he taught law at Oxford and became an inaugural professor of law at the newly founded London School of Economics. Dicey emerged as Britain's foremost jurist and constitutional theorist. The term *rule of law* had existed since the 1600s, but it was Dicey who popularized it and gave cogent rigour to the concept that no person is above the law, all are subject to the same laws, and such laws must be made openly by Parliament.

Dicey then came to grips with his country's typical disorganization on the legal front. Britain's criminal laws were scattered throughout dozens of dissimilar statutes, for example, and its constitution was no single written document but a hodge podge of acts and customs. He responded to this normal British muddle in 1885 with his landmark book *Introduction to the Study of the Law of the Constitution*, in which he expounded the principles he'd discerned to be part of Britain's "uncodified" constitution. This seminal work made Dicey renowned for asserting the principles of "parliamentary sovereignty."

The British parliament was an absolutely sovereign legislature, having the right to make or unmake any law. The freedom in which British subjects live Dicey pinned directly to the sovereignty of Parliament, and to impartial courts free from governmental interference. In harmony with this view of parliamentary sovereignty and to extend the importance of people living in freedom, Dicey then became the first strong advocate for referendums in the United Kingdom.

The central premise embraced by Dicey, and embedded in Canadian law and practice since the 1800s, is that referendums are compatible with parliamentary supremacy at our national and provincial levels. The common foundation of elected representatives in Parliament voting on issues and laws, and referendum verdicts by electors voting on major issues, is the power of sovereign people exercising free choice.

He discerned how "the people," meaning the much larger British electorate that had now become enfranchised, needed to exercise their power not only through representative institutions but also through the machinery of direct voting on issues. Dicey observed that the strengthening of popular government brought the rise of political parties, and because of that, how the prior high-water mark of Commons power was receding. Intensifying party loyalties had transformed the doctrine of sovereignty of Parliament into a mere cloak for the authority of government. Real power no longer rested with MPs. It had passed over to the party's leaders and organizers — the same transformation impacting Canada's parliamentary system, with ever-accelerating steps, from the 1860s to the present.

This led Dicey to embrace the referendum. Parliamentary traditionalists, unable to recognize the deeper trends that he saw, attacked direct voting as something that would devalue the authority of Parliament. In response, Dicey identified this issue-voting role for citizens as an important *new* part of British political institutions. The unique advantage of the referendum for Dicey, notes Vernon Bogdanor, "lay in its being a *democratic* check upon the excesses of popular government" and therefore "an instrument which suited the spirit of the age."[7]

If the referendum gave an electorate veto power over bills passed by Parliament, this would complete, in tandem with a broadly based electorate through significant extension to more people of the right to vote, the symmetrical transition required from absolute monarchy to constitutional monarchy. Until the eighteenth century, the monarch still had veto power over laws passed by Parliament. So now, reasoned Dicey, this power should pass to the electorate, finishing the process by which "the prerogatives of the Crown" would be transformed "into the privileges of the people."[8]

A.V. Dicey set out three further reasons for referendums. A ballot-box verdict could be the means for giving "formal acknowledgement of the doctrine which lies at the base of English democracy — that a law depends at bottom for its enactment on the consent of the nation as represented by the electors." Furthermore, the referendum would be a powerful weapon against "the wire-pullers in local constituencies," for it denied the fundamental premise that victory in a general election yielded a mandate for specific legislation. Dicey envisaged referendums as "the one available check on the recklessness of party leaders," although this would require citizen-initiated referendums because a ballot question wouldn't readily emerge from a political system those same reckless party leaders controlled. In 2011 this reality was demonstrated in British Columbia when the ballot question on sales tax harmonization came about thanks to a citizen-initiated process, not something the government in power wanted.

And even before Dicey's clarification of political theory, British Conservative leader Benjamin Disraeli in 1868 advanced a political realist's claim that a government required a "specific mandate" for truly major change. Prime Minister William Gladstone sought to disestablish the Irish Church, a major step he'd not informed the country about during the election. Disraeli said that even if technically Parliament had power to so alter the character of England and her institutions, there is "a moral exercise of power as well as a technical, and when you touch the principles on which the most ancient and influential institutions are founded, it is most wise that you should stay your hand unless you have assured yourselves of such an amount of popular sympathy and support as will make your legislation permanent and beneficial."[9]

Disraeli's pragmatic doctrine of specific mandate was in turn adopted by others. Lord Salisbury said: "There is a class of cases, small in number and varying in kind, in which the nation must be called into counsel and must decide the policy of the Government. It may be that the House of Commons in determining the opinion of the nation is wrong; and if there are grounds for entertaining that belief, it is always open to this House [of Lords], and indeed it is the duty of this House, to insist that the nation shall be consulted."[10]

This specific-mandate doctrine is grounded in the imperative that sovereign people be informed about a significant change to fundamental arrangements and have opportunity to give their deliberate consent. In 1901 Australians incorporated this concept in their constitution, requiring that a direct vote of the people ratify any amendment to the country's constitution. In 1992 Canada reached the same stage of democratic development when statute law required that people be made aware of major changes to fundamental arrangements, in the specific case of the Charlottetown Accord, and render a deliberate verdict on the proposed change at the ballot box.

CRITERIA FOR SEEKING A SPECIFIC MANDATE

Apart from significant constitutional change, what other subjects ought to require a specific mandate? No definitive list could itemize all the issues that have to be submitted to a direct vote and others that must never be. Distinguishing between the ambiguous general electoral mandate a government has, and issues requiring more specificity from the electorate, resides in the domain of statecraft. These half-dozen criteria, however, extracted from our history and experience, might help guide the exercise:

1. Does the proposed measure affect a positive principle going to the root of our institutions?
2. Is it one electors should consider, on the weight of pro and con arguments, separately from the personalities of politicians and party loyalties?
3. Will the measure's ultimate success depend upon buy-in of the governed?
4. Will a specific mandate help make the government stronger and more credible in negotiations on a crucial issue?
5. Can use of a ballot question help the country or province find its way out of an impasse?

6. Except for an emergency, is the major measure one the public wasn't informed about at election time and serious doubt exists whether the people would authorize?

To our detriment, we've generally underutilized one of democracy's rewarding, if risky, instruments of governing — getting a specific mandate about a transcending public issue through a referendum. The risk is never to the people.

HOW HARD IS ASKING A CLEAR QUESTION?

The preferred way to frame a ballot question, and the wording specified in a number of statutes, is "Are you in favour of …? Yes ___ No ___." This formulation leads to clarity about what is being asked. The simpler the question, the clearer the issue to be decided. The more direct it is the easier to force choice. The point is to elicit Yes or No, not Maybe or Don't Know.

Although Plato taught that asking the right question is often the most important thing, and despite Anton Chekhov reminding us that brevity is the handmaid of clarity, in this department of being brief and clear, a number of Canadian referendums have come up short. This wording by Premier René Lévesque for Quebec's 1980 referendum entered the record books for all-time foggiest:

> The Government of Quebec has made public its proposal to negotiate a new agreement with the rest of Canada, based on the equality of nations; this agreement would enable Quebec to acquire the exclusive power to make its laws, administer its taxes and establish relations abroad — in other words, sovereignty — and at the same time, to maintain with Canada an economic association including a common currency; any change in political status resulting from these negotiations will be submitted to the people through a referendum;
>
> *ON THESE TERMS, DO YOU AGREE TO GIVE THE GOVERNMENT OF QUEBEC THE MANDATE*

TO NEGOTIATE THE PROPOSED AGREEMENT BETWEEN QUEBEC AND CANADA? YES ___ NO ___.

Another exhibit in this ambiguous question category, and edging out Quebec's 1980 ballot for longest, was provided by the Northwest Territories for a vote on territorial division. A map showing the proposed boundaries was included on the ballot, not in accompanying material. The "question" itself, four paragraphs running to 186 words, lacked clarity because the extended preamble gave voters a lot of information better confined to the information pamphlet. The wording:

> On April 14, 1982, a majority of voters in an NWT-wide plebiscite voted to support the division of the Northwest Territories so as to allow the creation of a new Nunavut Territory with its own Nunavut government. The NWT Legislative Assembly and the Government of Canada accepted this result.
>
> In the Iqaluit Agreement of January 15, 1987, the Nunavut Constitutional Forum (NCF) and the Western Constitutional Forum (WCF) agreed that the boundary for division for the NWT would be the boundary separating the Tungavik Federation of Nunavut (TFN) land claim settlement area from the Inuvialuit and Dene-Métis land claim settlement areas. On April 19, 1991, the Government of Canada endorsed the compromise boundary shown on the map below.
>
> [Here a map of the Northwest Territories' proposed boundary line appeared on the ballot.]
>
> Division will occur in such a way as:
>
> - to maintain adequate levels of public services;
> - to respect the opportunity of residents in the Mackenzie Valley and Beaufort areas to develop new constitutional arrangements in the future for the western part of the NWT; and
> - to respect the employment status and location preferences of GNWT employees.

*ON THESE UNDERSTANDINGS, DO YOU SUPPORT
THE BOUNDARY FOR DIVISION SHOWN ON MAP
ABOVE? YES ___ NO ___.*

A couple of key rules are that the proposition be stated in a way that isn't loaded and that the ballot question be unambiguous. The directness of the ballot question "Are you in favour of adding fluoride to Toronto's drinking water?" leaves no doubt about what the issue is. The wording doesn't attempt to give a synopsis of the issue, nor explain it, because decades of experience with municipal ballot questions showed that people voting would already have heard fluoride's benefits explained by public health authorities and medical scientists, listened to denunciations by libertarians and conspiracy theorists about adding a chemical to the municipal water supply, weighed those concerns against the fact chlorine was already helping to keep the water safe to drink, and considered the low financial cost in tax dollars for widespread public benefit of improved dental health for everyone in the city. With any ballot question, which always *follows* a campaign period for debate and voter education of pros and cons, those casting ballots know why their choice is Yes or No — when the question is straightforward. When we cast a ballot to elect a representative, only the names of the candidates — not their bios and positions on issues — are presented for us to choose between.

MULTIPLE QUESTIONS ON ONE BALLOT

There is nothing wrong with combining several questions on a single ballot provided the consequences have been thought through. They hadn't been in Ottawa when city council put a question before city voters in 1933. The question asked local electors whether they favoured a council composed of a mayor and six councillors; a council with a mayor, four councillors, and eleven aldermen; or retaining the existing system. People voted about equally for all three options. With that ambiguous outcome, a sheepish city council took no action.[1]

Having a number of questions has proven possible in a variety of situations, however. When Newfoundlanders voted on their future after the Second World War, the first ballot offered three choices, which led to a second round of voting on only two options, the one about joining Confederation winning by a slight margin. When British Columbians voted on aboriginal land claim issues in 2002, eight different questions faced them on mail-in ballots. In 2016 Prince Edward Islanders saw a weighted ballot on which they ranked their preferences between five different electoral systems, learning in the bargain how weighted ballots might work in a preferential electoral system.

Asking someone their choice between options needs to clearly convey what the issue is, so the consequences of deciding one way or the other is also evident. Statutes and case law governing the referendum process specify that a ballot question be brief, clear, and answerable by either Yes or No.

Sometimes governments cloud a choice with ambiguity to camouflage their true intent, thinking they can fool gullible voters with what seems a low-risk option. Quebec's 1980 ballot question on "negotiating sovereignty-association" is a prime example. Yet even in confusing cases, political science research suggests that people sort out the crux of the choice facing them. The 1942 vote about releasing the government from its prior electoral commitment was, everyone knew, about green-lighting conscription. That 1980 vote in Quebec, despite the vague and convoluted question, was about Quebec separating from Confederation in one manner or another.

The danger of ambiguity about such a matter as the future of Canada, however, couldn't be allowed to just let drift into another separatist-sponsored referendum in Quebec, which prompted Prime Minister Chrétien to initiate a reference to the Supreme Court of Canada. Its 1998 landmark decision in *Reference Re Secession of Quebec* concluded that unilateral secession was illegal, would require a constitutional amendment, and that only a clear majority on a clear question could bring about any sort of obligation on the federal and provincial governments to negotiate secession.[2]

The Chrétien government then introduced "An Act to give effect to the requirement for clarity as set out in the opinion of the Supreme Court of Canada in the Quebec Secession Reference," or the Clarity Act for short. Enacted by Parliament in 2000, it stipulates that for any referendum about the secession of a Canadian province, Parliament has the power to determine whether the question is clear enough and the majority large enough to be recognized as a valid basis for negotiation.[3]

In response, Quebec's National Assembly responded by enacting Bill 99, "An Act respecting the exercise of the fundamental rights and prerogatives of the Quebec people and the Quebec State." It stipulates that Quebecers may determine unilaterally how to exercise their right to choose their political regime, including sovereignty, and the winning option in a referendum would be whichever side obtains 50 percent of the votes plus one.

The contest between federalists and separatists, more aptly understood as competing visions of Confederationists and independentists, is long-standing. A couple of colonial provinces participating in the negotiations for a combined federal state stayed out of 1867's new arrangement for some years. Nova Scotians voted in several elections for anti-Confederation candidates and elected a majority of them to the House of Assembly in Halifax and the House of Commons in Ottawa. Newfoundlanders didn't vote for the Confederation option in their first referendum, and only narrowly did so in the second. Quebecers twice voted on separation, with Confederation winning both times but only narrowly in the second round.

Sometimes people in these and other provinces vote in general elections to register protest against how Confederation operates. When the ballots are in general elections, it is impossible to discern clearly the message of disquiet or the measure of dissent. In the rarer cases of a referendum ballot, it has been slightly more obvious, but the unclear wording still makes interpretation problematic. Whether the "Terms of Union" for Newfoundland still had to be negotiated after the referendum, or the proposition for future negotiation of "sovereignty-association" portended nothing more than a nebulous outcome, reflected more the ambivalence of politicians than the ambiguity of ballot questions. Although it's important for referendums to have straight-up questions, they're impossible to pose when it's not clear what's really wanted.

Every component of our governance system — general elections, courtroom trials, royal commission inquiries, coroner's inquests, industrial arbitrations, referendums — is subject to strong conflicting pressures. None of them has a blemish-free record. General elections are abused when a premier opportunistically calls a snap election to win a surprise victory over temporarily weakened opposition, or to sidestep rather than confront a political dilemma, but nobody shocked by such abuses calls for abolition of elections. Nobody who sees a mistrial advocates abolition of the judicial system. Even ardent critics of the inordinate time and high cost of a royal commission or public inquiry don't assert we should never again have public investigations of intricate public matters. So why heed those who, disliking the controversial issues that referendums confront, oppose the procedure itself?

13

AREN'T SOME ISSUES JUST TOO COMPLEX?

Each time a referendum looms someone admonishes that controversial matters are too complex for a simplistic Yes or No answer. Canada's minister of democratic institutions asserted in 2016 that referendums "do not easily lend themselves to effectively deciding complex issues." In tandem with this problem of big-decision "complexity," it's suggested "the people" aren't capable of answering ballot questions, anyway, because the issues are obviously beyond their inexpert comprehension.

This recurring chorus of anti-democratic sentiment, expressed in new voices through the generations, is sometimes refreshed by new arguments. For example: referendums are no longer needed because opinion polling has been invented. Everybody can see how reliable opinion sampling is, with pre-voting surveys in May 2013 revealing that the NDP, not the Liberals, would govern British Columbia in the wake of that year's general election; in May 2015 that Wild Rose, not the NDP, would be in charge of Alberta's government; and in 2016 that President Hillary Clinton, not Donald Trump, would be living in the White House. More recently, another novel argument against referendums, already noted, is that they risk making people "emotional."

In 2016 a wave of arguments against citizens answering ballot questions, as a component of our democratic life, washed over Canada in the aftermath of Brexit and with the prospect of a national referendum on electoral reform. "Referendums and democracy don't mix," opined Janice Stein of the Munk School of Global Affairs at the University of Toronto. "In a functioning representative democracy, referenda are almost always a bad idea," said NDP veteran Robin Sears. Political observer Susan Delacourt wrote that "a simple yes-or-no referendum" on electoral reform had likely become a non-starter in Canada due to the "raw simplicity" of the Leave or Remain question for voters in the United Kingdom and ensuing "regrets" about a majority choosing to leave the European Community.

But political columnist Jeffrey Simpson of the *Globe and Mail* countered that "the electoral system is too important to be left to the politicians" and argued his case for why the people should choose the best system by referendum. Gordon Gibson, who'd chaired British Columbia's citizens' assembly on electoral reform, likewise contended a referendum should be held. Neither considered the subject "too complex" for voters.

Andrew Coyne, balancing the case, said the merit of Canadians having a referendum on the electoral system ought to be evaluated according to Canadian circumstances and our own democratic approaches, not the "alleged lessons from Brexit" that referendum opponents were advancing.

ARE PROHIBITION, CONSCRIPTION, AND CONSTITUTIONS COMPLEX?

When Canadians voted in 1898, the issue involved prohibiting alcohol's manufacture, distribution, sale, and consumption. Such a policy had economic, religious, social, and cultural dimensions interwoven with political and legal aspects, with prohibition support often underpinned by a zealous Protestant social movement for "moral uplift," and ardent opposition from free-spending distillers, brewers, tavern owners, and drinkers. Men had the vote. Women did not, but they campaigned actively to influence the referendum outcome. By any standard, the 1898 referendum instigated by Prime Minister Laurier's Liberals encompassed a lot of "complexities."

The second time Canadians answered a ballot question was in the middle of a cataclysmic world war. Voters in 1940 had given an electoral mandate, based on the Liberals' solemn campaign promise to never impose conscription for overseas military service, which handily resulted in the party's re-election. But by 1942, Prime Minister King's Liberal government wanted to reverse that mandate and bring in conscription. National survival in the face of global warfare whose outcome was gravely uncertain, political ethics about honouring the bond of trust with voters, the detrimental and distracting impact on war preparations of a three-month referendum, and the contentious issue of ordering Canadians overseas to wage war and risk death and maiming all contributed many layers to the 1942 ballot question's "complexity."

The third time we went to the polls, the ballot question asked whether we approved fundamental changes in our Constitution that would dramatically alter the exercise of power in eight major areas, from aboriginal governance to offshore mineral rights. A full catechism of "complexities" for each of the interwoven components in the Charlottetown Accord exceeds space limitations here but are elaborated in Chapter 18, "Voting on Confederation," to a greater degree.

These referendums on alcohol, conscription, and fundamental rewriting of our Constitution were laced with complexities. Yet, looking back, who would contend there was any better way to tackle those challenging decisions than through a direct vote by the people who would have to live with the consequences?

DECISIONS REDUCE TO "RAW SIMPLICITY" OF YES OR NO

The reality of making decisions, whether by public ballot or around the cabinet table, in a constituent assembly or at the family table, is that after hearing pros and cons and taking time to "think it over," the outcome must always be Yes or No. An uncertain response with many caveats is useless in making a decision. There is no place on the ballot for Maybe.

Cabinets and parliaments must decide every issue that arises one way or the other. Will we sign a trade treaty with the United States? Yes or No? Shall we declare war on Nazi Germany? Yes or No? When I voted as an MP in the House of Commons, the choice following debate over a measure's many dimensions was either Yea or Nay. Of course, a third option was to abstain, and sometimes an MP refused to stand and be counted, just as some voters stay home from the polls. Such neutrality might salve one's conscience or sidestep a private dilemma, but it doesn't get the decision made. Others have to decide the matter by their votes, because uncast ballots and abstentions don't do the job for a self-governing democracy.

Despite all the jostling considerations, the most complex decisions come down, in the end, to Yes or No. In the personal choices of life — Will I marry this person? Should we buy this house? Shall I stop smoking? — the answer can only be Yes, or No. At the end of a difficult criminal trial, the accused must either be convicted or acquitted. Even grand matters fraught with competing interests require either a red or a green light: building the St. Lawrence Seaway, developing nuclear-powered generating stations, fighting a war in Korea or Afghanistan, constructing pipelines for oil and natural gas, decriminalizing marijuana, allowing death with dignity for terminally ill individuals.

Acknowledging that issues are "complex," and especially that they're made to appear that way by Canada's academics, public commentators, and government consultants whose livelihoods depend on others deferring to them for explanation and comprehension, doesn't erase the fact that decisions must be made. At some point, somewhere, somebody up or down the line says either Yes, or No.

ARE REFERENDUMS MORE COMPLEX THAN ELECTIONS?

If, as critics of ballot questions contend, people aren't able to understand complex issues in a referendum, how do we possibly manage when faced with a general election? It is hard to conjure anything more complex than the choice presented to voters during an all-inclusive election. We want the best of all programs, but they're offered by different parties. We want one person as prime minister, but prefer the local candidate of a different party. We only get one ballot, and on it we must make a single choice.

In a referendum campaign, voting takes place after a period of debate about pros and cons, but there is only one issue to decide. The focus is on a principle, not personalities. How much clearer, simpler, and democratic could that be?

When answering a ballot question, just one important issue is getting decided; when voting in an election, the keys to complete power of government are being handed over. Based on the comparison, and applying the logic of those who oppose citizens voting in a referendum because the issue is "too complex," we should have abolished general elections long ago.

THE CONCEIT OF EXPERTISE

This feigned apprehension about the complexity of issues, and this attitude that mere citizens shouldn't get to vote on them, is grounded in several factors, among them the fact some legislators don't want their already limited legislative role diluted any further by a process that shares it with their electors. Another is that some legislators are reluctant to declare their stance on a contentious issue, as a referendum would inevitably require, fearing it could erode their own voter support. Third, the political establishment's determined control over processes affecting the public agenda has permeated the thinking of some academics and public commentators, particularly those with close affinity to the centres of power, a relationship that in some cases is enhanced by lucrative consulting contracts.

Finally, quite a few people, whether for reasons of higher education or higher income, infused with a precocious sense of social superiority, dismiss "the people" as ignorant folk liable to be influenced like sheep or swayed as a mob. It helps to demonize one's enemy by depersonalizing them. So this swath of Canada's political class now refers to citizens as "demographics" and labels where people reside not as named communities but area codes and postal codes. Detached and amorphous, it becomes easier not to engage individuals as fellow citizens in a self-governing democratic society, easier to think in clinically manipulative terms and impersonal abstractions.

Their conceit is that "the experts" understand things, grasp truth, and know reality, while "the people" have mere whims and opinions. It is wrong for every voter to get a ballot, they easily conclude, because not all voters are equal.

This mixture of ingredients leads those who accept such premises to oppose Canadians ever expressing support or opposition to a measure by answering Yes or No to a ballot question.

CONDEMNING REFERENDUMS AS "NOT PART OF DEMOCRACY"

Unlike the mere sideswipes others take against referendums, professor Janice Stein comes at this with a complete and articulate embrace of bundled arguments. And because her extensive airtime on CBC Television and TVO bathe the public in her contention that "referendums and democracy don't mix," professor Stein's long-held anti-referendum views, such as were published through the auspices of TVO on June 24, 2016, provide a convenient teaching moment. Her catalogue of complaint begins:

How well do referendums serve democracy? Not well, whether they fail or pass. Not well, because leaders always have to simplify complex decisions into a "yes" or "no" question. Not well, because referendums often give prominence to issues that are not at the top of voters' priorities, as Brexit did. Not well, because representatives have the chance through their party leaders to craft compromises. Voters do not: it's up or down. Not well, because leaders in a referendum campaign have every incentive to over-simplify and overdramatize, playing on people's fears to get out the vote. Not well, because referendums inflame passions and leave in their wake divided countries and divided families. It is for all these reasons that we elect representatives who form governments.

There's more to her argument, but before proceeding to them it's best to first deconstruct these interlocked opinions. Stein, in critiquing referendums because they "simplify complex decisions" so they can be answered Yes or No by the people, expresses preference for what she posits as the alternative — elected representatives of the people voting instead on compromises. Where was the "compromise" when MPs voted to declare war against Germany in 1939? What compromise attended the Trudeau government's 1970 replacement of Canada's entrenched Imperial system of measurement with metric? Whether that non-existent ballot question about going metric had received either a majority Yes or No, Canadians would have gained a surer grasp of the far-reaching implications of the move than its expert proponents displayed. In Parliament it was either "up or down" for every vote, from implementing the GST or ending capital punishment to ratifying the Free Trade Agreement or criminalizing abortion. Along with all other "elected representatives," I faced the same black-and-white possibility facing voters on a ballot question. The watertight compartments between simple questions, complex issues, compromises, and who is best to vote on them exist only in the theoretical configuration fantasized by professor Stein in order to exclude referendums as, somehow, not part of "democracy."

Next argument up is that ballot questions "give prominence to issues" not at the top of voters' priorities. This "top-of-mind" ranking is a nebulous concept upon which to oppose citizens answering a question in a democratic society. Actual experience in Canada provides stronger grounding than do imputed concepts about what scholars assume to be voter priorities. Janice Stein's theory reverses effect and cause. The reason referendums about restricting or prohibiting people's access to alcoholic beverages took place nationally and in all provinces, as well as in hundreds of "local option" municipalities, was that the contentious policy had long been a dominant public issue with implications for just about everybody. The reason Quebecers voted in two referendums on separation in 1980 and 1995, and all Canadians voted in 1992 on a constitutional package intended to deal with the same issue, is that "national unity" had been so "prominent" as to dominate our public life for three full decades. Ongoing experiences in Canada constitute a more relevant standard for evaluating when and why referendums are appropriate than vaguely conceptualized criteria about which issues are worthy of "prominence," or the fiction that some ranking exists "at the top of voters' priorities" that allows detached observers to certify which concerns ought to be addressed and which not.

Stein's third contention that "referendums and democracy don't mix" is stated this way: "Leaders in a referendum campaign have every incentive to oversimplify and overdramatize, playing on people's fears to get out the vote." If you substitute "*election* campaign" for "*referendum* campaign" in that sentence, what comes up on the screen is a parade of Canadian elections in which leaders oversimplified, overdramatized, and played on people's fears "to get out the vote." The professor's artificial segregation of one component of a self-governing society from its other working parts leads inexorably to the conclusion that *elections and democracy* don't mix, either.

A fourth damnation of ballot questions by Janice Stein, echoed in 2016 public comments by cabinet minister Maryam Monsef and public commentator Robin Sears, is that "referendums inflame passions and leave in their wake divided countries and divided families." What referendums actually do is provoke thought. A crucial public policy is placed before Canadians, among the most highly educated people in the world. As the referendum campaign gets under way, intelligent people are beneficiaries of a comprehensive system of communications and news reporting organizations that for several weeks becomes a nationwide or provincial "teach-in" on the pros and cons of the ballot question. Simultaneously, election officials conducting the referendum send all households a "publicity pamphlet," if required as it typically is by statute, in which both sides get equal space to explain to voters its side of the issue. Community halls fill with public meetings for discussion and debate, broadcasters host panels to evaluate the issue's implications, families and friends talk over the prospects for voting one way or the other, and a democratic society comes into its own. Although other countries cope with this trauma of decision-making, the emotional fragility of Canadians is now touted as reason to save us from having to answer a ballot question.

Emotion necessarily flows in and through these experiences because we are humans and because what we are asked to decide is significant for us. To worry that a ballot question will "inflame passions" should cause a professor of international relations such as Stein to cancel classes rather than broach the intensely controversial issues that necessarily constitute her curriculum and that should, if properly taught, certainly make students emotional. If *conduct* of public affairs is to be entirely cerebral and unemotional, so by logical extension should be the *study* of public affairs — in the sanitized, dehumanized, detached universe idealized by one who denounces "pure democracy." To say referendums "leave in their wake divided countries and divided families" is sophistry, suggesting the referendum actually *caused* the division, rather than serves to accurately reveal a pre-existing but previously unquantified condition.

Proceeding now to more of professor Stein's case, as published by TVO, we enter the universe of controlled democracy where experts know best. Arguing that, by a majority favouring the United Kingdom leaving the European Union, "voters did not behave as they were expected to." She expects that voters "usually favour the status quo" and "are risk-averse, especially when they're reasonably comfortable." Such assertions about voter behaviour and expectations of other people bring little credit to the "science" of politics. This supposition that "risk-averse" voters mostly favour things staying as they are ignores how an all-male electorate in British Columbia answered Yes to women getting voting rights a century ago, or how a decade and a half ago Northwest Territories voters approved *fundamental change* in their governmental arrangements — and how, in between, other referendum results didn't maintain the status quo on public utilities, denominational schools, availability of alcohol, marketing of agricultural products, or adding fluoride to municipal water supplies.

To advance her case that voters really aren't up to deciding *any* public measure by ballot, Stein alleges that in the European Union "some members have had to schedule a second referendum in order to overcome voters' aversion to changing the status quo." Translation: the dumb people just didn't get it at first. "All the experts thought the same pattern would prevail in Britain," she added about Brexit.

Experience with referendums about the European Union was not, however, quite as asserted. When a European constitution was drafted in 2005, each member country had to ratify it before it took effect. The Dutch held a referendum, and so did the French upon hearing that the British might do so. No other country, when following its own path to ratification, included a referendum.

Voters in the Netherlands and France rejected the European constitution after extensive debate about every conceivable merit and disadvantage it had for their country. No second referendum took place in either. In both countries, the political parties and elected representatives were fully engaged, together with the people, thrashing out the issues. The proposed referendum in the United Kingdom never took place.

Only in Ireland, several years later, did *two* referendums occur. The vote was on the Lisbon Treaty, whose negotiated adjustments would accommodate the European Community's operations alongside the sovereign operations of member countries. In 2008 Irish voters turned down the treaty, many hearing from Roman Catholic pulpits that it would prevent Ireland from maintaining its staunch "pro-life" anti-abortion laws. Ireland's refusal to ratify, in light of that vote, prevented the treaty coming into force despite every other member state having approved it. To break the impasse, clarifications were made about Irish sovereignty and in 2009, sixteen months after the first vote, 67 percent of voters in Ireland's second referendum approved the Lisbon Treaty, overcoming a sole member country's blockage of E.U. reforms. The "second round of voting" was not because slow-witted folks had to get up to speed, but resulted from a deliberate process and negotiated compromise, and achieving clarity about who had final say on abortion law, the outcome of a democratic dialectic in which the first referendum proved indispensable.

In Europe, where Stein stated "some members" had to schedule "a second referendum in order to overcome voters' aversion to changing the status quo," the only other country to do this, apart from that unique case of Ireland, was the United Kingdom. A ballot question about the United Kingdom's membership in the European Union first took place in 1975. The second, Brexit, was in 2016, forty years later. And the muddled politics of Britain's unhappy connection with the continent is hardly a precedent from which a scholar ought to extract ironclad conclusions about European referendums and apply them to Canada.

To conclude her case that referendums and democracy are incompatible, Janice Stein triumphantly dismissed the Brexit impulse of U.K. voters. "Swept up in a wave of populist anger against elites, laced with a heavy dose of xenophobia and seasoned with a dash of nostalgia, they voted to break with Europe and go it alone." But it wasn't that simplistic. Britons never got a vote in the early 1970s when Edward Heath's government first negotiated the United Kingdom's terms of entry into the European Community, to endorse that fundamental change for their country. Pressure for electors to have a say resulted in the 1975 referendum, at which time a majority of Britons favoured the still-new arrangement. By 2016, however, with so much having changed in the European Community over four decades, and revised terms having been negotiated by Britain's government, Prime Minister David Cameron accepted the need for electors to ratify the arrangement, and in the process, re-evaluate their country's long-standing lukewarm adhesion to Continental Europe.

Jeffrey Simpson placed Brexit in this context on June 23, 2016, in the *Globe and Mail*, viewing the "Leave" victory not in sweeping generalizations about populist anger and xenophobia, but the truer forces of Britain's own direct experience since the early 1970s living its "long, unhappy marriage of convenience" with the European Community.

It is neither the complexity of the issue, nor the preference of so-called policy experts, but rather the need for a clear verdict on a key issue that opens the possibility of resolving the dilemma of choice by a majority of informed citizens collectively answering Yes or No.

Even the biggest decisions are ultimately answered by a cabinet, a parliament, a jury, or an entire voting population with either Yes or No, Stay or Go. Experts themselves will never agree on the same conclusion, nor will those elected or appointed to public offices. When facing an irresolvable conundrum about a vital public question, the best resolution can be to force the choice. After all, in a democratic, self-governing system of government, the most authoritative voice with the greatest political legitimacy is that of the sovereign people, the folks in all walks of life in all parts of our country who daily experience our universe of realities and are competent to weigh in on something important that will affect who we are and what we do.

14

TO VOTE ON THE PRINCIPLE,
OR THE PACKAGE?

Our first two national referendums were on principles (whether to impose prohibition, whether to release the government from its pledge not to impose conscription), while the third was on a complete package (the Charlottetown Accord's extensive and interconnected constitutional amendments).

The pros and cons of asking people to vote on the principle of something, or on its details, have been weighed ever since Parliament first debated this in 1898. Some MPs wanted the electorate to deal with prohibition in principle. Others argued it only made sense for the people to consider a detailed bill that went beyond general opinion.

Justice Minister David Mills was in a predicament. He'd previously said in the Commons, "There should be a well-considered Bill prepared, and the vote should be taken upon it." Mills asserted, "The question is not whether the public favour prohibition in the abstract. It is whether they are ready honestly to carry it out in the concrete. The abstract position does not mean anything." Now a minister bound by the doctrine of cabinet solidarity, Mills was obliged to support the Laurier government's plan for a simple ballot question on the principle of prohibition alone. Not for the first time did a parliamentarian confront the public dilemma of personal opinion and a previously stated conclusion that had to be subordinated to the party's official position on an issue. It is, in fact, common diet on Parliament Hill.

Other parliamentarians, some newspaper editors, and the liquor interests also considered it problematic for electors to express their opinions only on the principle of prohibition in broad terms. However, this broad-brush approach — prohibition, Yes or No, rather than the detailed legislation to implement it — was favoured by the prohibition movement and by Prime Minister Laurier.

In support of his government's bill for a direct vote on the principle of prohibition, Laurier addressed a number of the issues raised in this debate. A major one was the loss of government revenues from liquor tax that would result from prohibition. "In the matter of the falling-off in revenue, should such a law be enacted, that is a question we thought better to leave to the electors themselves to ponder over and to consider, and to state their judgment upon in the best way they thought fit," Laurier explained.

At this time the Government of Canada was reaping $7 million a year from taxes on liquor, a significant portion of the public revenue. The minister of finance would just have to provide other sources of revenue if the excise taxes flowing into the public treasury from the liquor traffic dried up. The PM suggested more tax revenue could come from coffee, tea, sugar, or tobacco, but then added, upon reflection, that the finance minister "cannot put a single penny more duty on tobacco. If he were to put any heavier duty upon tobacco it is well known that it would not produce any revenue at all."

The PM addressed whether and to what extent this revenue aspect should be included in the question submitted to the voters and whether a rider should be added to the ballot requiring the government to implement prohibition legislation if a majority voted in the affirmative — in short, making it a referendum rather than a plebiscite. He didn't want to require voters to decide specifically on how the additional revenue should be made up, or oblige the government to act in a certain way given the voting results. Laurier rejected the idea of any riders to the ballot, and likewise turned back the idea of submitting to voters a detailed bill on prohibition, wanting lots of room to manoeuvre.

"All these considerations might well have formed part of the question to be submitted to the electors," the PM told the Commons, "but we thought it better to leave the question unhampered by these considerations, so that every man would be free to give his vote on the simple question, according to his own judgment and conscience."

• • •

Deciding whether a ballot should ask approval in principle, or present a specific plan that includes the hard trade-offs and working details, has been a recurring topic ever since that inaugural parliamentary debate in 1898. In 2016 Prime Minister Justin Trudeau's government had an electoral mandate on the clear principle that it would replace the first-past-the-post electoral system by a method of electing MPs that more "fairly" reflected the levels of popular vote that parties and their candidates received from Canadian electors. Yet many still called for a referendum on the Liberal's specific plan, which, it turned out, was something the prime minister didn't have.

In cases in which the new model electoral system is ready to roll out before voters, we've seen a recurring pattern in five provinces where the complexities of the proposed voting system bogs down discussion. From British Columbia to Ontario, through New Brunswick and Prince Edward Island, the quest for electoral change was accompanied by complaints, after the proposed new electoral method failed to win approval, that many facing their provincial ballot question on the subject "did not understand the proposed system."

We've now had enough such votes to see a pattern of inept political communication that gives voters a sense they need to know how the system works, rather than understand what outcome it could produce. Most citizens voting for a party promising a child tax credit don't know how the calculations are made, just that they'll get a cheque in the mail. Wilfrid Laurier knew that it was enough to address the principle, not try to work out the details during a campaign, such as trying to make regular citizens familiar with the mind-numbing details of an electoral system's inner workings.

A benefit of our federal system is that one province can try something new — such as health care insurance, votes for women, a minimum wage for workers, election finance reform, mandatory seat belts, a human rights code — while governments and residents of other provinces observe how that works out. If the experiment seems an improvement over the status quo, other jurisdictions in time replicate the measure, adjusted to their regional standards. Profiting from this kind of "leadership by example" with electoral system changes in one province would be a good way to observe how it really works. This tried-and-true Canadian pattern requires only that some leader has the vision to start.

• • •

For a century and a half, a parade of nation-defining issues has marched through our political arena. The broad concept of each plan then encounters the specifics of implementation, and we regularly hear it said that "the devil is in the details." Working out the trade-offs, integrating jostling interests, and watering down the grip of effective measures to achieve necessary compromise is the work of elected representatives, public servants, the courts, special interest groups, and associations. It won't escape Canadians wanting to improve this democratic operation and enhance political accountability that a refinement of process is needed to close the yawning gap between general electoral mandates and specific issue mandates, between major public issues and citizens' limited connection to them, and between broad principles and specific laws and programs. Nor will it escape democrats that the necessary connector is a revamped twenty-first-century Parliament operating in harmony with Canada's sovereign people.

15

CONTINUING ADULT EDUCATION

Putting a ballot question before electors is no gambler's toss of the dice because, before voting, those considering whether to answer Yes or No get a crash course on the pros and cons of the issue at hand.

A.V. Dicey discerned how a referendum could motivate education in public affairs. Voting on a specific issue required an elector "to decide public issues upon the weight of the argument, and not on the basis of party loyalties." This, he reasoned, enabled voters "to distinguish men from measures."[1]

Motivation, always key to learning, comes from the issue being one of transcending importance whose outcome, once decided, everyone in the voting community will either benefit from or pay the consequences for. There is minimal risk in a self-governing democratic country like ours, with well-educated people and comprehensive communications networks, submitting any matter to a vote of adult citizens. There is, rather, maximum reward in people becoming more deeply educated about a major issue affecting the course of our public affairs.

TRUSTING CITIZENS TO STUDY AND DECIDE

A core component of Canada's justice system is acceptance of citizen juries hearing evidence and then rendering Yes or No verdicts on the fate of someone's life. They don't convict or acquit at the start of the trial, but after they've heard and seen everything the defence counsel and Crown prosecutor present as evidence, and even then, only after withdrawing to deliberate on all they've learned, and to discuss it for as long as it takes to render an informed and well-thrashed-out decision.

Those chosen for jury duty are regular citizens, and in our system can't be lawyers because their professional training makes them, even if only sub-consciously, subjective "experts" who might overlay the case with their own legal thinking rather than weigh all evidence objectively and take instruction from the judge.

Juries are thus a form of "semi-direct democracy," too. This right to trial by jury places an accused individual in the hands of citizen peers, not a panel of legal experts. And just as referendums are really "semi-direct" democracy, so criminal trials take place *within* institutional structures and according to established procedures, channelled in a variety of ways to uphold rule of law, ensure due process, and balance interests. Men and women chosen at random hear testimony and examine exhibits, then decide, under instruc-tion from the judge about how to weigh the evidence, themselves. They ask questions about anything that needs to be clarified.

CLEARLY PRESENTING THE ARGUMENTS OF BOTH SIDES

A principle in any judicial process is to "hear the other side," which also applies to the referendum process. A century ago, when Canadians began to upgrade referendum procedures, one advance was the invention of a "publi-city pamphlet" that a neutral public official such as the lieutenant governor, clerk of the legislature, or chief election officer sent to the household of each voter. In that era before radio, television, and the Internet, this printed medium was all-important for clear presentation by both Yes and No sides of their arguments in their own words. Saskatchewan's 1916 Direct Legislation Act, for instance, provided this key educational component of the campaign. Each side got equal length (five hundred words) to state its case.

This educational practice has understandably been carried into mod-ern times because informing voters about the issue being addressed and the choice being forced is the prime requirement of the whole democratic exercise. The U.K. statute for Britain's 1975 referendum on the European Common Market included this essential provision. A couple of years later the Quebec Referendum Act, an admirably contemporary statute, repli-cated the provision. I not only included it in my Canada Referendum and Plebiscite Act, but in addition to the traditional paper-printed "pamphlet" also provided for voter education using state-of-the-art information media.

JOURNALISTS SAVE US FROM TWILIGHT ZONE POLITICS

Because a core rationale for a referendum is that citizens will cast an informed ballot, it is vital, as in all other aspects of maintaining a free and democratic society, for arm's-length information to be in circulation by which citizens can inform themselves.

News media free from government control are indispensable in presenting information about issues. And on an operational level, an election or referendum campaign without diversified media reporting would just not be comprehensible. All participants in the process — leaders, candidates or advocates for Yes and No, organizers, reporters, election officials, and voters — depend on open communication. If television and computer screens went black, radios fell silent, and newspapers vanished completely, the body politic would have no central nervous system. We'd be left in a twilight zone with billboards, leaflets, and people shouting at puzzled passersby with megaphones.

Journalism's prized role in the twentieth century is being upended by the digital revolution, by "everyone" now able to be a journalist with hand-held cameras and devices to upload and forward "breaking news," and by a subjective sense of breathless urgency replacing balance, gravitas, and objectivity. Operations of professional journalism continue to be consolidated and trimmed by increasingly concentrated media ownership, and starved for resources in the harsh economics of contemporary publishing. Even so, a free press working arm's-length from government is what keeps Canadian democracy alive. And the new opportunities of our digital age for deeper, faster, and wider education about issues and decision-making have opened refreshing and radical channels that are rebooting democracy.

We benefit from extensive media and diverse sources of information. Few countries have a higher per capita ratio of media outlets to citizens, even fewer as high a percentage of well-educated and literate people. If the referendum process can't be a success in Canada, where could it ever be?

LEARNING ON A NEED-TO-KNOW BASIS

We're constantly bombarded by "too much information," so subconsciously block most of it out. The wash of advertising about motor vehicles or mortgages floats past without registering — until the day we're ready to buy a car or purchase a house, when we suddenly have reason to open our receptors and glom onto all of it. Facing a ballot question likewise prompts a need to know.

Referendums contribute to our continuing adult education the dynamic necessity of absorbing all the information we can that is streaming from news outlets and other sources about a specific issue — because we're going to have to make an important choice about it.

The need to cast an informed ballot imposes on citizens a vested interest in studying the issue. A looming voting day engenders a degree of attention and achieves public education that otherwise simply doesn't occur. It's not that, in theory, we're uncaring about vitally important subjects. But I've never met a courtroom lawyer who prepares for a trial she isn't going to litigate, a student who crams all night for an exam he doesn't have to write, or busy people focusing assiduously on public issues nobody ever asks their serious opinion about.

The referendum is the trial, the exam. It creates a rare nexus between the individual and the issue. The approaching deadline for casting one's vote accelerates the learning curve. Whatever the outcome, that increased understanding about a major public concern enriches our country.

16

REFERENDUMS REVEAL, DO NOT CREATE, DIVISIONS

Maryam Monsef, while minister for Canada's democratic institutions, claimed referendums "have often led to deep divisions within Canadian and other societies." They do not. There's a difference between dynamite and a mirror. A ballot question doesn't create rifts; it reveals existing fault lines.

Such revelation, moreover, is a good thing. An accurate record of how Canadians in the various parts of our country think about a controversial subject has never harmed governance. On the contrary, this insight helped us navigate a mid-course through treacherous shoals of conflict.

STEERING THE SHIP OF STATE BY THE LIGHT OF REFERENDUMS

Prime Minister Laurier and the entire country had to come to terms with the drive by well-organized forces hoping to free society from the problems alcohol spawned by getting rid of "demon rum" altogether, countered by an equal and opposite force of many with stubborn attachment to liquor, and the business interests of those who distilled, brewed, fermented, bottled, distributed, and sold alcoholic beverages.

The 1898 vote on prohibition held a mirror to those divisions in Canadian society and throughout the country's regions. The prohibition vote *showed* fundamental division in country. The voting, and all the heated debate preceding it, did not *create* the dichotomy reflected in the ballot counts. The referendum's accurate measure of deep-seated and pre-existing conditions clarified the need to proceed with caution, a point made in a more dramatic fashion than anything else could. A referendum is criticized as a blunt tool, but sometimes whacking a mule's rear with a two-by-four is the only way to convey that it's time to move.

Another benefit of referendums — how they can actually contribute to "peace, order, and good government" — begins to appear only long after the ballots are counted. Those who advocated or opposed conscription in the dire days of the Second World War had to acknowledge, in dispassionate moments as time passed, the sanity of Prime Minister King's gradualism — "conscription if necessary, but not necessarily conscription" — because everybody could plainly see in the 1942 referendum results the risk of winning the war and losing the country had he rushed mandatory enlistment for overseas military service.

The division in our society over conscription was certainly not *created* by that referendum, as routinely alleged. It had existed, particularly between French-speaking and English-speaking Canadians, since the 1860s, when each community had broadly dissimilar views about raising an armed force to defend against military aggression from the United States; it was revived in the period 1914 to 1918, when this deep fault line reappeared in the 1917 general election results amid the First World War conscription crisis, and again came to the fore in 1940's general election as a pivotal issue on which parties campaigned with heartfelt intensity.

SHALLOW GRASP OF DEEP HUMAN TENDENCIES

Those expressing fears that the use of ballot questions will change people's fundamental values and core beliefs in short order — the duration of a referendum campaign — have nothing to fear. Past about age eight, and certainly by thirteen years of age, a traumatic experience is required to alter the basic world view and its grounding values we absorb in early childhood. What people express in marking a ballot, whether to answer a question or elect a representative, is a small manifestation of a much larger process compressing their lifetime acquisition of beliefs, values, attitudes, and memories.

Shallow understanding of the process by which humans develop our outlooks and what we respond to in campaigns is matched, in many cases, by how opponents of referendums similarly fail to see issue-voting as part of a much broader process for governance. Those focusing only on the numbers added up on voting night and getting agitated about the newly recorded evidence of people's pre-existing beliefs and considered opinions miss how the balloting is but part of a much larger phenomenon.

Not to ask a ballot question is to avoid looking in the mirror. A referendum *exposes* whatever division or gulf of opinion already exists within the community. It clarifies the depth of disagreement. It shows the breadth of consensus. It does so with a conclusiveness opinion polling can never achieve. It provides a deliberated expression of political reality. The direct voice of the people is an irrefutable alternative to the opinions of pundits who fill the airwaves, chat rooms, and columns with suppositions about what the people think and personal opinions on what decision is best for the country.

REFERENDUMS IN THE AGE OF OPINION POLLING

Referendums predated the invention of opinion polls, as noted earlier, leading some to suggest ballot questions have had their day, that to continue issue-voting in our modern era is time-warped politics. This reasoning suffers from the fallacious assumption that ballot questions and pollsters' questions are essentially the same.

A referendum asks a single question; pollsters pose several. A ballot question gets answered once; a pollster might phone back next week. A referendum vote is proceeded by a campaign of information, education, and debate, allowing time for reflection before voting; a pollster might be at your door or on the line when you've just climbed out of the shower, or are immersed in something entirely unrelated to public policy, or not had time to ponder the point he or she is asking about.

A referendum is a formal procedure, like going to mass or a concert, and involves all the voting citizens of our country or province at the same time, the same way, for the same purpose. A poll is none of those things. A poll comes with a margin of error; validly cast ballots present a precise and accurate number. An opinion tossed off to a stranger's question, with no consequence, is not a marked ballot on which you've inscribed your verdict and taken your part in shaping our future. A "representative sample" is not the same as millions of votes. A ballot is conclusive, the way opinion polls can never be.

That is not to say these two realms are unconnected. From the outset, polling's number crunching has been as intrinsic to referendums as it became to elections — not as a substitute for a ballot question but to determine whether, as Lucien Bouchard would put it much later, "winning conditions" exist. The wartime ballot question in 1942 on conscription was incredibly sensitive, not only for its domestic impact but the international message it conveyed and how Nazi propaganda might exploit the result. As Prime Minister King contemplated a country-wide vote on conscription, he turned to Sol F. Rae (father of the estimable Bob Rae), a senior official at the Department of External Affairs, who had a compelling interest in how Canada was going to raise more troops to defeat Nazi Germany.

To determine, in advance, whether the PM's prospective venture into ballot-box democracy would help or hinder this objective, Rae invited George Gallup, whose polling organization had been tapping into American public opinion since the mid-1930s, up to Ottawa to discuss conducting one of his "scientific polls" for the Canadian government. Could George find out how the public would respond to a decision by King to turn his back on his promise that there would be no conscription?

The two men reached an agreement. The results had to be kept top-secret by Gallup and reported only to Rae, the prime minister, and depending on what he found, a couple of Ottawa's most senior civil servants.

The contract first covered conducting the secret poll, then helping develop a strategy to deal with public opinion going into the 1942 plebiscite. This inaugurated the role of pollsters working to determine voting strategy and direct campaign tactics in Canada, for referendums and elections alike, based on their polling. Having started, there would be no end.

The proliferation of polls measures their status as a tool favoured by political parties to gauge public feelings about candidates and issues. The politicians' belief in the supposed superiority of polls can be gleaned from the fact that pollsters and polling are not denigrated as being "divisive."

17

VOTING ON DEMOCRACY

Canada's "democratic deficit," a European term given currency here by Prime Minister Paul Martin, is no new thing. A hundred years ago the Progressive Movement and United Farmers were promoting "direct democracy" and forming governments, impacting Canada's public life by their resolute drive to democratize the machinery of government, limit the ways patronage was soiling public administration, and curb how business interests controlled the legislature. Already in this century, a drive by citizens protesting existing democratic arrangements has produced more referendums on democratic ways and means. We've had provincial votes about changing the electoral system, balancing government budgets, and empowering citizens to initiate ballot propositions and recall elected representatives. In all, voting on the nature of Canadian democracy itself has been a variety pack, including surprising twists and sobering lessons.

DIRECT LEGISLATION BY THE PEOPLE

The pioneering effort to reconstitute democratic procedures took dramatic form in western Canada. Electors, empowered by statute to engage in creating provincial legislation, gained an alternate law-making channel that potentially would be more open to community needs than legislatures, where parties funded by special interests controlled the agenda.

Saskatchewan's Direct Legislation Act, a product of Premier Walter Scott's Liberal government in 1912, stipulated that no new law could take effect until ninety days after the end of a legislative session, to permit a vote by the people to ratify or reject it. During that period, if a petition signed by 5 percent of voters requested the measure be voted on, the statute's operation would be delayed, pending the referendum outcome. Excepted were acts authorizing government spending and ones that two-thirds of the legislators had voted exempt.

A two-way street, Saskatchewan's Direct Legislation Act also enabled electors to propose non-spending measures by an "initiative" petition. For this, signatures of at least 8 percent of electors were required. Once the attorney general certified the measure constitutional, the legislation had to be enacted without substantial alteration at the next session. If it wasn't, the citizen-proposed measure would go to a vote of the electors themselves. If a majority approved, the measure had to be enacted at the next session and become law upon Royal Assent.

The Direct Legislation League of Saskatchewan, in its advocacy for such a statute, had circulated a model bill and was dismayed by how the legislature modified their draft. The league felt the inserted category of exempt "emergency measures" was so broad that many bills would never reach the people, and was angered that exemption of money bills kept control of the public purse from the public. It was a hard-core tussle about who was really in the driver's seat, because a principle of Canadian parliamentary government is that only an elected ministry can propose measures for public spending. Private members' bills, facing this same limitation, can't include spending. The league was rightly miffed, however, that the legislature even removed its proposal for distribution of a "publicity pamphlet" containing succinct views by proponents of each side for a bill the people would vote on to ensure voters would understand the pros and cons.

Premier Walter Scott felt the modified Direct Legislation Act balanced competing interests. It received Royal Assent on January 11, 1913. Traditionalists, seeing no precedent for it in Britain, protested against law-making by referendum. Scott blanched, and his government introduced An Act to Submit to the Electors the Question of the Adoption of the Direct Legislation Act.[1] As its title suggests, there would be a referendum on the Direct Legislation Act itself.

When the balloting took place, the requisite 30 percent of electors failed to endorse the Direct Legislation Act. The Liberals immediately repealed it and refused all requests for another vote or further legislation.[2]

. . .

Alberta's legislature was undaunted by the clamour next door. Both Liberals and Conservatives listened sympathetically to the Direct Legislation League of Alberta, and the Liberal government of Premier Arthur Sifton, supported by the Conservative Opposition, enacted a Direct Legislation Act in March 1913. It, too, provided for legislation to be approved by vote of the people, and initiation of legislation by electors, closer to the league's model statute, though Alberta's legislators also tweaked a few provisions. A clear ballot question on the issue, rather than the entire act itself, could be submitted to electors. A law failing ratification had to be repealed.

In Manitoba, early efforts by the province's Direct Legislation League were rebuffed by Conservative premier Rodmond Roblin, who believed direct legislation incompatible with the British parliamentary system. The Liberals spotted opportunity, and leader Tobias Norris tucked direct legislation into their campaign platform. They lost 1914's election but won another a year later. The 1916 session quickly passed Manitoba's Initiative and Referendum Act by a unanimous vote, because the vanquished Tories, in replacing Roblin with a fresh leader, had also become converts to direct democracy.

Manitoba's act allowed for provincial laws to be made and repealed by direct vote of the electors, instead of exclusively by the legislature, by processes similar to those in the Saskatchewan and Alberta acts, but contained two important advances. If the legislature authorized an expenditure over $100,000, large for public spending in that era, the money could be held back three months pending popular approval. Second, provision was made for voter education.

Meanwhile, Alberta's Direct Legislation Act was already in service. Electors initiated a petition seeking prohibition of alcohol. On July 21, 1915, the provincial government put a ballot question to voters. In this wartime balloting, when temperance forces sought to lever Canada's military effort by removing alcohol from the equation, Albertans voted overwhelmingly for prohibition. Implementing the voters' choice, the legislature enacted the Liquor Act in 1916. Before long, Nat Bell Liquor Company faced charges of violating this prohibition law. Championing provincial alcohol interests against the rising tide of prohibition, Nat Bell fought back by boldly challenging the entire legislative regime as unconstitutional. However, the law was held to be valid.

Alberta's Direct Legislation Act, having withstood challenge, was used a number of times in 1920, 1923, 1948, and 1957. The act remained in force until 1958 when a citizen inquired about using it.[3] Alberta's timid deputy attorney general of the day proffered a cautious legal opinion to the Social Credit government that the act was possibly beyond the province's constitutional powers — based on a judicial decision about Manitoba's similar statute, not by taking account of consistent repeated use by Albertans of their own statute, nor that it had been upheld as constitutionally valid in the *Nat Bell* case.

•   •   •

The court case pertaining to Manitoba's Initiative and Referendum Act was itself odd from start to finish. Enacted in 1916, in fulfillment of the Liberal government's electoral mandate, "the enthusiasm with which it was passed soon disappeared," notes historian Agar Adamson, "and the Norris government decided to refer the act to the courts to test its constitutionality."[4]

Manitoba's premier received the verdict, rendered by judges in England unsympathetic to Canadian-style democratic power-sharing, that the act infringed the role of the Crown's representative. Tobias Norris took his colonial cue. His government didn't craft a replacement bill to address the position of the lieutenant governor, as clever legislative drafters are adept at doing, in a manner to satisfy formal requirements yet allow ballot-question democracy as the elected representatives in the legislature had enacted.

Manitoba's direct legislation engendered debates among lawyers, judges, law professors, and elected representatives, but not among citizens of the province in the manner intended, because no measure was ever submitted to the voters under the Initiative and Referendum Act, nor did Manitobans initiate even a single legislative measure by the means it provided.

British Columbia's Direct Legislation Act was enacted in 1919 after the B.C. Liberals led by John Oliver committed to such a measure in their election platform. The act received Royal Assent on March 29, 1919, just months before the Judicial Committee of the Privy Council declared Manitoba's version of the statute unconstitutional. In the shadow of Manitoba's impugned direct-voting statute, Premier Oliver became nervous about British Columbia's. The statute's proclamation was withheld, according to the province's attorney general, "due to the uncertainty as to its constitutional validity."[5] British Columbia's act, though long on the statute books, complete with vice-regal signature, was never proclaimed in force.

• • •

Canada's "direct-democracy" movement didn't peter out because Westerners exhausted themselves participating in public decisions and voting to guide their legislators about enacting laws. It ended, rather, because they had little chance to do so. Premiers in Manitoba, Saskatchewan, and British Columbia had opportunistically sponsored initiative and referendum measures for temporary electoral advantage. Rather than advance citizen-centred democracy, however, Norris challenged his own act in the courts, Oliver kept his direct-voting statute on the shelf unused, while Scott at least submitted his law to Saskatchewanians before repealing it when a majority failed to ratify the measure. Only in Alberta was the act put to effective use — indeed, with its constitutionality judicially upheld. Only in the 1950s, when timid men came to occupy the seat of government in Edmonton, was Alberta's Direct Democracy Act repealed.

In other ways, however, western Canadian society's democratic grassroots were sprouting healthy shoots. Voters at the polls answered ballot questions on wide-ranging topics, including democratic methods, under provisions of other referendum-enabling statutes.

VOTING ON VOTING ITSELF — DO YOU FAVOUR CHANGING THE ELECTORAL SYSTEM?

The question of whether to adopt the "single transferable vote," or STV, was put to B.C. voters in a referendum held in conjunction with a May 17, 2005, provincial election. In Canadian democratic practice, as earlier noted, a simple majority of 50 percent plus one is required to decide a matter. However, intent on preordaining defeat, the B.C. government imposed an extraordinary *double majority* threshold. The new STV system would have to be approved by 60 percent of voters province-wide *and* by a majority of voters in 60 percent of the province's seventy-nine electoral districts. One hurdle was cleared easily when STV won majority approval in seventy-seven, or all but two, ridings. British Columbians also gave STV a comfortable 57 percent approval, far more than normally needed to win, but short of the new 60 percent mark.

With such a perverse outcome, the government, after being roundly condemned for thwarting democracy, announced a second referendum on STV. This time voters would see the revised electoral boundaries for the proposed new system. Equal public funding would support information campaigns by supporters and opponents of STV. However, the same exceptional voting thresholds would apply as for the 2005 referendum.

In the second round of voting, in May 2009, despite STV support from current and former politicians, the Canadian Taxpayers Federation, prominent artists, and environmentalists, the proposal fell far short of the required 60 percent level, winning only 39 percent of votes province-wide, and majority support in just seven of eighty-five electoral districts.

• • •

In Prince Edward Island, meanwhile, lopsided election results produced under the first-past-the-post system created a legislative assembly in which opposition parties had only a couple of seats, despite winning 45 percent of the popular vote. In January 2003, the government appointed the island's retired chief justice, the amiable and wise Norman Carruthers, to examine "the important issue of electoral reform" so that the assembly could "continue to be relevant and effective."

Following study and hearings, he recommended to Progressive Conservative Premier Pat Binns that the best alternatives were either the "mixed-member proportional" or "single transferable vote" methods. Of the pair, Commissioner Carruthers felt mixed-member proportional the preferable choice. Resembling the existing electoral system, it would preserve the traditional relationship between voters and their elected member, while "allowing each elector a more meaningful role" because additional seats would be allocated according to popular vote, resulting in a "mixed-member" assembly (members elected in two different ways) with fewer "wasted ballots."

Carruthers stipulated that changing the electoral system should be approved by the people in a referendum. He proposed that a modified version of the B.C. Citizens' Assembly on Electoral Reform study the matter further and draft a clear referendum question. In December 2004, an eight-person body was duly created, the Commission on Prince Edward Island's Electoral Future, which conducted public education about first-past-the-post and mixed-member proportional systems, ensured the definition of a "majority" fully reflected "the diversity of Prince Edward Island," and framed the ballot question.

The commission recommended mixed-member proportional. The government put the choice to a vote by Islanders on November 28, 2005, for which the commission also recommended the approval threshold remain at the normal 50 percent plus one. Premier Binns overruled that. He'd wanted the commission to recommend British Columbia's super-majority rules. The premier said his government wouldn't be bound by anything less than 60 percent in favour of MMP.

A 64 percent majority of voters answered No, anyway. Proponents for electoral reform claimed lack of public education and inadequate referendum funding caused a much lower voter turnout than normal for island elections. As a result, the entrenched system remained in place and produced its next imbalanced result in 2015 when Liberals got 40.8 percent of popular support, won eighteen seats, and formed a majority government, outnumbering the Opposition members two to one. In that election, Progressive Conservatives with 37.4 percent support won eight seats; New Democrats, with 11 percent, none; Greens, with 10.8 percent, one. Predictably, the surge for electoral reform again came to the fore.

Taking a different tack for a second non-binding vote in 2016, Islanders were asked to choose between *five* potential voting systems, one of them the existing first-past-the-post system, by ranking each in preference on a scale of one-to-five. Four runoff rounds of counting eliminated the least preferred options until "mixed-member proportional" came out on top with 54 percent support by combining everyone's first, second, third, and fourth preferences. In this final round, the existing system got 43 percent of votes.

The result was touted as a "win" for MMP. However, only 36 percent of eligible voters cast ballots, far below the Islanders' usual high turnout for general elections. Premier Wade MacLauchlan, whose Liberals now felt comfortable with their majority of seats under Prince Edward Island's unreformed system, "doubted" the result could be said to "constitute a clear expression of the will of Islanders." He discussed the results with his caucus. Nobody bet next season's lobster catch on implementation of MMP for Prince Edward Island.

• • •

In 2006 New Brunswick Premier Bernard Lord announced a referendum on changing the electoral system after the Commission on Legislative Democracy he'd established recommended a system of "regional MMP" and a binding referendum. However, his Conservative government was edged out by the Liberals before the referendum took place. Shawn Graham, the new premier who'd come to power under the existing electoral system, called for further study of all available voting methods and pointedly rejected the idea of a referendum.

By 2010, Graham had been replaced by Progressive Conservative Premier David Alward, who won with a large popular vote. He in turn was replaced in 2014 by Liberal Premier Brian Gallant. New Brunswick had somehow completed its ongoing study of electoral reform and recommended that a referendum be held on changing the first-past-the-post system. On March 30, 2017, Premier Gallant announced the referendum would be held in 2020 after yet another provincial election under the existing system. Some New Brunswickers believe the next infestation of spruce budworm will come and go through the province's forests before the electoral system gets changed.

In 2003 Ontario Premier Dalton McGuinty's new Liberal government created a Democratic Renewal Secretariat. Three years later it set up a Citizens' Assembly on Electoral Reform, which recommended after a year a mixed-member proportional system for Ontario. The result of MMP would be a combination of members elected in local districts in the traditional way plus additional members elected for the province at large from party lists reflecting the overall levels of popular support received by the various parties. A referendum on changing the voting system was held in conjunction with the October 10, 2007, provincial election. Despite a commitment to "democratic renewal," the Liberals copied British Columbia's "double majority" rules that didn't apply to other democratic decisions. Implementing MMP would need approval by at least 60 percent of votes in a district *and* more than a majority of votes in 50 percent or more of Ontario's 64 electoral districts.

In addition to this high hurdle, McGuinty's Liberals abandoned their own creation during the campaign. When a complaint to the Ontario Election Office alleged imbalance in how the referendum issue was being presented, the campaigning Liberals seized this pretext to stand back from supporting

MMP. When a referendum and election take place at the same time, candidates focus on winning their seats more than any ballot issue. Most let the measure fend for itself with little support or effective explanation. Progressive Conservatives opposed changing the electoral system. It was unsurprising that the proposed MMP electoral system won 36.9 percent of the popular vote, with 63.1 percent of voters preferring to keep what they knew. That same day Dalton McGuinty's Liberals were re-elected under first-past-the-post, a "majority government" having just 42.25 percent of the popular vote.

VOTING TO EMPOWER CITIZENS THROUGH INITIATIVE AND RECALL

British Columbians cast ballots in 1991 to decide whether to give themselves "initiative" and "recall" powers — long-standing pillars of the direct-democracy movement.

Recall is a method citizens can use to require accountability from their elected officials, although its use is controversial. It had been implemented in Alberta by the Social Credit government, but the first time recall was attempted, the elected representative whom voters were trying to unseat was Alberta's Socred premier. Seeing his own measure boomerang, William Aberhart's Social Credit government had the Alberta legislature repeal the law in 1937.

Recall and impeachment are similar in that elected officials may be removed from office between elections by either process, but impeachment is initiated by the legislature while recall is the citizens' remedy. The legal mechanism of recall enables a specified percentage of voters to petition for an election to remove an identified elected official, and if the vote favours removal, a by-election takes place to fill the resulting vacancy.

The ballot question for 1991's October 17 referendum on the initiative procedure asked, *Should voters be given the right, by legislation, to propose questions that the government of British Columbia must submit to the voters by referendum?* This issue had arisen in the provincial assembly during earlier debate on the Referendum Act, British Columbia's newest version of enabling legislation for ballot-question democracy. MLAs keen on direct voting criticized the bill for not giving electors the power of initiative. The Referendum Act could have been amended to that effect at the time; instead, the government gave its commitment to hold a referendum on whether to establish the legal right for citizens to initiate ballot questions.

The second question, on "recall," was *Should voters be given the right by legislation to vote between elections for the removal of their member of the Legislative Assembly?* This measure had its genesis in a spate of political scandals, and a feeling that several elected representatives had proven themselves unworthy of public trust.

Both questions were devised by the Social Credit government of Premier Rita Johnston and channelled a political appetite for more hands-on democracy, which at the time was also being nourished in national politics by the Reform Party.

The two ballot questions, addressing process rather than substantive issues, reflected a new mood in the country as people increasingly attuned to political accountability. Politicians were perceived by a significant number of Canadians as part of the problem more than its solution. Polling suggested people wanted greater direct participation in public affairs. Canadians' prior deference to authority was in decline.

The right of initiative, Rita Johnston said, went "to the heart of direct democracy — the ability of the citizen to initiate new programs and new policies." The premier said everyone, including members of the cabinet and the Social Credit caucus, were free to vote as they wished but that she would vote Yes to both questions. So, he announced, would B.C. Attorney General Russell Fraser, minister responsible for the referendum.

Johnston explained the recall and initiative measures, if approved, would require legislation to be implemented. Different models of such legislation were available from Australia, Switzerland, and the United States, but her government didn't "intend to dictate any specific model." It would be a vote on the principle, not the details. She wanted a "made-in-B.C. model of direct democracy." New Democratic Party leader Mike Harcourt also supported voter-initiated referendums and confirmed he'd honour the referendum results if his party formed the government.

To familiarize voters with the referendum process, as well as the pros and cons of both ballot questions, the government established a referendum office for public inquiries, with a toll-free province-wide phone number. The provincial secretary provided impartial, factual information about the referendum and the ballot questions. The elections office distributed information on balloting procedures. General information and views about the questions came from political parties, policy organizations, interested individuals, and news media. For the public information campaign itself, material was delivered to all households in the province and made available to the public in every government office and all British Columbia public libraries. The entire effort cost $1.7 million. There were no spending limits on the campaigns sponsoring referendum positions.

The 1991 referendum was held at the same time as the provincial election. Ballots for both questions were available to voters at their regular polling stations and when marked were deposited in separate ballot boxes from the candidate votes. Approval required only a simple majority, more than 50 percent of validly cast ballots. No minimum number was required. The ballots for MLA candidates were counted first and the results made public, the greater priority, and then referendum ballots were tallied. Although the ballots were counted and reported by constituency, the results were aggregated on a province-wide basis.

The results were convincing. For recall, Chief Electoral Officer Bob Patterson reported 1,058,137 votes in favour, 248,432 against, and 128,171 rejected ballots. Those numbers represented 73.75 percent for recall, 17.3 percent against, and 8.9 percent ballots spoiled. Counting only the valid votes, Yes had 80.99 percent, No had 19.1. For citizens to have a right of initiative, a slightly higher number voted in favour; in percentage terms, a Yes vote of 74 percent, No of 15.1, and rejected ballots at 10.7. Expressed in terms of valid votes cast, 83.03 percent supported the initiative, and 16.97 percent were opposed.

The same day, British Columbians had, by electing a majority of NDP members to the legislature, chosen a new premier, Mike Harcourt. He'd pledged during the election that an NDP government would follow the referendum mandate from the people. True to his word, British Columbia's Recall and Initiative Act was enacted and came into force on February 24, 1995.

18

VOTING TO RATIFY, JOIN, AND SUBDIVIDE CONFEDERATION

For as long as Confederation has existed, electors have been casting ballots in relation to it in one way or another — to approve, join, subdivide, make over, or leave. This chapter revisits the first three of these democratic experiences.

Back when a number of British North American colonies were negotiating to create Canada under the 1867 federal constitution that now governs ten provinces and three territories, a strongly held view was that voters ought to ratify such a major change in advance to give Confederation legitimacy and achieve a public embrace of forming a new country.

This concept was worthy enough that four of the thirteen other British colonies in North America that had earlier rebelled against King George III to form the United States — Connecticut, Massachusetts, New Hampshire, and Rhode Island — required a vote by their electors on the new constitutions replacing the old colonial charters, which "should take effect only after they had been considered, voted upon, and approved by the State's voters."[1] The test wasn't to prove whether one felt loyal to the Crown or rebelled against it. The vote was recognition of the need to gain popular endorsement for a fundamental change that would affect all concerned — the colonial state entering a larger political union, the United States, whose long-term success would depend on people buying into the deal.

Many members of Parliament in the pre-Confederation version of "Canada" — a constitutional union of two provinces, Canada East and Canada West, whose names in 1867 would change to Quebec and Ontario — felt the same imperative as those American colonists. They wanted to get popular ratification from those potentially becoming part of an enlarged new union. In 1866 twenty of Canada East's elected representatives petitioned the secretary of state for colonies in Britain to restrain implementing Confederation *until* the colonial governments in British North America had a mandate from their people to create a larger country with a new constitution.

In support of their case, the MPs noted the irony that all elected representatives then advocating Confederation — not the least of them being John A. Macdonald — had previously spoken against the idea. What logic held that political leaders could change their minds yet not give *everyone* affected a chance to go through the same reasoning process? Confederation hadn't been mentioned in either the 1861 or 1863 general elections, so these MPs correctly noted that the people had given no electoral mandate to proceed with so fundamental a change. The people of Lower Canada had "never had an opportunity of pronouncing a decision upon the question," they pointed out. "Proper regard for their rights" and "every principle of sound statesmanship" required postponement of the final decision until it could be shown that "the measure be a good one and the people are really in favour of it."

They added that because the current Parliament of Canada would expire in the summer of 1867 and the existing Parliament of Nova Scotia the following spring, those pending general elections should take place "and would necessarily turn on the question of Confederation." The desirability of political union and the conditions on which it would be acceptable would be fully debated, they emphasized, resulting in "an election of Parliaments representing the settled convictions and the matured purposes of the people."

A general election, of course, never turns on a single issue, no matter how important, yet this was the only option in that pre-referendum era. Candidates advocating a particular policy and winning a majority of seats were deemed to have "an electoral mandate," and as crude as this mechanism can be, it is better than no public debate and vote on a transformative issue.

Those MPs reasoned that if a majority was favourable to Confederation, then decisions by parliaments elected under those circumstances "would go far to ensure the success of a system which at best could only be regarded as an experiment." Confederation should be attempted only under the most favourable conditions and that, they argued, would include affirmative mandates in the pending elections. If the results were adverse to Confederation, however, "that fact alone would demonstrate the wisdom of the delay for which we plead."

The petitioners traced promotion of Confederation "to the party or personal exigencies of Canadian politicians, and not a spontaneous or general desire among the people for fundamental changes in their political institutions, or in their political relations." The petition further argued that details of the federal union agreement hadn't been examined, in the way clauses of a bill are considered, in any of the provincial parliaments; that in Canada and Nova Scotia the people hadn't had an opportunity of pronouncing on either the principle or the details; and that in New Brunswick, where an election had recently been held, "the people cannot be said to have assented to the Quebec scheme," which was the only definite plan of union then under consideration.

That draft Confederation plan, worked out at Quebec City when delegates passed seventy-two resolutions to more explicitly express fundamental decisions made earlier at Charlottetown, included the constitutional framework for a new country. "We seek delay," the MPs concluded, "not to frustrate the purpose of a majority of our countrymen, but to prevent their being surprised, against their will, or without their consent, into a political change which, however obnoxious or oppressive to them it might prove, could not be reversed without such an agitation as every well-wisher of his country must desire to avert."[2]

The petition wasn't acted upon. Parliament in the United Kingdom enacted the British North America Act, 1867, in the form colonial political leaders had drafted it under close guidance from John A. Macdonald.

Decades later historian and political scientist R. MacGregor Dawson concluded the cold shoulder given to their appeal was "the consistent reluctance to submit the question of federation to any popular verdict."[3] The most forcible opponent of popular ratification was Macdonald, who'd previously disdained Confederation, then changed his mind. The irony in his reason for not taking the matter to the people was that "the fickle public" couldn't be relied upon. This desire to avoid an election or any form of ballot question, Dawson explained, "was conveniently explained as being in accord with British ideas of the functions of a representative legislature; but it also sprang from a shaky belief in the solid virtues of popular government."

Denying a direct vote on the constitutional question of Confederation meant contending views cropped up instead through the second-best procedure — a general election. That, indeed, was all the twenty MPs from Lower Canada ever sought.

. . .

Across Atlantic Canada, absence of a process by which electors could directly debate and vote on the consequences of participating in Confederation saw the electoral system used as the next best thing. Voting for representatives who espoused strong views on Confederation transformed elections into a referendum-like procedure. In the 1860s, Nova Scotians, New Brunswickers, Prince Edward Islanders, and Newfoundlanders realigned themselves into either the "Confederation Party" or "Anti-Confederation Party." Lines blurred as Liberals and Conservatives, the era's primary political affiliations, reoriented themselves for battle over union. Although many Conservatives were for Confederation and many Liberals opposed, such partisan distinctions largely became secondary to supporting either Confederation or Anti-Confederation candidates.

In Nova Scotia, Conservative Charles Tupper, a "Father of Confederation," had been elected Nova Scotia's premier with a majority in 1863 and didn't have to go to the polls until after Confederation took effect on July 1, 1867. Tupper's majority in the assembly voted Nova Scotia into Confederation. He also organized a Confederation Party to counteract the Anti-Confederation Party led by Joseph Howe. Tupper then resigned to enter federal politics and was replaced as premier and leader of the Confederation Party by lawyer Hiram Blanchard, a Liberal in the House of Assembly who supported union. When the provincial election took place on September 18, 1867, Blanchard was unable to lead the Confederation Party to victory. Anti-Confederation candidates captured thirty-six of thirty-eight seats and formed a government under separatist Premier William Annand, a newspaper editor.

In that same trip to the polls, Nova Scotia voters also elected MPs to fill the new Canadian province's nineteen seats in the House of Commons in Ottawa. Anti-Confederation candidates won all but one of them. Among the Anti-Confederate MPs was Joseph Howe, Nova Scotia's champion in achieving responsible government and skilled writer and publisher, who'd strongly opposed Confederation. In a sense, Howe's group was an earlier version of the one led a dozen decades later by Lucien Bouchard, head of the Bloc Québécois separatist MPs in Parliament. The lone pro-Confederation MP from Nova Scotia was Charles Tupper.

Years later historian Peter B. Waite would say it was "fortunate for Confederation" that Charles Tupper didn't "test his electorate" in the province until after the new constitutional arrangement had taken effect. "Then, too late, it was clear that 65 percent of Nova Scotians opposed Confederation."[4]

The *general* opposition of many Nova Scotians to Confederation was rooted in their existing self-government and identity, the Maritime community's natural affinity to Britain, historic and economic ties with the New England states, and the fact they'd had no say in the matter. In the 1860s, Nova Scotia burgeoned in general prosperity. Throughout the Atlantic region, people knew Confederation would reorient commercial life toward the interior of the continent, unattractive to those whose economic well-being was anchored by international commerce and ocean shipping.

Despite Nova Scotia's Anti-Confederation election results, Britain's Colonial Office in London refused to allow the province to secede from Confederation. That forced Anti-Confederation leader Joseph Howe to "accept the inevitable," as historian Colin D. Howell put it, "agreeing to enter Sir John A. Macdonald's government in return for an increased provincial subsidy in 1869."[5]

Binding Nova Scotia to Confederation took deal-making at the top levels of government, from brute exercise of power by London to payment of money by Ottawa. As for regular folk living with the consequences of being incorporated into a much larger and different country, they'd have to wait for another election when Confederation and Anti-Confederation candidates would again square off as stand-ins loosely approximating a Yes/No referendum on union.

By 1886, Nova Scotia's secession movement was being led by Liberal premier William S. Fielding. Campaigning in a provincial election to "repeal" Confederation, or alternatively gain further increased subsidies from Ottawa, Fielding's Liberals won twenty-nine of thirty-eight seats. Strongest separatist support came from areas tied to the traditional Maritime economy and the international shipping trade. Opposition to secession was greatest in areas beginning to industrialize, particularly coal mining areas and towns along the Inter-Colonial Railway linking the province to the continental interior.

Nova Scotia's separatist movement under Fielding was somewhat counterbalanced the following year in the federal election of February 22, 1887, when the pro-Confederation Conservative Party won fourteen of Nova Scotia's twenty-one House of Commons seats. For difficult decades, the Confederation issue simmered, and sometimes boiled over, with general elections the crude proxy for a referendum, providing the only ballot voters had to express their verdict on union.

• • •

New Brunswick's Anti-Confederation Party, a coalition of Conservatives and "Reformers" (as Liberals often called themselves in those days), led by Albert J. Smith, won the 1865 election, but lost power two years later to the Confederation Party led by Peter Mitchell. The legislature produced by that election approved joining Confederation by a vote of thirty-eight to one, with the result that Confederation 150 years ago would begin with four provinces. In 1867's federal election, Anti-Confederates won five of New Brunswick's fifteen seats in the House of Commons.

People in the Atlantic region almost instinctively invented a referendum-like process, for the sheer need of one. Voters focused on a transcending issue, the way they do in referendums, with little heed to partisan loyalties. In New Brunswick, Anti-Confederation leader Albert Smith and Confederation leader Peter Mitchell were both Conservatives, while Samuel Leonard Tilley, a Liberal, was the most prominent leader of the Confederation forces. Tilley, like Howe in Nova Scotia, would eventually be enticed by John A. Macdonald into his government.

New Brunswickers were less worried than other Atlantic people about increasing links with the more proximate Quebec and Ontario economies, and the province's Acadians saw advantages in a political union with French-speaking people in both those provinces. By 1870, the Confederate and Anti-Confederate parties in New Brunswick, having served their purpose, dissolved and earlier Liberal and Tory alignments reasserted themselves.

Prince Edward Island, despite hosting the first of three conferences devising Confederation, stayed aloof from joining. The colony was prospering in the 1860s, and, acculturated by the Islanders' mentality, was jealous of its independence. In 1873, however, deep in debt from constructing a railway, the humbled province bailed itself out by joining Canada in exchange for Ottawa assuming its heavy financial obligations.

It was the same for Newfoundlanders. Despite even greater economic difficulties, a majority sought to remain outside Confederation and pursue their independent destiny. In an 1869 election, they elected twenty-one Anti-Confederation members to the legislative assembly, only nine for the Confederation Party.

Politics over these years became polarized between Confederation's supporters and opponents — with a wide range of dubious claims, plenty of "emotion," and other familiar aspects of decision-making by ballot that today Canadian critics of referendums still criticize. In a democracy, the views of people will out. If one means for expressing views is unavailable, the force of people's beliefs will soon invent another. Whether beliefs about a major issue get vented in an election or through a referendum, it is not the voting process that "causes deep divisions." Rather, in a healing democratic way, this ability to debate and mark ballots channels them.

VOTING TO JOIN CONFEDERATION, 1948

For England's first overseas colony, Newfoundland, the prospect of joining thirteen other British colonies on the Atlantic seaboard to overthrow the British Crown never interested them in the way that it tempted quite a few Nova Scotians. Nor were Newfoundland's inhabitants much interested in joining Confederation. They didn't join in 1867, or in the years following, the way Prince Edward Island belatedly did. Instead, Newfoundlanders evolved into a self-governing British "dominion" as Canada itself would.

Newfoundland acquired powers of responsible government, an elected legislature, and self-governing dominion status with its own currency, customs duties, postal service, and other attributes of a country. In the 1930s, however, Newfoundland's chronically fragile economy sputtered to a standstill amid worldwide depression. Financial bankruptcy exacerbated violence raging between Catholics and Protestants. Britain closed down the government, boarded up the legislature, and imposed direct rule from London under a system known as commission government. Being run by appointed commissioners was an ignominious fate: Newfoundland became Britain's only colony to achieve self-government and then lose it.

After the Second World War, a referendum on Newfoundland's future was proposed by the Labour government of British Prime Minister Clement Atlee. He'd toured Newfoundland after the war, appalled by conditions he found "worse than the most poverty-stricken parts of rural Portugal." Britain was itself desperately coming to grips with its own financial predicament, severing colonial ties rather than renewing them. Unlike the African colonies, which would gain independence during the 1950s and 1960s and get financial and technical assistance from Britain, this sort of deal was impossible for Newfoundland in the hard postwar years when Britons themselves remained on rations.

In 1946 the British announced elections to choose a constituent assembly. One delegate to the Newfoundland National Convention, Joseph Smallwood, was elected by a wide margin in Gander. When he arrived in St. John's that September, Smallwood found few others shared his hope for Newfoundland joining Confederation. The national convention's mandate was to "make recommendations to His Majesty's Government as to possible forms of future governments to be put before the people at a national referendum."[6] Newfoundlanders would exercise their right of self-determination democratically, by ballot.

The convention's sessions became protracted. Gordon Bradley, Smallwood, and several others left for Ottawa, a delegation to clarify possible terms of union with Canada. Cabinet took a long time digesting all the implications. Prime Minister King and Justice Minister Louis St. Laurent learned payments to Newfoundland might exceed money going to the Maritime Provinces of Nova Scotia, New Brunswick, and Prince Edward Island *combined* and "recoiled in horror at such a politically impossible outlay."[7] But in Ottawa, not for the first time, political emotion trumped financial circumspection. Canada's government realized it had no choice except, in a phrase of the day, to "complete Confederation." Being stingy about money had, after all, jeopardized negotiations with Newfoundland about joining Confederation in the nineteenth century. After ninety-nine days in Ottawa and a steady flow of telegrams demanding their return to St. John's, Bradley and the delegation resurfaced in the city and reported Canada's "terms of union" to the Newfoundland National Convention.

In the meantime, other possibilities had been considered. Pragmatic Newfoundlanders hoped to remain under commission government. Others advocated a return to dominion status and self-government, a small but independent country under the British Crown. A different group led by prominent St. John's businessman Chesley Crosbie, father of John Crosbie of subsequent political fame in both Newfoundland and Canadian politics, actively sought terms of economic union with the United States. A close link had been forged between Newfoundlanders and Americans during the Second World War, with U.S. airbases and personnel becoming the largest component of the economy.

Only a minority of delegates wanted Confederation. However, fate handed a face card to Smallwood and the confederates. The government commission, still running things and in exclusive control of radio broadcasting, transmitted full daily broadcasts of proceedings from the national convention, a sensible prelude to the referendum by raising voters' awareness of the issues. Of all delegates attending, Smallwood alone was a professional broadcaster. Using his radio experience to his advantage, he went over the delegates' heads, reaching directly the scattered Newfoundlanders listening earnestly beside their radios in towns and outports.

When the Newfoundland National Convention finally voted on options it would recommend for the referendum, it produced only two choices: return to self-government with dominion status, or retention of commission government. Delegates defeated, by twenty-nine to sixteen, the motion to include Confederation on the ballot. Like their nineteenth-century Anti-Confederation ancestors, these delegates imagined they'd thwarted what the majority of them didn't want. As it turned out, they'd committed a first-class political blunder. By denying the people the right to make a full choice about their future in the referendum, they created an issue and galvanized a cause. Bradley, Smallwood, and their small but well-organized band of confederates promptly charged that twenty-nine "dictators" were denying the people the right to choose.[8]

Gordon Bradley, taking quickly to the airwaves, attacked the "dictators" and appealed for a mass petition of protest from the people to the governor. Because these very same radio listeners had attentively followed the convention proceedings, some fifty thousand of them got the point and promptly signed the petition. The British government was equally dismayed by this bizarre recommendation from the convention — a referendum asking Newfoundlanders if they wished to remain in primitive colonial status under commission government, or wanted to go it alone as an independent self-governing country — neither option financially viable. The British contrasted those two choices with the prospect of joining prosperous Canada, which had offered terms of union that seemed comparatively irresistible. Keen to be rid of its problem colony, the British saw Canada as Newfoundland's safest harbour, both willing and able to pay the high costs — for national pride in "completing Confederation."

So, demonstrating the limited influence of a colonial constituent assembly upon an imperial power, the British government simply changed their recommendation by adding a third option: join Canada as a province. At the end of all their labours, observed historian S.J.R. Noel, "the National Convention might just as well never have met."[9] Yet the convention had at least served to launch the Confederationists into the referendum campaign under the leadership of Joey Smallwood.

Newfoundlanders would go to the polls on June 3, 1948, to choose (1) responsible government, (2) joining Canada, or (3) staying under commission government. The referendum campaign took shape quickly and was vigorously fought: forcing choice wouldn't be easy. The convention, in voting down the Confederation option because most delegates didn't want it, had also recommended just two options so that voters faced a clear choice on their future. The British, insisting that three possible futures be on offer, created a scenario in which, when ballots were counted the night of June 3, voters had given majority support to none. Responsible government got 69,400 votes (44.5 percent), Confederation won 64,066 (41.1 percent), and commission government, 22,311 (14.3 percent).

The British, having stipulated a clear majority would be needed, had added another requirement: if a second ballot was required, the option with fewest votes would be dropped in the runoff referendum. The second round of voting took place on July 22, 1948.

Those advocating the responsible government option — Newfoundland's big money interests — had plenty of financial resources, but their forces were divided and poorly organized. On the Confederation side, Smallwood's appeal to the "toiling masses" had established a populist touch, though very large amounts of campaign money had come secretly from Ottawa — not the Government of Canada, but the governing Liberal Party, which envisaged a particular future for the new island province. Smallwood had given no formal commitment to join the Liberals, but while he collected desperately needed votes from any pro-Confederation Tories, in Ottawa it was safely assumed he would do so when the voting was over. After Newfoundland became a province, it would have seven seats in Parliament, not a large number but "a useful addition to Liberal ranks," as Richard Gwyn observed. "Campaign funds were a small price to pay for them."[10]

In the second campaign, Newfoundland's deep undercurrents of religious bigotry again roiled to the surface. In earlier times, election riots in Newfoundland sparked by impassioned animosities between Catholics and Protestants resulted in deaths. The 1948 campaign didn't overheat that far, but the Catholic hierarchy's support of responsible government and opposition to Confederation dramatically changed the political temperature. Archbishop Roche of Newfoundland "threw all of his very considerable influence into the fight," and his church magazine, *The Monitor*, became "an openly political instrument in the cause of responsible government."[11] In language strikingly similar to that of earlier French-Canadian nationalists in Quebec, notes historian Noel, the Roman Catholic leadership did not deny that an independent Newfoundland would be poor but argued against material blandishments in favour of the preservation, in isolation, of simple spiritual values. Partisan entry into the campaign by the archbishop and the Catholic establishment became a misjudged action because it provoked an equal and opposite reaction from Protestants, changing the campaign's flow abruptly. Protestants outnumbered Catholics two to one. Sectarianism rose to a fever pitch. This "sharpening of denominational lines in the second ballot could only benefit the Confederates."[12]

Other factors changed, too. With more than twenty-two thousand people (14 percent of electors) having voted for commission government, their support was up for grabs, their ballots enough to turn the tide. Economic forces also played a part: areas where fishing was the primary occupation mostly wanted Confederation, which would expand markets, while the merchant and professional classes of St. John's clung to the responsible government choice because that was how they'd continue to control the economy and exploit Newfoundlanders, getting richer by means of the low prices for fish and seal skins they grudgingly forked over to impoverished fishermen. There was, however, an exhilarating crescendo to the campaign's final days when several prestigious Newfoundlanders and leading lights of St. John's society broke ranks to publicly endorse the Confederation option.

The outcome was close: 78,323 votes (52.3 percent) for joining Canada versus 71,344 votes (47.4 percent) for responsible government. The overwhelming turnout, about 85 percent of electors, was almost as high as for the first ballot.

In Ottawa the referendum returns were nervously awaited. Before the vote, Prime Minister King pledged that the Canadian government would accept the colony into Confederation, provided Newfoundlanders demonstrated their decision for Canada "clearly and beyond all possibility of misunderstanding." As Richard Gwyn commented, the margin of seven thousand votes "hardly fulfilled King's conditions." What would happen now?

The prime minister's grey mood, and his well-honed penchant for fussy delay and obfuscation, could easily turn this "unclear" result into drifting confusion that would enable Newfoundland's power brokers in St. John's to press on with their eventual plan to link up with the Americans as a state of the Union. However, the PM's principal secretary, Jack Pickersgill, vibrated with excited energy at the prospect of his home province, Newfoundland, becoming Canada's tenth province. He understood King enough to anticipate his diffident state of mind. The morning after the vote Pickersgill swiftly studied statistics from all of King's previous election campaigns. By 10:00 a.m., when the prime minister telephoned, he was surprised by his secretary's enthusiasm.

"Mr. King, it is wonderful!" the Newfoundlander replied when asked his opinion on the voting. "Do you realize this is a larger majority than you received in any election except 1940?"

Following a pause while Pickersgill's comparison sunk in, Canada's now-smiling prime minister replied, "I hadn't realized that at all. That puts a different light on the whole situation."

Through the autumn of 1948, negotiations between representatives of Newfoundland and Canada produced final terms of union, even better for Newfoundland than those originally negotiated in 1947 and presented by Gordon Bradley to the national convention in St. John's. Only one member of the Newfoundland delegation, Chesley Crosbie — who'd wanted Newfoundland to become a state in the *American* federal union and campaigned with a bottle of Coke in his hand — refused to sign the Terms of Union. The British were relieved, and got smartly about other business.

On March 31, 1949, Newfoundland joined Canada as the tenth province. This fulfilled the mandate, conclusively if grudgingly given, as the people of Newfoundland voted themselves into Confederation. The issues had been ventilated and examined from every angle. All Newfoundlanders had participated in forcing the choice.

VOTING TO SUBDIVIDE CANADA: 1982, 1992

When Newfoundlanders voted to join Confederation, bringing new land to our country as an additional province, it was a contrast. Most provinces and territories resulted from subdividing the vast northern half of a continent already under Canadian jurisdiction.

After Confederation, the Northwest Territories' broad continental expanse was sectioned for the province of Manitoba in 1870, Yukon Territory in 1898, the provinces Alberta and Saskatchewan in 1905, and northward expansion of Quebec and Ontario boundaries by 1912. The new boundaries of the reduced Northwest Territories were retained until the end of the twentieth century when a trio of referendums contributed to a final subdivision of it, establishing the eastern Arctic as Canada's third territory, Nunavut.

In 1963 legislation was introduced in Parliament to divide the Northwest Territories into the Mackenzie (west) and Nunassiaq (east) territories, but with little support the proposal died. The government named A.W.R. Carrothers, law dean at the University of Western Ontario, head of a commission to study the evolution of governance in the territory, including division. Three years later his report concluded "within the next decade" no division should occur. Carrothers acknowledged, though, that the Northwest Territories' sheer size probably made division inevitable eventually. His concerns: two separate governments would have less success dealing with Ottawa; fragmented hunting, trapping, and fishing areas would require aboriginal people to abide by the laws of two territories; the dividing line, once drawn, couldn't easily be relocated for changing circumstances; and division would slow the advance to provincial status.[13] The Northwest Territorial Council's session in November 1966, despite approving Carrothers's report, criticized his failure to adequately consult the people throughout the Northwest Territories. Many of his concerns were more theoretical than realistic, the North as seen by a Southern Canadian. The council stressed that any division of the Northwest Territories should be left for territorial people themselves to decide.[14]

The report suppressed talk of division for a decade. But in 1974 the Inuit Tapirisat of Canada, representing the eastern Arctic's seventeen thousand Inuit people, proposed settling their unresolved land claims through the concept of "Nunavut," a separate eastern territory with its own government.

Following this plan's 1979 cabinet-level tweaking in Ottawa, the Inuit Tapirisat unanimously approved it in October 1980 at an annual general assembly held at Coppermine, Northwest Territories. *Nunavut*, meaning "our land" in Inuktitut, had now become the raison d'être for territorial division.

Inspired by this resurgence of division as a viable political act, the N.W.T. Legislative Assembly in 1980 declared its "commitment in principle to a major division of the present Northwest Territories into an eastern and a western territory, subject to the expressed will, by public debate and by plebiscite, of the people of the Northwest Territories showing preference for the establishment of one or two new territories."[15] The assembly also confirmed that if a majority voted Yes to the ballot question, this would be its mandate to request the Government of Canada to divide the Northwest Territories.

Under the proposal, Nunavut, the eastern half, would have a new capital, and the western half, *Denendeh*, meaning "Land of the People," would have Yellowknife as its capital. Both would have jurisdiction and government powers in their reconstituted territories. Because neither section was inhabited exclusively by Inuit or Dene, it was important for any new regime to combine aboriginal self-government with community (or public) government.

Preparing for the ballot question in 1981, the Legislative Assembly enacted a Plebiscite Ordinance.[16] N.W.T. legislators were resolved that only "true Northerners" should vote on land and governance policy and imposed on new residents a three-year waiting period before they could vote. A better filter to screen temporary workers and transients from voting is achieved by defining "ordinary residency," as all Canadian election and referendum statutes do, in a way that eliminates as voters individuals just staying on an interim basis. Three years was far outside Canadian norms, and also excessive by the standards of both Yukon and the Northwest Territories' own Elections Ordinances in which the rule is one-year residency before voting. The Charter's stricture to impose only a "reasonable limit that could be demonstrably justified in a free and democratic society" seemed offended.

Northern residents wanted to challenge their unfair disfranchisement by a court challenge, and as a member of the Northwest Territories Bar, I assisted their case.[17] One of the plaintiffs, an Inuit woman born and raised in the North, had lived several years in northern Alberta before returning home to the Arctic. She discovered she had to wait three years to qualify for answering a ballot question. But with voting approaching, the court was unwilling to interfere with the legislature's three-year hurdle.

• • •

Balloting on territorial division took place on April 14, 1982, with nearly nineteen thousand electors on the voting lists. Voting followed general referendum patterns. Turnout was 53 percent, of whom 56 percent said Yes to division, 44 percent, No.

A major step forward, forcing the choice put unaccustomed pressure upon all Northerners to reach a consensus and raised the stakes for N.W.T. aboriginal organizations and the federal government to resolve their impasse in land claims negotiation. "The extent to which native people can meet these two challenges," suggested policy analysts Frances Abel and Mark Dickerson, "may well depend upon how strongly they desire control of their own affairs."[18]

This vote was the first opportunity for northern residents to collectively register their views about a specific change in the constitutional status of their government. Until 1982 decisions about the Northwest Territories' boundaries and constitutional arrangements resulted from top-down decisions taken by people not residing in the territory. This initiative by northern aboriginal organizations to propose division, and the response of the N.W.T. Legislative Assembly to put a ballot question before the people, introduced authentic democracy and ended top-down governing of the North. In November 1982, Indian Affairs and Northern Development Minister John Munro announced the Government of Canada's agreement to division, conditional on prior resolution of land claim issues.

Within the territories, division was referred to the Constitutional Alliance of the Northwest Territories, a body composed of both the Nunavut and Western constitutional forums. By January 15, 1987, the alliance reached agreement on both the boundary and a plan to implement division of the territories. Two months later the N.W.T. Legislative Assembly approved the "Iqaluit Agreement" and recommended a ballot question on the proposed boundary. But the vote didn't occur in 1987. In October 1989, the Legislative Assembly was still debating the creation of Nunavut.

Progress was slow because of significant disagreements over how to combine "community self-government" and "aboriginal self-government" in the

Northwest Territories. Because the two systems are closely interrelated but not identical, comprehensive constitutional planning had to carefully distinguish between them. The situation's complexity involved diverse peoples having different interests scattered across an immense territory. Contrasting views between Inuit and the Dene and Métis trace back centuries, although these aboriginal groups share common outlooks when dealing with the non-aboriginal population and Southern influences. Most Northerners, whether Aboriginal or non-Aboriginal, share a common goal: autonomy and self-government represented by provincial (or province-like) status.

Intersecting these cross-currents, the land claims process added further complication. Some claims had already been settled, others were pending, while more remained stalled. In some cases, boundary disputes existed between aboriginal groups. For the all-important boundary that would divide the territories, Dene of the western Arctic and Inuit of the eastern Arctic couldn't agree on the proposed line. Also, land claims settlements were raising political disgruntlement elsewhere in Canada as taxpayers in the South faced paying multi-million-dollar settlements such as a $580 million bill for Nunavut to benefit seventeen thousand Inuit people.

Also slowing progress were serious concerns about a system of government based on race. The discriminatory three-year residency requirement restricting voting in the plebiscite was public evidence of a predisposition by Northern lawmakers to enact double standards. The N.W.T. Plebiscite Ordinance was a flashing red light about legal rights based on clumsily disguised racial criteria. This was seen by some, including lawyers immersed in work for aboriginal communities, as risking a Canadian form of apartheid, governance in which race would be the criteria for allocating rights. Yet striving for a more ethnically integrated system remained the focus, a quest helped by the non-racial approach of Northern Quebec Inuit leaders preparing for their own ballot question on governance in 1987.

• • •

On May 4, 1992, the Northwest Territories held its second referendum on division, this time about the exact location of the new boundary line. It was proposed to run north from the Manitoba-Saskatchewan boundary, zigzag west, then north again above the Alberta-Saskatchewan boundary to the North Pole.

Amendments to the Plebiscite Ordinance gave voting rights to a Canadian citizen who'd be eighteen by voting day and who'd lived in the Northwest Territories since May 4, 1989 — still three years. Although the Northwest Territories had fifty-eight thousand residents, the voters' list showed only about twenty-six thousand registered, some nine thousand in the eastern Arctic and seventeen thousand in the western Arctic.

The ballot question was long and confusing, as noted in Chapter 12. The information pamphlet, published in ten languages, asserted that "while a plebiscite is similar to a territorial election, it is held only to collect information," making it seem like census-taking.

From Ottawa, cabinet minister Tom Siddon and his Indian Affairs and Northern Development officials vigorously declared, in advance of a plebiscite, that division would proceed regardless of the balloting outcome — a majority No vote would not be grounds for scuttling Nunavut. This political intimidation of voters was unworthy of anyone seeking formation of a democratic consensus and public co-operation with government action. Given this edict from Ottawa, it seemed there was no reason anyone should even bother to vote.

In such a swirling context, the long-awaited boundary-line vote proceeded. Results from the 171 polls produced a margin of 54 percent Yes to 46 percent No. The campaign period offered a forum for popular participation in the evolution toward Nunavut, with the ballots providing an accurate reading of public sentiment on an extremely complex issue. Support for Nunavut in the eastern Northwest Territories, where four of five people are Inuit, reflected the same pattern as in the 1982 vote. Both referendums encapsulated the strong drive in the eastern Arctic to create Nunavut, which would give Inuit peoples effective control of a government slated to be created by 1999.

Voter response in the western half of the Northwest Territories was harder to analyze. Dene and Métis in principle supported Nunavut but opposed, in the words of Dene National Chief Bill Erasmus, "the imposition of a line and a method for determining legitimacy that does not take into account our inherent right, as a nation, to determine our own future."[19] Most land claims in the western Arctic were nowhere close to resolution.

Western Arctic non-Aboriginals found themselves in a particular quandary facing the ballot question. Residents in Inuvik whom I interviewed at the time had decided to set aside practical considerations, such as concern about "creating a second bureaucracy that would be expensive and inefficient," to vote, instead, "on principle." Ironically, they ended up casting ballots on opposing sides of the question.[20] Yellowknife Chamber of Commerce President Jane Groenewegen said that "we're in a no-win situation" because a Yes vote would support the Inuit while "shooting ourselves in the foot" and a No vote meant "raining on the Nunavut parade."[21]

In the western Arctic, opposition to further dividing the Northwest Territories came from non-aboriginal residents viewing it as a needless expense and from the Dene seeing the proposed boundary line as violating respect for their traditional hunting and burial grounds. The Dene also opposed on principle any aboriginal peoples extinguishing their land rights, which had been central to the 1991 agreement between Ottawa and the Tungavik Federation of Nunavut (TFN).

In the May 4 referendum, a majority in the eastern Arctic, where voter turnout was high, cast ballots in favour of the division. In the western Arctic, with low voter turnout, the majority voted against division.

· · ·

A third ballot question helped to further advance this contentious project later that same year. In November 1992, the Inuit themselves voted on their land claim deal, an integral component of the Nunavut proposal, and on the splitting of the Northwest Territories. Their agreement had evolved dramatically from earlier proposals, through negotiations over many years, and been signed on October 30, 1992, by the Government of Canada, the Government of the Northwest Territories, and the Tungavik Federation of Nunuvat. Under its terms, Ottawa would pay the Inuit $1.15 billion over fourteen years and confirm outright Inuit ownership of 350,000 square kilometres of land (an area half the size of Alberta) in exchange for the Inuit giving up aboriginal title to more than 80 percent of their traditional lands, territory the federal government and TFN would henceforth manage jointly. The Inuit would have the right to hunt, fish, and trap anywhere in Nunavut.

Voting between November 3 and 5, Inuit residents of the eastern Arctic overwhelmingly said Yes to the political accord. Of eligible voters, 9,648 went to their polling stations, an 80 percent turnout. People who didn't cast ballots were counted as No votes, an unusual step, which nevertheless still made the 69 percent Yes a high level of approval.

"The people of the eastern Arctic have sought a new jurisdiction in this country consistent with their desire to govern themselves and manage their own affairs," I said November 17 in the House of Commons, referring to the three referendum results. Throughout the process, the people and government of the Northwest Territories had been direct participants, creating the legislation for ballot questions in 1981, approving division by a majority vote in 1982, ratifying location of the boundary line in May 1992, and the Inuit in the eastern Arctic voting in November 1992 to adopt the plan for partnership participation in Nunavut. "Accordingly," I informed the Commons, "the Government of Canada will be introducing legislation at the same time of the claim settlement legislation, to divide the Northwest Territories and set up Nunavut. A happy day, particularly because the people themselves have been directly involved in making these decisions."

In Nunavut, 17,500 eastern Arctic Inuit have de facto self-government through the territorial legislature because they constitute 85 percent of the population, but other Canadians living there are equally eligible to vote. Although costly to maintain, Nunavut represents a system of government where local control prevails, where aboriginal self-government operates, yet where all residents participate within a public framework not based on race but on the legal equality of each person. The goal had been reached by pre-eminently democratic means, including direct voting by the people affected. Though non-binding, the three votes in 1982 and 1992 were stages in building historic momentum. Nunavut represented Inuit aspirations, grown stronger over the preceding two decades, to set up their own homeland, while for Ottawa, Nunavut became "a key symbol in its attempt to show Canadians and the world it is committed to native issues,"[22] and how combining aboriginal self-government with public community government is a basis for the harmony needed for successful government by and for all people living in the North.

VOTING TO BREAK CONFEDERATION: ROUND ONE, 1980

By spring 1980, a decade of turbulent political events had culminated in Quebecers facing a ballot choice on their province's future in Confederation. Back in 1969, Premier Jean-Jacques Bertrand had introduced Bill 55, the Referendum Act, in Quebec's National Assembly, and named a legislative Commission on the Constitution with himself as chair. Both measures had been promised by the Union Nationale in the election that brought the party back to power, and the diminutive, peppery premier was moving swiftly to implement the electoral mandate given his nationalist formation by voters.

Bertrand's ardent minister for the civil service, Marcel Masse, was especially strong for a referendum on constitutional matters. On November 20, 1969, he'd stated that a focused vote would be the best way to decide whether Quebec should secede from Canada. Addressing the International Relations Club at Université de Montréal, Masse said the question should be clearly worded: *Are you in favour of independence for Quebec?* He sought a referendum on the issue, rather than having it subsumed in a general election, because he wanted a clear decision, and one reached by the people of Quebec. "The day Quebec decides on its independence, it will certainly not be up to Ottawa, or Paris, or Abidjan," he declared. "It is to be decided by Quebec!"

The prospect of the province departing the union raised the uncertainty of how the Government of Canada would respond. Quebecers had the right to know, explained Masse, if they wish to proclaim independence now, what attitude Ottawa and Prime Minister Trudeau would take. "Will they leave the province free to decide, or will they use measures to crush the separatists, the *indépendantists*?"

The Quebec Liberal Party under Jean Lesage, still smarting from being ousted from office, was unsettled about holding a referendum. Yet Liberals saw the importance of people voting, so, wanting to be on the right side of history and to not abandon the Quebec cause to stronger nationalists, proposed several worthy amendments to Bill 55. One required distribution of information on the ballot question to the public, another creation of a Constitutional Council to oversee operation of any referendum.

By December, Quebec newspapers, covering these developments in the context of the Quebec government's "veiled threats of separatism," considered the positive role a referendum could play. A December 11 *Quebec Chronicle-Telegraph* editorial, "Referendum Only Answer to Classify Separatism," took exception to statements by Premier Bertrand and Marcel Masse about Quebec's possible move toward separatism. The editors considered their pronouncements just a lever for Quebec's government to extract its objectives from an upcoming constitutional conference.

When asked about Quebec voting to secede from Confederation in the near future, Premier Bertrand said it all depended on how patient Quebec's population might be. But Marcel Masse, profoundly passionate in his commitment to the cause, went all out: "Not only the Parti Québécois, but any government," he asserted, meaning the incumbent Union Nationale government, too, "could take Quebec to separatism, when Quebec wants to."

Again the *Chronicle-Telegraph* saw both sides. Commenting that "these honourable gentlemen have no right to use this reference on behalf of the Quebec electorate" despite whatever "secret desires" might burn in the hearts of some Union Nationale members, the paper said "it is believed by a great majority that Quebec will always be a strong and progressive Canadian province." However, because even editorial writers can't know what the people think, they hedged their bet: "But only a referendum will really tell. For this, the 'moment of truth' has arrived for all Quebecers, and for Canada — the sooner the better."[1]

By 1971, constitutional negotiations in British Columbia's capital city had produced an agreement, called the Victoria Charter, for changes in principle to the Constitution. Representing Quebec was Premier Robert Bourassa, whose Liberals had now replaced the Union Nationale government. In Victoria he agreed to the charter but back in Quebec City the premier withdrew support for the amendments, even though they'd been crafted to accommodate requirements of a more assertive Quebec. Under intense pressure from powerful Liberal cabinet minister Claude Castonguay and vigorous protest from *Le Devoir*'s influential editor Claude Ryan, the novice premier reversed his public commitment, creating adverse long-term consequences. With Quebec's Liberal government no longer supporting the Victoria Charter, putting the plan to provincial electors in a referendum never happened.

Interest in direct voting waned briefly but revived in the next wave of nationalist planning for Quebec's future. In the early 1970s, Jacques-Yvan Morin advised Parti Québécois leader René Lévesque that their route to power lay through skirting the traumatic question of separation from Canada and concentrating instead on social and economic issues and the record of Premier Bourassa's now-beleaguered Liberal government. Morin, top adviser to Quebec governments on constitutional matters from 1963 until 1971, had become a prominent member of the separatist party. His expedient for avoiding the hard issue of separatism was merely delay. The PQ still advocated a referendum on separating from Confederation, but now at some unspecified future date.

• • •

Also propelling 1980's referendum on Quebec's relationship with Confederation was the larger force of French-speaking Canadians' centuries-long "national" experience of surviving in British North America by withstanding assimilation.

In this historic quest, Quebec by 1980 had reinvented itself from within. For two decades, a revolution dubbed *tranquille* or "quiet" because it was transformative rather than violent had changed the province in education and agriculture, family life, and business enterprise. At first the exhilaration of throwing over the corporatist nationalism of the Maurice Duplessis era and the reactionary control of the Catholic Church fuelled the emerging new Quebec. Then *épanouissement*, or "liberation," energized further conquests.

That the province had changed internally was only half the story. As important, Quebec's shifting relations with Canada and the world formed a dynamic context for the future. By 1980, Quebecers faced a confusing tableau of change and continuity. Constitutionally, the change first came informally, within the existing framework of laws and institutions, through the "co-operative federalism" initiated by Prime Minister Lester Pearson. This was then extended by an "opting-out" formula by which Pearson's Liberal government allowed Quebec increasing freedom within Canada. A province not wanting to participate in a new Canada-wide program could set up an equivalent program and get federal funding, as Quebec did with its pension plan and other programs.

Continuity lay in the enduring threat Quebecers felt that the French language and culture would be submerged in a sea of English-speaking North Americans. Also, despite a federal system's benefits in allowing provinces their own government and jurisdictions, the divided loyalties that a two-tier state also fosters produced frustrating compromises and divided limited energies and resources into two separate orders of governance on the same territory over the same people. All that, plus the everlasting struggle to achieve mutual respect between French-speaking and English-speaking communities, made a country of their own appealing to many Québécois.

This amalgam of forces was hardly new. The confrontations they produce had played out before: at the turn of the twentieth century between Wilfrid Laurier and Henri Bourassa, in mid-century between Louis St. Laurent and Maurice Duplessis, and now these enduring dilemmas were being framed by Pierre Trudeau and René Lévesque. But this time the issue would be addressed not just by political leaders, clerics, editorial writers, and others atop Quebec's hierarchy. Now *all* voters in the province would collectively have their say on the fundamental reality of being a Quebecer. For the first time, the political culture of Quebec and the focused potential of ballot-box democracy reflected and reinforced one another. As Marcel Masse had emphasized, a referendum would be sharp and clear the way elections never could be.

• • •

Jacques-Yvan Morin's *étapiste* approach of gradual steps rather than one bold and alarming jump helped separatists avoid the deal-breaker issue of Quebec's outright independence. The Parti Québécois convention of 1974 officially adopted this strategy of gradualism. For true believers, though, the longer-term goal remained an independent country. After 1974 the Parti

Québécois refined *étapisme* into stages that appeared moderate and consensual: attainment of power through general election, a period of preparation, a first referendum on a mandate to negotiate with Ottawa, negotiations, a second referendum, conclusion of economic association with Canada, and declaration of independence.

Step one of this acclimatizing journey was successfully completed on November 15, 1976, when the Parti Québécois won the general election and took power. Across the country Canadians suddenly took seriously the prospect that the talk about Confederation breaking up would now be translated into action. With a separatist government controlling power in Quebec, the referendum became a topic of constant public discussion as the second phase of "preparation" began.

The Referendum Act initiated by the Union Nationale as Bill 55 in 1969 never became law, so on December 21, 1977, the Parti Québécois government introduced its own legislation, and by June 23, 1978, it had received third reading and Royal Assent. Quebec now had a permanent enabling statute by which the government could force the Confederation choice by ballot at the time of its choosing. The act included a key British precedent from the United Kingdom's 1975 referendum on the European Common Market: the "umbrella" requirement for two committees representing the Yes and No sides. Forcing all supporters of one option to work together, or at least coordinate campaign messaging and control campaign financing, benefits voters by ensuring a rational referendum process. The umbrella committees bring together disparate elements the way political parties do in election campaigns. In the ranks of Quebec's sovereignists and federalists are found the devout and the agnostic, capitalists and unionists, conservatives and socialists, Francophones, Anglophones, and Allophones (people whose first language is neither French nor English), the wealthy and the poor. By 1980, the advantage sovereignists had over federalists was that these differences had been smoothed over during a half decade devoted to a single higher purpose: unifying the separatist movement within the political party created by René Lévesque.

Meanwhile, other components of "preparation" ranged across a broad front. One was a sustained effort at providing good government — an end in itself, to be sure — but also a means of assuaging fears among those distrustful of a "separatist" government. This phase also entailed the subterranean work of political organization, with patient building and rebuilding of PQ campaign structures all across the province. More visible was the PQ's campaign of preparing the public mind.

A constant flow of publicity and promotion from the government's many departments and agencies reinforced a sense of cultural strength and national pride. The *péquistes* themselves had appropriated the symbols of Quebec: Maurice Duplessis's blue-and-white fleur-de-lys provincial flag, Gilles Vigneault's song "Mon pays" and celebratory ballad "Les gens du pays," and the very name *Québécois* for the party itself. The *péquistes* so completely insinuated their ideology and power quest into the historic destiny of Quebec that the two now appeared, to many, synonymous.

• • •

As the PQ government prepared for its referendum, Prime Minister Pierre Trudeau envisaged off-setting Canada-wide ballot questions on measures dealing with Confederation and the Constitution.

"Create counterweights" had long been a core concept of his political philosophy. In 1977 he'd proposed referendum legislation to enable a counterbalancing vote to any referendum launched by the Parti Québécois government on the separation question. On October 19 that year, the PM told the Commons his government would introduce legislation for national referendums. The national unity group in the Privy Council Office was drafting the bill and also preparing analysis of "unacceptable aspects" of the Quebec government's White Paper on Referendums.

Trudeau explained to MPs on October 20 that his government's intent in enacting enabling legislation for referendums "would not be to change in any sense our parliamentary system." He believed "the responsibility for legislation and policies should rest in Parliament." Accepting that Canadians live under a form of representative democracy, and not seeking to change that, he added that his government "would not want enabling legislation which would permit any government at any time to come forward with referendums to solve problems that the House of Commons or the government find too hot to handle." Rather, direct voting "would be a tool used perhaps only for a limited number of years to permit us to deal with constitutional questions and questions of national unity." An Act Respecting

Public Referendums in Canada on Questions Relating to the Constitution of Canada, short title the Canada Referendum Act, was accordingly introduced on April 3, 1978. The same bill was reintroduced that autumn in a new session of Parliament on October 18, 1978, and advanced to debate on second reading on January 2, 1979.

When Marc Lalonde, minister of intergovernmental relations, spoke in the Commons on December 12, 1978, in support of the Trudeau government's referendum plans, he specifically emphasized "circumstances when such direct involvement of the Canadian public could be of the utmost importance." Most significantly, he began with a referendum's educational role. "It could serve to acquaint the large majority of our citizens with the importance and character of proposals for constitutional changes," he noted, "and permit the people to express themselves directly on these proposals." Even if the proposals were supported by the great majority of federal and provincial governments and by the important political parties, "such public participation on the process of constitutional change could be very valuable."

Lalonde stressed that a ballot question is no substitute for Parliament or for the rules of constitutional amendment. It is "an addition to the present procedures which might provide extra relevance or legitimacy." He rightly linked legitimacy and consent of the governed as being essential in a democratic society. "This involvement of the public in the constitutional reform could directly demonstrate the legitimacy of the Constitution and help transform this legal document — which is out of necessity somewhat dry — into a people's statement of their basic principles which would guide them over many decades." A political pragmatist, Lalonde also believed direct public involvement "could serve to guide the federal and provincial governments, should the process of constitutional revision ever become blocked."

The House of Commons again echoed earlier shopworn debates over whether direct voting is compatible with a parliamentary system. Some MPs dwelt on the types of issues that were, or weren't, referendum-worthy. Many MPs, especially Liberals, seeing Pierre Trudeau and Marc Lalonde favour referendums, became inspired to support direct voting on issues, highlighting again, just as Laurier and King had earlier, a prime minister's overarching influence in Canada's parliamentary system and how by their magnetism they can attract MPs to policies and programs such as direct democracy.

This was as close as Canada had yet come to getting general enabling legislation for referendums on the statute books. Yet the vaunted bill never came to a vote. There was resistance in the cabinet. Despite two of the government's most senior leaders, the PM and the minister of intergovernmental affairs, wanting the measure enacted, a third strong Quebecer didn't. Jean Chrétien vowed the referendum legislation would only become law "over my dead body." The measure died on the order paper when the Thirtieth Parliament was dissolved, leading to the general election of May 22, 1979, in which the Trudeau government was defeated.

• • •

Meanwhile, in Quebec, step three of the PQ program — the referendum itself — occurred more or less on schedule. Even here the instinct for *étapisme* prevailed. The ballot question came first, a third of a year before announcement of the referendum date. Its wording, holding the *Guinness World Records* for longest referendum question until ousted by one from the Northwest Territories in 1982, was announced December 20, 1979, in the midst of the federal election campaign:

> *The Government of Quebec has made public its proposal to negotiate a new agreement with the rest of Canada, based on the equality of nations; this agreement would enable Quebec to acquire the exclusive power to make its laws, levy its taxes, and establish relations abroad — in other words, sovereignty — and at the same time, to maintain with Canada an economic association including a common currency; no change in political status resulting from these negotiations will be effected without approval by the people through another referendum; on these terms, do you give the Government of Quebec the mandate to negotiate the proposed agreement between Quebec and Canada?*

The PQ government sought to improve its chances by softening the hard goal of sovereignty-association, and consistent with *étapisme*, focus more obtusely only on form, strategy, and procedure — a mandate to negotiate.

Yet Quebecers knew what they were being asked to decide. It was, after all, the perennial question. Even so, one could rightly wonder what, exactly, "sovereignty-association" entailed.

The ballot question's concept of "sovereignty for Quebec and a new form of association with Canada" shrouded truth in generalities and couched ambition in ambiguity. For Lévesque, it was less a question, more a quest to discover Confederation's outer limits of flexibility, in order to attain the best of both worlds.

Although "sovereignty-association" contained trace elements from Quebec's long history, since Lévesque built on prior concepts of others, the expression *sovereignty-association* was his own creation. In the early 1960s, he'd begun calling for an "associate state" relationship between Quebec and the rest of Canada. He wasn't alone in seeking to verbalize a different Quebec-Canada relationship.

In 1964 Liberal Premier Jean Lesage, senior spokesperson for Quebec's Quiet Revolution, toured western Canada to promote "particular status" for the province, which journalist Peter Desbarats saw as "another catch-phrase used at the time to describe Quebec's political objectives in Confederation." A different term came into vogue in 1965's federal election when the New Democratic Party supported a "two-nation" theory. To Desbarats, this formulation "illustrated both the benevolence and vagueness of English-Canada's response to Quebec's new sense of special destiny."[2]

Two years later the Progressive Conservative Party of Canada adopted *deux nations* as some sort of policy. Like most slogan definitions of a revamped federalism, the "two-nations" theory appeared to recognize Quebec as the national homeland of French Canadians without venturing very far into the concept's implications.

After 1966, when Daniel Johnson led the Union Nationale back to power in Quebec with his pledge for "equality or independence," Quebec's nationalistic Liberals, ousted from office by even stronger nationalists, became obsessed with trying to define anew the terms of Quebec's "special status" in Confederation.[3] There was no end to expressing this old idea in new ways. One version described Quebec as a "distinct society within Canada." In time that got truncated to *distinct society*, a meaningless term because the province and its society were only "distinct" *within* Confederation's edifice, not separate from it.

A province governed by a codified law system unique to it, having linguistic and religious majorities not matched in other provinces, a social order evolved from a feudal landholding system and parish structure unknown elsewhere in Canada, a land colonized by one European monarchy, then conquered militarily by another the way no other part of Canada had been, was unquestionably distinct *within Canada*.

It was in this political and intellectual climate that Lévesque rebranded Quebec independence as "sovereignty-association," his own best answer to the four-hundred-year-old question about how to be French in America. His book *Option Quebec* explained how a sovereign Quebec state (with its own army, laws, and external relations) would remain in an economic or customs union with Canada.[4] Lévesque quit the Liberal Party to openly advocate the cause. He launched Mouvement Souveraineté-Association to accommodate the various ideologies, organizational structures, personalities, rivalries, and competing tactics of disparate elements in Quebec society that supported independence. Without unity the separatists' innumerable fracture lines hobbled purposeful action. It was from this disparate yet single-minded collectivity that in turn the Parti Québécois next emerged, Lévesque its leader, "sovereignty-association" its centrepiece program, and from 1976, the reins of power his.

• • •

On April 15, 1980, a confident Premier Lévesque announced the date everyone in Quebec and across Canada had been in suspense waiting for: May 20, 1980. This would be the "historic day," he said, when a popular vote on the question of sovereignty-association would give Quebecers the chance to declare "if they are satisfied with their position as a permanent minority in the present regime, or if they want a new deal." The premier emphasized the "equality" of Quebecers and the need to end minority status with other Canadians.

Key to the referendum was formation of the two umbrella organizations to align the many pro and con groups and focus debate. Members of the National Assembly and groups supporting either option had to register with the umbrella committees. The Referendum Act restricted campaign activities of political parties and groups to the two committees.

All federal parties, the Quebec Liberal Party, and some Union Nationale members of the National Assembly joined the No committee. The Parti Québécois and some former Union Nationale members of the assembly formed the core of the Yes committee.[5] The *péquistes*, anticipating reasonable unanimity on their side of the question and relative peace under the Yes umbrella, hoped that forcing the disparate groups opposed to Quebec's departure from Confederation into a single structure would produce organizational calamity. Yet Claude Ryan, editor of *Le Devoir* and now leader of the Quebec Liberal Party and chair of the No committee, saw only harmony in his ranks.

At a preliminary No committee gathering in Quebec City, authorized representatives from eight political parties, four federal and four provincial, plus representatives from seven non-partisan organizations, publicly agreed to coordinate their efforts. Ryan found their discussions "cordial" and the parties involved "mutually respectful."[6]

However, although the referendum question had been public since mid-December 1979, the No committee only held its first organizational meeting on March 27, 1980 — not eight weeks from voting. Only now did federal Liberals catch "their first glimpse of Ryan's disorganization." A big organizational chart on display had many boxes, most void of any name. A plan "had been devised but there were no people yet to make it work." This situation, reported authors Robert Sheppard and Michael Valpy, combined with Ryan's repeated snubbing of his federal counterparts, nearly fulfilled "the PQ's prophesy that all the squabbling groups would congregate under the No umbrella."[7]

The struggle itself ranged from the economics of Quebec and the pocketbook of individual Quebecers, to Quebec's cultural life in the French language, newly recognized rights and freedoms, historical imperatives, and the inherited attitudes of people — be they aboriginal voters, *pure laine* Quebecers with centuries of family history, or new French-speaking citizens from Haiti or Allophones from elsewhere. The gravity of the issue required all political leaders to clarify their position on Quebec's future relationship with Canada. Responses were emotional and intellectual, boring and humorous. Witnessing it all, stand-up comedian Yves Deschamps concluded: "All we want is an independent Quebec within a strong and united Canada!"

Central to the Yes campaign were three theses advanced in the Quebec government's 118-page white paper *La nouvelle entente Québec-Canada*, published in French- and English-language editions at the end of 1979. First, the *Québécois* have a unique history that justifies an independent destiny as a people. Second, sustained efforts to make federalism work on behalf of the people of Quebec had borne little fruit, and federalism promised an unsatisfactory future. Third, Quebec is a land with a future of its own, rich in human and material resources. Throughout the document, it was clear that although the ballot question asked only for a mandate to negotiate an altered relationship with Confederation, the government's long-term intent was making Quebec an independent country.

On January 10, 1980 the Liberal Party of Quebec countered with *A New Canadian Federation,* its 141-page document with twenty-nine recommendations for federal-provincial relations, the thoroughness and detail of it reflecting the careful hand of Claude Ryan. Rather blandly, this policy statement became known, from the colour of its cover, as the "Beige Paper." Like the PQ, the Liberals presented a history of Quebec, but one substantially at variance with the PQ version. Because Liberals believed a constantly better deal was attainable for Quebec within Confederation, the Beige Paper concentrated on how Liberal negotiators would seek division of provincial and federal powers in a made-over Confederation agreement.

The Quebec Liberal position on constitutional change was also a response to Pierre Trudeau and the federal Liberals' view of Canada's future, sharing their advocacy for a renewed federalism while parting company by envisaging a more decentralized federation. The Quebec Liberals argued that the Canadian Constitution would protect the "distinct personality" of Quebec and ensure the principle of "equal partnership" between the federal and provincial governments. They proposed amending the Constitution in line with the Victoria Charter, a remarkable shift in Claude Ryan's thinking; this could all have been over in 1971 if he hadn't forced Robert Bourassa to renounce that earlier constitutional agreement.

The Parti Québécois denounced the Beige Paper. So did the powerful nationalist Saint-Jean-Baptiste Society, describing it as a "Black Paper" in which Mr. Ryan was "throwing sand in the eyes of Quebecers."[8]

Meanwhile, in Ottawa, the recently elected Progressive Conservative Prime Minister Joe Clark claimed Ryan's views of the "new federation" paralleled his own but reserved the right to disagree on individual elements.[9] For their part, the federal Liberals sought to put the Beige Paper on the back burner and simply echoed Pierre Trudeau's benign observation that the proposals constituted "a very good basis for discussion," saying little more. Trudeau could hardly repudiate his provincial counterpart, noted political observer R.B. Byers, "but the gap between the Beige Paper proposals and the more centralist views of the federal Liberals loomed large."[10]

The Quebec National Assembly debated the wording of the ballot question in March, and from then until April 14, the two sides concentrated on organizing their campaigns, set to officially begin on April 15. A dominant pre-campaign issue was how the referendum could be a mechanism for securing change. Each side, suggest authors Kenneth McRoberts and Dale Posgate, claimed to have the best strategy for changing the Quebec-Canada relationship. "Proponents of the Yes vote argued that only a successful referendum could *débloquer* the present impasse in discussion of a new Canadian Constitution. Proponents for No countered that a Yes vote would in fact reinforce the impasse, since sovereignty-association is unacceptable to the rest of Canada."[11]

All principal players agreed the question raised by the referendum should be settled in Quebec. "This referendum will involve Quebecers only," said Premier Lévesque emphatically, echoing Marcel Masse's assertion more than a decade earlier. "Any intervention, federal or otherwise, would be rejected as a manifestation of insupportable tutelage."[12] Claude Ryan envisaged the federal Liberals having "exactly the same role on the committee as the by-then decrepit Union Nationale party." Federal participation was "acceptable," Ryan told federal Liberals, but the Quebec Liberal Party was fully capable of handling the referendum on its own.[13] Joe Clark's Progressive Conservative government fell in line with this hands-off stance, explaining that the prime minister should "stay out of the battle entirely and so preserve his authority for the morning after R-Day"[14] as if contemplating a Yes win.

Then, as is invariably the case in a campaign, something unexpected happened.

• • •

The federal Liberals defeated Joe Clark's government in a budget vote in the House, bringing on a general election.[15] Pierre Trudeau, who'd retired, first reprised his position as party leader and then reclaimed the prime ministership. He'd turned the balance in the Commons by winning seventy-three of Quebec's seventy-five seats. Collapse of the Clark government surprised just about everyone, but in Quebec it utterly dismayed *péquistes*. The PQ had plotted its referendum strategy around a federal villain expected to be invisible.

Pierre Trudeau had criticized Joe Clark repeatedly for not defending federal interests in Quebec. During the election campaign, Trudeau mostly avoided the referendum topic and what it implied, though in one departure in Newfoundland, "his eyes flashed and his voice crackled with emotion." Trudeau, observed national political writer Jeffrey Simpson, was "eloquent, *engagé*, and electric while he defended his conception of Canada."[16] Trudeau echoed Laurier and other French Canadians who saw all Canada, not just one province, as their home. "I want to offer you a large vision and a grander dream. It's a vision where Canadians grow strong by helping each other. That's why the Liberal Party is not asking you to choose between Newfoundland and Canada. And in my province ... I've been telling my people that they don't have to choose between Quebec and Canada. You choose the better of both worlds."[17]

For "Operation Truth," as some called the referendum, the elements of political battle now realigned. Not only was Lévesque forced to change his approach, but the methodical plodding of Claude Ryan, who'd been making No pilgrimages to all the smaller centres and familiar parishes of Quebec, was jostled aside by the assertive federal Liberals craving a big-league showdown.

Pierre Trudeau had been writing since the 1950s in opposition to nationalist tendencies. His view of history taught that a country should never base itself upon a single religion, nationality, or ideology; doing so had caused innumerable religious, national, and ideological wars. States, being imperfect, shouldn't claim absolute sovereignty. Man belongs to himself first of all, not to any particular race or language. In French Canada especially, nationalism often valued too highly all that distinguished it from others and resisted all change, even progress, from the outside. In Trudeau's view, a nationalistic government becomes essentially intolerant, discriminatory, and totalitarian. Since nationalism could destroy either French or English Canada from within, the better approach would be to renounce nationalism and pursue broader, more humane ideals.[18]

Trudeau's quest to make his well-developed intellectual understanding triumph in the Yes/No arena of the referendum would require something special.

Claude Ryan debated the literal wording of the ballot question in an arid and academic fashion. René Lévesque spoke about its higher meaning, appealing to Quebecers' pride, the continuity of history, and to equality. When the battle lines first formed, one choice was a formalistic seeking of a renewed Canada through a methodical restructuring of the Constitution. The other was an unstructured and instinctive adventure to establish a new country outside Confederation. That pivotal choice was now about to be reframed.

• • •

On March 3, 1980, just eleven weeks before referendum day, the new Liberal cabinet was sworn in at Ottawa. Fourteen of thirty-three portfolios went to French Canadians. An exhausted Jean Chrétien, who'd become justice minister, agreed to assume responsibility for the federal side of the referendum campaign, his third major campaign in a year. This "brought to the fight the emotional patriotism that had been missing from the federalist side," observed Sheppard and Valpy about Chrétien, "as well as a seemingly untiring talent for placating the haughty differences between Trudeau and Ryan."[19]

On April 15, Trudeau addressed the Commons shortly after Lévesque announced the May 20 date for referendum voting. A month earlier Claude Ryan had spoken in the Quebec assembly with clinical logic and professorial detachment appraising Lévesque's "sovereignty-association" concept. Trudeau now spoke in the same manner, but as prime minister of Canada. What Lévesque pledged to Quebecers — the satisfaction of sovereignty blended with the assurance of association — simply couldn't be achieved. Trudeau stressed that the dual goals of sovereignty and association were inseparable. The PM explained that association was a goal Lévesque could never "negotiate," because premiers of the other nine provinces had already rejected the idea. Thus, without association, there could be no sovereignty-association. Should Lévesque decide to "negotiate" directly with Ottawa, continued Trudeau, he as prime minister couldn't grant association because Quebecers had just given him and his Liberal MPs "a massive mandate to exercise sovereignty over Quebec and the rest of the country."[20]

Trudeau deduced that all Lévesque could achieve with a strong Yes vote would be an impasse. The PM's reasoning might have seemed abstract to English-speaking Canadians, but for many Quebecers, as Richard Gwyn noted, "it went straight to the heart of the matter." After Trudeau's speech, for the first time, *péquiste* spokespersons on hotline shows "found themselves having to explain to callers why a Yes vote would lead anywhere except deadlock."[21]

Premier Lévesque believed the other premiers would negotiate association, that indeed, they would negotiate just about anything. Yet in the public mind, Trudeau had successfully planted significant doubt about Lévesque's proposal.

The referendum question, at this elevated level of politics, now resolved itself into a matter of trust. Quebecers had heard endlessly about different constitutional possibilities, often expressed in slogans. But the deeper issue for most Quebecers involved something more. It centred on the ability to discern and illuminate — as George-Étienne Cartier, John A. Macdonald, Wilfrid Laurier, Henri Bourassa, Louis St. Laurent, and Pierre Trudeau each had in their turn — how to make the best of both worlds. As Quebecers increasingly focused on marking their ballots, choosing between Yes or No boiled down to whether the PQ's option was credible.[22]

During the *péquistes'* "preparation phase" for the referendum, they'd aimed to establish trust for themselves and credibility for the sovereignty-association option. The No campaign's new thrust was to destroy all such credibility, working a pincer movement. Ryan's methodical campaign and detailed Beige Paper pleaded for rational constitutional progress, while on a second front the federal Liberals, especially Trudeau and Chrétien, launched a more aggressive campaign to undermine credibility of the PQ option and trust in Lévesque. Arguing against separatism with "extreme tactical subtlety," the prime minister rejected the PQ's option and showed that Lévesque couldn't deliver it.[23]

Yet Trudeau recognized the general desire for change. To ignore this force would be to forfeit victory. The PM pledged immediate moves on serious constitutional reform if the No side won. He avoided details, because his views would have appeared too centrist for the campaign's tactical needs and Claude Ryan's stance, but he wanted to harness the impetus for change and bring about constitutional amendments he himself envisaged — patriation, entrenching the "economic union" within the Constitution, and a Charter of Rights and Freedoms.

In this enlarged context, the "renovated federalism" that Ryan proposed in the Beige Paper now appeared the more credible option, even though Trudeau never endorsed the concept because he considered it too decentralist. Despite their differences, Trudeau and Ryan both understood the real debate in the referendum was about separation. Ryan thus promoted his Beige Paper proposals as a workable approach for the future, a contrast to the utopian, less credible, and economically dangerous PQ option, while Trudeau undermined the separatists' credibility. In combination the two Liberal leaders gave Quebecers the clear impression there could be major change in Confederation's design.

Yet the voting outcome, polling suggested, remained uncertain. An extra boost was still needed.

• • •

Late in the campaign Trudeau made a promise to Quebecers during an electrifying performance deep in the heart of *péquiste* territory at the Paul Sauvé Arena in East End Montreal. In what he called "a most solemn commitment," Canada's prime minister pledged that, following a No vote, "we would immediately take action to renew the Constitution and we will not stop until we have done that." He announced Quebec MPs were laying themselves and their parliamentary seats on the line in telling Quebecers to vote No. Then the prime minister added "a solemn declaration to all Canadians." He told people in "the other provinces that we will not agree to your interpreting a No vote as an indication that everything is fine and can remain as it was before."[24]

The campaign necessarily also dealt with economic issues because Lévesque's option envisaged a continuing economic union with Canada, thus making projections about sovereignty's economic impact on Quebec and Canada central to the debate. Economists and businessmen joined politicians to offer the electorate a cornucopia of statistics and scenarios.

Lévesque and the *péquistes* referred with proud confidence to Quebec's vast natural resources, portraying the province as an advanced industrial society of six million people; standing twenty-third in world GNP and ninth in world GNP per capita. The PQ view was that Quebec would be economically viable with or without an association with Canada.

The *péquistes* argued that economic relationships between Quebec and the other provinces in Confederation constituted a two-way street. In the event of a complete rupture between Quebec and the rest of the country, they admitted that of the 181,000 jobs in Quebec depending on trade with Ontario, 130,000 could be lost rapidly without association, but argued that the reverse was the same, the impact just as real. A split would cost Ontario up to 85,000 of its 190,000 jobs dependent on trade with Quebec. "With that degree of interdependence," commented John Fitzmaurice, "the mutual interest in an association was self-evident."[25]

Against this, the No camp, particularly Ottawa's federalist Liberals, "made heavy and demagogic use of the economic arguments to paint an apocalyptic picture of the dangers of separation."[26] Their data made a strong argument about the general level of Quebecers' economic well-being, progress in industrial expansion, emergence of new service industries, and growth of economic activity in virtually all sectors — all achieved within the context of Quebec as part of Confederation. Appealing not only to self-interest but to fear, federalists orchestrated the parade of Brink's trucks, presumably laden with securities and money, leaving Montreal and crossing over to the safe haven of Ontario at the provincial border, a visual drama that television news relayed to electors on the eve of voting.

The umbrella committees and the campaign rules controlled advertising and publicity, but not all temptations were resisted. The Liberal government in Ottawa and the Parti Québécois government in Quebec City both advertised in ways that broke the spirit, if not the letter, of the Referendum Act. The Department of National Health and Welfare's advertising in Quebec against alcohol abuse (*Non, merci ... ça se dit bien*) conveniently duplicated the *Non, Merci* slogan of the No campaign while mocking campaign spending limits. The federal government refused to submit to the umbrella committee regime, denouncing it as infringing freedom of expression and freedom of association. The Government of Canada's campaign became such an irritant to the Quebec government and the Parti Québécois that it ended up before the courts. The Superior Court of Quebec refused to intervene, saying it lacked jurisdiction to issue a restraining injunction against Ottawa.[27] As well, Quebec's Referendum Council ruled the federal government wasn't bound by the Referendum Act.[28] Such alleged impotence of Quebec's statute law governing a referendum in the province was then contested in court, with the Quebec Court of Appeal holding that "since the statute did not explicitly refer to the federal government, it was not bound to obey it."[29] The federal government quickly erected billboard ads throughout

Quebec to reiterate Ottawa's sudden concern about the scourge of "alcohol abuse" with its simple clear message: *Non, Merci!*

Two wrongs don't make a right, but they might offset each other. The televised presentation of the debates of the National Assembly on the referendum question, while technically outside the referendum period, didn't allocate equal time to the Yes and No sides. And just as Ottawa exhibited grave concern for alcohol abuse in Quebec, the provincial government suddenly became fixated on automobile safety. An advertising campaign for increased seat-belt use inundated Quebecers with reminders to "fasten up" in a wordplay that also meant "fasten yourself to Quebec."

Another provincial government intervention in the campaign was repeated publicity of the referendum question in full-page advertisements and television broadcasts. These advertisements seemed like Yes advertising because the *péquiste* government had crafted the wording to encourage a Yes answer. However, instructing Quebec voters on the ballot question fell to the director general of elections, whose office is neutral in such matters, rather than Quebec's PQ government, which had a stake in the outcome.

Campaign interventions by entities outside the Yes and No umbrella organizations also took the form of institutional advertisements in newspapers and company statements containing strong implications about the importance of a particular result in the referendum. Whenever a referendum engages a fundamental issue, each side can be expected to promote its cause to the limit. Overall, interventions by the federal and provincial governments and others seem to have cancelled themselves out. Moreover, news media generally provided balanced presentation of the question and the campaign, independent from the advertising campaigns.

Given the weight and consequences of issues at play, it isn't surprising that emotion was at the forefront. Fistfights erupted at family reunions and elsewhere, leaving emotional scars on the participants, including members of Jean Chrétien's extended family. Despite these physical expressions of political views, the campaign was remarkably tolerant. Quebecers showed how to have fun with an issue, with the jests of stand-up comedians, quips in the street, face-painting with red maple leaves and blue fleur-de-lys, rival posters on the same apartment balcony, signs on the backs of buses, the fleece of a roadside sheep painted *Bààà-oui*. Quebecers' *joie de vivre* helped transform even this primordial struggle in charming ways.

• • •

On May 20, 1980, 3,473,752 Québécois voted on the question of granting their provincial government a mandate to negotiate with the rest of Canada the Parti Québécois' formula of sovereignty-association. "The choice should be as easy," René Lévesque had encouraged voters, "for the heart as for the mind."

The result was hardly lopsided, yet it was unequivocal: 59.56 percent voted No, and 40.44 percent Yes. The participation rate of the electorate was extremely high at 85.61 percent. Rejected ballots constituted 1.74 percent of the total. In absolute numbers, 1,485,761 Quebecers supported the Yes option, and 2,187,991 rejected it.

Many opinion polls had been published prior to the vote. One of them, the final Hamilton-Pinard survey, which most closely approximated the balloting results, indicated women more stridently opposed separation than men. During the campaign, PQ cabinet minister Lise Payette committed an apparent faux pas by criticizing women not supporting the PQ option as "Yvettes" — a stereotype for old-fashioned unliberated housewives of Quebec. This accusation triggered a fourteen-thousand-strong protest rally from the province's women. Research by pollsters and political scientists suggested a sizable majority of middle-aged and older voters, especially women, rejected the PQ's option on voting day.

While the referendum was defeated generally throughout the province, the margins were most decisive in metropolitan Montreal. Of the total provincial votes, Montrealers cast more than a third (34.5 percent), with over two-thirds (67 percent) refusing a mandate to negotiate sovereignty-association. Significantly, this result was fairy uniform across the city's linguistic and cultural communities. The province's concentrated anglophone population in Montreal voted well over 90 percent against the PQ option, a big number, although fewer than 24 percent of Montreal's voters are Anglophones and only five of the city's thirty-seven ridings contained a majority of Anglophones. Montreal's francophone ridings *also* voted No by significant margins, with some 60 percent of Montreal's Francophones rejecting the PQ option. "Voting appeared to have been close enough in the rest of the province to make the scale of the government's defeat attributable, above all," suggested political scientist Elliot Feldman, "to its failure in Montreal."[30]

After the vote, deeper statistical analysis and interpretation of voting patterns continued to be made. Of Quebec's 110 ridings — which were the counting areas for referendum ballots — the PQ won seventy-one in 1976's general election, but only fifteen of them gave majority support to the PQ option in the referendum. Only one riding in the province, after not electing a PQ member to the assembly in 1976, voted a majority Yes. Such differences might be attributed to the different natures of an election race and a referendum vote, but another statistic effectively nullified that consideration. In 1976 the PQ won twenty-nine ridings by more than 50 percent of the popular vote, and in 1980 fully eighteen of these twenty-nine ridings voted more than 50 percent *against* the government's referendum proposal. In short, ridings that delivered a PQ majority in 1976 rejected the party's most deeply desired policy.[31] The PQ's *étapiste* plan had been to win government by playing down the referendum on separation. The two rounds of voting, in 1976 and 1980, suggest that many Quebecers just wanted good government for their province, not to break up Confederation. A second important lesson that can be gleaned from comparing the results of the two campaigns is that a general election covers a diverse range of relatively smaller matters, but a referendum is exclusively focused on one transcending issue and that forcing a specific choice clarifies a hard decision the way nothing else can.

Some post-referendum interpretations sought to justify the May 20, 1980, results in ways to fuel the sovereignist cause. For instance, participating as a panellist at Université de Montréal in an April 3, 1992, colloquium on *"Démocratie et référendum — la procédure référendaire: bilan et perspectives,"* I debated one of my co-panellists, professor André Bernard of Université du Québec à Montréal, over his analysis of the francophone and anglophone vote. He argued that "real Québécois" (meaning Francophones) had voted Yes, and that the referendum was just another example of how French Canada's authentic voice was constrained by the prevailing structures and arrangements. Bernard's interpretation was underpinned by emotional and xenophobic appeal to Quebec nationalists. I suggested he couldn't have it both ways. If policies were to be *based on the position and legitimate needs of French-speaking people*, then one had to take account of the million Canadian Francophones living outside Quebec — not simply turn one's back on them, which was implicit in the sovereignist project for an independent Quebec and explicit in the extent to which Canada's "French Fact" was being identified with the Province of Quebec to the neglect, and even dismissal, of Francophones residing elsewhere throughout Canada. On the other hand, if the sovereignist project was *based on Quebec as a political entity, and asserting rights and powers for Quebec as a nation-state jurisdiction with distinct borders*, it required that everyone residing within Quebec's boundaries be taken into account and treated equally. To differentiate between residents within Quebec, as André Bernard was, and suggest the votes of some shouldn't count in determining public policy, was the same thinking, I contended, that led to apartheid in South Africa and segregation in the United States.

• • •

In the immediate aftermath of 1980's referendum, the broad political interpretations of the process and its result were positive and optimistic. Federalist forces interpreted the outcome as a clear indication by Quebecers to proceed with the renewal of Confederation.

Ahead would be efforts to entrench Canada's economic union within the Constitution, craft an amending formula so future changes to the Constitution could be made in Canada, not Britain, and inaugurate Pierre Trudeau's envisaged Charter of Rights and Freedoms, which he'd first promoted as justice minister at the Canadian Bar Association's 1967 annual meeting in Quebec City.

Another overdue feature of constitutional renewal was to deal with Parliament's unnecessary second house, which all provinces having them had abolished without anyone missing their redundant presence. Trudeau's own justice minister, John Turner, had concluded in his University of British Columbia thesis more than two decades earlier that Canada's Senate was "a functionless oddity." Yet premiers who governed without the needless duplication of a second legislative chamber, including newly created unicameral provinces Alberta and Saskatchewan, joined in this quixotic mission for an extreme makeover of Parliament's unaccountable law-making body, even seeking to separate the Senate from its dismal past by rebranding it as the "House of the Federation."

But as "First Ministers Conferences" dragged through the early 1980s, intransigent premiers balked at many of the PM's proposals — from how to provide veto rights in amending the Constitution so smaller provinces wouldn't be overpowered, to provisions ending interprovincial trade barriers and otherwise making Confederation an economic union as well as a political one. Facing stalemate, Prime Minister Trudeau proposed a referendum. He envisaged taking his proposals over the premiers' heads to Canadian voters directly — not the first time he'd seen the utility of the people themselves helping force a choice.

20

VOTING ON CONFEDERATION'S MAKEOVER: GETTING TO THE CHARLOTTETOWN ACCORD

The major effort to change the Constitution promised by Prime Minister Trudeau in exchange for a No vote in Quebec's 1980 referendum had produced by 1981 the Charter of Rights and Freedoms and a constitution-amending formula, but not the "entrenchment of the economic union in the Constitution" he had ardently sought, nor, most ironic of all, no buy-in from Quebec.

Quebec's exclusion was not because the province had a separatist government but because of how the deal had been reached by the first ministers. A motion condemning the constitutional changes without Quebec's ratification passed unanimously in the National Assembly, including support from all Liberals members. Quebec remained legally bound by the Constitution, but political disenchantment was summed up by how the province's National Assembly symbolically invoked the Constitution's "notwithstanding" clause for all legislation. Brian Mulroney said, "Quebec had been abandoned on the snowbank!"

In 1984 Mulroney's Progressive Conservatives brought a change of government to Ottawa, winning the general election with organizational support in Quebec from Liberal leader Robert Bourassa. A year later Canada's new PM and Quebec's resurrected premier, who'd suffered humiliating elector defeat in 1976 but led the provincial Liberals back into office in December 1985, sought to complete this unfinished constitutional business. An agreement on several amendments was reached by all premiers and the PM. This "Meech Lake Accord" was a determined act by federalist Quebecers, as Prime Minister Mulroney put it, "to reintegrate the province constitutionally back into the Canadian family."

The accord contained no surprises. It was short, incorporating points considered essential by Premier Bourassa, adjusted to perspectives of several other premiers. Recognizing that Quebec constituted "a distinct society within Canada" was one point, a statement of fact to accommodate the province's sociological and cultural uniqueness without dishonouring the country's other regions. A second point established the principle of equality of all provinces. A third resolved jurisdictional overlap on immigration. There was some tweaking of the amending formula for future constitutional changes. Another provision dealt with "opting out," already an established practice since the 1960s, whereby *any province* could sidestep a "national program" of the federal government by creating a comparable program of its own and get funding from Ottawa to operate it. Likewise, the reality of the Supreme Court of Canada, created by an act of Parliament in 1875, would be formally entrenched in the Constitution. Finally, the Meech Lake Accord sought to constitutionalize "executive federalism" by requiring annual first ministers' conferences, even specifying for 1988's agenda the topics of fisheries and the Senate.

The accord was initially well received. At a University of Ottawa conference on the subject, former Liberal cabinet minister Monique Bégin held up the signature page, bearing the names of all first ministers representing different political parties, and called it "the most beautiful document in Canada." Polling showed strong support in Quebec and across the country, too, where grateful relief greeted reconciliation of long-standing distemper over Quebec's role in Confederation. The agreement even included the motion Parliament and all ten provincial legislatures would pass to green-light these several constitutional amendments.

At this juncture critics of "executive federalism" complained the deal had been thrashed out by "eleven men in suits in the backrooms" who also controlled the legislatures that would vote ratification. The most effective answer to this valid criticism about an insider process changing our country's constitution *should* have been a national referendum to ratify the proposed changes.

The legislatures would still need to pass their set-piece motions, but the people would first deliberate on the matter and signal to elected representatives by a majority vote Yes or No whether there was public buy-in for the Meech Lake Accord. By directly asking citizens *Are you in favour of implementing the Meech Lake Accord?* when those who'd negotiated it were on hand to explain their agreement and when public interest was both focused on the accord and supportive of national reconciliation, the probability was that a majority Yes vote would not only speed ratification but increase the accord's political legitimacy by the best available means for a self-governing democracy.

• • •

However, legislators had a three-year deadline, until June 1990, to ratify. Why the first ministers gave themselves so leisurely a timetable rather than a deadline commensurate with the gravity of the matter remains one of those "What if …?" speculations of our political history. Lulled into complacency by that amount of time, and simultaneously encountering the governing establishment's short-sighted opposition to citizens voting on important issues, the Mulroney government failed to hold a national referendum. The fact there was no enabling law under which to do so was conveniently invoked by those opposed to ballot questions, which readily sealed the decision for those who assumed approving Meech Lake would be a slam dunk.

The Mulroney government would, instead of a referendum, just leave the easy matter of provincial ratification to the custodial guidance of a single federal cabinet minister. Lowell Murray, a long-time Tory backroom presence whose accomplishments were more than offset by a consistent pattern of political misjudgments, had been repaid for his allegiance to the party with a Senate seat by Prime Minister Joe Clark, then named government leader in the upper house by Prime Minister Mulroney. Now, in the context of gaining ratification of the Meech Lake Accord, he was handed the country's most sensitive portfolio as minister for federal-provincial relations.

Premier Bourassa expected fairly rapid approval. He envisaged Quebec's National Assembly voting to ratify Meech after all the other provinces had done so — a symbolic final act in "rejoining the Canadian family." Senator Murray pursued his obscure backstage methods. Time passed. With nothing happening, a chagrined Robert Bourassa decided he had to kick-start the process and get the fading accord back on the public radar. Quebec's legislative assembly thus became *first* to vote approval of the amendments. Elsewhere across the country, those with less than charitable views about French Canadians figured the deal must be really good for Quebec, given its "rush" to endorse it.

Steady passage of time was an enemy of ratification in other ways, too. Elections in New Brunswick and Newfoundland brought to office as premiers

Frank McKenna and Clyde Wells, both of whom discovered unusual theoretical grounds to oppose the Meech Lake Accord. The Newfoundland legislature had by this time already ratified the accord, but Wells had his newly elected majority rescind the province's motion. Now the process was actually running in reverse gear. New Brunswick's legislature, having not yet voted on the motion and under new management with McKenna, would postpone for a couple more years.

These reversals and delays gave time for doubt to foment about the accord. Former prime minister Trudeau, rather than gratefully and gracefully accepting that Brian Mulroney and Robert Bourassa had managed to complete his unfinished business, attacked the accord. He puzzlingly claimed it "gives too much to the provinces," yet the accord was constitutionalizing the Supreme Court of Canada, the well-established opting-out formula, confirming Quebec as "a distinct society within Canada," ending jurisdictional overlap on immigration, and the like. Yukon and the Northwest Territories went to court claiming exclusion and prejudice, a claim not upheld yet one that caused questions that could have been addressed when territorial voters weighed such assertions in the process of debating a referendum question, had there only been one.

The three-year deadline came up in June 1990. New Brunswick's legislature voted to affirm the accord as the deadline loomed, but by then Frank McKenna's deliberate delay had already taken its toll on the accord and been milked by the premier for all its political nutrition. Newfoundland was still out, with Clyde Wells seemingly no longer in communication on the issue. Manitoba had a requirement for public hearings on constitutional changes, prior to them being voted on by the legislature. After all this time, the hearings had still not taken place. To short-circuit the system, so the ratification vote could occur as pages of the calendar now became hands of the clock, unanimous consent of the assembly was required. It was repeatedly denied by a lone MLA.

In desperation, before the deadline expired, marathon first minister bargaining got under way at Ottawa's conference centre behind closed doors. Intermittent updates reported tentative progress, or word of some new problem, adding fuel to commentators' speculations as live television coverage outside the closed proceedings captured Canadians' anxious attention. This politically traumatizing way to amend a constitution was executive federalism's stunning alternative to the rational and democratic procedure of

putting the Meech Lake Accord to Canadian voters for open and deliberative collective approval or rejection three years before.

But because executive federalists operated in their established pattern
of excluding the sovereign people, this last-ditch round of negotiations
was only capable of producing more of the same. *If* the accord was ratified
before time ran out, the now-chastened Mulroney government pledged,
grievances would be dealt with in *yet another round* of negotiations. In
this pressure-cooker atmosphere, premiers were promised constitutional
amendment for a "Triple-E" Senate by 1995. Women were promised that
their rights under Section 28 of the Charter would be tucked under the further protection of the Meech Lake Accord's amendments, the way multi-
culturalism and aboriginal rights had been. The territories were promised a
role in future appointments of Supreme Court judges. Aboriginal peoples
and the territories were promised consultation on future constitutional
changes. Those who felt generally aggrieved because they misconstrued
how Quebec seemed to be the primary focus of the Meech Lake Accord
— not understanding that its purpose had explicitly been to overcome
the humiliating inability to get Quebec's agreement to Prime Minister
Trudeau's constitutional round — were themselves now promised "a statement of constitutional recognition." There was a nod to each complaint, a
sop to every wounded feeling.

Yet even in such desperate moments, Ottawa couldn't bring itself to
allow citizens a direct vote on constitutional matters. Rather than saying a referendum would be held to approve this wide array of significant
pledged constitutional amendments, the Mulroney government's only
response to the rising tide of protest about public exclusion was a promise
of "mandatory public hearings prior to adopting constitutional amendments." That didn't mean people had to attend them, just that governments had to hold them. In the culture of executive federalism, making
public meetings "mandatory" was meant to sound a note of grave intent.
What was the point of going to a meeting after a finalized package of
amendments had been negotiated but before elected representatives voted
on them? This was, at best, a cosmetic insult to the sovereign people.

• • •

In the aftermath of the Meech Lake Accord's three-year death throes, which caused some to recognize the embarrassing shortcoming of a national political system said to be "democratic," three provinces took remedial action.

B.C. Premier Bill Vander Zalm assessed Canadian criticism of the closed-circuit process for ratifying constitutional change and brought forth the Constitutional Amendment Approval Act of 1991. On March 12, 1991, the premier told members of the legislature that requiring a referendum on any proposed amendment to the Constitution of Canada *before* a resolution for that purpose is introduced in the legislature was "a first in the country." Vander Zalm expressed confidence that British Columbia's law requiring direct public participation in ratifying constitutional change would be followed by other provinces. Indeed, it was.

Alberta Premier Don Getty introduced the Constitutional Referendum Act in the legislature on March 19, 1992, to enable a province-wide vote on any proposed constitutional amendments. "Before any resolution to amend the Constitution of Canada can be passed by this Assembly a referendum must be held," explained Getty, "and it will be binding upon this Government to implement the results of that referendum." The Constitutional Referendum Act of Alberta received Royal Assent and became law in the spring of 1992.

In Saskatchewan, in conjunction with an October 1991 general election, Premier Grant Devine included a ballot question on a similar law for his province, which voters approved. But his government was defeated and the measure didn't become law under Roy Romanow, the new premier.

Quebec's response was similar, but necessarily more complex given the national humiliation with failure to get even the minimum requirements of Meech Lake accepted. The province's political leaders, with the benefit of a comprehensive referendum statute already in place, didn't need to take this threshold step as British Columbia and Alberta did but could focus directly instead on resetting the context for Quebec's future in Confederation. Premier Bourassa announced a period to develop a clear proposal that Quebecers would endorse or reject in a referendum on October 26, 1992. If, within that time, the federal government came up with a further package of constitutional amendments, Quebec would make it the ballot question. If there was no such proposal from Ottawa, a provincial plan would instead be the subject of the referendum and Quebecers would decide for themselves the future of Confederation.

• • •

In parts of what are today's Canada, constitutional arrangements have been revised a number of times, transformed by such milestone makeovers such as the Quebec Act in 1774, the Constitutional Act in 1791, the Act of Union in 1840, and the British North America Act, 1867, which created Confederation. Then, over 150 years as the country evolved, amendments to the 1867 constitution have accommodated six more provinces, changed boundaries of provinces and territories, and revised jurisdictional powers. During the twentieth century, amendments came on average once every five years. In 1922 the Supreme Court of Canada introduced an apt metaphor, likening Confederation's charter document to "a living tree" that grew and changed as the country advanced in new ways. This growing creation branched out into the equality of women and the enshrined constitutional status of aboriginal peoples. It extended to the new age of telecommunications as Ottawa's 1867 jurisdiction over postal service and telegraphy reached to encompass interprovincial telephony, radio, television, then telecommunications and the digital era as they spread a new communications canopy over our country. The expanding Constitution covered an altered era of government involvement in health care and social assistance. Continuous constitutional growth, over time, became intrinsic to Confederation's evolution.

Although this quest to live in harmony with our Constitution and change it when needed had been a worthy hallmark of democratic self-government, it then mutated into a preoccupation with constitution-making from the 1960s on. Rather than intermittently lopping off dead branches (for example, repealing spent provisions) and pruning so new growth could occur (for instance, switching responsibility for unemployment insurance to federal jurisdiction in 1940), the formerly pragmatic process escalated into attempts at extreme makeovers.

This phenomenon generated self-perpetuating rounds of conferences and gave birth to "executive federalism" as an *alternate* political forum for political insiders to game new constitutional designs for the country, an esoteric realm that Canada's sovereign people could only observe as bill-paying spectators. By the 1990s, executive federalism had so overwhelmed the governance landscape that it consumed political capital, preoccupied talented officials, spawned innumerable seminars and colloquiums on campuses and in countless conference centres, sidetracked attention and intellectual effort, drained human energy, cost billions in public funds, and diverted attention from substantive issues impacting Canada's economy and society. Televised first ministers' conferences became the public face of executive federalism, but these set-piece shows, like leaders' opening statements at international conferences, provided just a narrow and formalistic glimpse of this unaccountable and increasingly bureaucratic federal-provincial phenomenon. In tandem, a growing cluster of constitutional scholars, law professors, and media commentators rose to the status of "experts" in this prestigious white-collar industry.

This escapist drive to achieve "national unity" through constitutional negotiations sidelined other issues impacting the lives of all Canadians, thereby creating a *new* division in the country, or what today would be called "a disconnect," between the people and those in public office. Addressing and resolving substantive Canadian problems would have generated a more dynamic and unified country, if achieved by normal and accountable political resolution. Yet nothing, it seemed, could curtail this dysfunctional methodology of executive federalism. The ever-expanding, all-inclusive tendency to redirect major issues into this process "constitutionalized" heavy-duty political subjects that other countries openly confront and work out in their democratically accountable legislatures.

When the Meech Lake Accord languished, demonstrating executive federalism's inability to deliver results, the perverse outcome was not to abandon this dead-end detour from proven practice but to reinforce it. That last-ditch first ministers' conference in Ottawa — as Clyde Wells dishonoured his pledge to put the motion to a vote of Newfoundland's assembly, and while Manitoba MLA Elijah Harper defiantly withheld his consent, stalling all other members of the provincial assembly beyond the deadline for voting on their motion — produced a catalogue of *additional* issues the political leaders undertook to address next. Those commitments were ostensibly made on the condition that the holdout Newfoundland and Manitoba legislatures voted to amend the Constitution in accord with the Meech Lake deal, but when neither province did, that failure couldn't stop the momentum of this compulsive process to redraft the Constitution.

• • •

Now the Meech Lake negotiations, which had been a final focused attempt to bring Quebec back into "the Canadian family," was re-characterized as merely having been "the Quebec Round" of constitutional change. The concept of a new "Canada Round," which Opposition Leader Chrétien advocated and Prime Minister Mulroney accepted, envisaged that *every* constitutional change proposed from any part of Canada would be examined for possible inclusion in a new constitutional package. For openers, those subjects identified at the last rites for Meech — attention to women, aboriginal Canadians, territories, and the fate of the problematic Senate — got swept into the hopper for this open-ended constitutional marathon. The insatiable process then accelerated to the point where every group and region, each minority and special interest, sought to see itself individually reflected in the Constitution. Failure hadn't discouraged executive federalists, nor caused them to abandon this arid means of national advancement. The drive to constitutionalize our country's political agenda had now shifted into overdrive.

It was hard at the time, given the political, media, and cultural embrace in Canada of executive federalism's methodology, to recognize its inherent flaw: parading as "constitutional" matters that were primarily "political," and doing so through a process devised, operated, and accountable principally to political leaders and public servants, without connection to the grounding realism of the sovereign people to whom the Constitution ultimately belonged.

Because of the now decades-long momentum for an extreme constitutional makeover, there were few stones left unturned. Following consultations with "grassroots Canadians," the Spicer Royal Commission had presented many proposals on topics that could have been taken up in Parliament and provincial legislatures but which were now viewed as "constitutional" issues. The Mulroney government blended them with its own post–Meech Lake ideas for constitutional change, which it had been quietly developing through 1990 and 1991. In September 1991, Constitutional Affairs Minister Joe Clark presented Parliament with these proposals, some twenty-eight in all. This package was subjected to more public hearings all across Canada, conducted by a large parliamentary committee of MPs and senators, which then produced its own report, refining the government's proposals and distilling public reaction to them. All this constitutional grist was then milled again by Clark and the provincial government representatives from March through July 1992. Meanwhile, a series of six regional conferences — a forum that was a hybrid of town-hall meeting and con-stituent assembly, in which experts, advocacy groups, and citizens discussed the main constitutional issues — took place, held on weekends and televised nationally. The regional conference in Alberta discussed, for example, the "Triple-E Senate," while the meeting in Halifax contemplated "asymmet-ric" federalism as a means of accommodating Quebec's requirements within Canada. Not scheduled but agreed to under indigenous protest was a bonus conference to assess aboriginal self-government.

By the end of it, every conceivable proposal for amending the Constitution had been studied to brain-numbing exhaustion. Yet dur-ing early summer 1992, news reports of meetings between Clark and the premiers explained elaborate new proposals for an elected and empowered Senate. With that, Canadians had proof positive that the executive federal-ists had overheated to a dangerous degree.

While our country's ever-enlarging political class continued aloft, many Canadians, on the ground, couldn't avoid more sombre discussions about the continuing economic uncertainty resulting from the recession, issues of trade treaties, business changes, and industrial restructuring. Canadians became impatient with their politicians' preoccupation with constitutional topics in the face of grave economic dislocations and the country's social problems, environmental concerns, and international relations in a danger-ously changing post–Cold War world.

· · ·

Prime Minister Mulroney was launching yet another round of constitutional negotiations, which would become the most far-reaching since the conferen-ces that produced the 1867 Constitution and Confederation.

At an early stage, in July 1992, the intensive working of executive fed-eralism saw Constitutional Affairs Minister Joe Clark and provincial leaders reach an agreement on a package of constitutional proposals that Clark, in the immediate moment, dubbed "historic." During its brief life, this agree-ment became known as the Pearson Accord, having been negotiated at the External Affairs building named for Prime Minister Lester B. Pearson. Prime Minister Mulroney, attending meetings in Europe, was disconcerted to hear of the apparent finality pronounced about this constitutional package, since it was already being vilified in Quebec. Upon his return, Mulroney sized up the situation and concluded that *yet another* negotiating effort was needed to find a compromise that could be approved in Quebec. The prime minister reconvened all the parties during August, first in Ottawa, then in Charlottetown, for a further try. His approach in Charlottetown was to include in the accord only items on which there was unanimous consent, because the prime minister knew better than to hold a referendum for approval of a package containing elements any government objected to.

Accordingly, a number of provisions were deleted from the draft and placed instead in a separate "political accord." The political accord was to become the agenda for *further* meetings to resolve outstanding issues, once amending the Constitution on the basis of the Charlottetown Accord itself had been concluded. It was the same formula applied by executive federalists for reaching the Meech Lake Accord: agree on some points now, agree to further conferences of first ministers later, and even make them a constitutional requirement, to ensure a never-ending cycle of attempts to deal with political issues in the Constitution's formal structure.

That so many points were unanimously agreed upon in Charlottetown, the prime minister told me later, was due to the backdrop reality of the referendum. The premiers realized if agreement couldn't be reached in Charlottetown, the national leaders would simply return to Ottawa and bring in a package of proposals that reflected, in their opinion, the needs and consensus in the country, and with the support of the two other major parties in Parliament, take the proposed amendments directly to the people in a referendum. That prospect, in Prime Minister Mulroney's estimation, motivated the premiers at Charlottetown to actively seek a compromise all could endorse.

The Charlottetown Accord certainly epitomized political compromise. It was achieved mostly by the continuous addition of new features wanted by one premier to offset some concession to a stickler premier from another region. In some respects, it even seemed to square the circle, by reconciling three contending visions of Canada: the equality of provinces, the equality of citizens, and the equality of the two founding linguistic groups. The Constitution, as amended, would achieve the first by equal representation of every province in an elected Senate; the second by the Charter of Rights and Freedoms, which already accorded equality to individuals; the third by recognition of Quebec as a "distinct society within Canada" and promotion of

English-language minority rights in Quebec and French-language minority rights elsewhere in the county.

A "Canada Clause" would spruce up the workmanlike nature of the 1867 Constitution, long on practical details but short on poetic expression. In an era of meaninglessly generalized corporate "mission statements," it seemed necessary, to some, that we should add gloss to the Constitution with wording to "express fundamental Canadian values" and guide courts when interpreting the Constitution.

The existing Constitution provided for the political union of the county. Now provisions would state *policy objectives* underlying Canada's "social and economic union" — further evidence of the impulse to overload the constitutional vehicle. These social and economic goals, though comforting, would only be hortatory — not obligatory as far as governments were concerned. The "goal of full employment," for example, didn't give an unemployed worker a constitutional right to sue the government for a job. Other noble objectives included working together to strengthen the Canadian economic union; free movement of persons, goods, services, and capital; ensuring all Canadians a reasonable standard of living; and fostering sustainable and equitable development. There were more, touching on economic disparities, equalization, and regional development. As well, five social policy aspirations to be expressed in the amended Constitution would provide throughout Canada a comprehensive, universal, portable, publicly administered, and accessible health care system (already existing as statutory standards in the Canada Health Act); adequate social services and benefits so all individuals in Canada had reasonable access to housing, food, and other basic necessities; high-quality primary and secondary education for all individuals with reasonable access ensured to post-secondary education; the rights of workers to organize and bargain collectively; and protecting, preserving, and sustaining "the integrity of the environment" for present and future generations. It was as if the campaign platforms of every party that had ever contested a Canadian election had been run through the blender to top up the Constitution — all honourable sentiments and laudable goals, none of them justiciable rights.

The Charlottetown Accord hardly stopped there, however. It recommended changes for the House of Commons and Senate. On the principle of the equality of citizens through representation by population and to offset the loss of Senate seats by Canada's more populous provinces, the existing 295-member House would be enlarged to 337: the additional forty-two seats to be allocated would go eighteen each to Ontario and Quebec, four to British Columbia, and two to Alberta. Quebec would be guaranteed 25 percent of the seats in the House of Commons in recognition of Canada's linguistic duality.

Attributes of the proposed new Senate were equal provincial representation with six seats per province and one per territory for a total of sixty-two senators. Senators would be elected. Additionally, the Senate would have aboriginal representation, with numbers and method of election to follow. Changes to the law-making powers of Parliament's second chamber were to make it "effective," since its ineffectual nature was a matter of public record. Ratification of appointments to Canadian boards and agencies, for example, would be subject to an absolute veto by senators.

The Charlottetown Accord proposed that the Supreme Court Act's existing provisions about the court's composition be put in the Constitution to entrench what had already existed for more than a century. Why not?

• • •

Quebec's place within Confederation was addressed in thirty-one different ways in the Charlottetown Accord. One acknowledged, in the Canada Clause, that "Quebec constitutes within Canada a distinct society, which includes a French-speaking majority, a unique culture, and a civil law tradition." The accord dealt with divisions of constitutional powers between Ottawa and the provincial governments such as had already occurred through normal democratic politics when the federal government agreed to pay reasonable compensation to a province that chose not to participate in a new Government of Canada program in an area of exclusive provincial jurisdiction, as long as that province carried on a program or initiative compatible with the national objectives.

Exclusive provincial jurisdiction was to be recognized in mining, forestry, tourism, housing, recreation, and municipal and urban affairs. Each province could require the Government of Canada to negotiate an agreement defining its roles in that province, and Ottawa would be required to provide reasonable compensation when asked to withdraw its operations from that province.

The accord envisaged a new partnership with Canada's aboriginal peoples, based on "respect, rights, and responsibilities," contemplating self-government arrangements within Confederation. These provisions were a major advance. Just months before, the Government of Canada had succumbed to pressure from aboriginal leaders criticizing its six regional conferences that glaringly excluded them, and reluctantly agreed to a conference on aboriginal issues relative to the Constitution. Even by the start of the August constitutional discussions under the prime minister's chairmanship, which was a prelude to the Charlottetown meeting, aboriginal representatives were kept away. Chief Ovide Mercredi led representatives of the Assembly of First Nations to stand vigil outside the conference centre, protesting their exclusion. However, by this stage so much had been wound into the negotiated bundle that adding the complex dimension of aboriginal self-government wasn't much of a stretch. Consequently, it was agreed to. One day Chief Mercredi stood apart from the process, a poignant symbol of aboriginal exclusion. The next he was indoors at the negotiating table being welcomed by the premiers, everyone soon standing before television cameras to explain progress with aboriginal issues among the proposals for constitutional change.

At this point only Canadians with disabilities considered themselves excluded as a constituency unidentified in the Charlottetown Accord. That was true, but as with aboriginal Canadians whose status had already been guaranteed in the Constitution, the entrenched Charter already guaranteed, in Section 15, full equality "before and under the law" and "the right to the equal protection and equal benefit of the law," without discrimination on the basis of mental or physical disability.

It was only because of the juggernaut momentum of executive federalism, which had itself become an alternate structure to the democratic institutions created by the Constitution, that any identifiable group or interest excluded from this all-inclusive "Canada Round" took umbrage at going unmentioned. The existing Constitution already established the Government of Canada's jurisdiction over aboriginal peoples and it was Ottawa's prerogative to create a "new partnership" with indigenous Canadians any time it wanted to — acting through Parliament.

• • •

On its own, nothing would change the stultifying recalcitrance of senior ministers in the Mulroney cabinet and ranking Ottawa advisers about a national referendum on the Constitution, no matter how significant the changes. Only when the possibility of a new package of amendments emerged did the PM accept reality: Canadian citizens in three of the country's biggest provinces would be voting on constitutional change, and unless there was a *national* referendum, all other citizens would be denied this right. Overriding many of his ministers and a large swath of the Progressive Conservative caucus, the PM ensured referendum legislation was enacted so that all Canadians — not just Quebecers, British Columbians, and Albertans — could play a citizen's part in a democratic country on October 26, 1992.

In June 1992, Parliament enacted the Referendum Act. In September Parliament approved wording for the ballot question: *Do you agree that the Constitution of Canada should be renewed on the basis of the Agreement reached on August 28, 1992?* On September 18, the referendum campaign was officially launched, the vote to come thirty-eight days later. Our third Canada-wide balloting on a major public question would be the first on constitutional affairs. The vote in Quebec, conducted on the same ballot question on the same day, took place under the Referendum Act of Quebec. Everywhere else in Canada it was run according the Canada Referendum Act. The Quebec act stipulated the existence of two mandatory umbrella committees, a strict limit on referendum campaign spending, restrictions on campaign donations, a six-month residency requirement for voters, and voting results tabulated on the basis of provincial electoral boundaries. Outside Quebec, in contrast, people were free to form whatever committees they wished, in whatever number they wanted, to support or oppose the referendum, provided only that the committees register with Elections Canada if they spend more than $5,000. No limit restricted the size or source of financial contributions to any campaign committee. If a particular committee reached its spending limit, another committee could simply be registered to carry on the campaign, like amoebas subdividing by binary fission. New committees could be registered right up to voting day. Voters could be put on the list as long as they were resident when the enumerator called; there was no six-month waiting period, as in Quebec. The results were tabulated according to the boundaries of federal constituencies.

When the Canada Referendum Act was debated in Parliament in the spring of 1992, the merits of Quebec's stricter regime were contrasted to the laissez-faire approach of the Mulroney government's legislation. Those designing the bill peered nervously over their shoulders at the Charter of Rights and Freedoms, fearful it might be invoked by the National Citizens Coalition to challenge limitations on freedom of speech as unconstitutional. Quebec's lawmakers weren't spooked by such suppositions and had a fair, balanced referendum statute with umbrella committees and stronger standards they were prepared to defend in court if need be, and to re-enact using the "notwithstanding" clause if a court did strike down such provisions.

Following Parliament's enactment of the Referendum Act, much detailed work had to be done. The act itself only established the basic framework for the referendum; officials at Elections Canada had to draft extensive regulations, adapting provisions from the Canada Elections Act wherever possible to fill the gaps. Even as the campaign was under way, more regulations would be promulgated: for instance, to prohibit broadcasting voting results in time zones where the polls hadn't closed.

The Referendum Act directed that, in addition to English and French, aboriginal languages be used for voting materials wherever appropriate. Elections Canada produced referendum material in twenty-eight aboriginal languages and provided broadcasts in some thirty-one languages. Elections Canada and Quebec's director general of elections provided a neutral framework within which the referendum campaign and voting could be conducted fairly, while the Yes and No forces provided its content. As with general elections, a referendum campaign's substance takes whatever form the rivals choose.

• • •

The Charlottetown Accord itself, subject of the referendum ballot question, was executive federalism's minor miracle: unanimous consent on a far-reaching package of major changes supported by the prime minister and Government of Canada, all ten provincial premiers and their governments, the two territorial leaders, and the four national aboriginal leaders. This compromise had been reached by four Progressive Conservative governments, four Liberal governments, four NDP governments, four aboriginal leaders, and one independent government. Opposition Leader Jean Chrétien and his Liberal Party of Canada supported the accord, as did NDP national leader Audrey McLaughlin and her party.

At the outset of the campaign, NDP leader McLaughlin, reflecting limited understanding of the referendum process, stated that her party would link the unity issue with the economy. In effect, she was trying to turn the referendum campaign into a mini-general election. The NDP would simultaneously promote national unity while attacking government economic policies. However, the Charlottetown Accord generated more than enough issues of its own to debate during the five-week campaign. The New Democrat plan to address economic concerns in this context was buried by events as soon as it was announced.

As the campaign began, it was broadly assumed the Yes side would carry the day and the only real test would come in Quebec, where an extra effort would be needed to ensure a majority (even a narrow one) would endorse the accord. This apparent advantage engendered complacency among those favouring the accord. The Yes campaign structure was unwieldy outside Quebec, lacking the organizational structure of two umbrella committees mandated by Quebec's referendum law. With organizational aspects of the Yes campaign floundering, its message to voters lacked traction.

It is more accurate, in fact, to speak of many different Yes messages. Some supporters spoke of the accord as "not being perfect, not the way I would have written it." These lukewarm proponents of Yes asked voters to accept it anyway. Others were alarmists. The Royal Bank of Canada unveiled on September 25 a study entitled "Unity or Disunity: An Economic Analysis of the Benefits and the Costs" and widely distributed copies of its report. The bank's chairman, Allan R. Taylor, convened a press conference in Ottawa to dramatize the high economic costs of a No vote. It was reminiscent of the financial community's scare tactics in 1980 during the Quebec referendum on separation. Eventually, the bank modified its analysis and softened its position, but others on the Yes side continued to stridently emphasize how a No vote would lead to Confederation's breakup. Many Yes spokespeople were emphasizing the consequences of the vote rather than the contents and meaning of the Charlottetown Accord itself.

When explaining the substance of the accord to the Canadian public and addressing Canadians' specific questions for which they wanted clear answers, the Yes campaign suffered an information short circuit. Those on the Yes side had blithely accepted the idea that because politicians were so poorly thought of, messengers, to be successful, ought to be non-politicians.

Accordingly, at the national and constituency levels, great effort was made by the Yes organizers to patch together committees of eminent persons and notable celebrities whose single most important shared attribute, apart from being Canadian, was their distance from the political process and any identifiable partisan affiliation. Although people of outstanding accomplishments and diverse backgrounds, most were unfamiliar with the trade-offs that had gone into forming the Charlottetown Accord. They also were light on the substance of the document and tentative about its political implications. After the difficult hiatus created by this gambit, more elected representatives came forward to take up the battle in a cause that had not only lost steam but was now losing support.

From the outset, three complaints were voiced about the referendum process. First, some Canadians said they were too confused or didn't know enough about the issue to vote on the question. However, no one casts a ballot on the first day of any campaign; they do so on the last. The five-week campaign enables people to hear the issues dissected so that individuals can reach informed conclusions. As the campaign progressed, there was certainly no shortage of material about the accord or summaries and interpretations of it. Even as voting day loomed in late October, however, many people remained undecided. This was understandable, because contradictory interpretations of the accord were authoritatively served up by respected people on both sides. The confusion said less about the intelligence of Canadians, more about the inherent nature of the Charlottetown Accord itself.

The second complaint emerged from the first. While the ballot question was straightforward — Yes or No to the August 28 Agreement?— the package of amendments itself embodied a wide variety of substantive changes to the Constitution. Why couldn't these issues be set out one by one, many people asked, so voters could separately decide on such matters as aboriginal self-government, Quebec's distinct status, an elected Senate, and the Canada Clause? But the people had to choose between Yes or No, just as would 295 MPs and several hundred provincial legislators. Each part of the accord had been negotiated in relation to the rest, and it was, like a union's collective agreement, an integrated deal that had to be ratified or rejected as a whole. It would be impossible to implement Canada-wide multiple-choice results if each voter could choose bits and reject pieces of the vast composite. The comprehensiveness of the accord, the *direct inevitable result* of decades of "constitutionalizing" our country's political agenda, was its greatest weakness. As long as this avenue continued to be pursued, it had to result — to be successful on its own terms — in an agreement that blended and compromised the constitutional demands of all major groups from Quebec nationalists to alienated Westerners, from second-status women to unrepresented Aboriginals. The Charlottetown Accord, as the product of this all-in approach, was as good as it gets.

Thus, on a profound level, what Canadians faced on October 26 was the basic issue of whether this "something for everybody" constitutional package could sustain Confederation. And in this realm, many Canadians resisted approving what was just too much change all at once. Their lament was that the reliable Canadian method of incremental change, in response to a single specific problem, had been jettisoned for an extreme makeover. This negative reaction, in many cases, also coalesced around a patriotic craving for a "Canadian" Constitution that spoke not of the parts within but of one Canada as a whole. People had had it with executive federalism and its unconstitutional forum in which premiers pretended to national leadership by stridently pursuing regional and parochial interests.

A third complaint was that a thirty-eight-day campaign was too short to properly come to grips with the many elements of the Charlottetown Accord. The timing, however, resulted from the long time it took the national negotiators to reach agreement, and Quebec's legislated requirement for a vote by October 26 at the latest. This resentment about the rush was augmented, for some, by the fact that it was *Quebec's* deadline that imposed a drum-tight timetable on the rest of the country.

Yet deadlines can also be inspirational, and force concentration. As with journalists writing to deadlines, students facing exams, or lawyers preparing for trial, the same learning dynamic kicked in as October 26 loomed. People studied the accord and its interpreting documents, tuned in to debates, participated in discussions. Had the vote not taken place until, say, March or April 1993, most people would likely not have begun to focus on it until a few weeks, or days, immediately before. Had Quebec not insisted on a fixed date to resolve the aching uncertainty about Confederation, we'd still be in constitutional discussions today.

•   •   •

Canadians for years had been subjected to excessive discussion about the Constitution, an endless all-pervasive topic. By autumn 1992, no other electorate in the world was as prepared to deal with an issue as Canadians were about our Constitution. Yet the Charlottetown Accord addressed so many major political subjects. Even Canadians, who'd by osmosis soaked up deep constitutional awareness, had to come to grips with some new issues. Once the campaign began in earnest, it was clear that regardless of the numbers for Yes and No tallied on the night of October 26, the country was gaining from this national "teach in" on all issues raised by the Charlottetown Accord — which was essentially everything about Canada.

Journalists and news organizations relished their indispensable role in the campaign. Among the ambitious broadcasting efforts were CBC Television's three Sunday-night productions devoted to referendum issues in the form of electronic, Canada-wide, town-hall meetings, with notable Canadians and diverse citizens discussing and debating the contents and implications of the accord. While such exercises shed light on the ballot question, other broadcasts generated heat, such as radio hotline shows in British Columbia that offered a megaphone for the accord's vociferous opponents. The country's newspapers and news magazines carried page after page of analysis and covered public battles and behind-the-scenes campaign manoeuvres. The French-language newsmagazine *L'actualité* printed transcribed telephone conversations between two of Premier Robert Bourassa's top advisers alleging with disparaging comments that he'd failed to bargain successfully for Quebec's interests. It was a news organization's effort not to attack the accord on its own terms but undermine the credibility and authority of the premier who had negotiated it.

Opinion polling again raised questions of cause and effect. Since the direct vote by all Canadians constituted a comprehensive "opinion poll," the pollsters' interim reports on how the electorate was thinking, based on "representative samples" of voters they contacted, interfered with the deliberative process by influencing its outcome. Polling reports that voters in Quebec were likely to reject the accord influenced many voters in other parts of the country. Those who were concerned about Quebecers voting one way and the rest of the country the other concluded they could safely vote No and not run the risk of "breaking up Canada." This pattern of safe second-guessing by voters, sometimes called "strategic voting," is only possible on the basis of opinion poll results released at intervals during a campaign. As part of the voters' decision-making process, polls become integral to an individual's evolving position as voting day approached.

· · ·

A referendum campaign can't be a watertight compartment for five weeks in a country like Canada, and developments with no direct bearing on the accord itself, such as apprehension over signing the North American Free Trade Agreement (NAFTA), made some imprint on the campaign.

The theory that referendums can separate personality from policy was most severely tested, however, by two prominent public figures, incumbent Prime Minister Brian Mulroney and former Prime Minister Pierre Trudeau. Both placed themselves front and centre in the proceedings. Once the referendum was called on September 18, Mulroney began making major appearances across Canada to urge a Yes vote. Rather than adopting the role of father to the nation, calmly instructing the electorate about the Charlottetown Accord and its many provisions, as he might have done in televised "fireside chats" from the national capital, even sharing such appearances with leaders of other parties who likewise supported the accord, Mulroney was in his element, as if in the thick of an election-style campaign.

Trudeau, meanwhile, had telegraphed his intent to become a prime antagonist in the referendum drama, announcing days in advance a statement he'd make by October 1. Twelve years earlier Trudeau had pledged to Quebecers that he'd work for renewal of Confederation; now he urged Canadians to reject amendments intended to do just that. In saying Canadians shouldn't be "intimidated" and just vote No, Trudeau lent the prestige of his persona to the same No side being championed by separatist diehards Jacques Parizeau and Lucien Bouchard, with their Parti Québécois and Bloc Québécois adherents, and by Alberta's generally anti-Quebec Preston Manning and the anti-French elements in his Reform Party of Canada. In places where Trudeau had once been vehemently denounced, he was now being lionized by those wanting to express their antipathy to Quebec.

It is hard to calibrate the impact of major political figures on that referendum campaign. Trudeau's appearance fortified both the separatists in Quebec, who wanted a No, and voters elsewhere in the country whose No vote was a putdown of Quebec. Even harder to evaluate was the impact Brian Mulroney had upon voters. His standing in popular opinion across Canada had certainly seen better days. A number of voters tried to discern whether approval or defeat of the Charlottetown Accord might hasten his departure from office. Others resolved to not vote Yes if approval of the accord would be interpreted as a victory for Mulroney. Talking with voters throughout the campaign, I found that such feelings, though strongly held, blended with many other factors, and in most instances, really couldn't be quantified.

All the same, *Maclean's* published a Decima poll after October 26 that sought to quantify people's main reasons for voting No: 8 percent said it was because they opposed Brian Mulroney, 15 because the provinces shouldn't be given more power, 22 because the accord was a poor one, and 27 percent because Quebec got too much. During the campaign, many Yes supporters felt the PM's strenuous efforts were counterproductive to the result he sought, on account of strong negative feelings about him. This reinforced the risk of campaigning in a referendum if one doesn't separate personality from the proposal as much as possible. Still, politics is rich with paradoxes. Should Mulroney, as prime minister of Canada, be faulted for trying so strongly to promote the Yes side? Twelve years earlier many criticized Prime Minister Joe Clark for deciding to sit out the 1980 referendum battle over sovereignty-association in Quebec. It's never easy being a politician.

• • •

By about October 3, the bottom seemed to have fallen out of the Yes campaign. The growing impact of Pierre Trudeau's methodical denunciation on October 1 of the Charlottetown Accord gave high respectability to supporting No. The financial markets by early October had accounted for the accord's probable defeat, with the Canadian dollar dipping on international money markets and domestic interest rates rising 2 percent, all of which provided its own chill. And Prime Minister Mulroney campaigning in Quebec, alarmed by the public's preoccupation with that taped cellphone conversation between Diane Wilhelmy and André Tremblay demeaning Premier Robert Bourassa's bargaining efforts for Quebec, resolved to jolt the Yes campaign back into focus. When he appeared in Sherbrooke for an evening rally to speak about the thirty-one gains Quebec had achieved under the accord,

Mulroney held up pages listing the items. Then he ripped them in half. His dramatic gesture, intended to show Quebecers how they'd jeopardize what had been negotiated for them if they voted No, yielded a photograph that appeared the next day on front pages of newspapers across Canada. Many voters thought the prime minister was ripping up the Charlottetown Accord and considered his theatrics excessive and inappropriate. In the eyes of many by this stage, there was very little that Brian Mulroney could do right. He'd get no benefit of any doubt.

• • •

As October progressed, the number of community meetings and local debates about the accord proliferated. The full text of the Charlottetown Accord was delivered to every household. A toll-free long-distance number was constantly in use by hundreds of thousands of citizens seeking more information. Day by day, Canadians struggled to make their own personal decisions, many moving back and forth between Yes and No trying to reach a final verdict. Pollsters continued to take the pulse of the body politic and reported that the accord seemed in jeopardy.

The dynamic of the campaign was that the Yes side spoke generally in favour of broad propositions and compromise, while those urging a No vote focused on just one or two specific shortcomings in the accord and made a compelling emotional case on that basis alone. The cumulative effect of so many specific negative attacks administered the accord the death of a thousand small wounds.

As polls closed at eight o'clock on the night of October 26, the first indication the accord was in serious trouble emerged with its defeat in Nova Scotia by a vote of 51.1 percent to 48.5 percent. In Atlantic Canada's other provinces, the Yes side emerged victorious: Newfoundland with 62.9 percent; Prince Edward Island, 73.6 percent; and New Brunswick, 61.3 percent. In Quebec, the crucible of constitutional change, voters rejected the accord 55.4 percent to 42.4 percent. In Ontario, where collectively voters hedged their bets by dividing equally into two camps, the photo-finish result gave Yes the slimmest of margins: 49.8 percent to 49.6 percent. By this point, the results already showed the accord's future was all behind it. As more returns came in from western Canada, that message became unequivocal.

Manitoba rejected the accord 61.7 to 37.9 percent. So did Saskatchewan, 55.1 percent to 45.5 percent. Alberta electors voiced their No with 60.2 percent of votes to 39.6 percent for Yes. British Columbia, which throughout the campaign had remained a world unto itself, recorded the highest No vote anywhere in the country with 67.8 percent opposing and only 31.9 percent in favour.

When the No side triumphed, many journalists and commentators opined that the people had turned against the elites, a line of "analysis" that is the cliché of referendum post-mortems. Yet millionaire Pierre Trudeau in 1992 was a member of Canada's elite. Likewise, Preston Manning, son of a provincial premier, a millionaire, and a national party leader, greatly resembled the political elites he consistently attacks. The Liberal Party of Manitoba under leader Sharon Carstairs and the Liberal Party of British Columbia under leader Gordon Wilson both opposed the accord. So did the National Action Committee on the Status of Women, led by Judy Rebick, and the National Citizens Coalition, led by David Sommerville. A range of notables from the financial, business, and academic communities supported No, as well. The Yes side had a preponderant share of prominent Canadians and also had the combined political strength — such as it proved to be! — of the national Progressive Conservative, Liberal, and New Democratic backroom campaign organizers. On balance, the "elites" were on both sides of the referendum question.

Overall, the national vote saw 44.8 percent of voters endorse amending the Constitution on the basis of the Charlottetown Accord, with 54.2 percent opposed. Critics of referendums relish saying they "divide" the country, but these results didn't split along linguistic or regional lines. A general and far-reaching vote instructed the governments of Canada not to proceed with constitutional amendments that had seemed only two months earlier guaranteed of success.

The governments had proposed; the people had disposed. As Canadians decided not to follow one road to re-constituting Confederation, we implicitly sought another. The referendum of October 1992 transformed Canadian public affairs by redirecting political forces along a needed new trajectory. A referendum, it turned out, was the only thing with enough conclusive force to end the quixotic thirty-year quest by Canada's political class to deal with our country's public issues indirectly in the Constitution rather than straight up through our legislatures.

21

VOTING TO BREAK CONFEDERATION: ROUND TWO, 1995

Throughout the evening of October 30, 1995, Canada's prime minister watched Quebec referendum tallies ebb and flow toward a separatist victory. Ballot counts took time. Of 5,087,009 eligible voters, 4,757,509 had cast ballots — 93.52 percent — larger than any turnout for a Canadian or provincial election in history. Between No and Yes, the razor-thin difference was 50.58 percent to 49.42 percent. The federalists had eked out a win with 54,288 votes, barely the number of fans to fill Montreal's Bell Centre for two Canadiens hockey games.

Jean Chrétien, a staunch federalist, had been in a bravura state of denial that separatists could succeed. Equally astonishing, the separatists themselves had done little concrete planning for what would happen if they won beyond dreamily thinking about France granting diplomatic recognition that would trigger a similar pattern throughout La Francophonie. Stunning revelations in *The Morning After*, Chantal Hébert and Jean Lapierre's 2014 book of interviews with top sovereignist and federalist leaders about the events of October 1995, have since disclosed that separatist Premier Jacques Parizeau and Bloc Québécois leader Lucien Bouchard had no blueprint beyond voting day — typical Canadian "muddling through" of major events with no clear plan.

• • •

Over the decade and a half since the 1980 referendum on separation, political forces had built inexorably to this second referendum, seemingly in six bounding steps. First, Prime Minister Pierre Trudeau, honouring his 1980 pledge to overhaul Canada's Constitution if Quebecers defeated the separatist option, initiated extensive constitutional negotiations that by November 1991 resulted in the PM and nine premiers — but not Quebec Premier René Lévesque — agreeing to patriate the Constitution and include in it a Charter of Rights and Freedoms. The resulting Constitution Act 1992 was then enacted — but without ratification by Quebec's National Assembly.

The second step, taken by Trudeau's successor Prime Minister Brian Mulroney and Lévesque's successor Premier Robert Bourassa, was to complete the "unfinished" constitutional business. The two, with all other premiers, negotiated constitutional amendments to address Quebec's concerns. The Meech Lake Accord, as already noted, clarified several of Ottawa's powers in relation to the provinces and recognized Quebec as "a distinct society within Canada." Ratification of the accord didn't go to a national referendum but dragged out over three years of inept political handling by Ottawa amid fierce isolated opposition in New Brunswick, Newfoundland, and Manitoba. The drama of ratification's failure during the summer of 1990 prompted justifiable outrage in Quebec. Support for sovereignty surged.

The third step was taken by Lucien Bouchard, a close personal friend of Prime Minister Mulroney, who'd appointed him to the cabinet. Bouchard betrayed his long-time friend and country by forming the Bloc Québécois, a breakaway separatist coalition of Progressive Conservative and Liberal MPs from Quebec as a new federal party in Parliament devoted to Quebec sovereignty.

The fourth was Premier Bourassa's proclamation, in the wake of the Meech Lake Accord's demise, that a referendum would be held in Quebec during 1992, with either sovereignty or a new constitutional agreement on the ballot. That sparked a major round of constitutional negotiations, resulting in the Charlottetown Accord's extensive package of constitutional amendments, which failed to win ratification in 1992's Canada-wide referendum.

Fifth came political realignment. A general election in 1993 brought a Liberal majority government to power in Ottawa under Prime Minister Chrétien, a veteran of these wars who'd been Canada's minister of justice during the 1980–81 constitutional discussions. Facing him across the Commons aisle was the Bloc Québécois led by Lucien Bouchard, who in the 1993 federal election won fifty-four seats with 49.3 percent of Quebec's vote, giving the separatists the ironic status of being "Her Majesty's Loyal Opposition."

Sixth, and finally, an election in Quebec the next year produced another change of the guard. The separatist Parti Québécois, led by Jacques Parizeau, returned to power by ousting the provincial Liberals, forming a majority government with 44.75 percent of the popular vote. The new government's campaign platform, and hence its electoral mandate, despite not being approved by even half the electors, included holding a referendum on sovereignty.

• • •

It took a lot of manoeuvring to get the referendum aligned because the separatist movement embraced hardliners and moderates and most had different opinions about a winning path. The earlier *étapiste* approach was history. The government introduced its Act Respecting the Future of Quebec, or "Sovereignty Bill," mailed a copy to every household in Quebec, and announced a National Commission on the Future of Quebec. Within the PQ, debate continued over what terms for sovereignty should be voted on in the referendum. Parizeau disdained the PQ's earlier quest for a continuing economic relationship with Confederation that would somehow be ambiguously coupled with sovereignty — René Lévesque's formulation. In 1980 he'd watched Ottawa successfully campaign to render the sovereignty-association concept a non-starter. Why repeat history?

Opposition in the sovereignty movement to the premier's hard-line stance for outright independence coalesced around Bloc Québécois leader Lucien Bouchard. He believed a ballot option lacking partnership with Canada would doom the vote with moderate nationalists who were more realistic about separation's economic impacts. Bouchard's position was reinforced by Deputy Premier Bernard Landry, and by Mario Dumont, popular young leader of another party, Action démocratique du Québec. They all wanted an option "softer" than Parizeau's. When the National Commission reported in April 1995 on its study about the future of Quebec, it confirmed that the public generally desired an economic partnership with Canada.

Given the circumstances, Parizeau agreed to a broader approach. He, Dumont, and Bouchard signed an agreement on June 12, 1995, outlining details of the Quebec-Canada partnership negotiation process, seeking "sovereignty" with an economic and social partnership to be negotiated and presented to the rest of Canada. The premier was content that their agreement allowed the Quebec government to declare immediate independence if negotiations weren't successful, or following a successful referendum. Despite a brilliant legal challenge by lawyer and former separatist Guy Bertrand, who sought injunctions to stop the referendum and bring on a trial to establish that separating from Confederation wasn't constitutional, the juggernaut advanced.

• • •

The referendum ballot asked, *Do you agree that Quebec should become sovereign after having made a formal offer to Canada for a new economic and political partnership within the scope of the bill respecting the future of Quebec and of the agreement signed on June 12, 1995?*

Ballot-question wording inevitably attracts critiques. Daniel Johnson, Jr., leading Quebec's Liberal Party, called it confusing and said it should have contained the word *country*, as in "a sovereign country."[1] Some argued it shouldn't have mentioned "partnership" proposals because no Canadian political leaders outside Quebec would negotiate a partnership with an independent Quebec, while a more legalistic version of the same point was that no entity existed capable of undertaking Confederation's divorce proceedings.[2] Some saw the question as misleading because it implied that agreement had already been reached between Canada and Quebec on June 12, rather than just among the three leaders of sovereignist parties in the province.

Under Quebec's referendum law, Jacques Parizeau chaired the Yes forces, Daniel Johnson the No campaign. As required by the Referendum Act, both committees contributed their messages for a brochure sent to every voter. Each side had a $5 million budget. Campaign spending by any person or entity outside the umbrella committee framework would be illegal.

The campaign began October 2 with a televised address by both leaders, Parizeau injecting urgency by stressing this vote might be the last opportunity for sovereignty in the foreseeable future, Johnson covering the referendum with the fog of fear by forecasting economic uncertainty that a Yes vote would provoke. The economic card, always played by the federalists, included Quebec's unclear position in the North American Free Trade Agreement, Quebec's inability to control the Canadian dollar, which it hoped to still use, and statements of pending doom from business leaders

Paul Desmarais of Power Corporation and Laurent Beaudoin of Bombardier Inc., influential men with thousands of employees and contractors.

Parizeau criticized such interventions, accusing Quebec business leaders of betraying their customers and workers, a line that resonated well with separatist militants but seemed only to highlight economic uncertainties that worried undecided voters. The Yes campaign stressed that any prospects for revamping Confederation were slim to non-existent, based on convincing evidence to date, so the only course was to vote Yes and prepare to leave.

After one week, polls showed Yes trailing significantly. Needing to kick-start separatist momentum, Parizeau named Lucien Bouchard chief negotiator for the partnership talks between Quebec and Canada following a Yes majority vote.[3] The move had a double impact, making popular Bouchard more prominent in the campaign while also emphasizing the Quebec-Canada "partnership" nature of the ballot question. The next rounds of polls showed gains, and before long a majority of Quebecers said they intended to vote Yes.[4] Bouchard's speeches, delivered everywhere and often, urged Quebecers to vote Yes and give a clear mandate for change. He said only a strong Yes would permit final solution of Confederation's enduring constitutional issues, and that a new partnership with "English Canada" would benefit all.[5]

• • •

Aboriginal leaders in Quebec strongly opposed separation. They had grievances about their relationship with Ottawa, but experience dealing with provincial and municipal governments had convinced aboriginal peoples that they would face an even harsher future in a country called Quebec outside Confederation. Affirming their own right to self-determination, the aboriginal leaders said forcing their peoples to join an independent Quebec without their consent would violate international law. If forced to decide, the aboriginal peoples of the province would separate from a separate Quebec and remain within Confederation.

Advancing from press conferences and demonstrations, the politically potent Cree of Northern Quebec decided to fight fire with fire. Their respected grand chief, Matthew Coon Come, published *Sovereign Injustice*, a well-researched and persuasive legal analysis of the plan for a forcible inclusion of the James Bay Cree and Cree territory into a sovereign Quebec. He made the case for his people's right to self-determination and maintaining their territories within Confederation. The Cree then held their own referendum.

With voting on October 24, the ballot question asked, *Do you consent, as a people, that the Government of Quebec separate the James Bay Cree and Cree traditional territory from Canada in the event of a Yes vote in the Quebec referendum?*

With more than three-quarters of eligible voters casting ballots, 96.3 percent voted to stay in Canada. The Cree uprising against separatists was soon reinforced by another referendum vote, this time by the Inuit of Nunavik, whose ballot asked plainly, *Do you agree that Quebec should become sovereign?*

With 96 percent answering No to that question, the prospective landscape of a partitioned Quebec began to resemble Swiss cheese with big holes in it. Nunavik land occupied the top third of the province. The Cree held extensive territory around James Bay and inland.

To increase pressure on the Yes side, aboriginal groups demanded "full-participant" status in any constitutional negotiations that might flow from the referendum.[6] The province's aboriginal communities, understanding fully the consequences of the choice being forced by Quebec's government, increased tension in the campaign by making real to Quebecers the serious consequences of partition.

· · ·

Jean Charest, the federal Progressive Conservative leader, sent a potent message to his fellow Quebecers when, at No rallies, he waved aloft his Canadian passport, one of the strongest in the world of international travel and an asset of citizenship foolish to abandon — a riveting image that reappeared on television newscasts and newspaper front pages.

From the start, the federalist No campaign had many disparate elements — provincial Liberals, federal Liberals, Progressive Conservatives, and others. There was touchiness about who should be prominent, and who had to be kept out of sight. Separatists cried foul each time someone beyond the province's borders took a stance on the referendum, which is why non-Quebec Liberals in Ottawa maintained low visibility as cabinet ministers, though several countered the Yes campaign by directing their departments to mail social payment cheques to Quebec households with a pro-Canada message, and by ordering scores of citizenship judges from across Canada into the province to accelerate turning upward of twenty thousand immigrants into voting citizens in time to cast a No ballot by late October. Even the prime minister, a proud Quebecer, was kept at bay for most of the campaign, until polling numbers for the Yes side sobered everyone to fear that Quebec's bolt from Confederation was only days away and it was time to muster "all hands on deck."

Jean Chrétien's addresses had been rare, but now near the end of the campaign, when the uncertain outcome finally sparked him to action, the PM spoke at an October 24 federalist rally in the largest arena of West Montreal, focusing some four thousand No supporters on Quebecers' emotional attachment to Canada, promising reforms that would give Quebec more power, startling everybody by reversing his (and Pierre Trudeau's) stance and declaring he would support recognition of Quebec as "a distinct society," and that he'd lead reforms to the Canadian Constitution.[7]

After that speech in Verdun Auditorium, the prime minister delivered an October 25 televised address promoting the virtues of Canadian federalism for Quebec, mentioning the shared values of all within Confederation and warning how Jacques Parizeau would use a Yes majority to declare independence from Canada.

Lucien Bouchard got equal airtime following the PM's segment, despite being a leader of the Yes campaign in Quebec striving to break Confederation, because as leader of the Official Opposition in Canada's Parliament, he was entitled to rebuttal. Bouchard recapped the animosities of the constitutional debate. When addressing French-speaking viewers, he criticized Jean Chrétien's behaviour, holding up for the TV camera a newspaper's front-page report on the 1982 constitutional deal that excluded Quebec, showing Trudeau and Chrétien laughing.[8] Knowing his margin of victory lay with swing voters who needed reassurance about a continuing relationship between a sovereign Quebec and Confederation, the separatist leader dwelt on the partnership element of the proposal. Addressing English-speaking Canadians, Bouchard said ending the interminable constitutional squabbling would be good for everyone, asked for understanding of the Yes side, and committed to "negotiate in good faith."[9]

If the PM, in desperation, would reverse his stance on "distinct society" to save Confederation, others were no longer prepared to let the separatists have an open playing field. The silenced non-Quebec ministers holed up in Ottawa broke through many hurdles and stirred up Canadians outside Quebec to join an October 27 "Unity Rally" in Montreal at Place du Canada sponsored by the city's business leaders. Fisheries Minister Brian Tobin of Newfoundland went on television, urging Canadians to get to Montreal and join the rally, which he dubbed "the crusade for Canada," to show support for Quebec remaining in Confederation. The prospect of Quebec becoming an independent country, creating a vast gap in the centre, leaving Canada with east and west sections like Pakistan after India's partition, caused thousands of emotional people to reach Montreal by chartered buses and flights with airline tickets 90 percent off in a "unity" sale. At times during the day, the throng at Place du Canada reached 125,000, with the people hearing speeches by Jean Chrétien, Jean Charest, and Daniel Johnson. Televised images panning the vast crowd with its oversized Canadian flag dramatized the showdown. It was impossible to say how the event influenced voting. Jean Charest believed the rally maintained No campaign momentum when it was most crucial. Daniel Johnson was anxious about the rally exacerbating tensions with English Canada. Lucien Bouchard rightly wondered why English Canada had failed to rally in the streets of Fredericton, Winnipeg, and St. John's this way to prevent the collapse of the Meech Lake Accord.

When voting took place, Quebec society's long-standing divisions in the perpetual quest for cultural survival were again revealed. Yes was the choice of some 60 percent of French-speaking Quebecers while about 95 percent of English-speaking voters and Allophones voted No.

The Yes side was strongest in heartland Saguenay–Lac-Saint-Jean, across sprawling Gaspé, the oddly named "Centre-du-Québec" (which isn't in the province's centre but along the St. Lawrence River's south shore encompassing such urban centres as Drummondville, Victoriaville, and Bécancour), and also in Montreal's and Quebec City's suburbs.

Northern Quebec's mostly aboriginal voters, the Outaouais region of western Quebec where many thousands of federal government employees live, the Eastern Townships with its Anglo heritage and long partnership between the two linguistic communities, and the Beauce, at peace in its natural beauty and wanting peace in its public affairs, all generally voted No.

The largest turnout of electors in Canadian history showed just how delicately balanced the tipping point had become. The proposal of June 12, 1995,

was rejected by 50.58 percent of Quebecers while 49.42 percent voted Yes —
a tissue-thin margin, significantly narrower than in the 1980 referendum.

Jacques Parizeau resigned as premier. Lucien Bouchard, elected the new
leader of the Parti Québécois, became premier. He announced that a third
referendum would be held once "winning conditions" arose, but meanwhile,
the government's priority would be to overhaul Quebec's economy. Daniel
Johnson resigned as leader of the provincial Liberals. Jean Charest, a man
seemingly destined to become prime minister of the country, succumbed to
intense pressure from federalists across Canada and in Quebec. He resigned
as national Progressive Conservative leader and then was acclaimed leader of
the Quebec Liberals — on a mission to keep Confederation whole.

22

VOTING ON PROHIBITION

Canadians accustomed to beer at sports events, sidewalk cafés serving alcohol, licensed drinking in restaurants and at social gatherings, and a wide array of distilled, vinted, and brewed products in convenient retail locations, would find earlier Canada a foreign land.

By the mid-1800s, the place was awash in a sea of booze, and in reaction, church groups, temperance organizations, and women's institutes lobbied governments and legislators to build dikes and stem the tide of "demon rum." Unregulated availability of alcohol caused significant social problems. Working men passed strategically located taverns between the factory and their homes on payday, often reaching a wretched wife and hungry children hours later, drunk and moneyless, to administer beatings. Anyone heading to the back of a general store could dip a ladle into a barrel of raw whiskey, down a "grunt," then return to the street for action.

Elections took place without ballots, but not without ample supplies of alcohol to influence a voter's choice, or to provide "courage from the bottle." Showing up at polling places to openly declare support for one of the candidates required inner fortification to face intimidating partisan enforcers, some wielding axe handles as clubs. Amendments to the Dominion Elections Act banned the sale of alcohol while polls were open, prohibited partisan activity in the vicinity of voting places, and gave electors a secret ballot, in response to Canada's alcohol-centric political culture.

There being no shared cluster of views about "the liquor question," society was divided between those who focused on the social evils, health problems, and personal calamities alcohol created, and those who associated alcohol with pleasure, freedom of choice, or their uncorked source of income.

In this context, a reasonable response was to advocate "temperance," on the principle that one should enjoy "everything in moderation." At first the social and religious campaign for temperance tried moral suasion to encourage moderate use of alcohol, or abstemiousness. However, the political and legal dimensions of the liquor question also had to be addressed. In 1878 Parliament enacted the Canada Temperance Act, better known as "the Scott Act" after its sponsor, Richard William Scott, a Liberal who'd been mayor of Bytown (Ottawa) and was secretary of state in Liberal Prime Minister Alexander Mackenzie's cabinet. Scott based his legislation on the pre-Confederation Canada Temperance Act of 1864, itself widely known as "the Dunkin Act," which introduced referendums to our country more than a century and a half ago.

That groundbreaking statute had been gamely pioneered by Christopher Dunkin, an editor, lawyer, teacher, and Conservative member of the pre-Confederation Canadian parliament representing Brome County in Quebec's Eastern Townships. Dunkin became minister of agriculture in Prime Minister Macdonald's first national government after Confederation. The Dunkin Act empowered communities to prohibit retail sale of alcohol *if a majority of the municipality's electors approved* — a radical power-to-the-people innovation. With the Scott Act in 1878, Parliament extended this "local option" provision to all of Canada.

Although it was a federal law, the statute didn't attempt to impose a single Canada-wide standard on liquor's availability. Seasoned politicians, even those supporting temperance, knew that would be impossible politically. So the Scott Act, like its precursor Dunkin Act, gave local voters their own choice. The Dunkin-Scott formula was doubly democratic. First, voters could present an "initiative" petition if they wanted to force a choice about liquor in their community. Second, all qualified electors could answer either Yes or No, with the majority view prevailing. This brought the issue close to home and gave people an enhanced sense of responsibility for their self-government.

The "local option" was a two-way street. If enough people in the municipality petitioned for the referendum, it had to be held; if enough petitioned for repeal, another vote had to take place. The municipal council had to implement the result, either closing taverns and hotel bars if the vote favoured prohibition, or issuing new liquor licences to qualifying applicants if the vote mandated repeal. A three-year cooling-off-and-adjustment period had to elapse between votes to reduce erratic swings between a city or county voting itself "dry," then returning "wet," then "dry" again, when voter support was closely divided between the options and a small handful of swing votes, perhaps tempted by financial or other inducements, could reverse the outcome. Only a simple majority was required — in the statute's words, "more than half of all votes polled."

The act detailed all steps, starting with presenting a petition from electors of a county or city wanting a vote to trigger the process and ending with the obligatory order-in-council imposing prohibition where it had been approved by voters. A complete code for conducting a referendum, the act was a Canadian precedent, as early as the 1870s, for a self-contained referendum statute establishing a poll, specifying duties for returning officers, voting procedures, proceedings after the poll closes, adding up the votes and tendering returns of the result, secrecy of voting, preservation of peace and good order, and preventing corrupt practices and illegal acts. All aspects of procedure, including the form and substance of the petition and details about the nature of the ballot paper, were clear.

Created in Canada by Conservatives and Liberals, the pre-Confederation Dunkin Act and its nationwide successor Scott Act constituted a substantive advance in democratic decision-making: a statutory right for citizens to determine a policy with which they and their neighbours would have to live.

Then temperance shifted to prohibition. When Prince Edward Island joined Confederation in 1873, it added to our country the island's eighty-seven thousand people and their history of alcohol use and abuse since the colony's beginnings. From the 1820s on, island groups promoting "temperance" and advocating "abstinence" sought to change individual behaviour, but after five decades of limited success, they wanted to confront the *context* of the problems created by alcohol and began demanding a law to completely abolish intoxicating drink from society itself. They sharpened "abstinence" to "total abstinence," or "prohibition."

By 1878, if anybody was ready for the Canada Temperance Act, it was Prince Edward Island's prohibition forces. As soon as the Scott Act came into force, local votes were initiated in Prince County (December 28, 1878), the City of Charlottetown (April 24, 1879), and Kings County (May 29, 1879).

This was followed up, in 1893, by a provincial referendum on December 13 that asked Islanders, *Are you in favour of prohibiting the importation, manufacture, and sale of intoxicating liquor within this province?* To that, 3,331 answered No, 10,585 said Yes.

Across Canada's five other English-speaking provinces, too, many municipalities began voting for prohibition under local option. Throughout the 1880s, enforcement problems emerged because of the patchwork of dry and wet communities within a province. Lots of money was being made producing and selling something sinful, or at least scarce, that people wanted. With alcohol harder to get, bootlegging prices soared. The liquor problem hadn't evaporated; it had just been bottled up in wet communities. As transportation improved, it became easier for people wanting a drink but residing in a dry town to simply make their way to a neighbouring wet community. Adoption of this accommodating pattern across the country's regions seemed to balance interests to an extent, but those provoked by what they saw wanted to hit back even harder at "demon rum."

Could every problem of alcohol not be solved, asked the abolitionists, by removing the source of the problem itself through a comprehensive ban on all liquor?

The Women's Christian Temperance Union (WCTU) and the Women's Institute, both of which had local chapters throughout the country, soared into action, their demands for female voting rights dovetailing with their campaigns for prohibition referendums. This juggernaut for moral uplift was present in much of Canada, especially the country's evangelical Protestant homes. Another component of this "zero-tolerance" crusade was the all-powerful Dominion Alliance for the Total Suppression of the Liquor Traffic. The overall quest of these groups seeking to curtail alcohol was to expand local option votes into province-wide bans, that is, prohibition voted in by the entire provincial electorate. A single overriding law could dry out any remaining wet municipal oases that were attracting thirsty folk from far and wide.

Manitoba began this drive in 1892, hoping to cut off the manufacture and sale of alcohol through the achievement of a Yes vote in a province-wide prohibition referendum, scheduled to be held on July 23. Prince Edward Island followed on December 13, 1893. Ontario voters began 1894 by answering a January 1 provincial ballot on liquor prohibition. On March 15 that year, so did Nova Scotians.

In each case, premiers, unable to withstand the relentless lobbying and higher appeal to public morality from Protestant churches and the WCTU, as well as pushback from distillers and publicans who contributed cash to their election campaigns, were forced to act. As noted earlier, they knew the liquor question divided their cabinets, split their caucuses, and would throw their provincial legislatures into acrimonious turmoil if they introduced government legislation on prohibition. So instead they tossed the "hot potato" to the people. Rather than bottle up the explosion inside a legislature, a province's dispersed electors could diffuse the impact of society's complex divisions on the liquor question. A ballot question was admirably democratic, and unique as a political escape valve. The referendums in Manitoba, Prince Edward Island, Ontario, and Nova Scotia kept the institutions of representative government intact, able to continue dealing with more routine issues, while allowing *everyone* to understand and share in working out the multi-layered liquor issue.

For zealous prohibitionists and Protestants, these province-wide votes opened visions of a higher path to "New Jerusalem." To reach the dazzling citadel on a hill, to make all of Canada a sanctuary of moral probity and joyous Christian living, they pushed for what had earlier been judged politically impossible: a single national law applicable to all. The Liberal Party of Canada, languishing on Parliament's Opposition benches in the Gay Nineties, became a receptive home for this idea. Keen to attract more voters, Liberals made "considerable overtures to the temperance vote, and obtained noteworthy support from it at the 1896 election," notes a historian of Canada's Prohibition era, J.A. Stevenson, "on the promise of an adequate Dominion measure of temperance reform."[1]

Joseph Schull, a biographer of Wilfrid Laurier, misrepresents this event by contending the PM agreed to the national vote only in "an unwary moment," and had been "lured" into promising a referendum on prohibition.[2] Laurier was never indifferent to the possibilities of direct voting, as Schull also purports to be the case, writing that after 1898's prohibition vote, "there would be no more off-hand referendums" for Laurier.

Although entitled to a personal view about referendums, Schull projected his private bias onto the statesman he portrayed. Wilfrid Laurier had *not* taken up the 1898 prohibition vote on a whim, nor was he lured through inattentiveness. The Liberal Party of Canada's constituency delegates had deliberately voted, in a well-attended policy convention in 1893, for a nationwide direct vote on prohibition. The matter hardly caught Laurier by surprise. For thirty-six months between this convention and the 1896 general election, he constantly heard commentary, pro and con, about a prohibition plebiscite. Both the party he led and Laurier himself clearly pledged a national vote on prohibition as part of their 1896 Liberal platform. The promise contributed to Laurier winning enough votes, in a country overwhelmingly Christian and church-based at the end of the nineteenth century, to form a government. He became prime minister knowing his electoral mandate included a prohibition plebiscite.

Debate on the Laurier government's Prohibition Plebiscite Act began in the spring of 1898, with Agriculture Minister Sidney Fisher the leadoff speaker. An elegant and rich bachelor farmer from Knowlton, Quebec, he'd been vice-president of the Dominion Alliance for the Total Suppression of the Liquor Traffic for fifteen years by the time the Liberal Party convened in 1893 when he presented the national convention his resolution, which it adopted, for a Canada-wide plebiscite on prohibiting alcohol. After the Liberals assumed office, it was Fisher, on behalf of the Laurier cabinet, who introduced the Prohibition Plebiscite legislation in the Commons.

Fisher dwelt on the relationship between parliamentarians and the general public in a plebiscite, emphasizing that the issue before the House was the bill to establish the voting procedures, not the question of prohibition itself. "That is a question which, by the very nature of this Bill, is to be removed from the arena of the House of Commons for the time being and relegated to the electorate of the country for them to declare their views upon." It would be "at the hustings where the question will be thrashed out," he added. Once the people "have declared their will in respect to this question, it will come back again to the floor of Parliament and will have to be dealt with again by the representatives of the people in Parliament."[3] It was an early, clear statement of how a ballot issue operated in partnership between the people and their representatives, or "semi-direct" democracy.

George Foster, a former Conservative minister who'd established the 1892 Royal Commission on Prohibition, which had been a delaying tactic by the Tories, insisted from the Opposition benches that the government shouldn't hold a plebiscite unless it was prepared to be bound by the majority view and act accordingly. He was arguing, in fact if not by name, for a binding referendum. Noting the Commons was being asked to approve a plebiscite costing $250,000, the anti-prohibitionist stated, "We have no business doing that unless the government and Parliament are prepared, if the vote is affirmative, to translate the will of the people into a stern, strong, prohibitory law."[4]

Thomas Sproule, a medical doctor, ardent leader of the Orange Lodge, and Ontario Conservative MP, strongly denounced the measure. "I am not in favour of the principle of a referendum. I have always held it is un-British and utterly opposed to British parliamentary usage." Sproule spoke highly of Ottawa's public servants, asserting the heads of departments are "charged with the duty of governing the country, and are bound to be sufficiently well-informed on the condition of things in the country" to be able to decide whether legislation is required on any subject "without asking a special vote of the people on that subject." Expressing filial loyalty to British institutions, Sproule sniffed and said, "We have the right to expect in a British Colony, where the government of the country is based on the same principles as that of the mother country, that the executive for the time being will take the responsibility of saying what the country requires and providing legislation to carry that out, without asking the people, by means of a referendum, whether they want a certain thing or not." Sproule's British-mindedness also induced him to oppose all immigration to Canada except from Britain, to express as an Orangeman wholesale anti-French views, and upholding what he expected "in a British Colony."[5]

Sproule's expressed conception of a "British" parliament was all it took to provoke similar views across party lines from MP George Casey, an Ontario Liberal. Although feeling "compelled to support the Bill because it was a promise made" by his Liberal Party during the election campaign, Casey felt equally "compelled to speak to the principle involved," which he disowned. "We do not seem to be aware that in adopting this Bill, we are taking a very grave step in a new direction, a direction which is entirely new to our Constitution. We should realize what we are doing when we refer a question to a popular vote which should be decided within the walls of this House."[6]

Casey and other MPs who trembled about doing something "entirely new to our Constitution" overlooked the fact that the Constitution had not only been written by Canadians but that it deviated substantially from anything the British had tried, including a federal system of government akin to the Six Nations Confederacy and the American Constitution's federated union. If any British principle was relevant, it was that Parliament was supreme and therefore could do whatever its members wanted to vote for — including holding a plebiscite.

• • •

Because problems flowing from alcohol abuse affected so many Canadian women every day, they emerged as effective leaders in the prohibition movement. Yet women didn't have the right to vote, let alone to be elected to Parliament. So while men in the Commons debated, women rallied outside on Parliament Hill on May 3 in a mass demonstration, having brought to Ottawa a "monster petition" asking for a vote on prohibition.

Conservative MP Nicholas Davin from Manitoba responded in the Commons by introducing an amendment of the Prohibition Plebiscite Act to include as voters, as he put it, "the ladies in every constituency in Canada who take an interest in public trends generally and above all in this question." When government MPs defeated it, Davin accused the Liberals of "a pedantic adherence to symmetry," the government having excluded women from voting on prohibition because they were excluded from electing MPs under the Franchise Act.[7]

Several MPs, leery about sharing decision-making with the Canadian electorate, were hotel owners. Others had financial interests in the liquor trade. At the same time a number of MPs had won their seats with the full backing of the temperance movement. All these men knew where their votes and money came from. These interests and imperatives remained unspoken as they advanced high-minded arguments about Parliament, national politics, constitutionality, and loyalty to British tradition. "According to our British system of parliamentary government the plebiscite is entirely out of place," Rufus Henry Pope, a cattle breeder and Conservative MP from the Eastern Townships, told the Commons that same spring day. "We are in this Parliament elected to deal with public questions, right or wrong, and to assume the fullest responsibility for the action we may take."[8]

Despite these objections, the vote on the Prohibition Plebiscite Act was carried "on division," meaning by a voice vote of Yeas and Nays — the loudest being the winning majority — not by a recorded vote, which would have created a public record of how every MP voted. In "assuming the fullest responsibility" for their actions, they agreeably sought anonymity.

• • •

Many Quebecers felt this battle for prohibition was an alien Protestant threat to their traditional Catholic way of life. Quebec's attorney general challenged Ottawa's power to impose its decision about liquor prohibition on a province, initiating a constitutional challenge he fought, through appeals, all the way to the Judicial Committee of the Privy Council. In London the Privy Council ruled that a federal law prohibiting the manufacture and sale of alcohol would be a valid exercise of Ottawa's jurisdiction.

Canadians would go to the polls on September 29, 1898, to answer, *Are you in favour of the passing of an Act prohibiting the importation, manufacture or sale of spirits, wine, ale, beer, cider and all other alcoholic liquors for use as beverages?*

The country erupted into a robust democratic exercise. Arguments pro and con were no longer presented only to assemblies of the like-minded. The campaign let everyone have their say, though voting, being restricted to male British subjects twenty-one years and over, wouldn't register the full strength of the prohibition movement. "The aggressively vocal legions of the Women's Christian Temperance Union," notes journalist and historian James H. Gray, "were not permitted to cast ballots."[9] Some 44 percent of eligible voters turned out to vote. Of them, 278,487 answered Yes to prohibition; 264,571, No — majority support for a federal prohibition law. To nobody's surprise, the proposition carried in every province except Quebec where voters handily rejected prohibition 122,614 to 25,582 votes.

The overall result gave everyone an accurate picture of where adult men of the country stood on the liquor issue. The plebiscite hadn't *created* division. The history of these times, and results of previous provincial and municipal referendums on prohibition, make clear how the 1898 vote reflected existing Canadian reality. It reminded all concerned that issues surrounding the liquor traffic couldn't be resolved on a uniform country-wide basis.

Prime Minister Laurier, reflecting upon the results, said the narrowness of the prohibition majority didn't justify the government taking any action. He refused to bring in a prohibition law. A relatively small majority of 13,687 votes for prohibition across the entire country was still a majority, but Quebecers had voted massively, about 80 percent, against the option. Much of the country was already "dry" under local option, anyway. Adept at interpreting democracy's numbers, Laurier left alcohol for provinces to regulate.

He didn't, however, abandon his belief in the necessity of consulting the people about a major policy in a referendum, despite Joseph Schull's statement about "no more off-hand referendums" for Laurier, intimating that the PM ostensibly repudiated them. During the First World War, Laurier still believed that the people had to debate and vote on fundamental questions. In 1917, as Opposition Leader, the Liberal statesman introduced a resolution in Parliament urging Prime Minister Borden's government to hold a referendum on conscription. Despite knowing a ballot question's risks, Laurier understood the rewards of ballot-box democracy. His official biographer's sanitizing interpretation, glibly dishing referendums, is part of an intellectual tradition that buries or dismisses the reality of participatory democracy in our evolution as a self-governing people.

Prime Minister Laurier's decision to leave prohibition to the provinces, for continued operation within provinces of the federal Scott Act, and for whatever additional measures they enacted, meant Ottawa was no longer the primary political forum for broad liquor policy.

• • •

First to enact prohibition on a province-wide basis was Prince Edward Island in 1901, following a June 1 referendum that year. Then other provinces and Yukon Territory (as a governance extension of British Columbia) brought in prohibition laws, as the Prohibition era reached its zenith. Quebec banned the importation of spirits, but not their domestic manufacture and sale. Quebecers rejected prohibition in a 1919 provincial referendum.

Then the tide turned. In 1920 British Columbians voted themselves wet again, with alcoholic beverages becoming available in British Columbia and Yukon through government stores. After a vote by Manitobans, the province inaugurated a system of government sale and control of alcohol in 1923. Albertans and Saskatchewanians opened the same door in 1924, Ontarians and New Brunswickers in 1927, and Nova Scotians by 1930. Prince Edward Islanders, first in and last out, voted to end "the noble experiment" in 1948.

With one national referendum and three dozen province-wide referendums, together with thousands of local-option referendums in municipalities across the country, the "liquor question" wins, hands down, for "Largest Number of Canadian Ballot Questions on Any One Issue." More than that, it proved the resilience of a federal system of government with divided jurisdictions across a transcontinental country. Wilfrid Laurier's decision, that really only became understandable by Canadians in light of the voting results, showed it was impossible to impose a single "national" program to deal with an issue more social and cultural than economic and legal, and that it was better for a culturally diverse country to let the trial and error of social experimentation work itself out province by province, just as the liquor question continued to be determined community by community. The system of "local option," begun before Confederation, continued under the Canada Temperance Act of 1878 for decades. Today "dry" enclaves can be found in Alberta, Manitoba, Newfoundland and Labrador, Yukon, the Northwest Territories, Nunavut, and northern communities of Ontario and Quebec, many of them aboriginal towns and villages that have used ballot questions in the modern era to curb alcohol abuse by majority vote on the issue by those most directly affected — local residents of the community.

Prohibition-era lore from the twentieth century remains indelibly part of popular culture. Prohibition has gone, but not the organized crime networks it spawned. Costly lessons about "zero tolerance" were learned, but not remembered by those who'd later launch a "war on drugs," which produced more victims than victories. Throughout this drama, referendums performed a central role, first entwined with how those driven to ameliorate a major social problem sought prohibition by democratic means, then how those recognizing the high costs of the flawed solution voted to end it.

23

VOTING ON CONSCRIPTION

The nature of Canada's 1942 plebiscite has been examined by scholars for its significance in Canadian public affairs and cited by referendum critics for "causing deep and emotional divisions" in Canadian society. Earlier chapters examined certain aspects of 1942's ballot question in terms of theory and practice of issue-voting in Canada. To round that out, this brief chapter focuses on the political imperatives of people voting in wartime, because events can only be understood in context.

In a sense, Canada's entry into the Second World War bore little resemblance to our commitment of forces in the First World War. In 1914 Britain's colonies, intrinsic parts of the empire, were dragged into war by the Mother Country, but by 1939 the country was more independent. Prime Minister Borden had insisted Canada be a signatory in our own right to the 1919 Treaty of Versailles, not be subsumed as a colony under Britain's signature. In 1931 the Statute of Westminster had granted self-governing colonies such as the Dominion of Canada full legal freedom. And realism had vaporized the romantic war lust of British-minded Canadians that had propelled all-out support for the empire's earlier wars.

In another sense, however, entering the Second World War was the same — in the way that most generals prepare for the next war by studying the prior one. Prime Minister Mackenzie King, acutely mindful of the politically disastrous impact on Canada of the 1914–18 war, thought only about avoiding its perils. He even deluded himself when trying to discern a path forward. King had been impressed in 1938 by Adolf Hitler, attired not in military uniform but business suit when meeting Canada's PM, as "a good leader." The prime minister's initial assessment of risk convinced him a limited war commitment was possible. And who, really, wouldn't want that? The searing scars of conscripting men for overseas "battles" that were nothing more than slaughtering fields galvanized many Canadians to vow "never again" would we re-enact that murderous fiasco.

The prime minister deliberately waited a week after Britain's entry into the war, to symbolize that independence within the empire meant something. Yet, on September 10, 1939, Parliament in Ottawa voted for war on Germany.

Some said it was essential to get a mandate from the people *before* taking the country into war. Others, remembering how 1917's bitter wartime election had been fought over conscription, opposed that idea, arguing it would be divisive. Prime Minister King told Opposition Leader John Bracken there would be no election for the war's duration in order to sideline partisanship and unite all Canadians against a common external threat. Relying on that, the dutiful Conservatives closed party headquarters, ceased fundraising, and stopped organizing to concentrate exclusively on supporting King's war efforts.

After six months pondering how to achieve an optimal balancing point, the PM called a general election for March 26, 1940. Quebec's Liberals had just ousted the Union Nationale provincial government with an ironclad campaign commitment to oppose conscription, and King saw the opportunity to do the same — codifying his policy on conscription as an electoral mandate while consolidating his grip on power to steer Canada with his plan to wage a "limited liability" war. Throughout the campaign, King removed the fractious conscription issue by solemnly promising Canadian voters there would be "no conscription for overseas military service."

Most voters remained haunted by the nightmarish agony of the war in Europe two decades earlier, with its relentless sacrificing of human lives and consumption of everything else Canada could supply. King's intent was to co-operate with Britain and its allies, but have military involvement subordinated to economic assistance, agricultural products, and industrial support. French-speaking Canadians, persuaded to support going to war on the prime minister's pledge of "participation without conscription," voted heavily to re-elect King's Liberals across Quebec.

The government implemented its "limited-liability" effort by placing Canada's war footing on industrial manufacturing, food production, the Commonwealth air training program, and merchant marine transport to resupply Britain with soldiers, food, medicine, and war *matériel*. But this wasn't the 1914 war when entire armies got bogged down in trenches for years and hundreds of thousands died to gain a hill or a kilometre of enemy territory. The aggressive lethal military force of Nazi Germany, Fascist Italy, and Imperial Japan was leading to the rapid and extensive territorial expansion of enemies on whom Canada had declared war. The prime minister received reports that more soldiers would be needed, that Canada itself was vulnerable to occupation. He became obsessed contemplating how to change his solemn promise on conscription because it was the cornerstone of his strong March 26, 1940, electoral mandate from Canadians. The prime minister and his candidates had been explicit and unconditional in their repeated commitment that a Liberal government wouldn't force men into military service for overseas battle.

By late 1941, the war's outcome was in grave doubt. If the Allies hoped to turn the tide, more sacrifice and more soldiers were needed. But after the first wave of young men and women keen to enlist had signed up in the war's early months, recruitment for overseas service had slowed to a trickle.

On May 7, 1941, Australian Prime Minister Robert Menzies spoke in our House of Commons. Australia's army was engaged on five continents, and he was touring its locations when he stopped over in Ottawa. "It is not for me to say to honourable members of this House what your duty is…. There has never yet been a parliament in a free British county which did not do its duty." He put in personal terms how he was "so utterly convinced that I must put into this task everything I have, that I will fail in no effort, that I will never spare myself in whatever may be necessary to achieve victory." He added, "Nothing else matters except that when this war is over we should live in a free world."

King's government risked a defenceless Canada, unable to maintain the ranks once heavy fighting produced its inevitable casualties.

The country was operating under the National Resources Mobilization Act of 1940, enacted shortly after Germany's swift conquest of France in June 1940. Section 3 empowered the government to impose compulsory duty for home defence only, explicitly not "to serve in the military outside of Canada and the territorial waters thereof." Throughout the autumn of 1941, as King's cabinet discussed full conscription, Quebec cabinet ministers constantly shored up King's anti-conscription predisposition. By November 14, King suggested a plebiscite on conscription might help extricate the Liberals from part of their dilemma.

On December 30, 1941, Winston Churchill, Britain's defiant wartime prime minister, delivered a galvanizing speech in our House of Commons, the first live broadcast from Parliament, heard by Canadians on CBC Radio and others around the globe through the BBC's world service. He described Canada's contribution to the war effort "in troops, in ships, in aircraft, in food, and in finance" as "magnificent." He sketched the year ahead, advising "the Canadian Army may be engaged in one of the most frightful battles the world has ever seen." He stirred deep emotion: "I think it extremely unlikely this war will end without the Canadian Army coming to close quarters with the Germans as their fathers did at Ypres, on the Somme, or on the Vimy Ridge." The packed House and public galleries felt the dire urgency in Churchill's public message, as did listeners across Canada. In private, Churchill impressed upon Prime Minister King the even graver threat that awaited.

The Conservative Opposition, devastated in 1940's surprise election, which by design had found the party utterly unprepared, had changed leaders, replacing a dispirited Robert Manion with Arthur Meighen, former prime minister and now in the Senate, who vowed to implement conscription "over the whole field of war."

In January 1942, Australia reversed its policy and implemented full conscription. Taking his cue from that, King decided that a similar course of action was necessary for Canada. However, always the careful politician, he decided that he needed to protect his government from the potential risks associated with such an action. On January 22, 1942, the speech from the throne stunned listeners. The Liberal government would "seek from the people, by means of a plebiscite, release from any obligation arising out of any past commitments restricting the methods of raising men for military service."

King had divined his path forward. Because Canada had no general enabling statute for direct voting, the Dominion Plebiscite Act, 1942, was introduced in the House of Commons. The bill, envisaging a ballot question on releasing the government from its election promise, implied, but didn't stipulate, that conscription would follow an affirmative vote. During February 1942's parliamentary exchanges, the House of Commons *Debates* would once again record evaluations of the risks and rewards of forcing choice by ballot.

Leading the Official Opposition in the Commons, R.B. Hanson admonished King, saying, "We cannot win this war by plebiscite. Germany does not carry on war by plebiscite. Let this government rise to the level of its duty! Let it not be afraid to lead! A plebiscite is not a policy! It is the negation, the avoidance, of a policy. It is a declaration of impotence!" Channelling the ardent voices of Canadian conscriptionists, Hanson next raised the spectre of future possibilities:

> What will the government do if the plebiscite is indecisive; if the majority is too small? Will it say that, expediency having failed, we shall try another course? And what if the plebiscite is rejected by the people of Canada? Will the government resign? Or will the Prime Minister endeavour to carry on, cabin'd, cribb'd, confined, by a self-imposed vow which renders it impossible to carry out his pledge to the people of Canada that he will meet total war with total effort?

King, responding that his government needed freedom from past commitments, as the shift from limited to total war was under way, said, "Three methods exist by which this release could be obtained." The first would be a general election. "In a general election at this time the issue of conscription for overseas service would become one of the issues and, in existing circumstances," he told the Commons, "would almost certainly be the main issue." The second would be "a referendum solely with reference to the question of conscription for overseas service." The third would be a plebiscite, "not to obtain a decision with respect to conscription, but solely with the object of releasing the Government" from its existing obligation.

The PM suggested pursuing whichever method "would occasion the least interference with the war effort of the country." Ruling out a general election, King stated his belief that the Liberal government still possessed "the confidence of the country" and that it wouldn't be "in the interest of the people themselves, in the existing crisis, to leave the country without a Parliament for the time it would take to hold a general election." Differentiating a general election from direct voting on a single question, he rightly noted how in an election "other issues enter in, so it would not be possible to say that the verdict of the people, whatever it might be, had related solely to the issue of the application of conscription for overseas service."

He also discounted a binding referendum, because "far from being left in the hands of the government, it would be a specific request to the people to make a decision with respect to conscription." Specific decisions should be debated in Parliament, so on this issue, the government should not be bound by a referendum but rather "should be given a free hand to take, subject to its responsibility to Parliament, any course of action which it may believe to be necessary at a time of *war.*"

King reiterated that he didn't believe it would be "fair to the people to ask them to make military decisions." In consulting the people by plebiscite, "the Government is not throwing on the people the responsibility of making a military decision. It is asking the people to give the Government full power and full responsibility to take whatever military decisions the Government, in the light of all its knowledge, believes to be necessary. In consulting the people, therefore, we are not shirking responsibility, we are asking for full responsibility."

The Commons debated all over again, from January 23 to March 4, the fundamentals of a people's mandate. Some MPs worked up fresh speeches; others cribbed ideas and phrases from *Hansard* reports of 1898's debate on the prohibition plebiscite. The only new dimension was the reservation that elected representatives had about the advisability of plebiscite voting during war. They had all just come through a wartime general election.

Speaking again on January 26, the prime minister himself recalled that 1940 election to make his new case. The question of conscription for overseas service had been submitted to the people of Canada in that general election, which he also noted had been held in wartime. During the campaign, leaders of all parties made their statements to the electorate. At its end the people of Canada decided against conscription for overseas service. "So far as I am concerned," stated King, "without any consultation of the people on that subject, I do not intend to take the responsibility of supporting any policy of conscription for service overseas."

Explaining how conscription had been viewed in 1940 by people remembering vividly the conscription crisis of 1917, King then reviewed the changed circumstances of the Second World War that made reconsidering the conscription policy necessary, *but only in consultation with the people.* Looking forward, if the government had to be free to act in accordance with its judgment and subject only to its responsibility to Parliament, "it is clear that means must be found of releasing the Government from any obligation arising out of any past commitments restricting the methods of raising men for military service," he told MPs.

• • •

In Quebec response to holding a plebiscite on military service was outrage. Critics charged that 1940's election promise against conscription had been given *specifically* to Quebecers.[1] This interpretation made complete sense because the pledge had been King's effort to avoid a recurrence of the toxic conscription crisis of 1917, which centred on French-speaking Canadians, and that caused him to make his 1940 "no-conscription" election promise. But with that election over and the Liberals secure in power, Quebecers protested, *all* Canadians would be asked to free the government from its pledge to French Canadians.[2] It wasn't a plebiscite that created high emotion. It was, first, the broken election promise, and second, the fact that a majority electorate favouring conscription would now join the voting to sanctify King's betrayal.

The intense feelings of betrayal in Quebec led to the formation of La Ligue pour la défense du Canada (LPDC), the war's most politically effective civic group. The LPDC, an umbrella organization bringing together labour union representatives, farmers, commercial travellers, and members of local service clubs, campaigned for a Non vote in the plebiscite. The organization proclaimed that its French-Canadian supporters would defend Canada from invasion but resist forced recruitment for overseas military service. André Laurendeau, journalist and organizer, who later was editor of *Le Devoir*, a Bloc populaire Canadien member of Quebec's legislature, and co-chair of the Royal Commission on Bilingualism and Biculturalism, led the potent organization, which had among its younger members future prime minister Pierre Trudeau and future Montreal mayor Jean Drapeau.

The LPDC had little money. Except for *Le Devoir,* virtually all French-language newspapers were supporting the government. The CBC refused Non representatives access to the public airwaves, while Yes supporters benefited from extensive national network time. In surmounting these hurdles, the LPDC relied upon superb campaign organization. Fuelled by passionate resolve, its supporters distributed the anti-conscription message to every potential voter. The message hit home to a nervous, frightened, and profoundly offended French Canada.

By contrast, the Yes campaign, for all its advantages, was a bust — especially where it mattered most — in Quebec. The government information office was drumming up support for the war effort, even though the plebiscite was meant by King not to heighten bellicose resolve but to determine whether he might revoke his promise and still retain Quebecers' favour. No public funds were allocated to reach voters, so "patriotic" distilleries and breweries funded advertising for the Yes campaign.[3] Across Canada speeches by politicians of all parties filled the airwaves and literature poured forth, but in Quebec few were willing to speak out against the clear will of the people.

Voting took place on April 27, 1942. Canadians were asked, *Are you in favour of releasing the government from any obligation arising out of any past commitments restricting the methods of raising men for military service?* The results showed that 2.95 million Canadians would release the government from its no-conscription pledge, and that 1.65 million refused to do so. Voters in eight of the nine provinces reversed the government's mandate. Ontario's 82.3 percent Yes vote was just slightly below the level garnered in Prince Edward Island. The lowest Yes votes were Alberta's 70.4 percent, and New Brunswick's 69.1. Other provinces, except for one, placed in between.

The one was Quebec, where 78.9 percent of electors refused to release the Liberals from their election-winning commitment. Every constituency with a francophone majority registered a strong Non verdict. This anti-conscription sentiment and resentment of the federal Liberals, however, wasn't only confined to Quebec; it also found expression in farming and non-British sections of Manitoba, Ontario, and New Brunswick. Vegreville riding in Alberta and Rosthern constituency in Saskatchewan, both with large Ukrainian and German populations, also voted No.

It had been a foregone conclusion that Canada as a whole would release King from his promise of 1940, but it wasn't Canada as a whole that had sought the promise in the first place. "It had been exacted specifically by and made specifically to Quebec," notes historian Ralph Allen. "It was King's earnest hope that Quebec would release him from it, too, or at least give him enough votes to remove part of the sting of race and sectionalism from the country's thorniest issue."[4]

Turning to the plebiscite so voters themselves could revisit their electoral mandate helped King reduce the Liberals' dilemma, but at the price of Minister of Transport P.J.A. Cardin's resignation, and ongoing threats of other cabinet ministers from Quebec departing as well.

• • •

On May 8, 1942, the prime minister told the Commons he would introduce legislation repealing Section 3 of the Mobilization Act and described his government's policy as "Not necessarily conscription, but conscription if necessary." On July 7, the House voted second reading and the bill carried by 158 to 54.

Although, as noted, critics of direct democracy claim 1942's vote was "divisive," implying that the process created a division between English-speaking and French-speaking Canadians, a clear-eyed interpretation is that, first, the plebiscite reflected long-existing divisions in Canada, and second, the gulf measured by Yes and No votes wasn't simplistically between Canada's two most domination linguistic communities but rather wove together a complex range of beliefs, values, and memories across Canada, including who was prepared, or not, to excuse a government for reversing the campaign pledge that led to its election.

Ironically, one could better argue that the plebiscite actually *promoted* national unity because the voting results helped King keep the country together through the military manpower crisis. The ballot counts unequivocally demonstrated to everybody how strongly Canadian views differed. There was no point, as King said, "winning the war and losing the country."[5] Despite antipathy toward the PM for his mincing ways — and the anti-French hostility in a substantial Anglo quarter summed up by its aggressive slogan "Make the frogs fight!" — grudging political acceptance accompanied King's conduct of the war, especially when his idea of "limited" engagement was transformed by conditions beyond the control of Canadians, and as it became clear the Second World War was utterly different from the First.

Directly because of the plebiscite results, the King government managed to successfully delay introducing conscription for overseas service another *twenty-six months.* Meanwhile, both the people and the government prosecuted the general war effort with increasing success. Canada transformed itself into a significant world player, with naval power, air force strength, wide-scale manufacturing of munitions and weaponry, ever-increasing supplies of food and clothing and medicines for those closer to battle overseas, and a closer partnership of our scientists and engineers with those of Britain and the United States to invent the atomic bomb.

In 1944, when conscription for overseas action finally took effect more than two years after the plebiscite, Canadians earlier conscripted for Home Defence were transported to Europe as well-trained soldiers.

The plebiscite, by offering an outlet for intense feelings of desperation over national survival and of bitterness about electoral betrayal, averted an even uglier conscription eruption, like the searing one of 1917, by helping King buy time to diffuse the crisis. In the bargain, the PM clarified for everyone the constructive role of direct voting, the supreme importance of the people's mandate, and the relationship between Canadians and parliamentarians. Historian Ralph Allen calls King's 1942 national ballot question "perhaps the most ingenious of all his compromises."[6]

24

VOTING ON ABORIGINAL QUESTIONS

North America's oldest political institution, self-government by aboriginal peoples, has been obscured and undermined over the past several centuries by an overlay of European-style governance. Tribal communities varied in how each selected and operated their power hierarchies, but a common feature of most was the ability to achieve collective consensus, thanks partly to the relatively small number of people involved, partly to the methods used.

After European contact and colonization, the ability of Canada's aboriginal peoples to self-govern was compromised by takeover of lands, policies of assimilation, and control mechanisms of the Indian Act. To guide democratic governance, Indian Act regulations provided for the selecting of aboriginal councils by using either election or traditional band custom, and also for the holding of referendums. The minister of Indian affairs can order a referendum, either in response to a band council's request or when a ballot question is deemed advisable. The question might authorize, if a majority agrees, surrender of title to aboriginal lands, but the vote can also be on "any other matter affecting the band."

Referendum voting is generally by secret ballot, but if a band council requests, or if the minister considers it advisable, band members can instead register their support or opposition to the proposition by a show of hands or some other manner the band council approves. The Indian Referendum Regulations not only set out detailed procedures for voting, and provisions for holding subsequent ballot questions, but also grounds for appeals to challenge or nullify the outcome because of a corrupt referendum practice or a violation of the regulations that affected voting results.

Some consider the confrontational nature of a Yes-No decision antithetical to aboriginal ways. The consensus-seeking pattern of deliberate discussion seems incompatible with a referendum sharply framing two sides of an issue and then deciding, by an up-or-down vote, which has majority support and "wins." However, referendums using a secret ballot have helped: they have been adopted by aboriginal choice in ratifying land claim settlements, adopting new systems of governance, and achieving the interests of aboriginal peoples in sensitive cases when open discussion of an issue and public coercion prevented a solution that most wanted but could not otherwise achieve. Communities voting to ban alcohol in order to end social abuse and related problems are a prime example of this.

VOTING TO PROHIBIT ALCOHOL ON RESERVES

On reserves where alcohol was permitted, aboriginal women and their children, victims of extreme circumstances because of drinking, could not, on their own, stand up to those who committed violent acts when drunk. Problems with alcohol weren't confined to males, either. A referendum with its secret ballot empowered aboriginal women, joined by a number of responsible men, to collectively achieve alcohol-free reserves — a result not attainable through open consensus-seeking because of family pressure and the social status of women. Such votes, often close, remain current events, today.

The Natuashish reserve in Labrador, inhabited by Mushuau Innu, has grappled with alcohol abuse ever since the Hudson's Bay Company began trading cheap booze for high-value furs in the 1830s. The community's 2008 effort to resolve its alcoholism problem included a referendum to ratify the band council's bylaw banning the sale, purchase, and possession of alcohol within the forty-three-square-kilometre community. First passed by a razor-thin margin of two votes, local prohibition was upheld by a wider margin in a subsequent referendum in March 2010.

The northern Yukon community of Old Crow, home of the Vuntut Gwitchin, similarly voted itself dry, and eastern Yukon's Ross River, under control of its Dena Council, made itself an alcohol-free community. Across the Northwest Territories seven aboriginal communities are dry today, while ten have controlled alcohol. Of the Northwest Territories' seven liquor stores, those at Fort Simpson and Norman Wells have daily limits and sales restrictions. In Nunavut six aboriginal communities have voted themselves dry, and fourteen have self-imposed committees whose members are locally elected to which anyone wanting alcohol must apply for permission to buy a limited quantity. Only five Nunavut localities have no liquor restrictions.

In Northern Ontario, four James Bay Cree communities remain dry although transport of alcohol onto the reserves is lightly enforced. Eight of Quebec's James Bay Cree communities have prohibition, while the ninth, Whapmagoostui, is a wet exception. Of the dry settlements, Chisasibi alone has a checkpoint to enforce the ban on bringing alcohol into the village.

To contend with a major social challenge, Aboriginals have turned to issue-voting and local control of decision-making, harmonizing referendum techniques with local custom.

REFERENDUM USE IN CHOOSING BAND GOVERNANCE

A different example of a referendum's pragmatic utility was tested by the Mohawks of Kanesatake. The band had a customary way for selecting its council, as the Indian Act envisaged, with clan mothers selecting the chief and councillors. Who, after all, knew better the character of adults than the mothers who'd watched them develop since infancy? However, not all Mohawks at Kanesatake accepted the authority of this clannish leadership; they wanted modern democratic methods. At stake was the legitimacy of the band's government.

The contest became so contentious that it made national news and reached the floor of the House of Commons. Kanesatake's modernists and traditionalists could never agree. Consensus-building through open discussion had floated far downstream. Was it time to force a choice? On April 16, 1991, Indian Affairs Minister Tom Siddon announced that a referendum would determine the form of government for Kanesatake by majority decision using a secret ballot. "Any future actions will be guided," he said, "by the democratic decision of the people."

The outcome was decisive enough to switch from the electoral college of clan mothers but not deep enough to eradicate the disputatious nature of the Kanesatake Mohawks themselves. Disagreement between modernists and traditionalists continued to hobble band government, no matter which method was used to select it. That is why, despite launching democratic council elections in 1991, the task of clarifying the roles of the chiefs, the grand chief, and an elders' council never got done. The referendum, though an alternative worth trying in the band's elusive quest for effective self-government, was no silver bullet to solve the deeper crisis.

Ever since elections were introduced in 1991, implementing the referendum results, Kanesatake traditionalists have boycotted them. They'd voted on the ballot question to reject elections under the Indian Act and adhere instead to the matrilineal system of government that existed before colonization. They would yield neither to majority vote nor modernity.

There are times a referendum can't produce any reward at all.

SETTING GROUND RULES FOR ABORIGINAL REFERENDUMS

Use of referendums by aboriginal peoples to clarify and force an important decision, as seen in these examples of voting on alcohol and on the method for selecting a band council, entwine established Canadian referendum procedures and aboriginal custom to achieve a unique, or particular, way of doing things.

For instance, with the Indian Act envisaging formation of band councils either by voting according to the mini-election statute tailored to band council elections and enacted as a schedule to the act, or by traditional custom for tribal selection of chiefs, many bands reverted to customary practice after voting on the choice by ballot question.

Blending the democratic "majority rules" approach of a referendum with traditional methods of aboriginal consensus-building has increasingly led to general acceptance in Canada's aboriginal community of a referendum's value in certain cases, though some bands want higher levels of voter support to endorse or ratify particular types of proposals. This is the case especially for the most essential issue of all: a land claim settlement involving surrender of aboriginal title to territory.

Specific cases involve the concept of "bylaw power" and how bylaws should be approved. A strong consensus emerged in the 1980s among aboriginal leaders for a bylaw power in the Indian Act that recognized a band's authority to determine its own election rules, incorporating local custom and tradition as it saw fit. This resulted in new self-government legislation, such as the Cree-Naskapi Act, which gave the nine Cree-Naskapi bands in Quebec authority to make bylaws for band council elections and terms of office, and the Sechelt Indian Band Self-Government Act, which empowers the Sechelt Band of British Columbia to do likewise.

There was general agreement that election rules developed under the proposed bylaw power should be voted on by band members in a referendum. Within aboriginal communities, some bands felt that a majority vote (50 percent plus one) of *all* members should be needed, the same requirement for approval of band membership codes; other bands suggested a majority vote by members attending a meeting held specifically to review the election rules would suffice — a rule similar to those for voting in referendums on such matters as land surrenders.[1]

Harmonizing traditional methods of decision-making in aboriginal communities with Parliament's enacted Indian Referendum Regulations governing votes on issues has reinforced ballot-question democracy as an integral component of governance in Canada.

NISGA'A PIONEER LAND CLAIM TREATY AND RATIFICATION BY REFERENDUM

The successful Nisga'a Treaty, ratified by a Nisga'a Nation referendum on November 7, 1998, and then enacted by British Columbia's legislature and the Parliament of Canada, is a stellar example of unflinching determination by indigenous people.

In 1887, Nisga'a chiefs travelled by water down the Pacific coast to Victoria to discuss the "Nisga'a Land Question," only to be turned away on the steps of the legislature by B.C. Premier William Smithe. They themselves didn't turn away from their issue, however. By 1949, Nisga'a Chief Frank Calder couldn't be turned back from the legislature. He'd been elected one of its members. By 1955, Chief Calder had also emerged as president of the Nisga'a Land Committee. By 1973, his own determination and the persistence of his people resulted in the landmark "Calder Decision" in which the Supreme Court of Canada confirmed that the Nisga'a held aboriginal title to their lands before settlers came, though leaving unresolved whether aboriginal title continued to exist. By 1982, amendments to the Constitution dealt with that further by recognizing the existence of aboriginal rights. Through more decades, responding with patient resolve to irreversible changes on their territory, the Nisga'a reacquired many powers ranging from fishing rights to operating health care services. The culmination of their unrelenting efforts finally came with the Nisga'a proceeding, under the Government of Canada's "comprehensive land claim policy," to negotiate a settlement directly with Ottawa, while the B.C. government monitored negotiations with observer status.

The Nisga'a was the only First Nation in British Columbia to participate in the new "comprehensive" regime for negotiations announced by the Trudeau government in 1976. Two and a half decades later the Nisga'a final agreement, with British Columbia now a party to the talks, had been hammered out, establishing rights of self-government for the Nisga'a people in the Nass River Valley, a northwestern sector of British Columbia. In 1996 the Nisga'a people agreed by a "show of hands" for Yes or No at a special tribal assembly in New Aiyansh, capital of the now self-governing jurisdiction, to proceed, on the basis of an agreement-in-principle reached in their negotiations with the federal and provincial governments. The document was signed a month later at New Aiyansh by Canada's Indian affairs minister, Ron Irwin, British Columbia's aboriginal affairs minister, John Cashore, and Nisga'a Tribal Council President Joseph Gosnell, Sr., making international news as a historic breakthrough and leading to negotiation of the final agreement. Two years later, on November 9, 1998, the Nisga's people ratified the final agreement by referendum. Voter turnout was 72 percent, with 61 percent voting Yes. By April 2000, the Nisga'a Final Agreement was enacted by British Columbia's legislature and then implemented through an act of Parliament to become a binding treaty between all three governments — the new Constitution of the Nisga'a people.

Despite this success, the determination and time needed to overcome the complexity of the Trudeau government's "comprehensive" system meant no other B.C. First Nation participated in this process. By 1993, a revamped structure for negotiating B.C. land claims had accordingly been established. Under both regimes, however, referendums formed an indispensable process for aboriginal communities in understanding and ratifying the final agreements that had been negotiated.

REFERENDUMS CENTRAL TO B.C. LAND CLAIMS

The three-party negotiations involving the Canadian government, B.C. government, and British Columbia's First Nations begin with a First Nation entering into claim negotiations, work through to an agreement-in-principle, then proceed until reaching a final agreement. Within this framework, substantive treaty negotiations settle intricate and interrelated subjects about self-government, resource use, land ownership, jurisdictions, and more. After the parties settle on a final agreement, the chief negotiators for Canada, British Columbia, and the First Nation in question each recommend it to their respective principals for ratification.

The sequential steps to full ratification begin with the First Nation community holding a referendum. Following First Nation ratification, the Province of British Columbia proceeds with a cabinet minister recommending the agreement for approval and then introducing settlement legislation in the assembly where the bill is debated and enacted. After provincial ratification, Ottawa follows a similar process through Parliament. The conclusion is a signing ceremony of all three parties, which makes the final agreement a binding treaty.

This process has resulted in a number of final agreements, with more in various stages of progress involving about two-thirds of the 281 First Nations in scattered distinct locations within British Columbia, ranging from remote pristine wilderness areas to developed urban spaces.

When a final agreement begins its concluding journey to become a treaty, the initial hurdle is ratification by the First Nation's people, and problems can arise that are common to political society generally. For instance, with royal commissions and parliamentary committees, the small team of individuals who have spent months immersed in the complexities of a subject and who at last have knitted together an agreement or solution they recommend to others for approval, risk dealing in an off-handed manner with people who are not "up to speed" and who have not had "ownership" of the project. Those who must be well informed about what they are asked to vote for, be they members of a legislature, members of Parliament, or in the case of a land claim final agreement, members of a First Nation, might understandably be almost indifferent to the matter. This challenge of a "culture gap" is not between Aboriginals and non-Aboriginals but between negotiators and non-negotiators. Experience in British Columbia shows that more attention to the ratification process for First Nation peoples whose rights and future are at stake on a ballot will better serve them and the land claims process itself.

LESSONS ABOUT LAND CLAIM REFERENDUMS

Of the first three final agreements to emerge from this structured system, two were approved, one rejected. The Tsawwassen First Nation, a seafaring people of the Coast Salish located south of Vancouver near the U.S. border, benefited from effective continuous communications among its close-knit community of 455 members. Its final agreement was ratified with the support of 70 percent of registered band voters in July 2007.

In contrast, members of the Lheidli T'enneh First Nation rejected their final agreement that same year. Of 273 eligible voters, 234 cast ballots, 111 Yes to 123 No. Those in charge didn't expect this outcome. When the final agreement was rejected, those with stewardship for the land claim expressed the usual comments of shock and surprise when voters have been taken for granted and when assumptions have been made about messages and communication.

The surprised B.C. Treaty Commission, having overall carriage of land claim negotiations, promptly surveyed members of the Lheidli T'enneh First Nation. The commission wanted to discover what missteps had been taken and what might help the referendum process better fulfill its educational role. There are few better wake-up calls to governing authorities than a majority No vote.

The Lheidli T'enneh treaty process had been driven by a "Community Treaty Council" comprising family representatives. In 2003, when this council approved the initial agreement-in-principle, only fifteen community members took part. In retrospect, the big mistake was to not hold a vote of the membership on the agreement-in-principle. Rather than waiting until the end of extensive negotiations, a preliminary referendum could have determined the general willingness of band members to have their negotiating team launch intricate lengthy negotiations toward a final agreement. For many band members, the community meetings held *after* negotiations had been concluded were their first opportunity to question and get answers about provisions that would, if approved by a majority, become a binding treaty.

By 2006, some community meetings about the land claim were held to expand the circle of the informed beyond the original fifteen members of the Community Treaty Council. But a majority of those present earned a $40 attendance honorarium each week, almost as much money as they got each month in Social Assistance. In retrospect, that $40 enticement to attend meetings was deemed a mistake, attracting people wanting cash more than answers about land claims.

Community Treaty Council members were supposed to provide information from each weekly meeting to their family and bring back questions or concerns to the next meeting. The council didn't want the chief or band councillors to participate in these meetings, unless they did so as family representatives. That created an exclusionary divide that led to misunderstanding about whether the band council even supported the negotiations, or whether, according to a more conspiratorial view, its members might become windfall beneficiaries of the treaty.

The fact that band members didn't understand the implications of what was happening was the direct result of abysmal communications. The essence of a referendum is that ballots be cast by informed voters. Community Treaty Council members weren't given communications support, nor training that would equip them to deliver information in an understandable way. Follow-up with family members, though part of the theoretical plan, didn't work in practice because not all council members adequately conveyed information to family members, due to the fact many lacked understanding themselves.

The comprehension level in the community was poor because of low literacy levels. Band members reported that many of the questions they did ask went unanswered. As a result, when meetings took place, Treaty Council members were generally quiet and didn't ask questions, except for "four or five who regularly asked questions and dominated proceedings." It was concluded after the referendum that the Community Treaty Council should have done a better job getting feedback and identifying and addressing concerns much earlier in the process.

A related problem was how the negotiators for all three parties (the two governments and the Lheidli T'enneh) exerted intense pressure to hold the band ratification vote quickly to "keep the momentum" — their own, not the community's. In August 2006, the negotiators completed their mandates and recommended that the Lheidli T'enneh membership vote on the final agreement by January 2007, a date later pushed back to March. Starting in November, information meetings for band members were held in eight of the dispersed Lheidli T'enneh community's locations. Because turnout was low, home visits were offered. Few took up the offer.

In February 2007, a massive package of information, meant to prepare them for voting, landed at the homes of all the band's far-flung members. The delivery included the complete final agreement and its appendices, a 108-page "plain-language" guide to the agreement, information sheets, and a video. Apart from the challenges in comprehending this daunting package due to low literacy levels in the community, the guide itself was intimidating for voters, most of whom had never been in the negotiation's information loop. Even the "plain-language" guide, while helpful in answering questions of many band members, was in this context incomprehensible. The Treaty Commission's investigation suggested professional communicators ought to have provided information to band members in a non-threatening way, answered questions, and gathered feedback.

A recurring point of importance with referendums is timing. In the midst of preparing for the Lheidli T'enneh treaty referendum, band council elections took place, running from nominations in January to voting for chief and council on March 8, the election and referendum campaigns overlapping, voting for band council taking place one week before referendum voting. The election confounded the treaty-making referendum because it brought to the fore a long-standing division in the community — one between those who sought to maintain the traditional ways of choosing the band's leaders and those more open to non-traditional alternatives. Since 1929, the Lheidli T'enneh custom for choosing chiefs had been replaced by the Indian Act's alternate election procedure. But, just as with the Kanesatake, competing views about the different systems continued to divide band members. That is why the election campaigns for band council became battles over nepotism, family privileges, and trust of office-holders, the fallout from which tainted consideration of the land claim settlement vote. The commission's survey found that voters' thinking mingled both rounds of voting: people voted No suspecting the same people would be in power under the proposed new system of governance with six representatives elected at large; people voted No, since the treaty was linked in their minds to a prevailing view among some members that band councils are, and had been, corrupt; that protections weren't adequate; that if implemented as a treaty the new arrangement would make the chief and treaty manager and their families rich.

Trust was clearly a problem, because negotiators, not from the community, were seen as outsiders and defenders of "the package" rather than servants or agents of the band membership. Developing their information campaign, the treaty team worked toward a Yes vote and with little thought about responding to those working for a No outcome. The negotiators considered the Lheidli T'enneh website the primary information tool, but it wasn't an important communication vehicle at all. Beyond the limitations of cyberspace, influential elders didn't trust what was written on paper, spoken by outsiders, or even less, seen on a computer screen.

Taking stock of the No majority's rejection of the final agreement, the survey concluded that the referendum came too fast for people to gain a basic understanding of the proposed treaty. Too much information was dumped on band members at once, and only shortly before the vote. The plain-language materials, although responsive to members' questions, were still too complex. There was poor communication among family heads. There was inadequate information on the financial value of the land settlement to the Lheidli T'enneh, and about governance, taxes, and the constitution. Band members needed more precision about safeguards, conflict-of-interest guidelines, and dispute resolution for members. Some were unable to weigh how their existing rights, including inherent aboriginal rights and their rights under the Indian Act, would be affected if the final agreement became a treaty.

Greater effort should have been made not to hold meetings but to get out and talk with individual community members. Extra steps were required to ensure clear and timely information reached people affected. Individuals were afraid to speak out for fear of a backlash, including loss of band benefits. Consequences of a No vote hadn't been communicated clearly so that band members looking for a better deal from government by rejecting the treaty — as if this was just a round in a bargaining session — were shocked following the rejection to discover there would be no further negotiations.

This candid portrait of a community preparing to vote on a specific issue of transcending importance, although drawn for one First Nation in British Columbia, closely resembles the intricate electoral dynamic across Canada whenever a referendum takes place. Rather than being disdainful of citizens coming to grips with life in a democracy — "the people can't understand complex issues" is the typical dismissal — it is by learning from shortcomings the way the B.C. Treaty Commission intended through its survey that leads to corrections going forward, just as the Canada Elections Act continuously benefits from experience and incremental improvement.

BRITISH COLUMBIA'S TREATY NEGOTIATION REFERENDUM

By 2001 in British Columbia, the Nisga'a Treaty had taken effect, many other treaties were under negotiation, and a provincial election was looming. The Opposition Liberal Party, in the campaign's run-up months and during the 2001 election itself, drew voters who opposed aboriginal self-government or who were upset by other issues forming part of the land claim negotiations. Because so many treaties remained to be negotiated with other First Nations in the province, these issues were not retrospective to the Nisga'a agreement but related to future land claim settlements. Even so, the Nisga'a agreement entered the picture, too. It had been negotiated and signed by British Columbia's NDP government, against which the Liberals were now campaigning. Liberal leader Gordon Campbell didn't say a Liberal government would revoke it, but he did commit to revisiting aboriginal land claim issues and negotiations by holding a referendum.

On May 16, 2001, the Campbell-led Liberals won a convincing victory with an absolute majority of votes and an overwhelming majority of seats in the legislature. At this stage in the province's history, no party could sidestep the state of the aboriginal peoples in British Columbia. The NDP focused on modernizing aboriginal rights. The Liberals had an agenda of specific actions: doubling British Columbia's First Citizens Fund to $72 million, creating a $30 million Economic Measures Fund for aboriginal business development, and signing more than two dozen "economic partnership agreements" worth $2.6 million for projects ranging from petroleum training to a wildlife advisory system.

But there was something more in the new government's plan: the Liberal view of land claims posited a "provincial-interest" component to balance specific aboriginal needs. The Liberals pledged "to establish a new relationship with aboriginal people" and envisaged "a successful treaty process" as being one that "will help aboriginal people reach their goals." Gordon Campbell judged those goals to be the same as those shared by all British Columbians: "health care when we need it, education that gives children an opportunity to build a bright future, and economic opportunities."

The premier stated, "We are committed to negotiating workable, affordable treaty settlements that will provide certainty, finality, and equality." He saw treaties as "offering a new era of hope, economic opportunity, and greater self-determination for all aboriginal people," then added, "but for too long, most British Columbians have felt shut out of the process." And he now had an electoral mandate to hold the referendum. Describing the vote as being "on principles for treaty negotiations," Premier Campbell told British Columbians it was "an opportunity for you to have a direct say on an issue of vital importance to us all."

British Columbia's 2002 referendum on issues relating to aboriginal land claims settlement took ballot-box democracy into a new realm. The ballot asked not one but eight questions. Voters answered them not at polling stations but by postal ballots. And the issues pitted the province's aboriginal minority against the non-aboriginal majority, since the electorate included all of British Columbia's voting population. The province's 4.4 million non-aboriginal voters would add their voices to British Columbia's 144,000 First Nations voters in answering questions about land claims. Many First Nations leaders in British Columbia challenged the validity of such a province-wide vote. They contested it through media statements, public protests, website campaigns, court challenges, and a referendum boycott.

The Treaty Negotiations Referendum Regulation of British Columbia was created by order-in-council on March 15, 2002, under authority of the Election Act. Despite adopting the practice of mail-in ballots for a referendum, it lacked the modern requirement for umbrella organizations to coordinate the Yes and No campaigns, failed to impose campaign spending limits, and provided no mechanism to track campaign spending.

These ballot questions, described by the government as "principles being considered to guide the Province's approach to treaty negotiations," were to be answered Yes or No:

- *Do you agree that the Provincial Government should adopt the principle that private property should not be expropriated for treaty settlements?*

- *Do you agree that the Provincial Government should adopt the principle that the terms and conditions of leases and licences should be respected; and fair compensation for unavoidable disruption of commercial interests should be ensured?*

- *Do you agree that the Provincial Government should adopt the principle that hunting, fishing and recreational opportunities on Crown land should be ensured for all British Columbians?*

- *Do you agree that the Provincial Government should adopt the principle that parks and protected areas should be maintained for the use and benefit of all British Columbians?*

- *Do you agree that the Provincial Government should adopt the principle that province-wide standards of resource management and environmental protection should continue to apply?*

- *Do you agree that the Provincial Government should adopt the principle that Aboriginal self-government should have the characteristics of local government, with powers delegated from Canada and British Columbia?*

- *Do you agree that the Provincial Government should adopt the principle that treaties should include mechanisms for harmonizing land use planning between Aboriginal governments and neighbouring local governments?*

- *Do you agree that the Provincial Government should adopt the principle that the existing tax exemptions for Aboriginal people should be phased out?*

If nothing else, this list made clear what British Columbia's negotiators were grappling with. As for what the First Nations were addressing, not included in this list, the subjects enumerated by the Council of British Columbia Indian Chiefs were equally extensive.[2]

Premier Campbell and his Liberal government campaigned for an overwhelming result. The government's information brochure *Your Guide to the Referendum*, widely distributed to electors, set out the B.C. negotiators explanations for each of the eight ballot questions in a way that suggested only one "correct" answer (Yes).

The premier, addressing voters, whipped up sentiment: "In the nine years since the treaty process was established by the province, federal government, and First Nations, almost half a billion dollars has been spent on negotiations — and not one settlement has been achieved. That's created uncertainty for all of us, Aboriginal and non-Aboriginal alike." His minister responsible for treaty negotiations, Attorney General Geoff Plant, instructed: "Answering yes to these questions will provide the province's negotiators with a clear mandate on issues that have arisen and will continue to arise in the course of negotiations."

The referendum focused British Columbia's long-standing controversies over land claim issues. The general public could no longer complain about having no say in the settlement process. But British Columbia's First Nations saw the questions reflecting only the provincial government's perspective on negotiations that involved *three* parties, making the referendum one-dimensional in the power struggle over provincial authority and aboriginal co-existing jurisdiction to govern lands used for living, forestry, mining, ecotourism, hunting, and recreation.

The official results showed some 36 percent of eligible voters cast ballots. Their affirmative responses to all eight questions ranged from 84 percent to 95 percent of valid votes. To British Columbia's aboriginal leaders, those numbers meant either that negotiations were at an end, or that the results were irrelevant. Premier Campbell met the press and interpreted the results as clear and positive support for the government's principles.

Since then, a half-dozen more treaties have been concluded, either within the established B.C. treaty process or independently outside it. More continue progressing through the complex and necessarily time-consuming process. The three-party negotiating structure continues to be challenged in court, and by rejection, on the part of certain aboriginal leaders who argue that aboriginal title to far too much land is being forfeited through the B.C. treaty process, with negotiating First Nations getting as little as 5 percent of their claimed land recognized. A November 21, 2007, court decision ruled that the Xeni Gwet'in First Nation had demonstrated aboriginal title to half of the Nemaiah Valley, and that the province had no power over these lands.

The referendum is an important part of how this works, helpful not just in forcing choice but compelling attention by band members to what is involved — just as happened when all Canadians had to think more closely about the nature and implications of aboriginal self-government in preparing to vote on the Charlottetown Accord.

25

VOTING ON WOMEN'S RIGHTS

The people of Canada's western provinces not only pioneered Prairie settlement, agriculture, and large-scale resource development but were catalysts in Canada's democratic evolution. New parties formed Farmer, Progressive, Social Credit, and Co-operative Commonwealth Federation (CCF)/New Democrat governments in several provinces, while Progressive, CCF/NDP, and Reform Party candidates elected by western Canadians represented them in the House of Commons. Western Canadians pushed the frontiers of direct voting on issues, their legislatures were first to extend voting rights to women, and a B.C. referendum won approval from an all-male electorate to grant women the franchise.

ENFRANCHISING WOMEN

The quest in British Columbia for equality rights in electing representatives achieved early success in 1873 when "this ocean-washed pioneer community gave women the right to vote in municipal affairs, and did not limit the privilege to unmarried women."[1] By 1885, the push to include this democratic right for provincial elections advanced further when Victoria's chapter of the Women's Christian Temperance Union (WCTU) petitioned the legislature to enfranchise females. The Victoria WCTU was no hard-core suffragist group, like its often violent counterparts in the United States and Britain, which demanded the vote for its own sake.

The WCTU's interest in female suffrage, as prohibition historian Ruth Spence notes, was longer-term and goal-specific, a dimension of the broader prohibition movement. Once women got the vote, they would use their new power to abolish the liquor traffic.[2]

Provincial legislators heard out the WCTU delegation, accepted the petition, and then got on with other business. Yet for the rest of the 1880s and through the 1890s, pressure steadily mounted to enfranchise women. More petitions and delegations arrived at the legislature in Victoria. The government opined that women really didn't want the vote, as evidenced by the relatively few signatories to the petitions, and comforted by that observation, ignored the appeals.[3] Several pro-prohibition MLAs, however, understanding the WCTU's two-step strategy, began introducing private members' bills to give women provincial voting rights. Eleven such bills were presented between 1886 and 1899, though none of them reached even second-reading or debate stage in the legislature.[4]

In 1896, to show a modicum of responsiveness, the government and legislature granted women the right to vote for their school trustees and to run as candidates for such offices themselves, provided they or their husbands possessed the requisite property qualifications. It was some advance, but connected women only to children and their schooling, acknowledged women's interest in local not provincial matters, and tied women's eligibility to property as a test of their stable presence in the community. After nearly two decades of strenuous effort, with only this limited "accomplishment," the energy of those leading this cause understandably ebbed and the women's suffrage movement lost momentum. Only two bills for provincial enfranchisement of women were introduced from 1900 to 1910, both of them crushed by the Conservative majority during debate on second reading.[5]

Like Pacific tides, however, a movement that ebbed would again flow. Serious social issues affecting women gained notoriety as fresh women's groups enlightened the public about the dire implications of women's inequality. The battle for women's suffrage opened along a wider front, confronting far more than "demon rum." One issue was the Dower Act's treatment of married women's property rights. Vancouver women's clubs petitioned for a new dower regime because married women's rights about property, education, marriage, and guardianship of children had no protection in law but "were contingent upon the characters of their husbands."[6]

In January 1910, the steely new resolve of women in Vancouver to secure legal equality in social legislation through the power of the ballot manifested itself with the formation of the "Pioneer" chapter of the Equality League with one explicit goal: "securing the franchise for women." Four months later, ramping up an ambitious provincial organization, the B.C. Political Equality League was established with female and male members. Vancouver's mayor, Louis Taylor, presided at its founding convention, strongly endorsing women's suffrage. One delegate, Mrs. Gordon Grant, said, "Women in British Columbia have got tired of going to the legislature and asking for amendments to the laws concerning them and being put off with polite assurances of consideration, which were forgotten as soon as the last 'good afternoon' had been spoken. In order to get needed legislation, they must have the vote."[7]

But men controlled the legislature. Elected by men alone, they determined who could vote for representatives to the assembly — a self-referencing closed circuit. The oft-lauded majesty of democratic government remained a sham when the entrance to law-making power was so tightly guarded. Was there no escaping this conundrum?

Disgusted by the government's joking manner in rejecting women's petitions, Mrs. C.R. Townley of the Equality League's Vancouver branch published a serious pamphlet on the legal status of women. Under the law, she noted, wives could be deserted and left destitute; minors' estates belonged entirely to the father, and even if he deserted his family, he still had legal claim to the earnings of his minor children; in certain circumstances, a husband could collect and use his wife's income; he could will his property, even her dower, away from her; and as sole guardian, he could will guardianship of children away from her and need not consult her on the children's education or marriage. Many cases before B.C. courts showed men abusing their superior legal status. A woman's legal right to seek an injunction restraining her husband if he deserted her, or from acquiring the wages of their minor children, wasn't widely known. Moreover, this judicial remedy was expensive and difficult.

Seeking to eliminate the worst of these anomalies, petitions generated by Equality League members sought specific reforms — fairer laws on inheritance, protection of dower rights, equal guardianship of children, a widow's right to automatically become sole guardian, consent of both parents to the marriage of minors, preventing a father willing children away from the mother, and granting a deserted wife the right to earnings of minor children without a court order. Of all these, Attorney General William Bowser was prepared only to see changes to the Dower Act, proposed in a private member's bill. Not being government legislation, he pointed out, members could vote for or against it in a free vote. In the final hours of the legislative session, the dower bill was allowed to go to second reading, which many women believed to be progress. But it was a hoax. MLAs wanted to appear sympathetic by voting for the bill, knowing it wouldn't reach third and final reading, so that even this one measure among many asked for wouldn't be enacted.

"What the Government hoped to gain by deliberately insulting the best organized section of women in the province is not clear," writes historian A.M. Adams. However, the "effect of its crude treatment was immediately noticeable as this group decided to go all out for the franchise. As Mrs. Townley herself put it, "Our women were intelligent enough to recognize at last the real value of their present influence with Parliament, and that the dignity of citizenship alone will make their wishes carry weight in the legislative halls."[8]

By this date, women were voting in New Zealand, Australia, Tasmania, Scandinavian countries, and American states Wyoming, Utah, Colorado, Idaho, Washington, and California. In each of these jurisdictions, said the Equality League's Elsie MacGill, "woman suffrage had been followed quickly by changes in social laws; by statutes that provided for equal rights of guardianship between parents; raised the age of marriage; protected the marriage survivor from poverty by will of the deceased spouse; enforced maintenance; prevented destitution." Here was prima facie evidence, she reasoned, "that only when women could threaten or cajole with full power of the ballot could they expect immediate sweeping reforms, for elsewhere such legislation lagged."[9]

Taking a constructive new tack, women actively demonstrated through their social work how they were responsible citizens worthy of being entrusted with the franchise. The onset of war in 1914 brought further momentum to the cause. Although the educational and public activities of the suffrage movement in British Columbia had again reached their prior high-water mark, instead of pushing to capitalize on their successful efforts, "the suffrage societies ceased campaigning as such to participate in the war effort." Seen as a matter of putting first things first, this switch paid dividends in the long run, notes Adams, because "valuable contributions made by these efficient groups and their temporary abandonment of their own interests added a great number of supporters to their cause."[10]

When suffrage agitation revived in 1916, former foes of women voting "vied with its friends in offering tribute to the services performed by women as partners in defence of the nation," explains Catherine Cleverdon about this changed mood.[11] Only organized labour, long outspoken in advocating voting rights for women, cooled its ardour for the cause because women were filling jobs performed by men before the war, and the unions feared this would remain the new peacetime condition, leaving men unemployed. On April 14, 1916, the *British Columbia Federalist* editorialized that "the capitalist, anxious to exploit cheap labour, would see that women got the vote to keep men from getting back their jobs."[12] In general, women earned respect doing "men's work" to win the war, leading even W.J. Bowser, who'd risen from attorney general to premier in 1915, to concede their entitlement to share in affairs of state.

Adding to this surge in British Columbia by 1916 were the triumphs for women's voting rights in the Prairie provinces. Saskatchewan and Alberta suffragists only had to arouse general public interest in the issue, then ask the provincial governments for the franchise. In both cases, the governments saw the justice of the request and granted it; a less friendly Manitoba government, however, put up stiffer opposition. But by 1916 all three had extended voting rights to women through votes of their all-male legislators alone. "Besides bringing encouragement to the active workers in the movement," notes Cleverdon, "this triple victory on their eastern flank rather piqued British Columbians who always gloried in their progressiveness."[13]

Nothing spurs action like falling behind others. B.C. Liberals, out of office and seeking support from those annoyed with their Conservative government, forged a working alliance with the suffragists, "a group of intelligent, well-organized, and politically minded (though disfranchised) citizens." In February 1916, Liberal leader H.C. Brewster declared the political and legal inequities existing between the sexes to be "unjust, undemocratic, and detrimental to our development" and would "not exist any longer in British Columbia under a Liberal government."[14]

The Tory's political position in British Columbia was now exceedingly tenuous. Four years before, the party had swept back into office and faced a meagre opposition of just two MLAs. But its popular support dissipated, and the party was weakened from strife and "open breaches" on the question of women's suffrage. A change of leadership in 1915, when Attorney General Bowser replaced Premier Richard McBride, was an attempted solution.[15]

At the start of 1916's legislative session, two Conservative MLAs introduced a private member's bill to grant women voting rights, and veteran Socialist member J.T.W. Place reintroduced his private member's bill for the same purpose. Then Premier Bowser astounded the legislature. He suggested these measures be withdrawn, because the government itself intended to bring in legislation to give women the vote as of January 1, 1917. There was only one catch: a referendum would decide whether the Women's Franchise Act would come into force.

Liberal leader Brewster attacked a referendum as unjust to women. They had already indicated their support for enfranchisement but would have no vote in the referendum. Mrs. Gordon Grant of Victoria, an early leader in Canada's feminist movement and the first woman elected to Victoria's school board, who each year led a delegation to the legislature seeking enhanced women's rights, opposed the referendum on "the unfairness of submitting the question to a purely male constituency and the fact that it would mean women would neglect their war work to campaign for a favourable vote."[16] By April, a large contingent representing every segment of women's society in British Columbia met the premier to voice unanimous opposition to the idea. On May 15 and 16, the Political Equality League, assembled in Vancouver for an emergency convention, telegraphed "a final appeal" to Bowser. The convention sought enactment of a woman's suffrage bill by the legislature without conditions and without a ballot question. However, British Columbia's premier remained firm on the referendum.

Debate in the legislature on Place's voting rights bill stretched over five days, growing steadily harsher, the recriminations ever more bitter. The Liberals argued Bowser could prove his sincerity about enfranchising women by doing it now so they could vote in the coming provincial election. Victoria's *Daily Times* suggested logically that the premier, given his record on women's suffrage, knew he'd receive little support at the polls from newly enfranchised females and thus was using the referendum as a tactic to sidetrack women's suffrage, a devious concession to something he disliked and feared.

On May 17, the premier was furious about the acrimonious debate, enforced party discipline, and ended discussion of the private member's bill by defeating the measure. He ordered the party whip to crack the Conservative members into line. Party discipline took "precedence over personal views for certain Conservative members," notes Catherine

Cleverdon, "who had voiced approval of woman suffrage on other occasions."[17] Bowser became "somewhat uneasy," adds Adams, "when three Conservatives voted in support of it," anyway.[18] The Conservatives still enjoyed a large majority, but by 1916, with the government's support withering, the premier couldn't tolerate elected representatives voting according to their convictions rather than following a command from the party's hierarchy. Most Conservative members had no trouble voting against Place's bill, though. It was normal procedure to defeat an Opposition member's initiative, especially since in this case political credit for women getting the vote would go to a Socialist.

The government members next voted to enact various bills Bowser had introduced, legislation that not only included women's right to vote but also to be elected to the legislature. The Women's Suffrage Referendum Act provided a simple majority would be enough to decide the issue. The Conservative government had also decided to hold a long-awaited referendum on prohibition. Both ballot issues would be voted on the same day as the provincial election, "the best date because of economy and bringing out the largest and fairest vote."[19] These measures, and others dealing with voting by underage soldiers and those serving overseas in the war, were pushed through the legislature by late May and received Royal Assent to become law on May 31, 1916.

• • •

Initially, B.C. suffragists viewed Premier Bowser's manoeuvre with suspicion because he'd found ways before to confound their quest for voting rights. So an adjusted strategy was required. To this date, the campaign of the suffragists "had been directed at women and members of the Legislative Assembly, but now the issue was to be decided by the male electorate and they had only a short time to convince it of the justice of their cause."[20] The suffragists of British Columbia, said Mrs. J.A. Clark, chair of Vancouver's Central Suffrage Referendum Association, "had expected to gain the vote through the usual method — parliamentary action — and were organized for that purpose only." For a referendum, "the women had a greater task on hand than they had expected, for this method would take much greater organization and meant far more detail to work out."[21]

Realizing the positive value of direct voting about the franchise issue, however, suffragist Helen Guttridge, secretary of the Pioneer Political Equality League in Vancouver, endorsed the referendum. "We did not ask for a referendum on women's suffrage, but since that has been given us we have admitted that after all it is probably the best thing for us, because the referendum has taken the question of women's suffrage entirely out of politics altogether. It has nothing to do with either party and we think that it is more desirable for us to receive our suffrage in that way, without reference to either party."[22]

The women of British Columbia had certainly not come this far to let opportunity slip away. The suffragists' campaign, noted the *Vancouver Sun*, was necessarily in the hands of volunteers because they had no campaign fund, no budget for newspaper advertisements, and no paid organizer. So the campaign was "fully utilized by the suffragists to impress upon voters by every means at their command the justice of letting women vote."[23]

Suffragists addressed election rallies. Suffragists held teas and garden parties to bond, galvanize, and win over support. Suffragists conducted drawing-room meetings to educate supporters and provide arguments for them to spread to others about the necessity of women voting. Suffragists spoke to workers at the Labour Temple to recapture support and assuage unionists' fears over the prospect of empowered women taking men's jobs. Suffragists distributed pamphlets and circulars. Suffragists pioneered campaigning by telephone.

Yet holding a referendum simultaneously with a general election, featuring Bowser versus Brewster, pulled the suffrage issue into the undertow of B.C. party politics. The Liberals were supportive. Party leader Brewster pledged, if elected, to legislate equal guardianship of children and grant women's suffrage even if the referendum failed. He voiced contempt for the Conservatives' referendum, viewing it as "another sign of repentance — or the despair of a drowning politician." As Adams notes, Brewster said that Conservative leader Bowser used the referendum device "first for the purpose of shelving prohibition for the time, then adapting it to get rid of female suffrage."[24]

The B.C. Conservatives, with the notable exceptions of several elected members and party spokesmen, opposed granting women the vote. Initially in the campaign, the Conservative Party said it would take no part in the women's suffrage question, reported Vancouver's *News-Advertiser* on September 14, 1916, "because it has been referred to the will of the people, and the will of the people is law to the government." Yet the Conservatives accommodated suffragists speaking at Tory election rallies. On the whole, concludes Adams, "the suffrage campaign was quietly conducted and lacked the bitterness and acrimony which marked the battles of the two organized factions of the concurrent prohibition campaign."[25]

The election campaign itself was so bitter that, when combined with the intense controversy aroused by the prohibition issue, keeping the public aware of the suffrage issue proved difficult. From Cleverdon's perspective, "in spite of the valiant efforts of the women, it would be erroneous to infer that women suffrage was more than a minor issue in the campaign as a whole."[26]

Contributing to a relatively low profile for the suffrage question during the campaign, Adams suggests, was that suffragists faced no organized opponent. "No anti-suffragist groups appeared opposing their claims, and newspapers which did not actively support the suffragists tacitly did so by not opposing them in print."[27] Letters to the editor during the campaign primarily expressed concern over prohibition and party issues. Ones on women voting were nearly always favourable, but rare.

However, as campaigning proceeded and it emerged that the general public supported women getting voting rights, Conservative candidates realized that silence on the issue could lose them support. Premier Bowser and his Tory forces began to vociferously support a Yes vote.

He no longer equivocated: "The public life of the country would not suffer by the women being co-electors with the men." Women would "raise the moral standard of the country." The premier even prophesied. "When the time comes for women to take part in public discussions and meetings," there would be "good order at the meetings and they will see that there will not be so much personal abuse as there has been in the campaign of 1916."[28]

Years of education and action by suffrage groups had gradually displaced prejudice against women. Even so, the B.C. campaign presented, as ballot issues always do, opportunity for all arguments to be expressed and weighed, with several hoary stances against women's suffrage ventilated one last time for electors to contemplate. Two of the "favourites," Adams notes, were that women's place was in the home and that politics was too rough for women. Against the first claim, suffragists pointed out that legislation affecting every aspect of the home was enacted by legislatures in which women had no voice. The second was countered by Reverend Principal Vance declaring, "If that is the case, in God's name, it's time women got into politics."

No voice was more eloquent or often quoted than that of the Canadian suffragist champion Nellie McClung. Her forceful reasoning flowed from its refined simplicity, and she took delight in tearing apart a foolish argument. Appealing to men who argued against giving women the vote, she asked, "Were you men asked what you were going to do with the ballot when you got it? Wasn't it given to you merely because you were a human being and twenty-one? You weren't asked whether you were intelligent, moral, or wise." Women, she explained, were asking for the vote on the same basis. "They want a voice in their own government because it is a sign of spiritual independence, a mark of individuality. They also want the ballot as a weapon with which to fight against the things that threaten home and children."[29]

By the time the election and referendum campaigns drew to a close, it seemed clear that "the poverty of the anti-suffragist arguments, the long years of intensive campaigning, the proven willingness of women to undertake civic duties together with their remarkable achievements in the war effort" would ensure approval in the referendum.[30] On voting day, the all-male electorate agreed by a ratio of two to one that women should vote.

• • •

In other ballot counts, the Liberals under Harlan Brewster formed a government, and B.C.'s civilian electorate voted for prohibition. The prohibition result was reversed, however, when the large military vote came in. Allegations of major irregularities creating the "wet" military majority resulted in a royal commission investigation, which reported that 8,505 of the military ballots ought to be rejected for irregularities — enough to tilt the balance back to prohibition. The Liberals accordingly brought in the B.C. Prohibition Act, and on October 1, 1917, the province became "dry."

The questionable overseas military votes also delayed proclaiming in force the previously enacted Bowser Suffrage Act of 1916, slated to be proclaimed in effect as law if approved by the referendum. So, when the new legislature began its first session on March 1, 1917, women remained disfranchised, despite the ballot question victory the year before. The fresh Liberal government took advantage of this time warp to get political credit themselves for giving women the vote. Premier Brewster introduced amendments to the Elections Act on March 27 that extended the franchise and enabled women to be elected to the legislature — identical to Bower's measure. It passed easily with support from the former premier and his Tory members, now on the Opposition benches. Third reading and Royal Assent on April 5, 1917, was accompanied by glorious festivities, including a victory dinner and celebrations at the legislature.

Propelled by the strong referendum outcome, further measures soon enhanced the legal status of women. An equal guardianship law was enacted. Amendments to the Municipal Elections Act meant women could be elected to city offices, finally complementing the right of municipal voting that B.C. women had won in 1873, nearly half a century earlier.

Within months of women's provincial political emancipation, Mary Ellen Smith won a by-election on January 24, 1918, filling the vacancy created by the death of her husband, Ralph Smith, the long-time champion of women's suffrage in the B.C. legislature. As British Columbia's first woman in the legislature, Smith was gifted with good looks, a pleasing personality, and political astuteness. She headed a strong drive for the next decade to improve social laws, including a minimum wage for women. When appointed a minister on March 24, 1921, she became the first woman cabinet member in the British Empire.

• • •

After the three Prairie provinces conferred voting rights on women in 1916, British Columbia and Ontario did so in 1917. Nova Scotia followed suit in 1918, New Brunswick in 1919, and Prince Edward Island by 1922. Newfoundland, a separate dominion not part of Confederation, enfranchised women in 1925. Quebec granted women the right to vote on April 25, 1940. Only in British Columbia was a referendum part of the process. Yet across Canada's evolving regional political cultures, influenced from other parts of the country and abroad, the long-term quest of achieving full rights for women required, as it still does, a variety of approaches.

British Columbia's women's suffrage referendum of 1916 is part of the story of how Canadian women won the right to vote. It demonstrates some reasons governments turn to ballot questions: not in a positive way to get public buy-in or a clear expression of elector's sentiment on a vital issue but to delay a question those in power are reluctant to address. A decade and a half later Virginia Woolf would muse: "The history of men's opposition to women's emancipation is more interesting perhaps than the story of that emancipation itself."[31]

Even so, forcing the voting rights issue to be publicly debated and decided by referendum enhanced the political skills of the province's equality-seeking women to a degree not needed in other provinces. Their mobilization and educational work for the campaign had beneficial residual effects after voting ended. The referendum thus played its part in overall Canadian political development as step by step the people came to understand the link between equality and democracy.

Women in British Columbia not only won voting rights but, as an ironic bonus, witnessed the Conservatives of Premier William J. Bowser, in a classic Canadian finale, end up campaigning for the very measure they so long sought to avoid.

PAYING FOR ABORTIONS

One of three ballot questions facing Saskatchewan voters, as part of their October 21, 1991, provincial election, asked whether abortions legally performed in Saskatchewan hospitals should be paid for by the government.

The freedom of a woman to undergo an abortion had been contested intensely in Canada, and Parliament had been unable to come up with a new law, voting on five different possibilities to replace the abortion-limiting section in the Criminal Code struck down on constitutional grounds by the Supreme Court. As a result of no legal impediment, the decision to abort could be made by a pregnant woman and her doctor. This freedom wasn't being directly challenged by the Saskatchewan government's ballot question, abortion being within federal not provincial jurisdiction. However, by framing the issue in terms of whether the public should pay for abortions, the Progressive Conservative government of Saskatchewan knew the question would draw militants on the issue to the polls.

The Referendum and Plebiscite Act enacted by Saskatchewan's legislature earlier in the year set ground rules for 1991's triple-header. The other two questions asked if Saskatchewan should introduce balanced budget legislation, and whether the province's people should approve by referendum any proposed changes to Canada's Constitution.

Premier Grant Devine's decision to top up the provincial election with ballot questions was an eleventh-hour electoral gamble. His Progressive Conservatives were down in the polls. In the campaign backrooms, his strategists envisaged that highlighting these hot-button issues would entice voters predisposed to the Conservatives who, voting against taxpayers funding abortions and for balanced budgets, would also mark their MLA ballot for a PC candidate while at the polling station. As an example of how to abuse the referendum process, this is excellent. The ballot questions had come principally from the government and Tory polling results, rather than resulting from public agitation on the issues, though a taxpayer group had done some lobbying for a balanced-budget law. The choices smacked of political opportunism, not a party's sincere embrace of participatory democracy.

The Saskatchewan statute didn't provide for umbrella committees, so no structure coordinated the various campaigns for or against any of the three ballot questions. Without umbrella committees, no start-up money was voted by the legislature to help launch campaigns that could highlight the pro and con arguments Saskatchewanians ought to consider when deciding on the questions.

Nor would the government itself promote the issues. The Referendum and Plebiscite Act, adopting an excellent provision long part of Saskatchewan's Election Act to ensure fair elections, precluded the Saskatchewan government from advertising during the campaign.

Although ballot questions can be stand-alone events, and arguably should be, the October 1991 plebiscite coincided with the provincial election, as noted. Given the Election Act's campaign spending limits, parties understandably put their limited money toward electing candidates rather than promoting or opposing any of the ballot questions. The absence of Saskatchewan's government and political parties from the ballot-issue campaigns left it up to private organizations and individuals to advocate for or against the questions. The abortion issue attracted the most campaign interest, including newspaper advertisements and public participation at rallies by militants of the cause. The Taxpayers Association of Saskatchewan, having promoted the balanced-budget question, urged a Yes vote.

The chief electoral officer's staff answered inquiries about plebiscite procedures, but in keeping with its neutral role didn't provide information pro or con for any of the questions. Premier Devine clarified at the outset that the people's verdict on the three questions wouldn't bind the government, which downplayed the importance of voting. This stance caused consternation among backroom Tory strategists who'd concocted the "Hail Mary!" plan to help draw support to Progressive Conservative candidates. By September 26, New Democrat leader Roy Romanow criticized the ballot questions as "a way to distract voters."

At their polling stations voters received four ballots, one to elect their representative to the legislature and a separate one for each question. Slightly more than 80 percent of Saskatchewan's 651,196 eligible voters came to the polls.

The question *Abortions are legally performed in some Saskatchewan hospitals. Should the government of Saskatchewan pay for abortion procedures?* got a No answer from 62.62 percent of voters, with Yes getting 37.58 percent. On the other two, close to 80 percent of Saskatchewanians approved having a referendum on constitutional changes, and a similar number, enactment of a law requiring a "balanced budget."

The government that sponsored the ballot issues, however, wouldn't be around to translate the results into laws. Voters had elected five times more New Democrats than Progressive Conservatives. Roy Romanow replaced Grant Devine as premier and proceeded with a different agenda, which didn't include restrictions on the rights and freedoms of women.

VOTING ON FOOD SUPPLY ISSUES

In 1951 the climax of a three-year battle between advocates of various forms of grain marketing came to a ballot issue vote in Manitoba. The November 24 referendum was held province-wide, with balloting confined to farmers growing oats and barley — an example of "sectoral" referendums part of Canadian democracy and agricultural supply management.

The issue had been festering since 1948, when Parliament enacted legislation to transfer sale of coarse grains from the open market to the Canadian Wheat Board, subject to passage of complementary legislation by the three Prairie provincial legislatures. Alberta and Saskatchewan readily did so, but Manitoba swirled with controversy and Premier D.L. Campbell refused to sponsor the legislation, arguing it was constitutionally unnecessary. The act, then introduced as a private member's bill, flooded the legislature with prolonged and bitter debate. When finally passed in April 1949, by a vote of thirty-six to twelve, four cabinet ministers voted against and eight in favour of transferring coarse grains to the Wheat Board's jurisdiction.[1]

Farmers accustomed to the "free-market" system for their oats and barley, selling mostly through the Winnipeg Grain Exchange, rankled at this coercion. The Wheat Board was a government-run monopoly. They lost their freedom to sell grain they owned, grown on their own land, on the open market, often at higher prices. They saw the government's Wheat Board effectively expropriating their asset. With each year's crop, resentment grew. By 1951, the provincial government decided to ask the coarse grain farmers by direct vote: *Do you wish to continue to sell your oats and barley as at present?*

Little campaigning preceded the voting. The issues had been thoroughly thrashed out during the preceding three years. The 51,803 Manitoba grain producers registered on the voters' list didn't need an information pamphlet to understand what was at stake for them. Supporters of monopoly marketing stressed the advantages of a stable market and safe sale price. Opponents claimed farmers could make more money selling coarse grains themselves through the Grain Exchange. The government remained neutral.[2]

With 68 percent of eligible grain producers across the province voting, 89 percent wanted to continue marketing their oats and barley through the Canadian Wheat Board. Premier Campbell pointed out, reported the *Winnipeg Free Press*, how farmers overcame problems of great distance to the polls and cold weather to vote. "This re-emphasizes that Manitoba farmers can be depended upon to show initiative and judgment in deciding any question referred to them."[3] Commenting on the weather and character of the province's farmers saved him taking a stance on the thorny issue itself.

Although critics felt the question's wording didn't force the real choice, the central issue had been faced and farmers got the opportunity to collectively decide a policy of great importance to them. Addressing the open-market faction, Stanley Jones, the Winnipeg Grain Exchange's president, issued a statement: "On behalf of all farmers who want freedom to market as they choose, including those who found themselves in this invidious position, the 3,900 growers who voted No and the thousands who failed to vote because they could not truly register their opinions, the Grain Exchange reiterates its undertaking to continue efforts to bring about as soon as possible freedom of choice in grain marketing."

On the Yes side, J.T. McLean of the Manitoba Federation of Agriculture and Co-operation saluted farmers who'd voted pro-monopoly "for their overwhelming vote in favour of marketing through the Wheat Board." He told the *Free Press* that the vote was "one of the more decisive and clear-cut demonstrations of unity of purpose ever made by Manitoba farmers."

In the bigger picture, it was also a demonstration of precision use of the referendum tool. This sectoral application of ballot questions treats as a single constituency a particular community of interest. It doesn't involve the entire electorate at large with no adhesion to the subject. It doesn't turn on where the voters might be geographically scattered but on their community as a directly affected constituency. Manitoba's ballot for grain producers demonstrated the pragmatic efficiency of such referendums when farmer votes force choices on a specialized issue typically related to a wide range of produce marketing — from peaches to asparagus, wheat and barley to milk, poultry, and eggs, Canada's supply management system.

•   •   •

The utility of sectoral referendums was gaining wider acceptance. In 1954, responding to a request from Prince Edward Island's Federation of Agriculture, Liberal Premier Alex Matheson's government put in place An Act to Provide for the Taking of Plebiscites on Questions of Public Interest.

Under this statute, two ballot questions submitted to voters on November 10 that year sought to resolve controversy over whether the P.E.I. Potato Marketing Board should continue, and if so, whether as "a compulsory one desk selling agency" — that is, as a government monopoly such as the Canada Wheat Board. Mail-in ballots were used, with a majority favouring continuation of the Board.

•   •   •

Ontario's large and politically important rural communities and farmer organizations have a history of intense controversy over marketing issues, punctuated with sectoral referendums for the producers concerned.

Under the Farm Products Marketing Act, if a majority of Ontario farmers vote in support of a marketing plan, it will be established. That is how the province came to have some two dozen marketing boards that since 1990 have been consolidated under supervision of the Ontario Farm Products Marketing Commission.

The Farm Products Marketing Act doesn't oblige the government to use a formal balloting procedure, because sometimes the number of producers is small enough to make a formal "opinion poll" conducted by secret ballot more practical and less costly to ascertain majority opinion on a proposed marketing plan. Otherwise, when a petition from a group of producers who are representative of farmers growing that product asks for a regime to regulate marketing of the product, the steps needed to establish the marketing system will be carried out — either by decision of Ontario's agriculture minister, or after a ballot question voted on by all affected producers shows majority support for marketing their product on a regulated basis.

In November 1957, for example, a petition to the Farm Products Marketing Board, signed by some three hundred Ontario producers of fresh peaches, requested a vote by peach growers and producers on revoking the marketing plan operating as the result of a prior petition in 1954. The agriculture minister announced a vote by peach farmers to get "a clear-cut expression of the growers' and producers' feelings."

In preparing the voters' list, producers with peach orchards of fewer than two acres, and farmers who sold directly to consumers, were excluded. This arbitrary decision about the legal right to vote soon landed in court. In *Freeman v. Farm Products Marketing Board*,[4] Chief Justice James C. McRuer of the High Court held that the act gave no authority whatsoever for this procedure and that the board had no power to define who would be regarded as "persons engaged in the production of a farm product."

"Regulations cannot go beyond the manner of taking the votes," said McRuer, who'd grown up on an Ontario farm near Ayr and appreciated first-hand the nature of farm production. "The Legislature has determined who is to be entitled to vote and the persons entitled to vote are persons engaged" in the production in question. "The Board cannot circumscribe rights given by the Legislature," emphasized McRuer, "or disfranchise persons who are entitled to vote."

Legal advisers to the minister of agriculture criticized McRuer's decision as meaning anyone in Ontario owning a single peach tree would be an eligible voter, a position they felt too extreme to be realistic. Others felt their reductionist argument too silly to be taken seriously. But government lawyers have an inside track. Since 1958 the Ontario government, rather than revising and clarifying the requirements for voter eligibility, simply chose not to hold further ballot questions under those sections of the act making it optional to do so.

· · ·

Use of farm-related balloting otherwise continued, when not departmental lawyers but Ontario farmers could trigger the mandatory vote. They valued a referendum's merit of informing people who are directly concerned, framing the issue and allowing everyone affected to have their say by secret ballot.

In 1988, as an example, Ontario asparagus growers recognized a need to unite to better manage their marketing efforts. Fresh asparagus prices had fallen 11 percent in six years, cash outlays had risen 42 percent in six years, acreage in production had declined 12 percent in two years, and market share was generally down. Growers, competing against one another and forcing prices lower, found that reduced prices meant poorer quality and cutting corners on standards. To solve the periodic surplus inventories that played havoc with their price structure, a unified marketing system was proposed.

The Ontario Asparagus Growers' Marketing Board, based in London, prepared a proposal for "A Fresh Asparagus Unified Marketing Plan" and distributed an educational kit to producers, news media, and government representatives in advance of conducting a vote on whether to implement the plan. The ballot, mailed to all asparagus growers on December 14, 1988, asked, *Are you in favour of the proposal to establish a centrally controlled marketing system for fresh wholesale asparagus produced in Ontario?* Marked ballots had to be postmarked by December 20. The result, with 61.5 percent of growers voting, showed 71 percent favoured the plan, which was then implemented by the government in accordance with the farmers' mandate.

After a while, a number of asparagus farmers judged their unified marketing program too rigid, sacrificing the flexibility that the concept of a "market" connotes. Soon they showed that in a democratic society what is born by the ballot can die by the ballot. A petition with sixty signatures from growers stated they wanted the Fresh Asparagus Unified Marketing Plan to cease operation. The Ontario Asparagus Growers' Marketing Board sent a ballot asking *all* growers if they wanted the plan to continue operating in the coming 1991 season. Fifty percent of the producers voted, of whom 67 percent no longer favoured the unified marketing system. Consequently, the plan was *suspended*, with the option — in recognition of the oscillating ways of a democracy — to reinstate it "if growers decide that two or three years down the road they want the Plan back in."[5]

Other Ontario farmers grow oats and barley on some 258,000 acres across the province, their crops totalling farm cash receipts of $82.8 million annually. An Oat and Barley Council, operating from 2001 to 2010, brought together the entire value chain. But with voluntary membership and insufficient revenues, it lapsed, leaving oat and barley growers unrepresented by a farm group. After a couple of years, an Oat and Barley

Representation Committee took shape and advanced a new proposal. Ryan Brown, vice-president of operations for Grain Farmers of Ontario, said this committee, which developed the proposal, also worked hard to enable everybody to vote.

As a result, in 2014, Ontario's oat and barley growers voted by mail-in ballot in a referendum conducted by the Farm Products Marketing Commission. It showed that 77 percent chose to join the Grain Farmers of Ontario, a problematic result, however, because only 15 percent of eligible voters cast ballots. Despite that low participation, at least the referendum methodology was keeping current with the times: prior to the grain growers voting, information about the proposal was posted on a website and discussed at meetings and during a webinar.

•   •   •

These samplings of sectoral votes by farmers within a province pale in comparison to the intensity of farm-marketing issues at interprovincial and national levels. Here, battle lines form between farmers wanting the security and strength of co-operative and collective approaches, versus those demanding freedom and refusing to be coerced. To add complexity, these marketing questions are interwoven with transportation issues, interprovincial trade barriers, financial constraints, political imperatives, and corporate complexities. "The marketing of agricultural products has had a turbulent history in Canada," wrote John McMurchy in 1990, a lawyer's classic understatement.[6]

In 1949 Parliament enacted the Agricultural Products Marketing Act to regulate extra-provincial trade, and by the 1960s most provinces had settled on a regime of marketing boards for specified agricultural products. Then, in 1966, Ottawa set up national marketing schemes under Crown corporations such as the Canadian Dairy Commission. Next, producers in many provinces, but especially Ontario and Quebec, began waging what was dubbed the "Chicken and Egg War" that escalated into front-page news by 1971 as provincial governments, drawn into the fray, used their powers to retaliate against one another's products. Ottawa responded with the Farm Products Marketing Agencies Act in 1972, under which the Canadian Egg Marketing Agency began operating on a national scale.

In the process, Canadians glimpsed how an implacable confrontation over farm products could spiral in an ever-mounting series of retaliatory measures. The federal system's contest between Ottawa and provincial governments added a complicating degree of jurisdictional overlap and confusion that ultimately had to be arbitrated by the Supreme Court of Canada in a landmark constitutional law ruling. That courtroom battle began in 1976 when Ontario initiated a judicial reference case on the constitutionality of the complex federal-provincial scheme. The Supreme Court sorted matters out somewhat by ruling on which parts of Ontario's Farm Products Marketing Act (for creating marketing agencies in Ontario and authorizing them to co-operate with similar agencies created by Canada and other provinces) and the Government of Canada's two statutes, the Agricultural Products Marketing Act (allowing the federal government to authorize provincial marketing agencies to regulate interprovincial and export trade) and the Farm Products Marketing Agencies Act (which authorized the federal government to establish national marketing agencies), were constitutionally valid.

However, in this conflicting and overlapping jurisdictional headache of federalism, as different governments deal with the same territory, people, and products, even more complex are the wheat-marketing programs on the Prairies. A hint of this was given in the case of Manitoba, at the start of this chapter, which included interwoven national and provincial statutes and producers balloting on marketing options. Prairie grain growers initially felt the strong hand of regulatory government during the First World War. From then, until a producer's ballot question in September 2011 when more than 60 percent of wheat producers voted to keep the Canada Wheat Board monopoly system, wheat marketing remained a magnet for intense emotions and important economic battles over the food supply.

Prime ministers were drawn into the issue. Robert Borden instituted, then expanded, control over Prairie grain marketing under War Measures Act provisions. Mackenzie King disbanded the arrangements during the prosperity of the 1920s. R.B. Bennett reinstituted the Wheat Board regime in 1935 in response to deep Prairie agonies amid the Great Depression and Dust Bowl drought conditions. Louis St. Laurent faced Wheat Board marketing challenges from U.S. government wheat sale deals. John Diefenbaker expanded the board's operations by authorizing controversial bulk sales of grain to Communist China. Prime Minister Pierre Trudeau's government introduced legislation to create federal provisions like those in Manitoba and Ontario, enabling direct votes by farmers to decide specific farm-organization issues. These 1971 amendments to the Canadian Wheat Board Act would have authorized Canada's chief electoral officer to conduct a plebiscite among producers of certain kinds of grains, but as with other referendum legislation of the Trudeau government, the bill never passed.

The 2011 referendum on whether to maintain the Wheat Board's marketing monopoly revealed overwhelming support for the status quo. But that didn't settle the controversy. Just as in 1949, when this very issue opened a wide rift in D.L. Campbell's Manitoba cabinet, the same deep feelings set the Harper Conservative government against the majority of Prairie wheat and barley farmers in 2011. Previously, when Stephen Harper was president of the National Citizens Coalition, he'd espoused a number of libertarian positions, from freeing citizens from the randomly imposed legal obligation to complete Statistics Canada's onerous long-form census return, to liberating farmers from the government monopoly so they could sell their grain as they pleased rather than be legally obliged to operate within the Canadian Wheat Board marketing system. He aligned himself with anti-board farmers who'd protested, trucked their own wheat across the U.S. border, and sold it to Americans, then formed "Farmers for Justice" when the Wheat Board overreacted, and with RCMP officers in tow, laid charges, obtained convictions, and saw farmers jailed for as long as 155 days — not for selling drugs or banned firearms but their own wheat. In Parliament, Stephen Harper advocated a two-track marketing system, with freedom for those who sought it, and when his Conservative Party gained a majority government, he proceeded to implement this plan, declaring in advance of a farmers' referendum that its results wouldn't deter his government's program.

The Wheat Board conducted its ballot question in anticipation of the Conservative government's legislation to eliminate the board's monopoly, hoping to use it as leverage to pressure Harper to scrap his project. Some 62 percent of Prairie wheat growers (22,764 farmers) voted to keep the Wheat Board as the sole marketing agent for their grain, while 38 percent (14,059 farmers) voted to eliminate the monopoly so they could sell their wheat on the open market. Of barley growers, just over half (51 percent), voted to maintain the monopoly, compared to 49 percent who favoured its elimination. The vote was held by mail-in ballot of farmers in the Wheat

Board's jurisdictional area of Manitoba, Saskatchewan, Alberta, and British Columbia's Peace River district. Participation in the referendum was 56 percent for wheat growers, 47 percent for barley growers, and 60 percent for farmers who grew both.

But the Conservatives countered with a different electoral mandate. The PM and the agriculture minister repeated that the board-run farmer vote would have no bearing on the matter because the Conservatives had campaigned to eliminate the monopoly and received a majority mandate from voters to carry out its plan. The Conservatives added that it shouldn't matter what the board's voting results were because a majority of farmers shouldn't be able to dictate to a minority how to sell their grain — the issue of protecting minority rights when holding a referendum. On July 31, 2014, the Canada Wheat Board's monopoly ended and farmers could sell their crops to whomever they chose. Those wanting to market through the Wheat Board still had that option.

• • •

In Canada's democratic dialectic not only do elections and referendums impact one another to alter policies and advance programs but so in some cases do rival mandates from the general electorate (given to Prime Minister Harper in an election) versus a specific electorate (voted by Prairie wheat and barley farmers).

Ballot-box democracy, as embedded in many decades of policy formation for Canadian farmers and food producers through sectoral referendums, is enabled by statutes passed in our legislatures. The results of voting have, in turn, given rise to marketing regimes likewise created by statute. So from yet another angle, it is clear that referendums have long been intrinsic to Canadian public affairs, and that this process is "semi-direct democracy" because legislators and voters work through interrelated steps.

27

BALLOTING ON EVERYTHING FROM TIME OF DAY TO A FIXED LINK

Growing awareness of the rewards of referendums gave rise to ballot questions on such diverse controversies as plans for health insurance, ownership of electric power companies, gambling, and Sunday shopping. To shed further light on the wide range of Canadian ballot issues, this chapter offers a sampler of two more – dealing with time and travel.

DECIDING THE TIME OF DAY BY BALLOT

As the world's second-largest country, our experience with Canada's sprawling share of geography includes trying to blend the artificial "time zones" imposed by humans onto nature's own alternating seasons.

From east to west, our transcontinental country contains six time zones (Newfoundland Standard, Atlantic Standard, Eastern Standard, Central Standard, Mountain Standard, and Pacific Standard) that put abrupt edges to the "time of day." From south to north, we also accommodate Earth's seasonal shifts between the lush Carolinian forest of our southernmost area and the High Arctic latitudes far above the treeline, which bask in twenty-four-hour sunlight in summer and are cloaked with twenty-four-hour darkness in winter. Into this variable mix entered the invention of Daylight Saving Time by which we advance clocks an hour in spring for daylight's extended run, then set the hands back again one hour in fall, according to a "saving" schedule that itself has even changed. What earlier began on the first Sunday in April is today the second Sunday in March. Daylight Saving no longer ends on the last Sunday of October, but the first Sunday in November.

Imposing an orderly, systematic measuring system leads to efficiency, uniformity, and predictability. Starting from the "zero point" for time and meridians at the Royal Observatory in Greenwich, southeast of London, England, Greenwich Mean Time begins the westerly march of hours around the globe, marked off by meridians of longitude. An efficient measuring system should take no account of seas or borders, cities or farming zones, but politics and economics interrupted the plotting of lines. The ninetieth meridian, just west of Thunder Bay, Ontario, being six zones removed from Greenwich, should be a time zone boundary but isn't. The seventh hour west of Greenwich should start on the 105th meridian, running between Saskatoon and Regina, but was set instead at the Saskatchewan-Manitoba border, the northern part of which is on the 102nd meridian. Why? So that all Saskatchewanians would live in the same time zone. Officials would have a hard time explaining that the neat lines of the province's borders, themselves an artificial creation, didn't coincide with another set of imposed lines, since both were being drawn by remote officials. So from the outset, some instinct operated to accommodate human community within the measured boundary lines of land.

From the early 1900s use of Daylight Saving Time, often called "Fast Time," was encouraged throughout Canada on a voluntary basis.[1] But during the First World War, Ottawa increasingly imposed emergency measures, from press censorship, internment camps, conscription, even a "temporary" income tax to pay for the war that is still being collected several wars and a century later. In this context, Parliament enacted legislation in 1918 to impose Daylight Saving Time, also as a temporary war measure. To get the time issue dealt with, Prime Minister Borden's government had to override strong protests of MPs representing rural constituencies distressed by the adverse economic and social impact of the decision. Ottawa was flooded with "vociferous complaints from farming communities who claimed Daylight Saving Time meant an hour's work per day lost, as cows could not be milked any earlier and heavy dew on the ground made field work impossible."[2]

The practice of Daylight Saving was popular with most city dwellers, however, where people's separation from nature is greater. Use of electricity for lighting, heating, and operating equipment enabled pushing daytime conditions into the night hours as offices and factories no longer had to shut down with darkness descending, and streetlights and electrified homes added more hours of visible activity to each winter's night.

Recognizing a political "hot potato," the federal government heeded the economic case made by farmers — so when the statute came up for renewal after the war, it was repealed. Ottawa, following Laurier's precedent with prohibition, would use the federal system's advantage of leaving provinces and municipalities free to adjust the contentious use of Daylight Saving Time to regional and local conditions in whatever way they saw best.

This handoff, however, produced a patchwork of time confusion. Municipalities in western Saskatchewan got the right to switch to nearby Alberta's Mountain Standard Time, and most did. Then municipalities in the southeastern section of the province gained the option of choosing between Mountain Standard Time like the western part of their province, or Central Standard Time like neighbouring Manitoba. Exercising such an option led to a mixed variety that, to implement, produced a confusing zigzag time-zone boundary jogging "west, north, west, south, west, south, east, south, east, south, west and south, taking Yorkton, Melville, and Estevan an hour away from the rest of the province, until at last it reached the U.S. border and regularity again."[3] Some Saskatchewan cities went to Central Time in summer but ran on Mountain Time in winter, calling this particular hybrid "Mountain Daylight Saving Time." At one point the only consistent city was Lloydminster, straddling the Saskatchewan-Alberta border, which compromised by staying on Mountain Time all year. Confusion became so great that railway men used special three-handed watches for Saskatchewan runs until finally the exasperated railways solved their problem by operating on Standard Time year-round.

Not only for Saskatchewanians but for Canadians generally, the question of time zones was controversial because switching impacted many aspects of rural life and farming.

The time of day again became a national issue during the Second World War when Mackenzie King's government took control for the same "wartime necessity" that motivated Robert Borden's government to do so in the First World War. The Liberals imposed Daylight Saving Time on the whole country for the war's duration. With the coming of peace and the lapsing of Ottawa's reign over setting the clocks of the nation, British Columbia's government filled the vacuum by heeding the wishes of its urban population (with more voters) and continued Daylight Saving Time for the summer months from 1945 until 1952.

All through these postwar years farming communities protested strongly. The Conservative MLA for Delta, Alex Hope, urged that the issue be put directly to the people of British Columbia in a referendum. Having seen how a ballot question could bring finality to a contentious issue, he claimed that farmers "would no longer complain about Daylight Saving Time if the province as a whole voted in favour."[4] Desiring to resolve the controversy, the B.C. government held a ballot question on the matter, with voting held in conjunction with the general election on June 12, 1952. The government also submitted the controversial liquor issue to a provincial vote at the same time.

Support and opposition to Daylight Saving Time divided between urban and rural voters. Neither the Yes or No side formed a campaign organization, nor did the provincial political parties take a stand on the issue. "Nobody is saying anything about Daylight Saving Time in the campaign," observed Vancouver's *Province* about this studied avoidance.

Daylight Saving won with 290,353 ballots cast in favour, 231,008 against. Alex Hope had been correct about the power of a referendum to calm farmers' protestations. After the vote, Daylight Saving Time was proclaimed under the authority of the Daylight Saving Act, 1919, "without incurring protests from the farming community."[5]

• • •

Four years later, seeing British Columbia's success, Saskatchewan hoped a ballot question might resolve its time dilemma, too, and set the stage by enacting the Time Question Plebiscite Act, 1956.

With the province's easterly and westerly communities not sharing a common time zone, Saskatchewanians puzzled over how to set their clocks, especially because most lacked the railroaders' three-hand timepieces. They were ready to let the majority view prevail. However, when electors got to the polls, they found the ballot confusing: first, they had to vote for or against Central Standard Time for the whole province, then, second, show their preference for the time to be used in their own locality.

Just over a third of eligible voters cast ballots. When tallied, they showed 101,292 opted for Central Standard Time, 19,380 for Central Daylight Saving, and 83,267 for Mountain Standard — results impossible to interpret in a single policy. Having ineptly posed a ballot question that didn't force a choice, the government then referred its problem to a legislative committee, accepting its eventual recommendation to put Saskatchewan on Mountain Standard Time in winter and Central Standard Time in summer, a "solution" that split the cabinet, the legislature, and the population.

Next came a provincial statute enabling each municipality to hold local ballot questions on adopting its own time, guaranteeing a further reign of confusion across Saskatchewan. In 1959, to end local freelancing, the act was repealed. By 1962, politically shamed by the railway companies' decisions to run on a single uniform regime of year-round Standard Time, the matter was again considered by a legislative committee. This one recommended bisecting Saskatchewan into two time zones: Central Standard in the east and Mountain Standard in the west, with numerous exceptions. Today everyone in Saskatchewan operates on Central Standard Time in the summer. In winter, western Saskatchewan is officially on Mountain Standard Time, unless electors by local vote have put their particular municipality on Central Standard Time.

Ballot-box democracy played some role in Saskatchewan's time saga, but only with about the same success solving the dilemma as all the other methods tried.

· · ·

Albertans, having been spectators for years of the time wars raging in their neighbouring provinces, went to the polls themselves to decide how best to set their clocks. After the Second World War, when Ottawa again relinquished the time field, a 1948 Alberta statute enforced use of Mountain Standard Time throughout the province. In April 1967, the Social Credit government, in response to pressure from the party's strong rural base, announced a ballot question on the time question, the first occasion for Albertans to express their choice directly on the issue. The ballot asked, *Do you favour province-wide daylight saving time?*

When voting ended, overall results were Yes 236,555, No 248,680, representing 48.75 percent in favour of Daylight Saving and 51.25 percent against, split largely along urban-rural lines. Outside Edmonton, Calgary, Lethbridge, and Medicine Hat, the vote overwhelmingly favoured retaining Mountain Standard Time year-round.

That vote, on May 23, 1967, was held in conjunction with a provincial election that returned Alberta's Social Credit government to office for a ninth term, with a massive majority in the legislature. After four more years of urbanization, increasing pressure mounted on the Socreds to hold a second vote on Daylight Saving Time. Again the same question was posed: *Do you favour province-wide daylight saving time?* Again the balloting was held in conjunction with a provincial general election — on August 30, 1971.

This time, however, the difference was in the campaign. In 1967 voters had been exposed to a vigorous No campaign, at the end of which No achieved a relatively narrow victory. For 1971 the "Yes for Daylight Saving Society," having pushed hard to get the referendum, fought even harder for the extra hour.

This round resulted in 386,846 votes for Yes to 242,431 for No. Province-wide Daylight Saving Time had been approved by 61.47 percent of the electorate.

The farmers resigned themselves to the outcome. "I wasn't surprised by the vote," said W.D. Lea, president of Unifarm, an official spokesperson for some thirty thousand Alberta farmers. "As farmers, we have a lot of other matters that are more urgent to contend with than Daylight Saving Time." The vitriol had been drawn from the issue. Everybody who wanted had had their say — twice. On April 25, 1972, Alberta implemented Daylight Saving Time.

· · ·

The Daylight Saving issue continued ticking in British Columbia where, on August 30, 1972, another ballot question was posed, and like the time referendum two decades earlier, was held in conjunction with a provincial election. Voters were asked, *Are you in favour of Pacific Standard Time, including Pacific Daylight Saving Time, as is applicable now throughout the province?*

This vote, though provincially sponsored, wasn't conducted throughout British Columbia but in five northern electoral districts most impacted economically — a variant on the sectoral referendum. The results were 63.38 percent No to 34.24 percent Yes. Such use of a referendum in farming and outlying areas, where economic and social patterns better fitted the rhythm of Standard Time, showed more successfully than in Saskatchewan that the intelligent use of a ballot question — in this case on a regional basis for those directly impacted — can provide appropriate flexibility and address a particular need, akin to holding several by-elections on the same day to fill vacancies in the legislature. It helped, of course, that British Columbia's geography was also more compatible with this north-south arrangement.

The "time" issue reminds us how governments can't do things for people without also doing things to people. Some folks were forced to set their clocks by a majority view. In most cases, the grudging acceptance by those who "lost" an hour was grounded in knowing that in a democracy that's how majority rule works, and that the process at least gave everyone a chance to be heard and be counted.

BALLOTING ABOUT A BRIDGE TO CANADA'S MAINLAND

Of the three island colonies of British North America that are today part of Canada, only one was near enough to the continental mainland to contemplate a tunnel or bridge. Vancouver Island and Newfoundland maintained their coveted separateness with boats and planes, but Prince Edward Island long flirted with the notion of a dual personality as both an island and a piece of the mainland.

The identity of Canada's smallest province is captured in its official name: Prince Edward *Island.* Few Islanders know much about Prince Edward himself, but all understand the benefit of crossing water to get to their province and most value their sea moat for keeping people "from away" away. An Islander's state of being "unto one's self" has a primordial quality, which is why the political, economic, social, and cultural aspects — not to mention practical transportation realities — of Prince Edward Island's relationship to the mainland loomed so large for so long.

When Prince Edward Island became a Canadian province in 1873, its Confederation agreement required Ottawa to provide "efficient steam service for the reliable conveyance of mail and passengers between the Island and the Dominion, winter and summer, thus placing the Island in continuous communication with the Intercontinental Railway and the railway system of the Dominion."[6]

"Efficient steam service" wasn't restricted to coal-fired ferries but included the possibility of steam locomotives pulling trains. Indeed, the P.E.I. government had been going broke constructing a provincial railway, and getting bailed out of its debt by the terms of union with Canada gave new lease to the Islanders' railway dream — as reference to "the railway system of the Dominion" signalled. In 1885 a tunnel under the Northumberland Strait was proposed for better year-round communication and transportation between island and mainland. Planning for this tunnel was carried out in 1895. With the advent in 1917 of an ice-breaking ferry and more reliable year-round service, that project faded. Then other concepts took its place as over the years new plans were touted for reliable transportation to and from the island, including railway and highway tunnels, a bridge, and a causeway. The word *reliable* was interpreted to rule out airplanes and boats.

The explicit promise of a bridge, or sometimes a tunnel, rose and fell in tidal regularity with the coming and going of election campaigns. Although the introduction of air travel reduced the pressures to actually *do* anything new — the reliable ferry service was kept modern, while simultaneously preserving the reality of "island" culture — the concept of a "fixed crossing" such as a bridge, causeway, or tunnel emerged again with proposals from both sides of the House of Commons between 1956 and 1965.

In this matter, progress is measured not in days but decades. After federal Liberal Party leader Lester Pearson promised a causeway when he lost the 1962 general election, and a year later, in the 1963 election, repeated the same pledge but this time formed a national government, work on approaches to the causeway began. In 1966 construction started on the bridge-causeway combination itself. This project was terminated in 1968, however, after the costly access roads had been built, because the rapid speed of this project was getting out of hand.

A couple of more decades slipped along unnoticed, then some feasibility studies were made in the 1980s. This work eliminated the causeway on grounds of potential future environmental damage. Next to fade into even darker oblivion was the old railway tunnel idea because, in rethinking that option, someone opined that it wouldn't provide "a continuous link," the mantra for this elusive dream, since railways ran on timetables and the intervals between train service were getting much longer. Pragmatists added that a railway tunnel would be neither quieter nor more convenient than the existing ferry service, already paid for and operating efficiently.

During the 1980s, some desultory rounds of discussions took place intermittently, the way the premiers of Prince Edward Island, Nova Scotia, and

New Brunswick got together in the 1860s, and at intervals since, to discuss Maritime Union; after several days of fine dining and discussion, they returned to their respective capitals in Halifax, Fredericton, and Charlottetown to carry on as before. "Important but not urgent at the present time" was a Maritime view on many issues. Emerging from those 1980s discussions about Prince Edward Island's future as an island, several public- and private-sector proposals reappeared for a long-ignored "fixed-link" crossing. By 1988, this led to a feasibility study by the Department of Public Works in Ottawa.

The "linking" concept involved a highway either over a bridge or through a tunnel. The federal government asked seven Canadian construction consortiums to submit plans and prices. Ottawa thought a likely cost would be $1 billion and estimated a half decade for construction to complete the fourteen-kilometre link between Borden on the island and Cape Tormentine on New Brunswick's coast. A fixed-link project could have significant long-lasting effects on the lifestyle and economy of Prince Edward Islanders, and on the biophysical environments of the island, the mainland, and the Northumberland Strait.

•   •   •

In mid-November 1987, federal government officials called for tenders to build the crossing. In conjunction with that, they launched "information meetings" across Prince Edward Island. Residents could ask questions about the crossing proposal and submit written comments on survey cards. Premier Joe Ghiz believed Islanders weren't getting a chance through this typical "public consultation" process of contemporary government in Canada to express their views adequately.

A week later, on November 23, 1987, the Liberal premier announced a province-wide vote. "After monitoring the federal government's version of providing information to Islanders," said Ghiz at a Charlottetown press conference announcing the plebiscite, "I am now prepared to say that a more effective process of consultation, debate, and exchange of opinion must take place."

Fortunately, the premier could utilize the carefully established ballot-question procedures in Prince Edward Island's existing Plebiscite Act. Islanders long embraced the value of plebiscitary democracy, having marked ballots to settle questions a number of times as far back as 1878. Had the province not already had on its statute books enabling legislation for such a vote, Joe Ghiz couldn't have acted with such dispatch and confidence.

Voting would take place January 18, 1988. Islanders would be asked whether they supported plans to build a physical connection to Canada's mainland. Rather than choosing between a specific structure such as bridge or tunnel, the issue was to be framed generically as to whether any "fixed link" was desired.

The fixed-link plebiscite did exactly what this democratic procedure is designed to accomplish. In the words of historian Douglas Baldwin, it "forced Islanders to think about their future."[7] This thinking turned on positive and negative economic dimensions and the cultural identity of island life. A fixed link would benefit agriculture through cheaper transportation, affect fishing with possible environmental damage, and help tourism through easier access. However, it could harm tourism by altering the uniqueness of "island" charm. Entering the New Year 1988, the issue aroused as much controversy as it had whenever contemplated in all prior decades.

People debated what really constituted economic and cultural "progress," with the opposing Yes and No groups choosing names that illustrated this dichotomy. The progressive pro-link supporters called themselves "Islanders for a Better Tomorrow," and the proud anti-link advocates defiantly dubbed themselves "Friends of the Island." Proponents of a stronger economy and a better materialistic lifestyle, notes Baldwin, conflicted with defenders of the environment and the "Island way of life." Certainly the ballot question didn't "create" this division, but it did give the dual nature of Prince Edward Island public expression and allowed it to be subjected to open discussion and reappraisal.

The compact province's relatively small number of residents — its population slightly larger in number than that of Oshawa, Ontario, and considerably smaller than that of Burnaby, British Columbia — means residents are able to pay close attention to the career of events within the identifiable terrain of their water-bound community. They didn't need the statutory five-week campaign to reach a verdict. Premier Ghiz told me, when we met in Charlottetown to review the legal side of things, that for the sake of families, news reporters, and campaigners, he was glad the Christmas and New Year's break provided a respite from the increasingly repetitive campaigning.

In the January 18, 1988, voting, Islanders voted 59 percent in favour of a fixed-link crossing. The project then progressed through work on the engineering studies, proceedings for environmental impact reviews, and the launching and adjudication of several court challenges.

. . .

Driving across the completed "fixed link" disappoints those expecting grand views, because the outer sides of the traffic lanes face solid bridge walls high enough to block the scenery. On windswept wintry days, the same barriers shield against blustery gales that would play havoc with motor vehicles.

As for an alternate "reliable" journey across the Northumberland Strait, the ferries are still running, one year-round and a second operating in summer. Islanders boarding them have, since January 18, 1988, an even better sense of just who they are, and what their island means to them. Joe Ghiz was satisfied his people had had a proper means for debating all points of view, then reaching a collective decision. The character of their island is of abiding interest to all the people, not just their elected representatives or government officials.

DEMOCRATIC ACCOUNTABILITY THROUGH MUNICIPAL BALLOT QUESTIONS

When we seek to measure the importance of something in Canada, we almost instinctively start with the national picture and next take in the provincial scene. However, that approach is misleading when it comes to referendums. Our three national ballot questions, and the more frequent use of provincial referendums — ranging from well over a dozen in British Columbia and Prince Edward Island to just one in New Brunswick, with other provinces at a half dozen or so — gives the wrong impression of just how import-ant referendums have been for many Canadians. For a very long time, they have been held at the municipal level and have numbered in the *thousands*. Although a "junior" level of government, municipalities in Canada are the senior player in ballot-box accountability.

Within a province, some municipalities are more predisposed than others to test issues by asking voters a ballot question. Even in the same town or city, there is an ebb and flow in how readily ballot questions are resorted to for municipal decision-making. It's the same with First Nations reserves where decision-making patterns vary but ballot questions are in the mix for quite a few.

Between provinces there is uneven use of municipal ballot questions, as well. Some, for instance in Quebec and Ontario, have deep-seated local control that emerged because widely scattered communities had their affairs and futures in their own hands. In other provinces, smaller in population and size, established at later dates in history, local government was often less autonomous and more directly controlled by the municipal affairs depart-ment in the provincial capital.

Ontario developed especially strong municipal governments from 1850, beginning with An Act to Provide, by One General Law, for the Erection of Municipal Corporations, and the Establishment of Regulations of Police, in and for the Several Counties, Cities, Towns, Townships and Villages in Upper-Canada.[1] Although the more convenient short title of this pre-Confederation statute is the Municipal Corporations Act, 1849, it is even more popularly known as "the Baldwin Act." Named for its sponsor, Robert Baldwin, co-premier and attorney general of Canada, when Canada West and Canada East operated as united provinces, this first municipal statute laid down a near-perfect structure for local self-rule across a vast territory of diverse regions and specialized settlements, from farm villages to mining towns, from manufacturing centres to institution-based communities. The Baldwin Act is authoritatively "regarded as the Magna Carta of municipal government in Canada."[2]

That's why local electors in Ontario, with this pre-Confederation 1840s foundation, viewed voting on municipal questions as instinctively right for a democratic country. Indeed, judges treated it like a "natural right" — meaning it inheres in the people by nature rather than having to be granted by a law-making body. "There is nothing in the Ontario Municipal Act permitting the council to take a plebiscite," observed Judge Myron Britton 115 years ago in the case of King v. Toronto, "and there is no express prohibition against their doing so." On this basis, he rejected a legal challenge and allowed a municipal referendum to proceed.[3] Prior to that, in 1887, another Ontario court refused to restrain a referendum when a challenger argued the ballot question was outside the legal competence of a municipality. Because there was no statutory prohibition of plebiscites, and because no injustice or injury could be shown by the plaintiff if the vote took place, the judge in Davies v. Toronto had no difficulty letting local electors have their say.[4] In 1903 Ontario's legislature confirmed this long-standing democratic practice, amending the Municipal Act to expressly confer statutory authority for voting on issues by local ratepayers through a non-binding ballot question.

Quebec's legislature likewise enacted many statutes providing ballot-box democracy, including the Cities and Towns Act, the Municipal Code (for villages and smaller rural settlements), the Education Act, the Municipal Public Utilities Sales Act, the Municipal Franchises Act, the Mining Towns Act, the Liquor Permit Control Act, the Temperance Act, and even the Act

Respecting Offences Relating to Alcoholic Beverages. For *pure laine* Quebec, the right to vote on issues is woven deeply into the original fabric.

• • •

In this context, local decision-making, typically entailing significant expenditure for a proposed project such as a library, arena, bridge, water treatment facility, or concert hall, included a ballot question to approve taking on the debt — because local ratepayers would have to pay it off through their taxes. If the majority was No, the ratepayers paid lower taxes and got by with fewer amenities. If Yes, locals got the benefit of such additional facilities, the community became better established, and the costs were borne over the life of the bond issued used to raise money for the construction. The choice being forced between Yes or No revolved around that trade-off.

In the process, this method for achieving local consensus provided democratic restraint on the tendency of councillors to spend money and gain ribbon-cutting glory and votes while leaving the unpleasant financial hangover for their successors. In practical terms, too, locals could keep an eye on the slow progress of construction, or the apparent wasteful use of materials — pressing their councillors for explanations and penning letters to the editor. In all, local ballot questions were an apt instrument for cost-benefit analysis, as weighed by people best able to judge — those paying the freight and enjoying the results. Ballot questions for municipal ratepayers in our country have been an ideal instrument for democratic accountability.

• • •

In Ontario this great system got sidelined in the 1960s and 1970s. In that era, spending by the provincial government shifted from frugal financial management to open-future expansion. The first Ontario budget to exceed $1 billion, tabled under Premier John Robarts, was major news. Working at Queen's Park as executive assistant to Attorney General Arthur Wishart at the time, I felt the sober awe that spread among provincial members over the scale of spending when within three years that amount doubled as Premier Bill Davis took the helm in 1971. By 2016, Ontario government yearly spending had risen to $134 billion, with that year's deficit of $5.7 billion getting added to the now-staggering public debt of $307 billion, making the province the most indebted sub-national jurisdiction in the world. With a population just one-third of California's, Ontario's debt load is more than double that of the biggest U.S. state.

In tandem with that spending rampage, Ontario's municipal governments also got themselves cemented in debt. The cause of this can be found largely in the eclipsed role of democratic accountability at the ballot box. Huge public debts occurred because spending restraints were removed.

At the national level, where similar trends occurred, and in the Province of Ontario, the Office of Comptroller General was emasculated. Traditionally, in our parliamentary system, where "supply" (money) must first be authorized by our elected representatives before it can be spent, the comptroller general was an official who controlled the amount that had been duly authorized for a project but for which not enough revenue had yet accumulated in the public treasury. This official could and did hold up projects and programs — otherwise ready to be rolled out — until money was available for them.

In the extended economic boom after the Second World War, people became used to prosperity and envisaged a limitless future. By the 1970s, a new idea was being preached: people didn't need to save up for something — a car, television set, new clothing, or house — *before* buying it. Instead, they could purchase on credit, enjoy the item now, and pay off the debt (with interest) in the future. This same thinking pervaded government, as finance ministers, using a one-sided application of Keynesian economics to justify spending into indebtedness, came to view the public accounts in an entirely different light.

During this transition from frugal accountability and fiscal prudence to freebooting financial indulgence, the Ontario Municipal Act was amended, a counterpart to removing the powers of Ontario's comptroller general. Instead of submitting a borrowing bylaw to local voters, a council could apply to the Ontario Municipal Board for a green light to spend the money. Control passed from local citizens on the scene to civil servants in politically remote Toronto. In the provincial capital, these officials took their cue from the debt-seeking provincial government and seldom refused a municipality's well-argued case for incurring more debt to upgrade some roads, replace a bridge, modernize a sewage treatment plant, or construct a new hockey arena. In this retreat from ballot-box accountability, tinkering with other statutory provisions reduced possibilities for ballot questions such as under the Fluoridation Act of Ontario.

With the link of democratic accountability broken, spending by municipalities skyrocketed. After the Mike Harris government made mandatory the publication of names and salaries of all public officials being paid more than $100,000 a year, this "Sunshine List" revealed tiny municipalities with as many as eight or ten such secure individuals on their payrolls.

· · ·

In 2015 British Columbia turned to this use of ballot-box financial accountability when Metropolitan Vancouver voters were asked to approve, or not, a new 0.5 percent regional sales tax, integrated with the provincial sales tax, to pay local government's share of a decade-long $7.5 billion transit plan to upgrade rapid transit, buy hundreds more buses, add new ferries, and build another bridge. At first this seemed promising.

Results were announced July 2. Almost 600,000 votes had been cast, evenly split between Yes and No in Vancouver, more heavily opposed in outlying municipalities where electors saw little public transit in the ten-year plan to service their areas. Of valid votes cast, 290,151, or 38.32 percent, said Yes. No ballots numbered 467,032, or 61.68 percent. The proposed transit tax had been defeated.

The next Sunday, on CBC Radio's network program *180*, I discussed why Vancouver's experience was a case study of Canada-wide funding challenges for urban transit systems, but equally a prime example of how *not* to conduct a referendum.

The Yes side had strong support from those in public office but suffered from a calamitous campaign. The No forces waged a far more effective effort. The subject of public transit understandably raised issues about the operations of TransLink, the regional public transportation authority. The real problems on that front were dramatically highlighted midway through the referendum campaign by the firing of TransLink's CEO.

Transit referendums are more routine in the United States where their successes in getting voter approval for funding — meaning voter endorsement of the transit program itself — flow from campaigns that can run for up to two years, not two months as was the case in Vancouver. Well-planned campaigns identify the pros *and* cons that will be argued, then develop a strategy to ensure the best message is conveyed on each issue. Given the short referendum period imposed by the province, all these advantages were lost, which caused the Yes side to flounder.

The all-important education campaign about a ballot issue, prior to voting, benefits from time and intelligence. The Yes side in Vancouver only began publicity efforts in March, with mail-in ballots in voters' hands from March 16 on, returnable from then until a May 29 deadline. "It was like the Yes side thought it had better not peak too early," reported Gary Mason in the *Globe and Mail*, "or perhaps someone suggested a plebiscite was like a general election and people wouldn't start thinking about the issue until just before voting began."[5] Meanwhile, the No side, with key support from the Canadian Taxpayers Federation, studied comparable U.S. experience and for months had already been influencing voters by vilifying whatever the Yes side stood for.

Although TransLink became a lightning rod, it didn't cause the Yes side to lose. For that, credit goes to the absence of a persuasive campaign. In addition, several mayors said publicly they'd find other ways to fund transit if the referendum didn't approve the new tax. Given that, why vote for it?

• • •

Across Canada, use of municipal ballot questions has declined in recent decades. That causes a downward spiral, as lack of familiarity and practice makes newcomers to politics uncertain about their role and inept when using them. Once mayors and councillors saw ballot questions as a normal part of community democracy. Today they often strive to avoid them.

Over time, efforts to reduce democratic accountability have changed political culture itself. Seldom today do municipal councillors feel the imperative to ask local voters to debate and vote on major issues. They are increasingly prone to commission opinion polls and hire consultants instead.

Ballot-box verdicts, however, reflected a community understanding that governance in a democratic society entails a partnership between citizens and those elected to represent them. That time now past was certainly not a golden age but it was an era when greater satisfaction attended public service and its outcomes.

29

CANADA'S PLACE
IN A UNIVERSE OF REFERENDUMS

As citizens of an international country, we Canadians work, study, invest, travel, live, and engage as participants and observers in public affairs abroad. From our United Nations engagement in world health, armed forces peacekeeping, and refugee placement, to our NATO alliance operations and world trading arrangements, on through wide-ranging global projects of Canadian non-governmental organizations and transnational business corporations, we absorb the international scene's impacts and exert influence on it. When others vote in referendums, this, too, is some part of our universe.

COLOMBIA'S 2016 REFERENDUM ON PEACE

From 1964 to 2016, Colombia suffered the longest-running internal war in the western hemisphere. Begun during the Cold War, the country's half-century battle between government forces and the Fuerzas Armadas Revolucionarias de Colombia (FARC) killed a quarter-million Colombians, displaced seven million more, and delivered cruel fates to uncountable others, who disappeared, were forcibly recruited, tortured, kidnapped, or otherwise afflicted. This Marxist-Leninist insurgency stubbornly endured into the twenty-first century in a haze of drug trafficking, land disputes, and the quirks of Colombian politics. That a modernizing, middle-income nation of fifty million would still have thousands of heavily armed FARC guerrillas living in the jungles and fighting a Communist revolution in 2016 bore testament to Colombia's fragmented geography and culture of political violence.

It was said "everybody wants peace" for Colombia and her people, and "everybody" included Canada. The country's internal displacement of people, exceeded only by Syria's ongoing internal war that began in 2011, brought many Colombians north, seeking refuge in Canada. Canadian taxpayers, through our federal government, paid $100 million in 2016, divided between bilateral assistance to the country and Colombia's "peace process."

After four prior attempts at peace negotiations, both sides were trying again, meeting over five years in Havana. In late 2016, the negotiations in Havana finally produced a peace accord. Members of the non-governmental organization Canadian Lawyers Without Borders, who'd been working since 2003 toward this goal, considered it "a model for other countries mired in insurgencies."

Implementing the accord required ratification by the people to achieve the requisite buy-in from a deeply scarred nation. From the very start of negotiations, President Juan Manuel Santos had stipulated any agreement would have to be endorsed by the people in a *plebiscito*. To give peace a chance, he knew support from the people was essential. FARC still had some 5,800 guerrilla fighters, most in jungle hideouts.

Canada wanted ratification to make the western hemisphere safer, a Canadian foreign policy goal, and to open up more bilateral business with the third-largest economy in South America. The "historic" agreement gained support from the United States, endorsement by the United Nations, the blessing of Pope Francis, even a song written and recorded by Ringo Starr. Canada's foreign minister, Stéphane Dion, arrived in Cartagena, Colombia, for the signing ceremony, showing our support for the widely celebrated peace agreement.

Within Colombia two former presidents who'd tried to make peace with FARC and failed, Álvaro Uribe and Andrés Pastrana Arango, were vehement leaders of the No campaign, while President Santos displayed confidence bordering on cockiness leading up to the October 2, 2016, referendum vote. The intensity of the campaign saw the choice narrowing, and when votes were tallied, even some of the accord's critics seem surprised it had been defeated — by 53,000 votes, or 0.43 percent. The immediate response outside Colombia, including by some vocal Canadians, was to lament that once again the referendum process — simplifying an issue to Yes or No — showed its shortcomings by creating this devastating setback.

However, the real result was an example of a ballot question's role in the democratic dialectic. After the October 2 vote, an intense six weeks of negotiation with a more humble President Santos and the others forged a much-improved revised peace agreement, incorporating issues that had emerged and only become clarified during the campaign, proving how dialogue and compromise in even a deeply polarized society can result in progress. This wouldn't have occurred without the referendum — as the prior half decade of negotiations bore witness. In November Colombia's Congress approved the revised peace accord. FARC began demobilizing under U.N. supervision, and Juan Manuel Santos received the Nobel Peace Prize.

BREXIT EXPOSES THE BRITISH CONUNDRUM

The decision to take Britain out of the European Union's common market of five hundred million people had certainly not been expected by Prime Minister David Cameron, who'd initiated the vote. As the Brexit campaign progressed, Canadians followed developments closely because our news media increased coverage once the result began to loom as less certain, and because any referendum about separating from a union has traction with us in the shadow of two prior Quebec ballot questions on this possibility.

Quebec separatists, close students of independence referendums by Basques, Catalans, Chechens, and Scots, found portents in the Brexit campaign for their next referendum about separating from Canada, speaking enthusiastically about a rising global quest for identifiable communities to regain self-identity through self-control. On the other hand, Prime Minister Justin Trudeau, pressed by journalists for a statement on the U.K. developments, stuck to our official line that Canada doesn't comment on elections or referendums in other countries. His forceful response measured just how much we'd disliked interfering foreigners commenting on Quebec's sovereignty referendums in 1980 and 1995.

The 2016 referendum, initiated by Prime Minister Cameron, was his country's second on U.K. membership in the European Community. The earlier referendum, in 1975, came *after* Britain's government took the historic decision without popular ratification to ditch its Commonwealth common market and make its own brave new world with Continental Europeans instead. Canada and a host of other Commonwealth countries, our diverse economies meshed through decades-long trade patterns with the United Kingdom, had to fend for ourselves. This led to our Free Trade Agreement with the United States, then NAFTA with Mexico included, and most recently our own trade treaty with the European Union.

Britain set its new trajectory in the early 1970s under Prime Minister Edward Heath at a time when former colonies, having achieved independence, could no longer be economically exploited as in the past. It was widely felt that "Britain had lost an empire and failed to find a role." The ambivalence of Britons showed up on many fronts. Powers of government were "devolved" to the United Kingdom's national parts, yet without giving Scotland, Wales, Northern Ireland, or England complete independence from one another. The United Kingdom joined the European Community but without the spirit of devotion needed for complete adhesion, keeping the British pound as currency, and refusing to join the Eurozone. Centuries of being a "distinct society" within Europe, fostered by an island mentality of people set apart, ensured that the United Kingdom would never embrace and be part of a united Europe in the manner of Germany, France, Italy, and the others. The referendum in 2016 didn't create this ancient dichotomy; it just revealed its current manifestation.

If Britain still had any remaining lessons to teach the world, it was the retrospective conclusion that the time for people to weigh in on transformative choice is *in advance* of fundamental change. A time and place for asking citizens to debate, reflect, and vote upon major matters most often is a general election, but it can also be through a referendum — and in this, "timing" is not about a month or year but rather in relation to the choice ahead.

AMERICA'S AGENDA-SETTING BALLOT PROPOSITIONS

There are no country-wide referendums in the United States because there is no national voting system. To elect the president and vice-president, the only national vote that Americans have, an Electoral College aggregates results from the individual electoral systems of all fifty states. For referendums, the constitutions and statutes of each state vary. In states whose political culture is especially democratic, such as along the Pacific coast, enabling provisions for ballot propositions are generous, accessible, and used as a natural extension of citizens taking charge of things that need to be addressed.

Ballot propositions have been known to cause seismic upheavals and reconfigure the political agenda in a state, spread across a number of states, and produce aftershocks here in Canada. Voting to revamp legal sanctions for cannabis use began in 1972 with California Proposition 19, was voted on in the 1980s in Georgia and Oregon, and in the 1990s formed ballot questions in Arizona, Washington, Alaska, Maine, and Nevada. Over the years, use of the initiative machinery to sort out more specific marijuana issues, such as taxing cannabis or treating possession as a minor misdemeanour, continued apace. Voters in Arizona have so far faced eight pot propositions; those in California and Oregon, seven; in Maine, Washington, and Nevada, there have been six; Alaskans and Coloradans voted on five. By 2016, twenty-five states had legalized marijuana for either medical or recreational use, with propositions on the ballots of four states for 2016's election cycle and more slated for voting in 2017 and 2018. Clearly, voting on propositions is a functioning part of the democratic dialectic in America, bringing onto the public agenda issues not advocated by candidates or parties. In Canada, with the Liberals winning an electoral mandate to change the law on marijuana, this U.S. experience became increasingly relevant to Canadian policy-makers.

California, Oregon, and the State of Washington have been active venues for citizen-initiated ballot questions — interesting because Canada's West Coast, too, is the leader in all categories of Canadian democracy. This Pacific-tinged political culture causes outsiders to dismiss healthy West Coast democracy as "excessive." Yet Californians, treasuring this dimension of their "open society" and the robust political accountability fostered by this voting system, have taken deliberate steps to upgrade operation of their citizen-initiated propositions, in response to serious critiques, by refining the legal framework. Moreover, California's well-educated voters have proven far more adept at "coping with intricate initiatives than had been presumed by political scientists," observed American authority Charles M. Price.[1]

Other assumptions about apathy, indifference, and susceptibility of voters seem just as open to challenge. Pollsters frequently report Americans "highly sensitive" to taxation issues, yet when researching state-level citizen initiatives in 1990 for my book *The People's Mandate*, I found ballot questions that would have required drastic tax cuts or limits on government spending were all defeated by voters in Massachusetts, Nebraska, Colorado, and Utah. "Radical" environmental reforms, which critics assumed to be a primary motivation of the electorate, didn't gain much support at the polling stations, either: far-reaching land-use and pollution measures were turned down by voters in California, Washington, Oregon, Michigan, and New York. Even the contention that voters won't support unpopular measures had evaporated with the November 1990 decision of Arizona voters to deny themselves a 20 percent reduction in automobile insurance premiums, while a ballot decision rendered by Oregon voters made wearing automobile seat belts mandatory despite a widespread assumption that American "keep government off my back" libertarian views would prevail.

In some states, this democratic machinery has worked for generations as an integral component of the political system and is seen as a natural part of self-government, embraced by legislators and citizens alike as a vital public agenda platform for a range of subjects, including amendment of the state constitution. Ballot-box democracy is embedded as an effective two-way partnership. In one direction, state legislators can refer issues and enacted statutes to the people for decision or ratification. Flowing the other way, citizens have the right of initiative — a parallel channel for getting issues onto the public agenda — which generates hundreds of signature petitions each year and culminates in many statewide and local ballot propositions taking place in conjunction with electing representatives.

This robust approach to democratic self-government has become a continuous and effective working partnership between citizens and elected representatives. On November 8, 2016, voters in the United States, in addition to electing Donald Trump the country's forty-fifth president, chose senators and members for the U.S. and state congresses, municipal officials, local judges, and school board members, then gave their verdicts on statewide and local ballot questions. The issues included sixty-nine measures referred to electors by their state legislature on constitutional amendments, two state statutes, seventy-one ballot propositions initiated by citizens through signature petitions, three "advisory" or non-binding questions, and eleven obligatory votes to approve bond issues. Not all made it through the judicial certification process, but those that did cumulatively generated 154 statewide ballot measures decided across thirty-five states, affecting more than 205 million Americans. Eight more had been voted on earlier in the year.

Most prominent were questions about gun control, health care, the minimum wage, taxes, and legalizing marijuana. Maine had a ballot proposition about reforming its electoral system. California, apart from many mainline issues, again set itself apart with environmental and edgy health concerns, from the first referendum in the United States for a statewide ban of single-use plastic bags at retail outlets, to requiring actors to wear condoms during the filming of pornographic movies in the state. California's mainline votes ran the gamut of gambling; the death penalty; allowing grocery and convenience stores to sell full-strength beer and wine; revising campaign finance and lobbying laws; penalties for identity theft; and a constitutional right to hunt, fish, and trap.

In addition, municipal lawmakers and activists across the United States put hundreds of local issues, affecting the everyday lives of citizens, onto ballots for voters to decide. Fully seven hundred important community issues became local ballot questions in populous California's November 2016 voting. Some were tailored specifically to the communities in which they were voted on, but others — dealing with marijuana use, a minimum wage, fracking, and LGBT discrimination — were small slices of larger statewide or national agendas, their proponents seeking to build momentum by accumulating a series of local victories.

Canadians declaim the length and cost of American presidential elections, yet the excessive news coverage of that spectacle obscures from our view how robust real democracy is at ground level across our neighbouring republic.

THE GOLD STANDARD OF SWISS REFERENDUMS

Swiss-pioneered measures for a citizen-centred democracy influenced many others a century ago, and not only those chomping at the limits of British-derived systems that thwarted democratic accountability and national progress. For instance, one Swiss procedure, the "popular veto," allowing electors to petition for a referendum on legislation already enacted by Parliament, spread to Italy. Swiss provisions for citizen-initiated ballot questions were also adopted by many American states seeking to emulate the gold standard of citizen-based governance.

Even for those confined within British systems, Switzerland's democratic methods held appeal. Manitoba, Saskatchewan, and Alberta, just opening up and taking advantage of their fresher start, as well as British Columbia, applied variants of Swiss issue-voting. Australia, too, saw the value of embedding a referendum provision in its constitution, making the document amendable only if a majority of voters ratified the change.

That sound Australian provision appealed to Prime Minister Pierre Trudeau when negotiating an amending formula for our Constitution, but regrettably he never succeeded in getting it adopted. Again, in 1991, when Prime Minister Brian Mulroney was taking his turn at constitutional negotiations, part of the extensive process included Canadian senators and MPs also glancing at this Australian provision for referendums to ratify amendments. However, rather than following Australia's well-established precedent and learning from the experience of a country so like our own in government structure, the Parliamentary Committee on the Process for Amending the Constitution chose to perpetuate our political establishment's anti-democratic predisposition. The committee focused on Switzerland, instead of Australia, and though this gave a surface appearance of "going to the source," it was just a deke. The committee quickly noted how referendums had been used, in its view, to "excess" by the Swiss. From there it was a short leap to an illogical conclusion: the parliamentarians refused to recommend that Canadians be allowed to ratify constitutional amendments. As its guilty sop to the notion of Canada as a "world-class" democracy, the best the committee could do was say a referendum "only be used as a supplementary procedure" if a government of the day decided holding one would be appropriate.

Looking selectively at referendum experience abroad had not guided but hindered our Canadian quest to be a citizen-centred democracy. Better to follow our own example.

30
REWARDS OF CITIZEN-CENTRED DEMOCRACY

Canadians hoping for something better than the ineffectual performance of moribund public institutions focus on the intended purpose of such bodies to emphasize patient-centred health care, student-centred education, and citizen-centred democracy — yet find it hard to dislodge the numb practices of hospitals, schools, and governments with their protectorate of entrenched professionals, dependent service clientele, and self-referencing bureaucracies.

Many didn't wait for a miracle to refresh Parliament and our legislatures, to revitalize our political parties or the public service, to revamp government programs for health services or practices of the education system. Instead, they sought alternate channels of action: non-governmental organizations to address public issues directly; use of social media to drive attention to a particular cause independent of governance structures and commercial news organizations; and the right to vote on constitutional change and establish, in the bargain, that our Constitution doesn't belong to those who govern but to the people.

The role of referendums plays just a small part in this bigger drama. However, by recognizing the people as ultimate sovereigns in our multi-layered structure of public institutions and state power, the referendum is intrinsic to citizen-centred Canadian democracy. So inherent, in fact, that referendum use can properly be considered part of our Constitution, which the Supreme Court defined as "the customs, conventions, and enactments of the written constitutional text as well as Canadian political and judicial institutions and processes." Our so-called "direct democracy" operates within a statutory framework enacted by legislatures and its verdicts are not self-implementing but take effect only through Canadian political institutions and processes.

Ballot questions and concerted efforts by a segment of Canada's political class to prevent them entwine with turning points in our political and constitutional evolution. Sometimes a referendum has been resorted to out of political desperation, or for trivial matters, or as an unwise exercise of statecraft about an issue not yet ripe for resolution. But annoying misuse of a democratic practice isn't unique to ballot questions. We've suffered opportunistic calling of elections, political delay by appointing royal commissions, and sidelining problematic individuals by parking them in the soft shadows of Parliament's second chamber. Sometimes such abuse is caused by narrowly partisan motives. Other times, especially in the case of referendums, it has been because the requirements and potentials of responsible government itself are poorly understood.

Yet alongside the inescapable risk of people in power misjudging or abusing this unique democratic tool, referendums bring far more rewards, such as the following Top Ten.

I. REALITY CHECK

All institutions make captives of those who serve them. Even those of us who believe we're free agents exercising independent judgment are bent to the will and ways of the institutionalized system in which we function: schoolteacher, soldier, union leader, bank manager, priest, journalist, lawyer, member of Parliament. For a decade, I strenuously kept in contact with my constituents, advanced every measure I could to enhance citizen-centred governance, and pushed back against the pressures to conform, admonished by a cabinet minister for independence in Commons voting: "You know the way the game is played!"

I didn't consider myself isolated from reality, but reading letters from individuals I'd worked with before becoming a parliamentarian, I was chagrined by their critique of some Mulroney government initiative because they just couldn't see the bigger picture. I didn't think I was living in a parliamentary bubble, and when the Charlottetown Accord emerged as the mother of all constitutional agreements, I campaigned for its ratification sincerely believing that the position of Quebec was finally being understood even as all related needs and interests from other sections of our country were simultaneously being accommodated. Yet when the Charlottetown Accord failed to win majority support from Canadians, and once everything quieted down, I reread the document in calm deliberation. I felt increasing relief that what I'd campaigned for had been defeated.

Years before I'd written, as part of my democrat's creed, "Probably nine times out of ten, the collective wisdom of a large body of informed voters will make a better decision than any small group convinced it knows best." On October 26, 1992, informed voters had reconfirmed a principle for democratic governance: If you can't persuade others that a major change is necessary, then it is necessary to not make that change.

After I lost my seat in the House of Commons, I reread letters I'd received while an elected representative. Many contained interpretations I now saw in a different light. I'd previously thought my friends and constituents just didn't see the big picture. However, what I held in my hands were accurate versions of a different reality.

The rawest reality we face in Canadian democratic procedures is not the diffuse electoral process. It is not the temporizing legislative process. It is the referendum process, which gives sovereign people a collective voice, an unfiltered reality check to recast conclusions of narrowcast experts, and when needed, enable course correction.

2. CREATE COUNTERWEIGHT

Pierre Elliott Trudeau's well-developed political philosophy about the exercise of state power included the necessity to "create counterweights." That is what his constitutionally entrenched Charter of Rights and Freedoms provides: an offset to uphold the freedom of citizens against those who would curtail it. He also saw how the sovereign people, through the channel of a referendum on constitutional questions, could be an essential counterweight to the governmental cluster of first ministers.

Brian Mulroney said the threat of Ottawa holding a national referendum on constitutional changes, if the first ministers continued to balk, forced them to make concessions and reach the agreements in the Charlottetown Accord.

However, there are more robust non-Canadian illustrations of the referendum's power in creating counterweight.

Along California's spectacular Pacific coast, developers filled scenic real estate with upscale residential projects, with no protest from hands-off state legislators or from municipal politicians, all of whose campaign budgets included generous contributions from the developers. The urgency of preserving unique landscape for public enjoyment in perpetuity wasn't on the politicians' agendas. Municipal councillors, in what they saw as win-win-win, approved outlying areas for residential development, slice after small slice, as payback to their election funders, to serve their community by creating jobs for local trades, and to increase tax assessment.

Nobody in office saw the larger picture *and* had the political freedom to restrain the process of parkland infilling — so concerned citizens signed an initiative petition and forced choice by a ballot proposition. The Coastal Conservation Act of California, enacted in 1976, drew its major provisions from that citizen-initiated proposition, which won majority voter support at the polls. The result, since enjoyed by millions: vaulting cliffs rising from white sandy strands and edged by irreplaceable redwood forests, public parklands forever — thanks *only* to the people's vote.

Another compelling example of referendum-as-counterweight is Italian. It's a bit like Brian Mulroney's example in which governments constrained by political pressures from taking action can be pushed to deal with an important issue just by the *prospect* of a referendum. In 1978, under Italy's initiative law, the Radical Party began collecting signatures on a petition to force a choice about the country's abortion law. Everyone would publicly debate controversial abortion policy and parliamentarians would be pressed to declare their stance, thereby in many cases reducing their re-electability. To circumvent the intensity of this referendum campaign, the Italian Parliament swiftly approved an abortion law.

Given the unflinching opposition to abortion by the Roman Catholic Church and widespread Catholic influence throughout Italian society, this change in abortion policy wouldn't otherwise have occurred. S.E. Finer made a detailed study of that counterweight-creating phenomenon. "Without this initiative threat, no such legislation would have been passed." It was, he concluded, "an instance of how the referendum device can break the parties' monopoly on issue definition."[1]

Similarly, back here in Canada, the result of British Columbia's 1916 referendum on enfranchising women was also used to leverage extension of other equality rights for women. During the Quebec referendum on separation in 1980, Prime Minister Trudeau pledged major constitutional changes *if* the No side carried the day. Referendums in the Northwest Territories about dividing the wide expanse and creating Nunavut in the eastern Arctic directly spurred settlement of Inuit land claims. When Prime Minister Harper became paralyzed in moving on his pledged reform or abolition of the Senate, Senator Hugh Segal, Green Party leader Elizabeth May, and others called for a referendum on the unelected and unaccountable second chamber, not because it would directly lead to change but because it would pressure legislators to deal one way or another with our country's embarrassing colonial relic. After Prince Edward Island's 2016 referendum on electoral reform, Fair Vote Canada and Equal Voice invoked the results, which supported proportional representation, to push the Trudeau Liberals on their fading promise to replace Canada's "unfair first-past-the-post" voting system for MPs. The point is that referendums can do more than force a choice; they can provide leverage for democratic politics.

Issue-voting by the people has potential to be a political counterweight to powerful, unresponsive governments. A century ago Canada's Progressives saw initiatives and referendums as an alternative, or at least a counterweight, to legislators manipulated by lobbyists and hobbled by party discipline. At the core of such thinking is recognition that the principal cause of corruption is concentrated, unaccountable power.

In this respect, Canadian referendums take on importance because the great power of contemporary government is no longer effectively counterbalanced by the people's elected representatives in the Commons or provincial legislatures. However, except in British Columbia, the "initiative" exists only for limited applications. The ability of citizens to trigger a ballot question, rather than waiting for government to hold a referendum, is a missing ingredient of responsible government that members of today's legislatures might well add to the toolbox of a citizen-centred democracy.

3. MANDATE CLARITY

When the Liberal Party formed a majority government in 2015 with its explicit pledge to change the electoral system, it floundered because the Trudeau government's replacement model for electing MPs had never been specified, and none was proffered even after a year in office. A cry went up from diverse Canadians for a referendum on the issue. Once again the ambiguous nature of a general election mandate, in this case pertaining to

"Canada's unfair electoral system," leaves too much that is too important to mincing interpretation and political opportunism.

That is why the "specific mandate" provided by a clear ballot question can break through deliberately spread political fog that obscures the issue and delays action. Whether to give women the vote in British Columbia, build a bridge from Prince Edward Island to the mainland, prohibit use of beverage alcohol or reinstate its availability, impose Daylight Saving Time, or ratify an aboriginal land claim treaty — nothing else clarifies an issue like a referendum campaign when all interested and eligible citizens participate directly and produce a collective deliberative verdict.

Clarifying a public mandate through a properly framed ballot question entails three dynamic elements. First is discovery. Just as an election campaign is "unpredictable" because events nobody anticipated emerge and take centre stage, a referendum campaign causes a shakeup that can bring new light and fresh insight to something that not long before seemed fixed on a set course. Colombia's 2016 referendum campaign on its peace accord drew out issues needing more satisfactory resolution than had been achieved during five protracted years of negotiations. When ratification of the accord failed, the urgent new imperative overtaking all concerned led to working out better solutions for problems clarified through citizens debating about how to vote.

Second is using a ballot question to clarify the mandate. The benefit of this reward is often denied by those in power, who prefer to interpret a vague general mandate from voters the way it suits them. Once the election is over, many leaders and their advisers break faith with the electorate. Within contemporary Canadian politics, elastic "electoral mandates" and the exercise of governing power by leaders who lie undermines the credibility of the system. Even if the leaders can be replaced, however, the willing violation of their pledged word dissolves the legitimacy of democratic government itself. That, once gone, is irreplaceable. To counter this, the role of ballot questions to clarify mandates is part of a multi-faceted democratic country founded on "responsible-government" accountability to the people.

The third dynamic element is how a specific mandate is implemented. This is where statecraft comes in. Although the voting produces numbers pro and con a measure, that might or might not lead to implementation of the majority view. Prime Minister Laurier could see, as could all Canadians, that prohibition would be better handled through the provinces rather than through Ottawa despite an overall majority favouring a national law. The very night of his constitutional referendum defeat by an overall majority vote, Prime Minister Mulroney could announce that "the Charlottetown Accord is history" and in those five words bring down the curtain on a process that, despite herculean efforts and the deep resolve of so many for so long, had been a path wrongly taken.

Seasoned prime ministers know that reading voting returns requires more than arithmetic, that sometimes the way to deal with an issue is to stop dealing with it. This, too, is how referendums bring clarity to a public mandate.

4. SAFETY VALVE

Pretty well every Canadian would agree that for a democratic society such as ours it is better to ventilate a public issue than bottle it up. The way a referendum allows this to be done is one of its most significant rewards, because more than each individual expressing her or his views, we get to hear the collective voice of the Canadian people.

The bum rap given to referendums — that issues are "oversimplified" by forcing a choice between Yes or No — overlooks the practicalities of free speech, open dialogue, developing a case, debating a proposition, and reaching consensus. Form and structure facilitate reasoning. A process for presenting pro and con arguments makes it possible for citizens to be heard instead of their voices being drowned out in an un-orchestrated cacophony. Student debates are structured to argue the negative and affirmative of an issue. Law courts are set up and operate within rules for lawyers to present the opposing cases of plaintiff and defendant. Broadcasting rules allow for the leader of the Opposition to also have airtime when the prime minister takes to the airwaves to make a major policy announcement. Elected representatives debate for or against a motion or bill, then vote either Yes to approve or No to defeat the measure.

A referendum, especially when the sides are organized by Yes and No umbrella committees to present content in an intelligible fashion, offers structure for ideas and arguments, a context in which it is possible for everyone interested to ventilate their ideas about the issue.

Every now and then contentious issues confound legislatures, split parties, and divide cabinets. Keeping big issues bottled up in representative institutions can be politically perilous for all concerned and can disrupt other necessary operations. Our history shows, at that point, the benefit of advancing to an all-inclusive referendum process — the safety valve of a democratic state.

5. CRASH COURSE

Education about a ballot issue is probably as important a reward from a referendum as the actual vote tallies at the campaign's end. A referendum forces us to think about an issue, reflect on possibilities, and together make an informed, collective choice about something central to our lives. And to help with this program of continuing adult education, the news media, in tandem with the Yes and No campaigns, ensure we have plenty to study and inwardly digest. It is a crash course because there's limited time before voting. It is not abstract learning because there is a specific question that must be answered on the fast-approaching date.

This incentive to learn about the ballot issue is rewarding not only for individual citizens but for the country or province as a whole because a population aware of a public measure's complexity and far-reaching effects will generally become more understanding of the multi-layered nature of issues politicians grapple with. The educational component of a referendum campaign, followed by deliberate casting of thousands or millions of ballots, has an outcome nothing else can match.

Some contend that ordinary citizens shouldn't vote on issues because they simply don't understand them the way experts do. Many major decisions in Canada have been made by a small number of people unaware of all the complexities, sometimes out of touch with changed conditions, and often influenced by vested interests whose power behind the scenes was never openly acknowledged. Are such decisions more valid in a democratic self-governing country than ones reached with the involvement of informed citizens?

People might not be fully up to speed on an issue the day a referendum is announced. They're the ones Canadian television networks seek out for "streeters," the selectively edited on-camera comments by pedestrians who blurt out something like "I don't know anything whatsoever about it!" It's part, witting or unwitting, of how those who like to control the Canadian storyline are readily dismissive of a democratic process to which they believe themselves superior.

However, by the time the campaign's tutorial ends on the eve of voting, the people certainly are up to speed. A voter entering the polling station to mark a ballot on a single issue probably understands the voting consequences better than he or she does in a multi-faceted general election. Getting ready to vote in a referendum is like studying for an exam with only one question — and when you know in advance what that question is.

Just as a general election is our trusted method to select between personalities, programs, promises, and performance, an educational referendum campaign, which culminates in answering a ballot question, is our focused means to choose a particular policy. It is often preferable because it provides clarity that an electoral mandate does not. It is, occasionally, the only suitable means for bridging an impasse. And in its wake, people are better informed about something important.

6. CITIZEN BUY-IN

Consent of the governed is the glue that holds Canadian democracy in place. There are a number of ways consent can be given, but any short list of them would include the referendum because the deliberative process and orderly public steps of issue-voting permit a reasonably objective evaluation by citizens and the formation of community consensus about an important issue at a particular time.

Opinion pollsters ask a "representative sample" of voters about their intentions, but a referendum involves everyone. Opinion sampling is usually an out-of-the-blue call, but the marking of a ballot is a deliberate procedure that comes at the end of a period of debate, education, and reflection. Opinion sampling generates a percentage of people for or against a measure today, a partial statement that another poll might contradict tomorrow. In contrast, a referendum is a public ritual. It entails each citizen creating an artifact through the marking of a ballot and then depositing it in a secure box or mailing it to the referendum office for counting. This individual act, repeated thousands or millions of times as each eligible voter comes forward, forms part of a serious collective exercise. It is a right of citizenship equal to all. It produces an outcome that generally puts a contentious matter to rest — because all concerned know they'd had their chance to pitch their strongest case to others, and because of Canadian understanding that in a democracy, while respecting minorities, the majority rules. There is no other way, certainly not through commercial opinion polling, to so effectively achieve community buy-in for a measure, or even community understanding of it when a majority rejects the proposed measure. There is never "consent" when those in power merely assume that a new policy or program is acceptable to the people.

7. POLITICAL ACCOUNTABILITY

The concept of "responsible government" introduced in the 1840s to British North American colonies was carried forward into the 1867 constitution for Confederation. Responsible government fused the elected assembly of people's representatives with ministers of the Crown in the same legislative body so that the former could hold accountable the latter for policies and practices of the government. The relationship established unequivocally that those wielding state power in the name of the monarch had to answer to the ultimate sovereign, the people, through their representatives.

This relationship is still embedded in the Constitution, but we've begun to refer in common speech more to "democratic accountability" than to "responsible government." The new term resonates better with contemporary Canadians. It connotes a clearer, even edgier, meaning. It implies that governmental accountability entails far more than what transpires in the Commons during Question Period or when MPs scrutinize and vote to approve the government's spending estimates for the upcoming fiscal year. It isn't limited to elected representatives in legislatures holding cabinet ministers and public officials to account. Democratic accountability includes the crucial role journalists, public policy organizations, and empowered citizens play in following public events and inquiring about them to spread word to others. It includes getting issues of governance before courts and tribunals for adjudication. Democratic accountability in Canada today broadly means that anything done by government must be answered for.

Rising awareness of the need for more accountability in the workings of government, both in Ottawa and in the provinces, gave renewed prominence to the auditor general, creation of new roles such as the parliamentary budget officer and ombudsmen with specified jurisdictions of vigilance, Access to Information statutes, registration of lobbyists with rules to curb and publicly disclose their activities, a "Sunshine List" exposing to daylight every year the names and salaries of high-pay civil servants, and online disclosure of spending by public office holders. The quest to achieve a citizen-centred democracy is part of this larger tapestry of accountability measures, which is also the context in which referendums, especially any initiated by citizens, make the constitutional concept of "responsible government" a working reality for Canada's sovereign people.

This need for democratic accountability emerged in the mid-1800s, with the visceral urge of colonists to get better control over local decision-making in Nova Scotia, Lower Canada (Quebec), and Upper Canada (Ontario) — the autocratic refusal of which led to armed insurrection in the latter two colonies by 1837. That revolutionary unrest provoked London to extend "responsible government" by 1840 to Britain's North American colonies that hadn't already overthrown the Crown and reconstituted themselves as a republic — the United States of America.

Part of our own story is reflected, with that point of departure, in how those Founding Fathers went to such lengths to institutionalize "limited government" in the American Constitution. The Americans crafted numerous checks and balances over executive power, institutionalizing separate roles for elected representatives and for the judiciary to each veto and restrain those wielding executive powers of government, and to initiate laws in the case of Congress and to strike down laws as unconstitutional in the case of the Supreme Court. In keeping with this constitution and the political culture it created over time, ballot propositions became a robust part of democratic governance at both state and municipal levels in the United States, with citizens generally having the legal and even constitutional right to initiate votes on a broad range of issues.

What we got with "responsible government" was the British monarchical system as it had evolved constitutionally by the mid-1800s: to *integrate* the legislative and executive functions of government, rather than counterbalance them; to *integrate* two sources of sovereignty by making the Crown and the people confusingly appear as one, rather than establish a single sovereign power in the people; and to enshrine as a stabilizing constitutional goal "peace, order, and good government," rather than the egalitarian principle that "all men are created equal" and a citizen-centric constitution whose goal is to enable "life, liberty, and the pursuit of happiness." In history's laboratory of democracy, Canada is the control, America the experiment.

The long view of Canadian history also shows that our use of referendums ebbs and flows in measure with our ambivalent embrace of democracy. When rising interest in ballot-issue democracy appeared during the 1970s, as if a new generation of Canadians was discovering for the first time the possibilities of being a political democracy, Agar Adamson smiled and published a 1980 article in *Policy Options* entitled "We Were Here Before: Referendums in Canadian Experience." He sought to teach Canadians enchanted by direct democracy's novelty that ballot-issue voting hadn't just been invented. He revealed our long-running connections with referendums, and that we have more history of forcing choice through ballot-box verdicts than most folks realized.

This mechanism for public accountability results from the same democratic instinct that drove our forebears to fight for and achieve responsible government. It is but one of many instruments in the toolbox of democracy. It is infrequently used because, like any untested tool, its unique purpose is poorly understood. Citizen voting on issues isn't institutionalized the way that our legislatures and courts are, nor constitutionalized the way that many of our other democratic rights are. Yet properly recognized for what it is, the referendum's reward is how it contributes to the ability of citizens to live in freedom while keeping an eye on what those entrusted with power of government are up to.

8. DEMOCRATIC VITALITY

The willingness to participate, to be self-reliant, and to accept that our future is in our own hands and not entrusted to "the system" are three hallmarks of a vital democratic society. Political scientists have additional indicia, even grids, on which to track a person's political psychology, ideological identity, or adhesion to the political system. But no matter how one calibrates it, most folks readily understand that a self-governing democracy like ours needs the fuel of human energy, emotion, and ideas. Passivity and lethargy won't let us realize our potential.

So the variety of ways individual Canadians can today become active in the community, and why others withdraw from involvement to the point of ignoring public issues and not even voting, makes a compelling inquiry into the health of the body politic, since that determines our capacity for self-government.

When examining cause and effect, a physician or forensic scientist not only studies the conditions that are present but looks for telltale signs in what might be absent. When looking for evidence for "democratic vitality," it is just as important to consider those who don't vote as those who do; to register which issues aren't on the public agenda instead of only those that are; even to see the ballot questions that are noticeable by their absence, the referendums that never took place to force public debate and collective choice on metrification of the measurement system, the Meech Lake constitutional changes, or dozens of other important questions affecting a positive principle of our country's government and the nature of a citizen's life that people never had a say in.

Here we see the threshold barrier of no referendum-enabling law on the statute books. Here we find the generally non-existent right of citizens to initiate ballot questions. Here we observe governments in British Columbia and Prince Edward Island setting higher levels for majority approval by the people to change the electoral system under which they got elected than they require for approval of far more sweeping measures they themselves enact in their legislature. Here are heard the voices of the political establishment and its coddling chorus who decry referendums and celebrate this void.

Absence of a normalized role for citizens to help make specific choices on transcending issues is the portrait of democracy in our country. We need to add this missing element to complete the picture, the way a detective sees not only what is present but especially looks for what is absent, to discover truth.

Recognizing this missing element, and others, in the operations of our democratic state is a way to begin remedial action. Getting to the root of why people turn away from politics and participation makes clearer what needs to be done. A particular "reward" of this is that it allows us to glimpse the irony of Canada's governing class purring in public about the democratic ways we honour, while behind the scenes ensuring that hurdles prevent those ways ever becoming robust.

9. GOVERNANCE PARTNERSHIP

The heart of "representative democracy" beats in the House of Commons, our provincial and territorial legislatures, and our local councils. Here the few, elected by our votes, represent the many. Invariably, those elected by their fellow citizens are impressed by the honour, feel the bond first forged in an election campaign and then sanctified at the ballot box, and in almost all cases strive to give worthy public service.

From the era when representative assemblies were first elected in the 1700s in colonies that today are part of Canada, down to the present era, just about everything in this link between electors and representatives has been transformed many times over. The growth of mass society, the speed of communications, the array of issues now the purview of public life, the year-round (rather than a month or less) sittings of legislative bodies, opinion polling's "representative samples" of the population's views and values that elected representatives heed, and the rigid control of political parties over candidates during elections and over elected representatives in the legislature submerge local interests and thereby mute the voices of electors. The bleak result is that today's "representatives" are mostly unknowns, and not just MPs. Who can name all thirty ministers in Justin Trudeau's cabinet, or Canada's ten provincial and three territorial premiers?

Referendums are absolutely no magic cure for shortcomings of contemporary democracy in the age of Internet politics and the obliteration of social and geographic boundaries. However, they are a macro part of "representative democracy" — the part when the many represent and speak for themselves. Referendum experience in Canada shows ballot-question democracy can sometimes maintain or restore genuine connection between citizens and elected representatives, at least when the public issue is big enough to be important to both. Elected representatives have a role in the issue being transferred directly to the sovereign people to force an open choice, take some role in the educational campaign and efforts of persuasion prior to voting, and will somehow be responsible for addressing the people's verdict delivered through the ballot boxes.

One elemental reward for a self-governing democracy is to experience that connection between governed and governors as tangible and two-way. This communal awareness, which can come with a referendum as well as in other ways, is found in the compatibility of decision-making that melds elected representatives and citizens in an interconnected process. This governance partnership is something specific and purposeful, its voting more potent than the diffuse focus of a general election with its numerous indirect linkages.

10. POPULAR SOVEREIGNTY

Despite the risk of this democratic tool's misuse, placing issues before citizens to force a collective choice has, overall, rewarded political life. Both directly and indirectly, referendums play a constructive part, sometimes even an indispensable role, in helping a self-governing people address issues not satisfactorily resolved through any other available means.

The free-floating ambiguity that impedes Canadian political life, much of it stemming from having institutionalized contending sovereigns — the People *and* the Crown — has resulted in politicians becoming tantalized by referendums and taking preliminary steps toward them, only to retreat into politics' amorphous twilight zone rather than use the device. They have no problem asking the sovereign people to give them the reins of power in a general election but balk at asking the same source of political legitimacy for ballots to help break a political impasse or to ratify a major change.

Premiers Walter Scott of Saskatchewan, Tobias Norris of Manitoba, and John Oliver of British Columbia all won elections a century ago promising referendums on legislative measures and giving the people a right to initiate ballot questions themselves. In Saskatchewan, Scott oversaw enactment of the Direct Legislation Act in 1912, but then had doubts and put the referendum statute itself to a ballot question for ratification. When it failed to get enough support, he repealed the measure and made no further attempt at connecting the people with the work of their elected legislators. In British Columbia in 1914, Oliver fulfilled his electoral promise to enact a Direct Legislation Act, but then, retreating in doubt, never had the statute proclaimed in force. In Manitoba, Norris in 1916 implemented his promise, too, with the Direct Legislation Act. However, he also backpedalled, referring his own government's enactment to the courts to opine on its constitutionality, and by the time the Law Lords in England were through, they'd found a technicality to strike the measure down. Meanwhile, Alberta Premier Arthur Sifton, no political wimp like the other three, fulfilled his promise. The legislature in Edmonton enacted the Direct Legislation law in 1913, which was virtually the same as the others, under which Albertans voted on a number of ballot questions during the following years. Success rate in honouring the sovereign people: one in four.

Prime Minister Pierre Trudeau proposed a national referendum as part of his arsenal of measures to counteract a ballot question in Quebec on that province breaking up Confederation. A prime consideration was that all Canadians, not only those residing in Quebec, should vote on a crucial province seceding from Canada, because such dramatic change would affect everyone in the destruction of our country. Trudeau also envisaged a national referendum for a different purpose: public ratification of new constitutional provisions his government was developing. But the prime minister failed to match words with action, because the Canada Referendum Act, which had been introduced in the Commons, wasn't proceeded with and died on the order paper. The PM also sought a national referendum to ratify constitutional changes and incorporated such a provision in drafts of the amending formula being negotiated. It wasn't a stretch: Australia had done this in 1901. But in a quagmire trying to reach agreement with ten different premiers, each advancing their own agenda and several opposed to a referendum, Trudeau caved in. He removed the referendum requirement for citizens to ratify constitutional amendments. When he subsequently hit new snags with the premiers over the best procedure for amending Canada's Constitution, the prime minister lamented with annoyed regret on November 5, 1981, having "not kept in the amending formula a reference to the ultimate sovereignty of the people as could be tested in a referendum." Prime Minister Trudeau even danced this referendum two-step — first forward, then back again — in 1971 when his government introduced legislation to enable direct votes, run by Canada's chief electoral officer, on Prairie grain farming issues. The bill never proceeded through Parliament to become law. Attempts to results: four to zero.

Alberta Premier Peter Lougheed decided to get a specific mandate from the people through a referendum that would disclose strong public endorsement for his government's energy policies, a counterweight against the Trudeau government's intrusion into the oil-producing province's energy jurisdiction. Lougheed's minister of intergovernmental affairs pronounced the Alberta Referendum Act as "an extremely important piece of legislation for this government" when he introduced it in the legislature on October 20, 1980. Yet for the next five months the bold measure never advanced beyond that introductory "first reading" and died on the order paper with prorogation on March 30, 1981. Success rate: zero for one.

Ambivalence about referendums by even strong political leaders, and ardent resistance to them by cabinet ministers, has paralyzed this country's ability to normalize procedures for the sovereign people; as Brian Mulroney put it at the time of his own belated embrace of referendums, "to do more than get a kick at the can every four years." He had failed to hold a referendum on the Meech Lake Accord, and only instituted a national referendum because three provinces, where voting on the Charlottetown Accord was happening, forced his hand. Rating re linking government and the sovereign people: one-half in two.

Earlier in the twentieth century, Wilfrid Laurier and Robert Borden wanted public clarity on such issues as sending Canadian soldiers overseas to war and dealing with the unaccountable exercise of law-making powers by Parliament's second chamber, but in the circumstances of the day couldn't get the referendums they hoped for, compounded by the fact that the political establishment's split personality in its relationship with the sovereign people had resulted in there being no enabling legislation for a referendum on the statute books, anyway. The compromise for holding 1898's ballot question on prohibition was a perfect token to self-doubting democrats: a one-off act that expired after the vote took place. As for the war, after it ended, Arthur Meighen, who'd enforced conscription as Borden's minister of justice and who'd himself become prime minister, deeply lamented that the issue had never been taken to the sovereign people for a mandate vote. For these three PMs: one notable breakthrough, many missed shots.

· · ·

The cycles of on-again, off-again interest in direct democracy as a component of our political life are noticeable. Today public awareness of the benefits that can flow from ballot-box democracy is much higher than it was. Holding referendums is more frequent, which in turn brings a familiarity with the process's risks and rewards necessary for good statecraft. Many opinion leaders today call for referendums on a number of subjects. While it is easier to propose something than to get it implemented, the prospect for reintegrating the Canadian people into decision-making on matters that positively affect us all is not an ephemeral wish but a political imperative. Even if a significant proposal is notionally within a government's electoral mandate — an increasingly fictitious concept, to be sure — there can be real benefit from a focused public examination, followed by free citizens collectively rendering a considered verdict on it.

Referendums have helped shape Canada's character at the national, and more frequently, provincial, municipal, and reserve levels of governance. This valuable instrument is neither appropriate nor necessary for issues that can be resolved through the deliberate working of routine Canadian procedures of governance. The referendum's enduring and symbolic potential is reserved for times when proper exercise of statecraft takes the risk and reaps the rewards of forcing choice, as a mature working of Canadian self-government, about a transcending issue with significant impact on the sovereign people.

Because of our Canadian ideology or mythology about being a rights-based, politically united, multi-culturally rich, socially pluralistic, and behaviourally tolerant country, the profound dislike of referendums by Canada's political class flows directly from the way a ballot question sometimes exposes how we aren't all those things. Those comfortably entrenched in power or entrapped by patterns of anti-democratic thinking allege that a referendum "creates" divisions — as if it is the cause of unwanted differences — rather than crediting this democratic procedure for revealing essential truths about our fracture lines. The referendum is the child who points to the naked monarch riding by in splendid procession, a scene adults are either too acclimatized or too fearful to acknowledge, and shouts out, "Look, Mommy, the King is wearing no clothes!"

To more honestly celebrate Canadian diversity, we best see its full extent.

CANADIAN BALLOT-ISSUE VOTES: NATIONAL, PROVINCIAL, TERRITORIAL

(Although not tabulated below, thousands of municipal ballot questions, dozens on reserves, and many sectoral direct votes on agricultural issues have also taken place.)

Jurisdiction	Date of Voting	Issue
Canada	Sept. 29, 1898	Prohibition of liquor by national law
	April 27, 1942	Release government from election mandate on conscription
	Oct. 26, 1992	Approval of Charlottetown Accord constitutional amendments
British Columbia	Nov. 25, 1909	Local option policy for liquor control
	Sept. 14, 1916	Women's suffrage
	same day	Prohibition of liquor
	Oct. 20, 1920	Temperance Act
	June 20, 1924	Sale of beer by the glass
	June 1, 1937	Public health insurance
	June 12, 1952	Daylight Saving Time
	same day	Regulation of sale of liquor
	Aug. 30, 1972	Daylight Saving Time (conducted in five electoral districts only)
	Oct. 17, 1991	Recall of elected MLAs
	same day	Right of citizens to initiate ballot questions

	May 15, 2002	First Nations land claims issues (eight questions)
	May 17, 2005	Proportional electoral system
	May 12, 2009	Proportional electoral system
	Aug. 5, 2011	Harmonized sales tax
Alberta	July 21, 1915	Prohibition of liquor
	Oct. 25, 1920	Prohibition of liquor
	Nov. 5, 1923	Temperance Act
	Aug. 17, 1948	Ownership of power companies
	Oct. 30, 1957	Permission for additional outlets for sale of liquor
	May 23, 1967	Daylight Saving Time
	Aug. 30, 1971	Daylight Saving Time
Saskatchewan	Nov. 27, 1913	Approval of Direct Legislation Act
	Dec. 11, 1916	Abolition of liquor stores
	Oct. 25, 1920	Importation of liquor into Saskatchewan
	July 16, 1924	Prohibition of liquor
	June 19, 1934	Sale of beer by the glass
	Oct. 31, 1956	Choice of local time zones
	Oct. 21, 1991	Requiring balanced provincial budget by statute
	same day	Ratification of constitutional amendments by referendum
	same day	Government payment for hospital-performed abortions
Manitoba	July 23, 1892	Prohibition of liquor
	April 2, 1902	Prohibition of liquor
	March 13, 1916	Temperance Act
	June 22, 1923	Government control of liquor sales
	July 11, 1923	Amendments to Temperance Act
	June 28, 1927	Three questions concerning sale of beer
	Nov. 24, 1952	Marketing of coarse grains

Ontario	Jan. 1, 1894	Prohibition of liquor
	Dec. 4, 1902	Prohibition of liquor
	Oct. 20, 1919	Four questions on Ontario Temperance Act and sale of beer
	April 18, 1921	Importation of liquor into Ontario
	Oct. 23, 1924	Repeal of Ontario Temperance Act
	Oct. 10, 2007	Proportional electoral system
Quebec	April 10, 1919	Prohibition of beer and wine
	May 20, 1980	Quebec to negotiate sovereignty-association with Canada
	Oct. 1, 1987	Constitutional future of Northern Quebec (voting in region only)
	Oct. 26, 1992	Approval of Charlottetown Accord constitutional amendments
	Oct. 30, 1995	Authority to proclaim Quebec an independent country
New Brunswick	May 14, 2001	Legalization of gambling using video lottery terminals
Nova Scotia	March 15, 1894	Prohibition of liquor
	Oct. 25, 1920	Regulation of sale of liquor
	Oct. 31, 1929	Retention of prohibition
	Oct. 16, 2004	Sunday shopping
Prince Edward Island	Dec. 28, 1878	Prohibition (Prince County)
	April 24, 1879	Prohibition (Charlottetown)
	May 29, 1879	Prohibition (Kings County)
	Dec. 13, 1893	Prohibition (province-wide)
	June 5, 1901	Prohibition
	Summer 1913	Opening of roads to automobile use
	Jan. 22, 1923	Prohibition
	July 18, 1929	Prohibition
	June 25, 1940	Prohibition (six questions concerning alcohol sale, permits)

	June 28, 1948	Approval of new Temperance Act
	Nov. 10, 1954	Two questions on role of P.E.I. Potato Marketing Board
	Jan. 18, 1988	Approval of fixed-link crossing (bridge) to mainland
	Nov. 3, 1997	Removal of all video lottery terminals from the province
	Nov. 28, 2005	Proportional electoral system
	Nov. 7, 2016	Proportional electoral system
Newfoundland	Nov. 4, 1915	Prohibition of liquor
	June 3, 1948	Decision on constitutional status: regaining responsible self-government; joining Canada; or continuing commission government
	July 22, 1948	Decision on constitutional status: joining Canada or regaining responsible self-government
	Sept. 5, 1995	Replacing of parochial schools with a mostly public school system
	Sept. 1, 1997	Replacing of parochial schools with a fully public school system
Northwest Territories	April 14, 1982	Question of territorial division
	May 5, 1992	Location of new boundary line
	Nov. 5, 1992	Creation of Nunavut (voting in eastern Arctic)
Nunavut	April 14, 1982	Question of territorial division (voting while part of Northwest Territories)
	Nov. 5, 1992	Location of Nunavut boundary as new Canadian territory
	Dec. 11, 1995	Choice of capital for Nunavut
	May 9, 2016	Authorizing Nunavut municipalities to sell municipal land

ACKNOWLEDGEMENTS

Dundurn publisher Kirk Howard inquired if I'd update my two prior Dundurn books on referendums to take account of Brexit and other dramatic developments on the "direct-democracy" front, which led to this new work. I'm grateful to Kirk for his attentive interest in keeping books on important Canadian subjects before the reading public, and am proud to be associated with him in this endeavour as he continues to navigate Canada's largest independent publishing house through the choppy waters of the always challenging book business.

As with my other recent Dundurn titles on Canadian political subjects — *Foreign Voices in the House*, *The Big Blue Machine*, and *Our Scandalous Senate* — I've been pleased to work with seasoned editor Dominic Farrell of Dundurn. Dominic's dedicated professionalism ensured thematic clarity to this work and the structure of its contents. By the same token, Michael Carroll has again devoted his intelligence and deployed his sharp eyes in the manuscript's detailed edit, resulting in a book of great accuracy. Thank you, Dominic and Michael.

Others at Dundurn also contributed to this book's evolution, and I especially thank vice-president Beth Bruder, executive assistant and contracts and administration services manager Sheila Douglas, sales and marketing director Margaret Bryant, sales manager Synora Van Drine, managing editor Kathryn Lane, director of design and production Jennifer Gallinger, senior designer Laura Boyle, project editor Elena Radic, ebooks and IT manager Carmen Giraudy, and publicist Kendra Martin.

Esteemed constitutional expert and political scientist Peter Russell has contributed a foreword, for which I am most grateful, to clarify the importance of ballot-question democracy in our Canadian context.

Peter, in addition to his outstanding work as a teacher and public commentator and leader of the Canadian Political Science Association and Churchill Society for the Advancement of Parliamentary Government, is a published author of well-deserved acclaim. In saluting his accomplishments, I wish to also acknowledge the legion of those who, like Peter, study, teach, write, and care about the role of citizens in democratic countries. Especially, I tip my hat to those who advance ways that the "initiative" process can empower people to not merely elect representatives to legislatures but also to write, circulate, debate, and more directly adopt important measures.

NOTES

PREFACE: A WORD ABOUT WORDS

1. Julien Côté, *Instruments of Direct Democracy*, 3rd ed. (Quebec City: Directeur général des élections du Québec, 2001), 5.

CHAPTER 2: ANVIL OF A SELF-GOVERNING PEOPLE

1. *Globe and Mail*, September 20, 1978, 2.

CHAPTER 4: THE SOVEREIGN PEOPLE OF CANADA

1. Gregory Tardi, "An Interlocutory Report on Referendum Litigation" (unpublished manuscript, 2002), 6.
2. J.A. Stevenson, *Before the Bar: Prohibition Pro and Con* (Toronto: J.M. Dent, 1919), 87.

CHAPTER 5: REFERENDUM LAW NORMALIZES DEMOCRATIC LIFE

1. Transcript of press conference, National Press Club, July 21, 1988, Library and Archives Canada, Ottawa.

CHAPTER 6: REFERENDUMS IN HARMONY WITH THE CONSTITUTION

1. 63 O.L.R. 645 (1929), 3 D.L.R. 629.
2. (1958) O.R. 349.

3. Reference of the statute was made under R.S.M. 1913, c. 38 to the Court of King's Bench (Mathers C.J.K.B.) Re Initiative and Referendum Act (1919) A.C. 935: 938 (1919) 3 W.W. R, 1, 48 D.L.R. 18.
4. Man. R. 1 (1917) 1 W.W.R. 1012, 32 D.L.R. 148.
5. (1919) A.C. 935 (1919) 3 W.W.R. 1, 48 D.L.R. 18.
6. (1922) 2 A.C., 128 (1922) 2 W.W.R. 30, 37 C.C.C. 129, 65 D.L.R. 1. (P.C.).
7. Berriedale Keith, "Notes on Imperial Constitutional Law," *Journal of Comparative Legislation and International Law* 4 (1922): 241.

CHAPTER 7: CHARTER PROTECTION OF MINORITY RIGHTS

1. Paul Adams, "Manitoba." In *Canadian Annual Review of Political and Public Affairs* (Toronto: University of Toronto Press, 1983), 264.
2. *Canadian News Facts*, October 15–30, 1983, 2962.
3. "Rights Referendums Undemocratic, Say Church Leaders," *Ottawa Citizen*, October 5, 1983.
4. *Ottawa Citizen*, October 26, 1983, 8.
5. Ibid.
6. *Windsor Star*, October 28, 1983.
7. *Report of the Chief Electoral Officer, Referendum of October 1, 1987, in Northern Quebec* (Sainte-Foy, Quebec, June 15, 1988).
8. Philippe Nadeau and Jean Rochon, "Referendum in Northern Quebec," *Rencontre*, Secrétariat aux affaires autochtones, Quebec City, December, 1987.
9. "Referendum Will Settle Split over Inuit Self-Rule," *Globe and Mail*, October 1, 1987.
10. *Le Devoir*, "La souveraineté-association au Nouveau-Québec inuit," September 30 and October 1, 1987.
11. *Edmonton Journal*, "A Foundation for Self-Determination," October 2, 1987.
12. *Toronto Star*, September 16, 2007.
13. *Hogan v. Newfoundland (Attorney General)* (1999) 173 Nfld. & P.E.I.R. 148 at 150-151, para. 1.
14. *Hogan v. Newfoundland (Attorney General)* (1999) 173 Nfld. & P.E.I.R. 148 at 156, para. 26.
15. *Hogan v. Newfoundland (Attorney General)* (1999) 183 D.L.R. (4th) 225.
16. (1999) 183 D.L.R. (4th) 225, at 293.
17. "What to Do with Your Referendum Ballot," www.ubcic.bc.ca. Last updated June 14, 2002, Archive of Events and Documents.

CHAPTER 8: JUST WHAT CONSTITUTES A "MAJORITY"?

1. *National Post*, October 9, 2001.
2. Wally Braul, "A Provincial Nisga'a Referendum? A Bad Idea!" Aboriginal Rights Coalition of British Columbia, October 2001, http://arcbc.tripod.com/nisgaa.htm.

CHAPTER 9: NO SUCH THING AS "DIRECT DEMOCRACY"

1. Peter Stüder, "The Limits of Direct Democracy," in *Sovereign People or Sovereign Governments*, ed. H.V. Kroeker (Montreal: Institute for Research on Public Policy, 1981), 95.

CHAPTER 11: "MANDATES" FROM THE PEOPLE

1. Harold D. Clarke, Jane Jensen, Lawrence LeDuc, and Jon H. Pammett, *Absent Mandate: The Politics of Discontent in Canada* (Toronto: Gage Publishing, 1984).
2. Vernon Bogdanor, *People and the Party System: The Referendum and Electoral Reform in British Politics* (Cambridge: Cambridge University Press, 1981), 259.
3. Jon H. Pammett, "Political Education and Democratic Participation." In *Political Education in Canada* (Halifax: Institute for Research on Public Policy, 1988), 221.
4. Arthur Meighen, "The Canadian Senate," *Queen's Quarterly* 44 (Summer 1937): 152–63.
5. "Opposition Parties Plan Thorough Debate on Free Trade," *Globe and Mail*, December 6, 1988.
6. Letter to the Editor, *Globe and Mail*, December 14, 1988.
7. Bogdanor, *People and the Party System*, 14.
8. A.V. Dicey, "Ought the Referendum to Be Introduced into England?" *Contemporary Review* (1890): 504.
9. Quoted in Bogdanor, 17.
10. Bogdanor, 17–18. See also Patricia Kelvin, "Development and Use of the Concept of the Electoral Mandate in British Politics, 1867–1911." Ph.D. thesis, University of London, 1977.

CHAPTER 12: HOW HARD IS ASKING A CLEAR QUESTION?

1. Kenneth Grant Crawford, *Canadian Municipal Government* (Toronto: University of Toronto Press, 1954), 156.

2. *Reference Re Secession of Quebec* (1998) 2 SCR 217.
3. An Act to give effect to the requirement for clarity as set out in the opinion of the Supreme Court of Canada in the Quebec Secession Reference. S.C. 2000, c. 26.

CHAPTER 15: CONTINUING ADULT EDUCATION

1. See Bogdanor, *People and the Party System*, 15.

CHAPTER 17: VOTING ON DEMOCRACY

1. S.S. 1912-13, c.2.
2. Elizabeth Chambers, "The Referendum and the Plebiscite," in *Politics in Saskatchewan*, Norman Ward and Duff Spafford, eds. (Don Mills, ON: Longmans Canada, 1968), 67.
3. Letter to the author from Legislative Counsel, Alberta Legislature, Edmonton, February 17, 1978. Repeal was effected by S.A. 1958, c. 72.
4. Agar Adamson, "We Were Here Before: The Referendum in Canadian Experience," *Policy Options* (March 1980): 51.
5. Audrey Marilyn Adams, "A Study of the Use of Plebiscites and Referendums by the Province of British Columbia," unpublished M.A. thesis, University of British Columbia, Department of Economics and Political Science, April 1958, 166.

CHAPTER 18: VOTING TO RATIFY, JOIN, AND SUBDIVIDE CONFEDERATION

1. Austin Ranney, "The United States of America," in David Butler and Austin Ranney, *Referendums: A Comparative Study of Practice and Theory* (Washington, DC: American Enterprise Institute for Public Policy Research, 1978), 68.
2. "Scrapbook Debates," *Montreal Herald*, October 31, 1866 (Library of Parliament, Ottawa).
3. R. MacGregor Dawson, *The Government of Canada*, 4th ed. (Toronto: University of Toronto Press, 1966), 41.
4. P.B. Waite, *Arduous Destiny: Canada 1874–1896* (Toronto: McClelland & Stewart, 1971). See also *The Canadian Encyclopedia*, vol. 1 (Edmonton: Hurtig Publishers, 1988), 489.
5. *The Canadian Encyclopedia*, vol. 1, 1856.
6. S.J.R. Noel, *Politics in Newfoundland* (Toronto: University of Toronto Press, 1971), 254.

7. Donald Creighton, *The Forked Road: Canada 1939–1959* (Toronto: McClelland & Stewart, 1976), 145.

8. Noel, *Politics in Newfoundland*, 257.

9. Noel, 255.

10. Richard Gwyn, *Smallwood: The Unlikely Revolutionary* (Toronto: McClelland & Stewart, 1968), 100.

11. Joey Smallwood, *I Chose Canada* (Toronto: Macmillan, 1973), quoted in Gwyn, *Smallwood*, 113.

12. Noel, 258.

13. A.W.R. Carrothers et al., *Report of the Advisory Commission on the Development of Government in the Northwest Territories* (Ottawa: Queen's Printer, 1966).

14. *Council of the Northwest Territories Debates, 3rd Session*, vol. 1 (Ottawa: Government of Canada, 1966), 147–48.

15. Quoted in "Nunavut: Vision or Illusion?" *Canadian Parliamentary Review* (Spring 1990), 6.

16. S.N.W.T. 1981 (3rd Session), c. 13.

17. *Almon et al v. Government of the Northwest Territories*, 1982.

18. Frances Abel and Mark O. Dickerson, "The 1982 Plebiscite on Division of the Northwest Territories: Regional Government and Federal Policy," *Canadian Public Policy* (March 1985), 6–9.

19. Letter from Dene National Chief Bill Erasmus to Indian Affairs Minister Tom Siddon, May 6, 1992.

20. Author's interview with residents of Inuvik, Northwest Territories, May 1992.

21. "NWT Split Wins Approval by Narrow 54% Majority," *Edmonton Journal*, May 5, 1992.

22. Miro Cernetig, "Turnout Is High for Vote on New Territory," *Globe and Mail*, May 5, 1992.

CHAPTER 19: VOTING TO BREAK CONFEDERATION: ROUND ONE, 1980

1. *Quebec Chronicle-Telegraph*, December 11, 1969, 4.

2. Peter Desbarats, *René: A Canadian in Search of a Country* (Toronto: McClelland & Stewart, 1975), 154.

3. Pierre Godin, *Daniel Johnson: 1964–1968 — la difficile recherche de l'égalité* (Montreal: Les Éditions de l'Homme, 1980). See also Daniel Johnson, *Égalité ou indépendance* (Montreal: Les Éditions de l'Homme, 1965).

4. René Lévesque, *My Quebec* (Toronto: Methuen, 1979). See especially Part 3, "Sovereignty-Association," 67–98.

5. Vincent Lemieux, "The Referendum and Canadian Democracy." In *Institutional Reforms for Representative Government* (Toronto: University of Toronto Press, 1985), 133.

6. Robert Sheppard and Michael Valpy, *The National Deal: The Fight for a Canadian Constitution* (Toronto: Fleet Books, 1982), 26–27.

7. Sheppard and Valpy, *The National Deal*, 26–27.

8. *Montreal Gazette*, January 11, 1980.

9. *Canadian Annual Review of Politics and Public Affairs 1980* (Toronto: University of Toronto Press, 1981), 41.

10. Jeffrey Simpson, *Discipline of Power: The Conservative Interlude and the Liberal Restoration* (Toronto: Personal Library Publishers, 1980), 348.

11. Kenneth McRoberts and Dale Posgate, *Quebec: Social Change and Political Crisis* (Toronto: McClelland & Stewart, 1980), 282.

12. Lévesque, *My Quebec*, 108.

13. Sheppard and Valpy, 27.

14. Richard Gwyn, *The Northern Magus* (Toronto: McClelland & Stewart, 1980), 369.

15. Simpson, *Discipline of Power*. See Chapter 1, "The Collapse of the Government," 3–47.

16. Simpson, 349.

17. Ibid.

18. Pierre Elliott Trudeau, *Nationalism and the French Canadians* (Montreal: Harvest House, 1963). See also Hugh Bingham Myers, *The Quebec Revolution* (Montreal: Harvest House, 1963).

19. Sheppard and Valpy, 22.

20. Gwyn, *Northern Magus*, 371. See also House of Commons *Debates*, April 15, 1980.

21. Gwyn, *Northern Magus*, 371.

22. John Fitzmaurice, *Québec and Canada: The Referendum of 20 May 1980 in Its Wider Context* (Hull, U.K.: University of Hull, 1981), 2.

23. Fitzmaurice, *Québec and Canada*, 24–25.

24. Sheppard and Valpy, 33.

25. Fitzmaurice, 24–25.

26. Ibid.

27. *Boucher v. Mediacom* (1980), C.S. 481.

28. *Conseil du référendum*, May 16, 1980.

29.   Fitzmaurice, 22.

30.   Elliot J. Feldman, ed., *The Quebec Referendum: What Happened and What Next?* (Cambridge, MA: Harvard University Press, 1980), 10.

31.   Feldman, *The Quebec Referendum*, 10.

CHAPTER 21: VOTING TO BREAK CONFEDERATION: ROUND TWO, 1995

1.   Mario Cardinal, *Breaking Point: Quebec, Canada, and the 1995 Referendum* (Montreal: Bayard Canada Books, 2005), 153.

2   John Ruypers, *Canadian and World Politics* (Toronto: Emond Montgomery Publications, 2005), 196.

3.   Cardinal, *Breaking Point*, 227. See also Lawrence Martin, *The Antagonist: Lucien Bouchard and the Politics of Delusion* (New York: Viking, 1997).

4.   Chantal Hébert and Jean Lapierre, *The Morning After: The 1995 Referendum and the Day That Almost Was* (Toronto: Knopf Canada, 2014), 12.

5.   Hébert and Lapierre, *The Morning After*, 120.

6.   Parliamentary Research Branch of the Library of Parliament, *Aboriginal Peoples and the 1995 Quebec Referendum: A Survey of the Issues* (Ottawa: February 1996).

7.   Cardinal, 304. See also Hébert and Lapierre, 245.

8.   Jean Chrétien, *My Years as Prime Minister* (Toronto: Vintage Canada, 2007), 147–48.

9.   Cardinal, 313–14.

CHAPTER 22: VOTING ON PROHIBITION

1.   Stevenson, *Before the Bar*, 87.

2.   Joseph Schull, *Laurier* (Toronto: Macmillan, 1965), 339–40.

3.   House of Commons *Debates*, Third Session, Eighth Parliament, vol. 47, 1898, 4688.

4.   House of Commons *Debates*, Third Session, Eighth Parliament, vol. 47, 1898, 4694–95.

5.   House of Commons *Debates*, Third Session, Eighth Parliament, vol. 47, 1898, 4712–13.

6.   House of Commons *Debates*, Third Session, Eighth Parliament, vol. 47, 1898, 4714–20.

7.   House of Commons *Debates*, Third Session, Eighth Parliament, vol. 47, 1898, 4728–29.

8.   House of Commons *Debates*, Third Session, Eighth Parliament, vol. 47, 1898, 4736.

9.   James H. Gray, *Booze: The Impact of Whisky on the Prairie West* (Toronto: Macmillan, 1972), 58.

CHAPTER 23: VOTING ON CONSCRIPTION

1.   André Laurendeau, *La crise de la conscription* (Montreal: Éditions du Jour, 1962). See especially Chapter 13, "Un plébiscite," 70–80.

2.   J.L. Granatstein, "Le Québec et le plébiscite de 1942 sur la conscription," *Revue d'histoire de l'Amérique française* 27, no. 1 (June 1973): 43–62.

3.   J.L. Granatstein and J.M. Hitsman, *Broken Promises: A History of Conscription in Canada* (Toronto: Oxford University Press, 1977), 171.

4.   Ralph Allen, *Ordeal by Fire: Canada 1910–1945* (Toronto: Doubleday, 1961), 416–17.

5.   See generally R. MacGregor Dawson, *The Conscription Crisis of 1944* (Toronto: University of Toronto Press, 1961).

6.   Allen, *Ordeal by Fire*, 416–17.

CHAPTER 24: VOTING ON ABORIGINAL QUESTIONS

1.   *Lands, Revenues, and Trusts Review, Phase II* (Ottawa: Indian Affairs and Northern Development, 1990), 114.

2.   See Chapter 7, "Charter Protection of Minority Rights."

CHAPTER 25: VOTING ON WOMEN'S RIGHTS

1.   Catherine Cleverdon, *The Woman Suffrage Movement in Canada* (Toronto: University of Toronto Press, 1950), 87.

2.   Ruth Spence, *Prohibition in Canada* (Toronto: Ontario Branch of the Dominion Alliance, 1920), 68.

3.   See Elsie Gregory MacGill, *My Mother the Judge: A Biography of Judge Helen Gregory MacGill* (Toronto: Ryerson Press, 1955).

4.   Adams, "A Study of the Use of Plebiscites and Referendums in the Province of British Columbia," 43.

5.   Ibid.

6.   Ibid., 44.

7.   Ibid., 47.

8.   Ibid., 46.

9.   MacGill, *My Mother the Judge*, 122–23. Quoted in Adams, "A Study of the

Use of Plebiscites and Referendums," note 152, 177.

10. Adams, "A Study of the Use of Plebiscites and Referendums," 15.

11. Cleverdon, *The Woman Suffrage Movement*, 93.

12. Ibid., 97.

13. Ibid., 94–95.

14. Ibid.

15. Adams, 52.

16. Cleverdon, 85, 96–97.

17. Ibid., 52.

18. Adams, 52.

19. *Canadian Annual Review* (1915), 734.

20. Adams, 53.

21. Report of Mrs. J.A. Clark, "Women Are Now on Equality with Men," (Vancouver) *News-Advertiser*, September 17, 1916. Quoted in Adams, "A Study of the Use of Plebiscites and Referendums," 180.

22. Adams, 180.

23. *Vancouver Sun*, August 14, 1916. Quoted in Adams, "A Study of the Use of Plebiscites and Referendums," 181.

24. Speech at an election rally at the Old Victoria Theatre, July 11, 1916, reported in the *Daily Times* (Victoria) the next day and cited by Adams, "A Study of the Use of Plebiscites and Referendums," 54.

25. Adams, 55, 181.

26. Cleverdon, 99.

27. Adams, 55, 181.

28. Adams, 55.

29. Cleverdon, 9.

30. Adams, 182.

31. Quoted in the *Globe and Mail*, May 11, 1992.

CHAPTER 26: VOTING ON FOOD SUPPLY ISSUES

1. *Winnipeg Free Press*, November 26, 1951.

2. *Winnipeg Free Press*, November 27, 1951.

3. *Winnipeg Free Press*, November 25, 1951.

4. (1958) O.R. 349.

5. Letter to author from Ontario Asparagus Growers' Marketing Board, August 21, 1991.

6. John C. McMurchy, *A History of Agricultural Legislation in Ontario* (Toronto: Ministry of Agriculture and Food, 1990), 14.

CHAPTER 27: BALLOTING ON EVERYTHING FROM TIME OF DAY TO A FIXED LINK

1. Malcolm M. Thomson, *The Beginning of the Long Dash: A History of Timekeeping in Canada* (Toronto: University of Toronto Press, 1978).
2. "Daylight Saving," *The Encyclopedia of Canada*, vol. 2 (Toronto: University Associates of Canada Limited, 1935), 187. See also "Time" in *The Canadian Encyclopedia*, vol. 4 (Edmonton: Hurtig, 1988), 2163.
3. *Canada Month*, Montreal, February 1962.
4. Adams, "A Study of the Use of Plebiscites and Referendums," 141.
5. Adams, 142.
6. "A Bridge of Sighs," *Atlantic Advocate* 78 (February 1988): 6–8.
7. Douglas Baldwin, *Land of the Red Soil* (Charlottetown: Ragweed Press, 1990), 178.

CHAPTER 28: DEMOCRATIC ACCOUNTABILITY THROUGH MUNICIPAL BALLOT QUESTIONS

1. 12 Vict. c. 81.
2. George Rust-D'Eye, Ophir Bar-Moshe, and Andrew James, *Ontario Municipal Law: A User's Manual*, 11th ed. (Toronto: Carswell, 2017), 8.
3. *King v. Toronto* (1902), 5 O.L.R. 163.
4. *Davies v. Toronto* (1887), 15 O.R. 33.
5. *Globe and Mail*, March 20, 2015.

CHAPTER 29: CANADA'S PLACE IN A UNIVERSE OF REFERENDUMS

1. Charles M. Price, "The Initiative: A Comparative State Analysis and Reassessment of a Western Phenomenon," in *Western Political Quarterly* 28 (June 1975): 260–61.

CHAPTER 30: REWARDS OF CITIZEN-CENTRED DEMOCRACY

1. S.E. Finer, *The Changing British Party System, 1945–1979* (Washington, DC: American Enterprise Institute for Public Policy Research, 1980). Quoted in Bogdanor, *People and the Party System*, 86.

BIBLIOGRAPHY

Adams, Audrey Marilyn. "A Study of the Use of Plebiscites and Referendums by the Province of British Columbia." M.A. thesis, University of British Columbia, Department of Economics and Political Science, April 1958.

Adamson, Agar. "We Were Here Before: The Referendum in Canadian Experience." *Policy Options* (March 1980): 51.

Alderson, Stanley. *Yea or Nay: Referendums in the United Kingdom*. London: Cassell, 1975.

Allen, Ralph. *Ordeal by Fire: Canada 1910–1945*. Toronto: Doubleday, 1961.

Anderson, Dewey. *Government Directly by the People*. Stanford: Stanford University Press, 1942.

Archer, Keith, et al. *Parameters of Power: Canada's Political Institutions*. Toronto: Thomson Publishing, 1999.

Armstrong, Elizabeth. *The Crisis of Quebec, 1917–1918*. Toronto: McClelland & Stewart, 1974.

Baldwin, Douglas. *Land of the Red Soil*. Charlottetown: Ragweed Press, 1990.

Bealey, Frank. *Democracy in the Contemporary State*. Oxford: Clarendon Press, 1988.

Beedham, Brian. "Full Democracy." *The Economist* (December 21, 1996).

Bélanger-Campeau Commission. *The Political and Constitutional Future of Quebec*. Quebec, March, 1991.

Bogdanor, Vernon. *The People and the Party System: The Referendum and Electoral Reform in British Politics*. Cambridge: Cambridge University Press, 1981.

Bonjour, Felix. *Real Democracy in Operation*. New York: Frederick A. Stokes Co., 1970.

Boyer, J. Patrick. *Direct Democracy: The History and Future of Referendums*. Toronto: Dundurn, 1992.

_____. *Election Law in Canada: The Law and Procedure of Federal, Provincial, and Territorial Elections.* 2 vols. Toronto: Butterworths, 1987.

_____. *Hands-On Democracy: How You Can Take Part in Canada's Renewal.* Toronto: Stoddart, 1993.

_____. *Lawmaking by the People: Referendums and Plebiscites in Canada.* Toronto: Butterworths, 1982.

_____. *Money and Message: The Law Governing Election Financing, Advertising, Broadcasting and Campaigning in Canada.* Toronto: Butterworths, 1983.

_____. *The People's Mandate: Referendums and a More Democratic Canada.* Toronto: Dundurn, 1992.

_____. *Political Rights: The Legal Framework of Elections in Canada.* Toronto: Butterworths, 1981.

Boyer, J. Patrick, et al. *Démocratie et référendum: la procédure référendaire.* Montreal: Université de Montréal, Québec-Amérique, 1992.

British Columbia Royal Commission on State Health Insurance and Maternity Benefits, Final Report. Victoria: King's Printer, 1932.

Broder, David S. *Democracy Derailed: Initiative Campaigns and the Power of Money.* New York: Harcourt, 2000.

Brown, K. Craig. *Robert Laird Borden: A Biography.* Toronto: Macmillan, 1975.

Brown, R. Craig, and J.M.S. Careless, eds. *The Canadians.* Toronto: Macmillan, 1967.

Brun, Henri, and Guy Tremblay. *Droit constitutionnel.* Cowansville, QC: Éditions Yvon Blais, 1982.

Butler, David, and Austin Ranney, eds. *Referendums: A Comparative Study of Practice and Theory.* Washington, DC: American Enterprise Institute for Public Policy Research, 1978.

_____. *Referendums Around the World: The Growing Use of Direct Democracy.* Washington, DC: American Enterprise Institute for Public Policy Research, 1994.

California Commission on Campaign Financing. *Democracy by Initiative: Shaping California's Fourth Branch of Government.* Los Angeles: Center for Responsive Government, 1992.

Canadian Annual Review of Politics and Public Affairs. Toronto: University of Toronto Press, 1981, 1983.

The Canadian Encyclopedia. Edmonton: Hurtig, 1988.

Canadian Parliamentary Review. Spring 1980.

Canadian Public Administration 10, no. 1 (March 1967).

Canadian Public Health Journal 26, no. 9 (September 1935).

Canadian Public Policy, March 1985.

Cardinal, Mario. *Breaking Point: Quebec, Canada, and the 1995 Referendum*. Montreal: Bayard Canada Books, 2005.

Carrothers, A.W.R., et al. *Report of the Advisory Commission on the Development of Government in the Northwest Territories*, vol. 1. Ottawa: Queen's Printer, 1966.

Chambers, Elizabeth, "The Referendum and the Plebiscite." In Norman Ward and Dull Spafford, eds. *Politics in Saskatchewan*. Don Mills, ON: Longmans, 1968.

Chief Electoral Officer of Canada. *The 1992 Federal Referendum: A Challenge Well Met*. Ottawa: Elections Canada, 1994.

Chief Electoral Officer of Quebec. *Instruments of Direct Democracy in Canada and Quebec*. 3rd ed. Sainte-Foy, QC: Directeur général des élections du Québec, 2001.

———. *Référendum 30 Octobre, 1995*. Sainte-Foy, QC: Directeur général des élections du Québec, 1995.

———. *Référendum 1995: rapport des résultats officiels du scrutin*. Sainte-Foy, QC: Directeur général des élections du Québec, 1995.

———. *Referendum of October 1, 1987 in Northern Quebec*. Sainte-Foy, QC: Directeur général des élections du Québec, 1988.

Chief Plebiscite Officer of Northwest Territories. *Report on the Plebiscite on Division of the Northwest Territories, 1982*. Yellowknife, NWT: Government of Northwest Territories, 1982.

Chrétien, Jean. *My Years as Prime Minister*. Toronto: Vintage Canada, 2007.

Clarke, Harold, et al. *Absent Mandate: Canadian Electoral Politics in an Era of Restructuring*. 3rd ed. Toronto: Gage, 1996.

Cleverdon, Catherine. *The Woman Suffrage Movement in Canada*. Toronto: University of Toronto Press, 1950.

Crawford, K.G. *Canadian Municipal Government*. Toronto: University of Toronto Press, 1954.

Crees of Quebec. *Sovereign Injustice: Forcible Inclusion of the James Bay Crees and Cree Territory into a Sovereign Quebec*. Nemaska, QC: Grand Council of the Crees of Quebec. 1995.

Creighton, Donald. *The Forked Road: Canada 1939–1959*. Toronto: McClelland & Stewart, 1976.

Cronin, Thomas E. *Direct Democracy: The Politics of Initiative, Referendum and Recall*. Cambridge, MA: Harvard University Press, 1989.

Dawson, K. MacGregor. *The Conscription Crisis of 1944*. Toronto: University of Toronto Press, 1961.

———. *The Government of Canada*. 4th ed. Toronto: University of Toronto Press, 1966.

Delroy, Steve, and Audrey Dubé. "From Reading Room to Committee Room." *Canadian Parliamentary Review* 13, no. 4 (1990).

Denquin, Jean-Marie. *Référendum et plébiscite.* Paris: Librairie générale de droit et de jurisprudence, 1976.

Deploige, Simon. *The Referendum in Switzerland.* London: King, 1898.

Desbarats, Peter. *René: A Canadian in Search of a Country.* Toronto: McClelland & Stewart, 1975.

DeWitt, Benjamin Parke. *The Progressive Movement.* New York: Macmillan, 1915.

Dyck, Rand. *Canadian Politics: Critical Approaches.* 2nd ed. Scarborough, ON: Nelson Canada, 1996.

Dyer, Gwyn. *War.* New York: Crown, 1985.

Encyclopaedia of Canada. Toronto: University Associates of Canada Limited, 1935.

Feldman, Elliott J., ed. *The Quebec Referendum: What Happened and What Next?* Cambridge, MA: Harvard University, 1980.

Finer, Herman. *Theory and Practice of Modern Government.* New York: Henry Holt, 1949.

Fitzmaurice, John. *Quebec and Canada: The Referendum of 20th May 1980 in Its Wider Context.* Hull, U.K.: University of Hull, 1981.

Forbes, H.D., ed. *Canadian Political Thought.* Toronto: Oxford University Press, 1985.

Fox, John, Robert Andersen, and Joseph Dubonnet. "The Polls and the 1995 Quebec Referendum." *Canadian Journal of Sociology* 24, no. 3 (1999): 411–24.

Fox, Paul, ed. *Politics: Canada.* 2nd ed. Toronto: McGraw-Hill, 1966.

Garland, Reverend M.A., and J.J. Talman. "Pioneer Drinking Habits and the Rise of the Temperance Agitation in Upper Canada prior to 1840." *Papers and Records of the Ontario Historical Society* 27 (1931): 341.

Godin, Pierre. *Daniel Johnson: 1964–1968, la difficile recherche de l'égalité.* Montreal: Les Éditions de l'Homme, 1980.

Goodhart, Philip. *Referendum.* London: Tom Stacey, 1971.

Gould, Lewis L., ed. *The Progressive Era.* Syracuse, NY: Syracuse University Press, 1974.

Granatstein, J.L. *The Politics of Survival: The Conservative Party of Canada, 1939–1945.* Toronto: University of Toronto Press, 1967.

Granatstein, J.L., and J.M. Hitsman. *Broken Promises: A History of Conscription in Canada.* Toronto: Oxford University Press, 1977.

Gray, James H. *Booze: The Impact of Whisky on the Prairie West.* Toronto: Macmillan, 1972.

Gywn, Richard. *The Northern Magus.* Toronto: McClelland & Stewart, 1980.

_____. *Smallwood: The Unlikely Revolutionary*. Toronto: McClelland & Stewart, 1968.

Hahn, Harlan. "Voting in Canadian Communities: A Taxonomy of Referendum Issues." *Canadian Journal of Political Science* 1(1968): 462.

Hailsham, Lord. *The Granada Guildhall Lecture, 1987*. London, November 10, 1987.

Haljan, David. *Constitutionalising Secession*. Oxford: Hart Publishers, 2014.

Hébert, Chantal, with Jean Lapierre. *The Morning After: The 1995 Quebec Referendum and the Day That Almost Was*. Toronto: Alfred A. Knopf Canada, 2014.

Hofstadter, Richard. *The Age of Reform*. New York: Random House, 1955.

Honey, Samuel Robinson. *The Referendum Among the English*. London: Macmillan, 1912.

Hughes, C.J. "The Referendum." *Parliamentary Affairs* 11 (1958).

Humphries, John M. *Proportional Representation: A Study in Methods of Election*. London: Methuen, 1911.

Indian Affairs and Northern Development. *Lands, Revenues and Trusts Review*. Phase II Report. Ottawa: Queen's Printer, 1990.

Jackson, Robert J., and Doreen Jackson. *Politics in Canada: Culture, Institutions, Behaviour and Public Policy*. 5th ed. Toronto: Prentice Hall, 1998.

Johnson, Daniel. *Égalité ou indépendance*. Outremont, QC: VLB, 1990.

Keith, Berriedale. "Notes on Imperial Constitutional Law." *Journal of Comparative Legislation and International Law* 4 (1922): 233.

Kobach, Kris. *The Referendum: Direct Democracy in Switzerland*. Aldershot, U.K.: Dartmouth Publishing, 1993.

Kroeker, H.V., ed. *Proceedings of a Conference Sponsored by the Institute for Research on Public Policy and the Government Studies Program*. Montreal: Institute for Research on Public Policy, 1981.

Lakeman, Enid, and James Douglas Lambert. *How Democracies Vote: A Study of Majority and Proportional Electoral Systems*. 3rd ed. London: Faber & Faber, 1970.

Laurendeau, André. *La crise de la conscription*. Montreal: Éditions du Jour, 1962.

Lederman, William R., and John D. Whyte. *Canadian Constitutional Law: Cases, Notes and Materials*. 2nd ed. Toronto: Butterworths, 1977.

LeDuc, Lawrence. *The Politics of Direct Democracy: Referendums in Global Perspective*. Peterborough, ON: Broadview Press, 2003.

Lévesque, René. *My Quebec*. Toronto: Methuen, 1979.

_____. *Option Québec*. Montreal: Les Éditions de l'Homme, 1968.

Link, Arthur S. *Woodrow Wilson and the Progressive Era*. New York: Harper & Row, 1954.

MacDonald Royal Commission. *Institutional Reforms for Representative Government*, vol. 38. Edited by Peter Aucoin. Toronto: University of Toronto Press, 1985.

Mandel, Eli, and David Taras, eds. *A Passion for Identity: An Introduction to Canadian Studies*. Toronto: Nelson Canada, 1988.

Manitoba Law Reform Commission. *Working Paper on Electoral Systems*. Winnipeg: 1976.

McGill, Elsie Gregory. *My Mother the Judge: A Biography of Judge Helen Gregory McGill*. Toronto: Ryerson Press, 1955.

McRoberts, Kenneth, and Dale Posgate. *Quebec: Social Change and Political Crisis*. Toronto: McClelland & Stewart, 1980.

Meighen, Arthur. *Unrevised and Unrepented*. Toronto: Clarke, Irwin, 1949.

Mills, Bob. "Direct Democracy." *Parliamentarian* 75, no. 4 (October 1994).

Mowry, George. *The California Progressives*. Berkeley, CA: University of California Press, 1951.

_____. *Theodore Roosevelt and the Progressive Movement*. Madison, WI: University of Wisconsin Press, 1946.

Munro, William Bennett. *American Influences on Canadian Government*. Toronto: Macmillan, 1929.

_____. *The Initiative, Referendum and Recall*. New York: Appleton, 1912.

Myers, Hugh Bingham. *The Quebec Revolution*. Montreal: Harvest House, 1963.

Noel, S.J.R. *Politics in Newfoundland*. Toronto: University of Toronto Press, 1971.

Oberholtzer, Ellis P. *The Referendum in America*. New York: Scribner, 1911.

Ontario Standing Committee on the Legislative Assembly. *Final Report on Referenda*. Toronto: Legislative Assembly, 1997.

Philpot, Robin. *Le référendum volé*. Montreal: Les Éditions des Intouchables, 2005.

Pope, Joseph, ed. *Confederation: Being a Series of Hitherto Unpublished Documents Bearing upon the British North America Act*. Toronto: Carswell, 1895.

Ranney, Austin, ed. *The Referendum Device*. Washington, DC: American Enterprise Institute for Public Policy Research, 1981.

Rappard, William E. "The Initiative and Referendum in Switzerland." *American Political Science Review* 6 (1912): 345–66.

Richardson, J.E. *Patterns of Australian Federalism*. Canberra: Australian National University, 1973.

Rogers, Ian MacFee. *The Law of Canadian Municipal Corporations*. 2nd ed. Toronto: Carswell, 1971.

Royal Commission on Dominion-Provincial Affairs. *Report*. Ottawa: Queen's Printer, 1940.

Russell, Peter H. *Constitutional Odyssey: Can Canadians Be a Sovereign People?* Toronto: University of Toronto Press, 1992.

Ryan, Claude. *A Stable Society: Quebec After the PQ.* Edited and translated by Robert Scully. Montreal: Éditions Heritage, 1978.

Schull, Joseph. *Laurier.* Toronto: Macmillan, 1965.

_____. *Ontario Since 1867.* Toronto: McClelland & Stewart, 1978.

Scott, Stephen A. "Constituent Authority and the Canadian Provinces." *McGill Law Journal* 12 (1966–67): 528.

Sharp, Clifford D. *The Case Against the Referendum.* London: Fabian Society, 1911.

Sheppard, Robert, and Michael Valpy. *The National Deal.* Toronto: Fleet Books, 1982.

Shortt, Adam, and Arthur George Doughty, eds. *Canada and Its Provinces.* Toronto: Publishers Association of Canada Limited, 1914.

Siegfried, André. *The Race Question in Canada.* Paris: Librairie Armand Cohn, 1906; English-language edition. London: Eveleigh Nash, 1907; republished in Carleton Library Series. Toronto: McClelland & Stewart, 1966.

Simpson, Jeffrey. *Discipline of Power: The Conservative Interlude and the Liberal Restoration.* Toronto: Personal Library Publishers, 1980.

Smallwood, Joey. *I Chose Canada.* Toronto: Macmillan, 1973.

Smith, Gordon. "The Functional Properties of the Referendum." *European Journal of Political Research* 4 (1976): 1–23.

Spafford, Duff, and Norman Ward, eds. *Politics in Saskatchewan.* Don Mills, ON: Longmans Canada, 1968.

Spence, Ruth E. *Prohibition in Canada.* Toronto: Ontario Branch of the Dominion Alliance, 1920.

Sproule-Jones, Mark, and Adrie van Klaveren. "Local Referenda and the Size of Municipality in British Columbia: A Note on Two of Their Interrelationships." *BC Studies* 8 (1970–71): 47–50.

Stevenson, J.A. *Before the Bar: Prohibition Pro and Con.* Toronto: J.M. Dent, 1919.

Strachey, John St. Lee. *The Referendum.* London: Unwin, 1924.

Strong, C.F. *Modern Political Constitutions: An Introduction to the Comparative Study of Their History and Existing Form.* London: Sidgwick & Jackson, 1963.

Tallian, Laura. *Direct Democracy: A Historical Analysis of the Initiative, Referendum and Recall Process.* Los Angeles: People's Lobby. 1977.

Tellier, Robert. *Municipal Code of the Province of Quebec.* Montreal: Wilson & Lafleur, 1975.

Thomson, Malcolm M. *The Beginning of the Long Dash: A History of Timekeeping in Canada.* Toronto: University of Toronto Press, 1978.

Trudeau, Pierre Elliott. *Nationalism and the French Canadians.* Montreal: Harvest House, 1963.

Waite, P.B. *Arduous Destiny: Canada 1874–1896*. Toronto: McClelland & Stewart, 1971.

Wambaugh, Sarah. *Plebiscites Since the World War*. Washington, DC: Carnegie Endowment for International Peace, 1933.

Ward, Norman. *The Canadian House of Commons: Representation*. Toronto: University of Toronto Press, 1950.

Weyl, Walter E. *The New Democracy*. New York: Macmillan, 1915.

Whyte, John D., and William R. Lederman. *Canadian Constitutional Law: Cases, Notes and Materials*. 2nd ed. Toronto: Butterworths, 1977.

Wood, L.A. *A History of Farmers' Movements in Canada*. Toronto: University of Toronto Press, 1975.

York, Geoffrey. *The Dispossessed: Life and Death in Native Canada*. Toronto: Lester & Orpen Dennys, 1989.

Zurcher, Arnold J. *The Experiment with Democracy in Central Europe*. New York: Oxford University Press, 1933.

INDEX